The Social Cure

A growing body of research shows that social networks and identities have a profound impact on mental and physical health. With such mounting evidence of the importance of social relationships in protecting health, the challenge we face is explaining why this should be the case. What is it that social groups offer that appears to be just as beneficial as a daily dose of vitamin C or regular exercise?

This edited book brings together the latest research on how group memberships, and the social identities associated with them, determine people's health and well-being. The volume provides a variety of perspectives from clinical, social, organisational, and applied fields that offer theoretical and empirical insights into these processes and their consequences. The contributions present a rich and novel analysis of core theoretical issues relating to the ways in which social identities, and factors associated with them (such as social support and a sense of community), can bolster individuals' sense of self and contribute to physical and mental health. In this way it is shown how social identities constitute a 'social cure', capable of promoting adjustment, coping, and well-being for individuals dealing with a range of illnesses, injuries, trauma, and stressors. In addition, these theories provide a platform for practical strategies that can maintain and enhance well-being, particularly among vulnerable populations.

Contributors to the book are at the forefront of these developments and the book's strength derives from its analysis of factors that shape the health and well-being of a broad range of groups. It presents powerful insights which have important implications for health, clinical, social, and organisational psychology and a range of cognate fields.

Jolanda Jetten is Professor of Social Psychology at the University of Queensland, Australia. She was awarded her PhD in 1997 from the University of Amsterdam. Her research is concerned with identity, group processes and intergroup relations. She is currently Chief Editor of the *British Journal of Social Psychology* and a BPS Spearman medalist.

Catherine Haslam is an Associate Professor at the University of Exeter, UK. She has published extensively on the neuropsychological dimensions of memory and identity. She initially trained and worked as a clinical psychologist and subsequently completed her PhD at the Australian National University in 1999.

S. Alexander Haslam is Professor of Social and Organisational Psychology at the University of Exeter, UK. His work focuses on the contribution of social identity to a range of social, organisational, and health outcomes. A Fellow of the Canadian Institute of Advanced Research, he is a former editor of the *European Journal of Social Psychology* and Kurt Lewin medalist.

The Social Cure

Identity, health and well-being

Edited by Jolanda Jetten, Catherine Haslam & S. Alexander Haslam

Routledge
Taylor & Francis Group

LONDON AND NEW YORK

First published 2012
by Psychology Press

Published 2014 by Routledge
2 Park Square, Milton Park, Abingdon, Oxfordshire OX14 4RN

Simultaneously published in the USA and Canada
by Psychology Press
711 Third Avenue, New York, NY 10017

*Routledge is an imprint of the Taylor and Francis Group, an
informa business*

First issued in paperback 2015

British Library Cataloguing in Publication Data
A catalogue record for this book is available from the British Library

Library of Congress Cataloging-in-Publication Data
The social cure : identity, health and well-being / edited by Jolanda
Jetten, Catherine Haslam & S. Alexander Haslam.
       p. cm.
   Includes bibliographical references and index.
   ISBN 978-1-84872-021-3 (hb)
1. Social networks–Psychological aspects. 2. Group identity. 3.
Health–Social aspects. 4. Well being–Social aspects. I. Jetten,
Jolanda. II. Haslam, Catherine. III. Haslam, S. Alexander. IV. Title.
   HM741.S633 2011
   302.3–dc22
                                                    2010050068

ISBN 978-1-84872-021-3 (hbk)
ISBN 978-1-138-89152-4 (pbk)
ISBN 978-0-203-81319-5 (ebk)

Typeset in Times by Garfield Morgan, Swansea, West Glamorgan
Cover design by Sandra Heath

Contents

Figures and tables

Figures

Tables

Contributors

Hymie Anisman, Department of Neuroscience, Carleton University, Ottawa, Ontario, K1S 5B6, Canada.
Email: hanisman@connect.carleton.ca

Christopher P. Barrington-Leigh, Institute for Health and Social Policy, McGill University, Charles Meredith House, 1130 Pine Avenue West, Montreal, H3A 1A3, Canada.
Email: cpbl@wellbeing.econ.ubc.ca

Nyla R. Branscombe, Department of Psychology, University of Kansas, 1415 Jayhawk Blvd., Lawrence, KS 66045, USA.
Email: nyla@ku.edu

Claudine Clucas, Research Department of Infection and Population Health, UCL, Royal Free Hospital, Rowland Hill Street, London, NW3 2PF, UK.
Email: c.clucas@ucl.ac.uk

Tracey Cronin, Department of Psychology, Social Science Research Building, Office 314, Carleton University, 1125 Colonel By Drive, Ottawa, K1S 5B6, Canada.
Email: tracey.cronin@yahoo.ca

Jacinta M. Douglas, School of Human Communication Sciences, La Trobe University, Bundoora, Victoria, 3086, Australia.
Email: J.Douglas@latrobe.edu.au

John Drury, School of Psychology, University of Sussex, Falmer, Brighton, BN1 9QH, UK.
Email: j.drury@sussex.ac.uk

Claire V. Farrow, School of Sport, Exercise and Health Sciences, Loughborough University, Ashby Road, Loughborough, Leicestershire, LE11 3TU, UK.
Email: C.V.Farrow@lboro.ac.uk

Saulo Fernández, Dept. Psicología Social y de las Organizacione, Universidad Nacional de Educacion a Distancia (UNED), Juan del Rosal, 10, 28040 Madrid, Spain.
Email: saulo@psi.uned.es

Angel Gómez, Dept. Psicología Social y de las Organizacione, Universidad Nacional de Educacion a Distancia (UNED), Juan del Rosal, 10, 28040 Madrid, Spain.
Email: agomez@psi.uned.es

Fergus Gracey, Consultant Clinical Neuropsychologist, Cambridgeshire and Peterborough NHS Foundation Trust, Cambridge Centre for Paediatric Neuropsychological Rehabilitation, Heron Court, Ida Darwin, Cambridge, CB21 5EE, UK.
Email: fergus.gracey@ozc.nhs.uk

Martin S. Hagger, School of Psychology, University of Nottingham, University Park, Nottingham, NG7 2RD, UK.
Email: martin.hagger@nottingham.ac.uk

S. Alexander Haslam, School of Psychology, College of Life and Environmental Sciences, University of Exeter, Exeter, EX4 4QG, UK.
Email: a.haslam@exeter.ac.uk

Catherine Haslam, School of Psychology, College of Life and Environmental Sciences, University of Exeter, Exeter, EX4 4QG, UK.
Email: c.haslam@exeter.ac.uk

John F. Helliwell, Department of Economics, University of British Columbia, #997-1873 East Mall, Vancouver, BC, V6T 1Z1, Canada.
Email: john.helliwell@ubc.ca

Jolanda Jetten, School of Psychology, University of Queensland, St. Lucia, QLD 4072, Australia.
Email: j.jetten@psy.uq.edu.au

Janelle M. Jones, School of Psychology, University of Queensland, St. Lucia, QLD 4072, Australia.
Email: j.m.jones@psy.uq.edu.au

Blerina Kellezi, Centre for Criminology, University of Oxford, Manor Road Building, Manor Road, Oxford, OX1 3UQ, UK.
Email: blerina.kellezi@crim.ox.ac.uk

Craig P. Knight, Prism, University of Exeter, Innovation Centre, Rennes Drive, Exeter, EX4 4RN, UK.
Email: Craig.P.Knight@exeter.ac.uk

Mark Levine, Department of Psychology, Lancaster University, Fylde College, Lancaster, LA1 4YF, UK.
Email: m.levine@lancaster.ac.uk

Kimberly Matheson, 503 Tory Bldg, Carleton University, Ottawa, Ontario, K1S 5B6, Canada.
Email: kim_matheson@carleton.ca

Tamara Ownsworth, School of Psychology and Griffith Institute of Health, Griffith University, Mt Gravatt, 4122, Australia.
Email: t.ownsworth@griffith.edu.au

Nancy A. Pachana, School of Psychology, The University of Queensland, Brisbane, QLD 4072, Australia.
Email: npachana@psy.uq.edu.au

Stephen D. Reicher, School of Psychology, University of St Andrews, St. Mary's College, South Street, St. Andrews, Fife, KY16 9JP, Scotland.
Email: sdr@st-andrews.ac.uk

Fabio Sani, School of Psychology, University of Dundee, Park Place, Dundee, DD1 4HN, Scotland.
Email: f.sani@dundee.ac.uk

Lindsay St. Claire, University of Bristol, Centre for Hearing and Balance Studies, 5th floor, 8 Woodland Road, Clifton, Bristol, BS8 1TN, UK.
Email: L.StClaire@bristol.ac.uk

Mark Tarrant, Peninsula College of Medicine and Dentistry, University of Exeter, St Luke's Campus, Heavitree Road, EX1 2LU, UK.
Email: mark.tarrant@pcmd.ac.uk

Rolf van Dick, Department of Psychology and Sports Sciences, Social Psychology / Institute of Psychology, Goethe University Frankfurt, Kettenhofweg 128, 60054 Frankfurt, Germany.
Email: van.Dick@psych.uni-frankfurt.de

W. Huw Williams, School of Psychology, College of Life and Environmental Sciences, University of Exeter, Exeter, EX4 4QG, UK.
Email: W.H.Williams@exeter.ac.uk

Preface

As we were in the process of compiling this volume, Clement Freud – the celebrated writer, chef, and broadcaster – passed away at the age of 84. Looking to sum up the life of this celebrated bonviveur, a number of commentators recalled Freud's observation that "if you resolve to give up smoking, drinking, and loving, you don't actually live longer; it just seems longer". In recognizing that time seems to pass more slowly when we are unhappy or depressed, Freud alludes to the fact that seemingly unhealthy activities (ones that are often indulged in the company of others) can paradoxically be better for us if they are the basis for a fulfilling social life. In this respect, Freud might be characterized as an unwitting advocate for "the social cure" – a phrase that speaks to the potential for people's health and well-being to be sustained and enhanced by their social relationships – in particular, those that derive from their membership in social groups.

Seeking to formalize some of the logic that underpins Freud's quip, this volume explores the theoretical and practical issues associated with attempting to develop and deliver this cure. The need for such a volume is evident from at least three recent developments in the field. First, in the last decade, a growing body of research has demonstrated that social groups and networks are important predictors and protectors of health and well-being. However, it is also clear that, after showing this to be the case, researchers have found it hard to explain the origin of such effects. What precisely is it about our membership of social groups that is so beneficial for health and well-being? It appeared to us, and also to many other researchers, that the social identity approach provides an ideal platform from which to start answering this question. Indeed, over the last few years, this recognition has informed multiple programmes of research that have fleshed out why and when social identity and social relationships more generally affect health and well-being. In light of this, we sensed that there was a clear need for a volume that would collocate this work and help to draw it together.

It was also apparent to us that interest in the relationship between identity and health was a focus for researchers not just in a single discipline, but in a wide range of disciplines and fields – not just different forms of psychology (social, organizational, clinical, health, neuro) but also sociology, political science, epidemiology, and economics. Accordingly, we sensed that a second need existed for a volume that brought together researchers at the forefront of these various developments and that showcased the variety of perspectives and insights that they bring to the subject. This is critical because a full analysis of the contribution that identity processes make to health and well-being must account for the way in which psychological, social, and clinical factors interact to determine the range of outcomes in which we are interested. In line with this point, one of the novel features of this book, and one of its manifest strengths, is that its contributors come from multiple disciplinary backgrounds and their various insights reflect engagement with a very broad range of social groups – from stressed office workers to survivors of war crimes, from people with hearing difficulties to those with skeletal dysplasia, from young people with acquired brain injury to elderly residents in care homes. By drawing on this breadth of expertise, the book not only captures the scale of the research agenda but is also in a position to promote the cross-fertilization of ideas across disciplines, and ultimately to provide broad-based theoretical advance.

Yet going beyond the need to present and integrate ideas in the cause of theoretical advance, we also perceived a third need that was far more practical. For when thinking about the ways in which social identity and group membership can provide a "social cure", we touch upon questions that are of far more than just academic interest. As the various chapters in this volume attest, "the social cure" is capable of promoting adjustment, coping, and well-being for us all regardless of whether we are dealing with stress, illness, or trauma – or simply the hurly-burly of everyday life. Importantly too, the magnitude of these curative effects is surprisingly large, and this makes it all the more important to translate theoretical advance into practice and policy. Clearly, if the potential for a social cure is real, then there is a moral imperative to seek answers to the question of how this can be delivered with a view to optimizing both health and well-being. Accordingly, our third goal in assembling this volume was to make progress in the task of specifying how identity resources can be harnessed by both practitioners and policy makers.

Our hope is that in its attempt to address these three needs, this volume – and the underlying quest both to understand and to undertake "the social cure" – will continue to inform and inspire research, practice and policy for many years to come. Yet in a book that celebrates the capacity for groups to enrich people's lives, it would be remiss of us not to conclude this brief exposition by drawing attention to the contribution of others to this collective endeavour. First, we would like to express our gratitude to all the contributors for their willingness to sign up to the enterprise and then to put their shoulders to the wheel. We would also like to thank the many colleagues who provided helpful comments and encouragement along the way and who gave us not only the benefit of their considerable experience but also the motivation to see the project through to its conclusion. We are grateful too to the team at Psychology Press – and to Sharla Plant in particular – for the hard work they have done on our behalf throughout the publication process. Our sincere thanks also go to the practitioners and staff in the various organizations with whom we have collaborated over the past decade and whose relentless enthusiasm has been both energizing and infectious. And last, but not least, we would like to thank the research organizations that provided us with the funding that was necessary to turn this project from a tentative proposal into a tangible product. Principle amongst these are the Economic and Social Research Council in the UK (RES-062-23-0135), the Australian Research Council, the University of Queensland in Australia, and the Canadian Institute for Advanced Research. In keeping with the major theme of this book, this support was instrumental in making this volume a reality. We hope that it, in turn, provides support for those seeking to create positive realities for others.

Jolanda Jetten
Brisbane

Catherine Haslam
S. Alexander Haslam
Exeter

November, 2010

Part I

Social identity, health, and well-being

1 The case for a social identity analysis of health and well-being

Jolanda Jetten
University of Queensland

S. Alexander Haslam
Catherine Haslam
University of Exeter

To understand just how important social contact is for humans, it is instructive to consider situations in which opportunities for social inter-action and engagement are lacking. Social isolation can have devastating consequences with profound negative effects on our resilience, health, and well-being. For example, in prison settings, solitary confinement is per-ceived to be the ultimate punishment – and denying a person contact with others is often the most effective way to break down his or her resistance. Stories about castaways (e.g., Robinson Crusoe) tell a similar tale: To be deprived of human contact for an extended period of time is extremely challenging and is the main obstacle that people face when adjusting to uninhabited environments. We also know that people are psychologically vulnerable when they are no longer able to pursue an active social life (e.g., as a result of illness or old age). Indeed, considerable evidence suggests that being cut off from social contact with friends, family, and other social groups is not just extremely upsetting, it can have significant negative consequences for health and even lead to an early death.

Given all this, it seems pertinent to ask why it is that we rarely use our understanding of the causes of social isolation as the basis for *cures* that can counter its harmful consequences. In the Western world at least, the idea that family, friends, work colleagues, and social groups more generally have a key role to play in helping us overcome a range of stressors – including illness, traumatic life-changes, and discriminatory treatment – does not appear to be all that intuitive. Thus, even though it is well understood that being socially isolated makes us vulnerable and represents a considerable health hazard, there is often a reluctance to acknowledge the other side of the coin: that being embedded in a social network provides real benefits for health and well-being. Indeed, this can be seen to constitute a major "blind spot" in the way that relevant parties (e.g., practitioners, theorists, and members of the general public) approach these issues. A key goal of this book is to expose – and take steps to eliminate – this blind spot.

The fact that this blind spot persists seems all the more remarkable in light of the wealth of evidence demonstrating the positive impact of social connectedness on health and well-being (see Haslam, Jetten, Postmes, & Haslam, 2009, for a review). For example, a recent meta-analysis has demonstrated that the magnitude of the effect of social relationships on mortality is comparable to quitting smoking, and exceeds that for obesity, high blood pressure, and physical inactivity (Holt-Lunstad, Smith, & Layton, 2010). Indeed, the fundamental message that emerges from this study is that people with adequate social relationships have a 50 percent greater likelihood of survival than those with poor relationships. Moreover, these effects appear to hold strong even after controlling for variables that are typically associated with adverse health (e.g., initial health status; for a review, see House, Umberson, & Landis, 1988).

All this highlights the fact that social relationships make an independent contribution to health outcomes. Thus, after reviewing the research evidence, in his book *Bowling Alone*, Robert Putnam concludes: "As a rough rule of thumb, if you belong to no groups but decide to join one, you cut your risk of dying over the next year in half" (2000, p. 331). This conclusion underlines the profound way in which we are affected by our social environment and the social relationships that we form with others. It also suggests that participating in group life is an important means by which we can inoculate ourselves against, and repel, threats to our mental and physical health.

Accepting that our mental and physical health is supported by social factors opens a whole new spectrum of curative possibilities. However, to apply these new cures effectively we must also understand the mechanisms through which social networks offer such protection. For even though the finding that social networks protect mental and physical health is well documented – and hence may not come as a complete surprise – the question that is more difficult to answer is why this is the case. Indeed, until recently, there was no clear theoretical framework that might allow us to understand the processes that underlie the relationship between social relationships and well-being. Yet over the last couple of years, this void has been partly filled through the development of psychological theorizing concerning the way in which identity processes impact on health and well-being. More particularly, this work proposes that an understanding of the dynamics of *social identity* holds great promise in providing the necessary theorizing to help us understand when and why social connections affect well-being.

Social identity refers to the sense of self that people derive from their membership in social groups, (e.g., family, work, community, etc.; Tajfel, 1978; Tajfel & Turner, 1979). It therefore reflects the fact that in thinking about who we are, we can define ourselves (and our sense of self) not just as "I" and "me", but also (and often more importantly) as "we" and "us". Historically, social identity research has tended to focus on the way in

scared of my own thoughts | thinking

scared to do that again b/c I don't want to end up where I was which these group-based identities determine how people from different groups relate to each other (e.g., to explain processes involved in stereotyping and discrimination). As a result, until recently, other consequences of group-based belonging – in particular, those that relate to well-being – were largely unexplored. Of late, however, there has been increasing interest in the specific role that group memberships (and the social identities associated with them) play in determining people's health and well-being. The scale of this growth can be gauged by considering the fact that since 1990 there has been a logarithmic increase in the number of research articles whose titles, abstracts or keywords reference "social identity" or "social identification" together with "health" or "well-being" (and a quadratic increase in the number of times that these publications have themselves been cited; see Haslam et al., 2009, for further details).

It seems highly likely that these trends will continue in the years ahead. Accordingly, our hope is that this edited book will serve a dual function: first, to document the progress that has recently been made in understanding the interplay between identity, health, and well-being and, second, to stimulate and inform future interest among researchers, practitioners, and policy makers. With this in mind, in compiling this volume, our purpose has been to bring together a variety of perspectives and views from leading researchers representing a range of disciplines (clinical, health, social, organizational, economic) as a means of providing theoretical and empirical insights into the ways in which social interactions and social connections affect health and well-being. More specifically, in the chapters that follow, the contributions all examine how social identities (and factors associated with them; e.g., social support, a sense of solidarity, and community) have the capacity to contribute to a "social cure" that is capable of promoting adjustment, coping, and well-being among individuals who are dealing with a range of illnesses, injuries, traumas, and stressors. The nature of the research that the various chapters cover is extremely diverse, but at their heart there is a clear focus on the way in which different aspects of group life interact with other factors (e.g., psychological, biological, medical) to determine health and well-being.

We realize that some readers may already be quite familiar with the social identity approach, but that others may not have had much exposure to this theoretical framework. Accordingly, we need to ensure a basic understanding of this approach before we can appreciate how this bears upon issues of well-being and health. In the next section, we therefore provide a short theoretical overview of key social identity principles and we discuss how these apply to health. Along the way, we will also identify the potential for a social identity analysis to address current "needs" in the field. In short, we argue that the value of a social identity analysis of health and well-being lies in the fact that this framework (a) provides a *social* analysis of health and well-being, (b) provides a *coherent* framework for understanding health and well-being, and (c) provides theoretical *tools* that allow us to design and implement interventions that can capitalize on our understanding of the importance of social relationships for health.

THE VALUE OF A SOCIAL IDENTITY APPROACH TO HEALTH AND WELL-BEING

The social identity approach is comprised of two related theories: social identity theory (SIT; Tajfel & Turner, 1979, 1986) and self-categorization theory (SCT; Turner, 1985; Turner, Hogg, Oakes, Reicher, & Wetherell, 1987). As noted above, both theories are central to our current purpose, and we therefore need to provide a short introduction to their core principles. For more extensive accounts, we refer readers either to the original writings by Tajfel and Turner (1979, 1986; Turner, 1982; Turner et al., 1987), or to more recent reviews and overviews (e.g., Haslam, 2004; Postmes & Branscombe, 2010; Turner, Oakes, Haslam, & McGarty, 1994).

Social identity theory was initially developed to explain group behaviour relating to intergroup conflict and discrimination. It does this with specific reference to the sense of self that individuals derive from membership of social groups – that is, their *social identity*. A key idea here is that in order to understand behaviour in various social contexts (in particular, those in which there is conflict, prejudice, and discrimination), it is necessary to recognize that individuals can define their sense of self ("who they think they are") in social and not just personal terms (i.e., as "us" and "we", not just "I" and "me").

Some of the assumptions that are central to the theory are: (a) that people generally strive to achieve or maintain a positive sense of self; (b) that in many social contexts an individual's self-concept will derive from significant group memberships and hence be defined in terms of social identity; and therefore (c) that when a particular social identity is salient, individuals strive to maintain positive social identity by positively differentiating their own group (the *ingroup*; e.g., as a woman, as an Australian) from other groups (*outgroups*; e.g., men, Americans; Tajfel & Turner, 1986).

These ideas were initially derived from a series of experiments in which Tajfel and colleagues randomly assigned people to one of two previously meaningless groups (e.g., groups supposedly defined on the basis of their liking for the abstract painters Klee and Kandinsky) and then asked them to allocate points signifying small amounts of money to members of their ingroup and members of the outgroup (Tajfel, Billig, Bundy, & Flament, 1971). In these experiments – which became known as the minimal group experiments – it was found that participants did not allocate points equally, but rather tended to display ingroup favouritism by giving more points to the ingroup than the outgroup. It appeared that through ingroup favouritism participants gained a positive social identity; an outcome that is all the more powerful when we consider that this was achieved via creation of groups that had no prior meaning.

These ideas about the importance of social identity for understanding social behaviour were subsequently refined and extended within self-categorization theory (Turner et al., 1987, 1994). This theory asserts that there are multiple levels at which we can define ourselves and that each has distinct implications for our behaviour. At the subordinate level people define themselves, and act, as individuals (compared to other individuals and in terms of personal identity; Turner, 1982); at the intermediate level they define themselves, and act, in terms of their membership of a specific group (compared to relevant outgroups and in terms of social identity); and at the superordinate level they define themselves, and act, as human (in contrast to other species).

levels?
so do we prioritize? different identities

The fact that there are different levels of self-categorization suggests that to understand individuals' interactions with the social world around them – including those interactions that have implications for mental and physical health and well-being – we need to appreciate the way in which people define and understand themselves in a given context or situation. Such an analysis suggests that individuals will respond differently depending on whether they define themselves as unique individuals (in terms of personal identity) or as group members (in terms of social identity; e.g., as stroke sufferers, older adults, or as students). As we will see in the chapters that follow, amongst other things, this will determine their perceptions of particular stressors, their responses to health messages, their interactions with health care providers, and their reactions to different forms of social support. For example, the particular group membership in terms of which a woman defines herself (e.g., as a patient, an employee, or a mother) will determine the significance of the stressors she confronts, the effectiveness of the health messages to which she is exposed, and the value of the care and support she receives.

→ affects their perception & runs to life

COVID-19 vax

However, these insights about the way in which individuals' behaviour is dictated by identity concerns (and the social contexts in which these are embedded) are rarely taken into account when studying health. Typically, health outcomes and behaviours are studied at the individual level and the role of group membership, shared group memberships, and shared social identity is left unexplored. One reason for this is that it is ultimately individuals who engage in health-related behaviours (e.g., smoking, drinking, exercising), individuals who suffer from an illness, and individuals who are exposed to health risks. More particularly, it is as individuals that they are often treated (e.g., in hospital or when visiting the doctor). Given this, it is perhaps not surprising that research into these various topics has been informed by approaches that focus largely – if not exclusively – on the abilities and capacities of individuals *as individuals*. For example, such approaches have explored the role of individual differences (e.g., in personality traits such as "hardiness", "resilience", or "extroversion") that might

identity concerns & health

buffer people against stressors and threats to health. Other research has focused on individuals' personal thinking styles in explaining variation in their ability to cope (e.g., examining the way in which individuals cope by cognitively reappraising stressful transitions; Brammer, 1992). This individual-level understanding is then translated into interventions that are equally individualistic. For example, these involve helping individuals to make lifestyle changes to minimize stress (Friedman & Rosenman, 1974), to relax in times of change, to assist in coping (see Cooper, 1990), or to foster a sense of optimism rather than pessimism (Brissette, Scheier, & Carver, 2002; Seligman, 2006).

Nevertheless, it is equally (if not more) true, that all the above activities are also structured by group membership. People engage in health behaviours in groups (e.g., clubs, families) and different groups engage in different types of health behaviour; people suffer illnesses in groups (e.g., at work, at school) and different groups are exposed to different types of illness (e.g., as a function of their social class, their occupation); and, finally, people's health is also managed in groups (e.g., in clinics, hospitals, and through various health campaigns). Thus, while health is always personal, it always has a social dimension too. Indeed, this insight is central to fields such as epidemiology, population health, health economics, and medical sociology.

Unfortunately, then, psychological or other accounts that focus only on the individual as an individual are limited in scope because they fail to come to grips with the social underpinnings of health and well-being. Indeed, the few studies that have measured both personality and social relationships (e.g., Cohen & Wills, 1985) all show that, on their own, individual-level accounts are incapable of explaining the all-important contribution of social relationships to individuals' well-being. At a theoretical level, such accounts cannot explain why it is the quality and diversity in our relationship with others that crucially determine our mental and physical health. More generally, if we accept that people are social animals with a fundamental and perhaps even evolutionary need for social connections (Cacioppo & Patrick, 2008), then it becomes clear that theories that focus only on the individualized individual are not well suited to the task of advancing our understanding of people's basic need for fulfilling social relationships. It is clear then, that *the field's first need is for an approach to health and well-being that is inherently social.*

An obvious question that arises from this assertion is what this social approach should look like. How should we conceptualize the social aspects of health? In this regard, it is important to bear in mind that "social" means different things to different people. Indeed, as a result, the field is plagued by myriad conceptualizations of the social. These include those who construe it in terms of social networks, social connectedness, social capital, interpersonal relationships, social roles, friendships, socio-structural factors, or self-complexity, just to name a few. These different conceptualizations are often used interchangeably despite the fact that they are derived from different theories and rely on different measurements of relevant constructs. And even if these concepts are distinguished, there is often no clear agreement among researchers as to how they differ or of how they relate to each other. This is problematic for a number of reasons. In particular, the diversity of conceptualizations, definitions, measures, and theories of the social stands in the way of the development of a common language, with which to understand the impact of social factors on health and well-being. In contrast to the medical model (against which it is often compared), this absence of a coherent model for understanding and tackling relevant issues has clearly hindered progress in the health field. Accordingly, *the field's second need is for a social approach that provides a coherent framework for understanding health and well-being.*

In thinking about the way forward, we argue that focusing simply on the benefits of different types of social relationship (e.g., those in small or large groups, those with "significant others" or professionals, those that involve formal or informal roles) is probably not the best way to make progress. This is because it seems unlikely that this issue can be resolved through a taxonomic approach. As we see it, a more promising way forward involves developing theory that focuses on the way in which self-definition is affected by social relationships. This is precisely where the social identity approach can help us. For if we conceptualize the impact of social relationships in identity-related terms, we not only clarify when and how those relationships are truly social, but we also have at our disposal a rich set of principles that can help us to understand when, why, and how these relationships affect well-being and health.

In this regard, self-categorization theory is particularly useful as it tries to disentangle the social psychological dynamics of the self. When do we define ourselves as group members rather than as individuals? What determines which group memberships define our sense of self in any given context? What are the consequences of self-definition in group-based terms? As already intimated, the theory's answer to such questions is based on the argument that social identification underpins all forms of group behaviour. As John Turner (1982) put it: "social identity makes group behaviour possible" (p. 21). In these terms, a group emerges when, and only when, a number of people perceive themselves as sharing a sense of identification with others who are members of the same social category or group (Turner, 1982, p. 15).

However, we all belong to many groups and therefore can categorize ourselves in many different ways (e.g., as a woman, an older adult, etc.). So which of these different social identities will be prominent in any given context? Self-categorization theory argues that this is an interactive product of (the *fit*) we perceive ourselves to have with a particular group and our *readiness* to use it (Oakes, Haslam, & Turner, 1994). For example, a woman is more likely to define herself as a woman (sharing group membership with other women) if this way of categorizing herself (i.e., her self-categorization) maps on to her understanding of the similarities and differences between women and men (e.g., in terms of attitudes and preferences), and if the group membership is meaningful to her (e.g., because she is a feminist). There are therefore a number of ways in which a particular social identity can become salient. One important route is through prior involvement in the group, as this increases the likelihood of the group membership becoming salient when contextual factors make it fitting.

Following up on these ideas, a further core insight of self-categorization theory is that through sharing a sense of identification with other ingroup members, we can influence, and be influenced by, those others. In other words, social identity is a basis for mutual social influence (Turner, 1991). This means that when people perceive themselves to share group membership with others in a given situation they are motivated to strive actively to reach agreement with them and to coordinate their behaviour in relation to activities that are relevant to that identity. A young woman who defines herself as a mother will seek out the best representatives of this group (e.g., experienced mothers) to validate her understanding of issues that affect mothers and use this group in formulating a response to those issues that affect mothers and children (e.g., when deciding how best to access health care).

Importantly too, when we define ourselves in terms of group membership, the perceived norms and values of that group will affect our individual behaviour when deciding what is the right and proper thing to do (e.g., in the case of mothers, whether it is a good idea to use formula milk). In a similar way, shared social identification of this form also provides the basis for various forms of productive social interaction between people – including the provision of social support, helping, and other acts of solidarity (Haslam et al., 2009). In the case of social support, for example, a shared sense of social identification between people increases the likelihood that they will provide each other with effective support and it is under these circumstances that we are most likely to see positive benefits for health and well-being.

More important for the present volume, though, is the fact that social identification processes can help us understand the basis of the health benefits associated with social group membership. For if we understand social relationships as having the capacity to sustain valued social identities, then we can begin to see why they are so critical for health and well-being. In particular, because social identities are central to our sense of self, the social relationships that inform those identities provide the all-important lens through which individuals see and understand social experience and on which basis they seek to tackle key life events. In this way identity-relevant relationships help us to understand and adjust to a range of demanding life transitions, whether they are planned (e.g., retirement, moving) or unplanned (e.g., retrenchment, illness). For the same reasons, our relationships with

ingroup membership & influence
– motivation
– actions

seek out the best of those who share a similar identity

health & social

identity relevant relationships help us with transition periods of our life fellow ingroup members determine our interpretation and response to key aspects of illness and wellness – including the way that symptoms are perceived and treated, the content of health-related norms and behaviours, and our response to various clinical outcomes (Haslam et al., 2009; Jetten, Haslam, Haslam, & Branscombe, 2009). What matters in all this is not whether the social aspects of keys processes are defined in terms of social roles, social networks, or even interpersonal relations. Instead, the social identity approach makes it clear that what matters most is the way that individuals' relationship with others is defined – and, most particularly, how those others contribute to the person's sense of self, both as an individual and as a group member. Accordingly, we would suggest that *the field's third need is for an identity-based approach that provides a coherent analysis of the role of the social self in health and well-being.*

But bringing together theoretical work on the relationship between social identity and health from a range of fields is not just exciting from a theoretical point of view. Equally important, such theorizing can be used to develop practical strategies for maintaining and enhancing well-being, particularly among vulnerable populations. Indeed, the value of any theorizing needs to be measured against its ability to provide insights that help research to make a material difference – in this case, by delivering benefits for both health and well-being. Using theory to inform developments in the delivery, management, and promotion of health care should also help make those interventions more efficient, better targeted, and more sustainable.

The success of the current enterprise therefore rests heavily on the ability of the social identity approach to health to make an actual difference in the field. Putting a different spin on Kurt Lewin's famous dictum that "there is nothing so practical as a good theory" (1951, p. 169), we would add that "there is nothing so practical as a good theory that affects practice". Indeed, a theory's value is tremendously magnified if it helps us not only to think about solutions to problems, but also to bring those solutions to fruition. In this respect, *the field's fourth need is for an approach that provides a framework for practical interventions that maintain and enhance health and well-being.* As we will see, the last part of this book contains a range of contributions that provide insights into the way that social identity theorizing can provide exactly this advance as a consequence of its ability to inform concrete interventions in a range of applied settings.

THE PRESENT VOLUME

The contributions brought together in this volume use social identity-related principles to understand people's responses to a range of health-related stressors (e.g., trauma, illness) in a range of settings (e.g., care homes, rehabilitation clinics, organizations, war zones), and among a wide range of groups and populations (e.g., survivors of atrocities, patient groups, older adults moving into care). The research programmes summarized in the various chapters are associated with key researchers and leading research groups in the field, and each provides a novel and intellectually stimulating perspective on core theoretical issues surrounding the role of identity-related processes in well-being. In asking us to appreciate the value of group life, the authors challenge us to change our perspective on the factors that influence health and well-being. They achieve this by providing a reasoned argument for a social identity approach to health, demonstrating the various situations in which social groups can be the source of either cure or harm, and helping us understand how we can translate the principles of social identity approaches into practice. In the remainder of this chapter we outline how these ideas inform the structure of the book and also briefly indicate the nature of the contributions that the different chapters make.

Part 1: Social identity, health, and well-being

Contributions in the first part speak to the need to develop an analysis of health and well-being that is both social and coherent. The authors provide critical insights into the relationship between social identity and health that move beyond traditional analyses that have tended to promote individualized understanding and management of health. Several chapters in this section provide a theoretical foundation for the links between social identity and well-being, and an examination of the processes that underlie this relationship. This section goes further, though, to provide an analysis of the economic value to society that social groups offer and in demonstrating this, the authors show that the capital we draw from social groups is typically of far greater value to our health than our material circumstances.

The chapter by Fabio Sani provides a comprehensive and insightful review of the literature concerning the way in which social identity processes determine physical and mental health. Central to Sani's argument is an emphasis on the quality of social relationships – a factor that he sees as a key determinant of whether or not social groups are beneficial to health. Accordingly, the stronger our ties with family, work colleagues, community or other groups, then the better our health, irrespective of whether this is assessed in terms of mortality, chronic illness, mood, pain, or life satisfaction. This in turn, creates what Sani refers to as a "virtuous circle" in which these relationships strengthen identification further and hence prove capable of delivering even more health-related benefits.

The chapter by Mark Tarrant, Martin Hagger, and Claire Farrow provides an overview of research showing that people's engagement in health-promoting behaviours is influenced and determined by social categorization processes. This chapter addresses directly the concern that many health professionals express about the general public's failure to engage in health-promoting behaviours. As Tarrant and colleagues argue, we can only overcome this barrier when we acknowledge that health behaviours do not occur in a "social vacuum". These authors present results of a number of empirical studies which show that the interpretation of health behaviours is critically determined by the types of behaviour that group members perceive to be ingroup-defining. The theorizing here helps us to understand when and how group membership can promote health (e.g., when group norms promote a healthy diet), but also when and how group membership can lead to detrimental health outcomes (e.g., when group norms promote binge drinking and unhealthy eating).

John Helliwell and Chris Barrington-Leigh broaden theorizing on the way identity affects health by examining macro-level links between health and social capital (examined in terms of both identity and connectedness). Based on large-scale national surveys in Canada, they assess the impact of social network size on subjective well-being as measured by the income changes that would produce equivalent increments in levels of life satisfaction. The findings of this analysis demonstrate that social identity and social capital make a substantial contribution to life satisfaction at the national level. Indeed, being able to count on relatives or friends in times of trouble is shown to have the same effect on well-being as tripling household income.

Part 2: Social identity, stigma, and coping

Building on the recognition that social identities play a part in the maintenance and protection of well-being and mental health (e.g., Haslam & Reicher, 2006; Levine, Cassidy, Brazier, & Reicher, 2002), an important question that remains to be answered is how people who face exclusion on the basis of group membership (e.g., ethnicity, gender, class) use identities as a resource to protect well-being and mental health. Interestingly, recent research suggests that when people are confronted with discrimination they do not necessarily downplay the importance of that identity. Rather, it appears that group-based rejection can lead them to nurture and embrace the excluded identity even more (e.g., Branscombe, Schmitt, & Harvey, 1999; Jetten, Branscombe, Schmitt, & Spears, 2001). In this way, identification with a minority or marginalized group may serve not only as a buffer against environmental threats (e.g., discrimination, exclusion, poverty), but also as a key resource that can be mobilized in order to manage and combat these threats. The second part brings together contributions that focus on these issues and on the challenges that people face when they are confronted with group-based discrimination and disadvantage.

Lindsay St. Claire and Claudine Clucas's work highlights the critical role that defining one's self in terms of an illness group (e.g., as a person with hearing problems or as a cold sufferer) has on the interpretation of physical symptoms. It also shows that this self-categorization in turn affects people's willingness to engage in health-promoting behaviours. In line with findings from the literature on stereotype threat, they also find that when a nega-tively valued category becomes cognitively salient (e.g., so that a person self-categorizes as an older adult), this tends to bring into play negative stereotypes that are then confirmed through ongoing interaction. These authors argue that being aware of these factors not only provides an explanation for a client's experience, but also a promising way to reduce the likelihood of negative outcomes, by drawing on other social relationships that are not defined solely in terms of illness.

Jolanda Jetten and Nancy Pachana focus on driving cessation among older adults and show that giving up a driving licence as a result of poor health does not just involve a change in mode of transport but also initiates a process of identity change whereby older adults perceive that they are making a transition from a relatively valued category (younger-old) to a more devalued category (old-old). This work offers a novel perspective from which to manage driving cessation. Central to this is an awareness that it is the change in people's relationship with others that is particularly critical in explaining adverse health outcomes. Accordingly, this identity change needs to be taken into account when examining long-term adjust-ment to driving cessation, a point that the authors discuss in relation to a theoretical model which integrates these and other findings from the literature.

Nyla Branscombe, Saulo Fernández, Angel Gómez, and Tracey Cronin show how coping strategies differ depending on whether stigma is defined as a threat to the group as a whole (i.e., collective-level threat) or whether it is perceived as a threat at the individual level. Their research involves work with a range of groups including people suffering from skeletal dysplasias that are the cause of disproportionate short stature (dwarfism). In coping with the stigma associated with this condition some people choose to adopt an individual-level coping strategy (i.e., undergoing limb-lengthening sur-gery and in this way moving away from the group), whilst others use a collective strategy (i.e., increasing their identification with the group as a way of challenging discrimination). Critically, the authors show that stra-tegy choice is driven by the norms embedded within a given culture. In Spain, where there is greater evidence of social exclusion associated with dwarfism, most opt for an individual strategy; however, in the USA, where there are stronger support networks, most adopt a collective strategy. This research nicely illustrates the critical role that society plays in determining how people protect themselves when faced with stigma and discrimination.

Kimberly Matheson and Hymie Anisman extend upon a psychological analysis of the relationship between social groups and health to consider the biological impact of stress reactions under conditions of group-based discrimination. In their analysis they focus on conditions of mild, pervasive discrimination (e.g., being the subject of close scrutiny as a result of one's ethnicity). They make the important point that while people often seem to emerge from these situations unharmed, they can remain sensitized to such an extent that the next time they occur, biological responses can be exaggerated, making them more prone to psychological and physical disorder in the long term. This chapter highlights the intimate relationship between social and biological factors and helps us to understand the physical wear-and-tear that a disconnection from others can cause.

Part 3: Social identity, stress, and trauma

The third part of the book brings together research from a range of health arenas to explore the way in which shared identity underpins group members' capacity to respond effectively to stressors. From the range of research presented, it is apparent that shared identity plays a central role in enabling people to cope effectively with challenging life events, and even to grow as a consequence. In all cases, though, it is apparent that positive outcomes are not straightforward consequences of group membership, but instead are structured by the nature of the social identities that underpin and bear upon group life.

S. Alexander Haslam, Stephen Reicher, and Mark Levine discuss the way in which people's experience of contact with others is affected by the extent to which they share social identity with them. Starting from the observation that previous research has failed to observe a straightforward link between social support and well-being, they systematically unpack the processes that might help us to understand the dynamics of this relationship. Importantly, they propose that beneficial effects will be most apparent when social support is interpreted in the spirit in which it is intended, and that this is more likely to occur when those who provide and receive that support perceive themselves to share a relevant social identity. This analysis provides novel insights and helps us to understand that while social interactions and social support can be a basis for a range of benefits, in the absence of shared social identity, social support and interaction can also have negative consequences.

Rolf van Dick and S. Alexander Haslam present a conceptual analysis of the way in which social identity moderates the stress–strain relationship in organizational contexts. They argue that stress is tempered by group dynamics and that we need to understand these dynamics to be able to deal effectively with the negative impact of workplace stress on well-being. The chapter presents empirical evidence that confirms the importance of social identification as a basis for effective stress management and also offers practical recommendations for managing and promoting well-being at work. In particular, a strong case is made for the need to move away from individual-level strategies which tend to preclude opportunities for positive forms of employee empowerment.

John Drury examines how group processes shape responses to another type of stressor – those that people confront in mass emergency situations. His work develops the argument that crowds affected by emergencies and disasters can be crucial sources of the solidarity, cooperation, coordinated action, and psychological support that is required for their own survival and recovery, independent of the interventions of emergency services. The chapter develops a model that applies social identity theorizing to mass emergency behaviour and suggests a new, dynamic, model of collective resilience. This model has fundamental implications not only for academic theories of crowd behaviour, but also for emergency preparedness and response, and the effective management of disasters.

Blerina Kellezi and Stephen Reicher identify ways in which identity dynamics affect coping and adjustment following the trauma of war. In the first instance, they provide an analysis of the way in which war crimes are typically aimed at undermining individuals' capacity to turn to the group for support. Consistent with this analysis, in their own research – conducted in the aftermath of the Kosovo conflict – they find that those victims of war crime who had been victimized in ways that violated sacred and important aspects of group life were least likely to be able to draw effective social support from others. On the other hand, the chapter provides a powerful demonstration of the way in which social groups can be curing in those circumstances where individuals' trauma can be reconciled with the norms and beliefs of the group. Together, this evidence brings to the fore complex issues concerning the capacity for groups to be both a curse and a cure – and points to the need for rehabilitation to be sensitive to the identity-based meaning of particular acts.

Part 4: Social identity, recovery, and rehabilitation

The impact of identity processes on health and well-being points to the capacity for a social identity approach not only to enrich academic understanding in these areas but also to play a key role in shaping health-related policy and practice. At a practical level, such work has the potential to inform developments in the delivery, management, and promotion of health care. More generally, it offers an integrative vision that generates enthusiasm and provides direction for a much larger body of work that is to follow. Speaking to this potential, the fourth part of this volume brings together contributions that examine how sensitivity to issues of social identity can inform recovery and rehabilitation – thereby translating theory into practice.

Jacinta Douglas shows that even people with severe cognitive impairment who appear to have lost many, if not all, elements of their past self (e.g., those related to work and to recreation), still have an understanding of "who they are". Moreover, this residual understanding of self is important for improving individuals' well-being and their capacity to deal with health-related challenges, a point that is demonstrated among people who have experienced severe traumatic brain injury. In this regard, Douglas demonstrates that adjustment and improvement in well-being among those with brain injury is contingent largely on practitioners' capacity to capitalize on existing relationships and to promote the development of new relationships. This analysis provides promising insights into mechanisms that trauma victims can draw from in the process of reconstructing their sense of self and coming to some understanding of the person they have become after injury.

Janelle Jones, Jolanda Jetten, S. Alexander Haslam, and W. Huw Williams also discuss the role of social identity in protecting well-being in a chapter that examines the process of disclosing information about one's acquired brain injury to others. The chapter argues that nondisclosure can protect individuals from discrimination, but that it often also stands in the way of individuals' ability to draw on the social support that can be provided by a range of formal and informal networks. Speaking to this argument, the chapter presents data from two large-scale studies of individuals with acquired brain injury. Amongst other things, these show that, when support is forthcoming, this can help to (re)build a person's sense of personal and social identity and thereby enhance well-being.

Identity change and rebuilding is also an underlying theme in the chapter by Fergus Gracey and Tamara Ownsworth. While these authors argue that multiple factors need to be taken into consideration in the context of identity reconstruction, they note that social relationships must be a focal point in helping people redefine themselves in ways that preserve some sense of continuity with the self as it was experienced prior to trauma. In emphasizing the importance of self-continuity in adjustment to life change, Gracey and Ownsworth move us beyond a purely "individualistic and biocognitive" analysis. In this way, their analysis provides a comprehensive analysis that ambitiously integrates different forms of knowledge and thereby supports the development of a social neuropsychological approach to rehabilitation.

Catherine Haslam, Jolanda Jetten, S. Alexander Haslam, and Craig Knight draw from theoretical insights into the way that identity informs well-being to develop interventions among older adults in care homes. Their chapter presents results from a number of intervention studies that examine the extent to which building new groups can have beneficial well-being effects for older adults in residential care. In particular, the chapter focuses on two studies that provide promising results – one examining the effectiveness of different forms of reminiscence therapy, the other looking at the effects of involving residents collectively in the process of redecorating a new care facility. In both cases it is clear that creating groups which serve to build a sense of shared identity among residents has positive effects on a range of important measures, including cognitive ability, identity strength, and well-being.

Part 5: Conclusion

Catherine Haslam, Jolanda Jetten, and S. Alexander Haslam use the book's final chapter to take stock of the current state of the field and of the substantial advances that have been made in understanding the relationship between identity and health. Going forward, their review also seeks to abstract the key messages that emerge from the preceding chapters for different groups of users: theorists, clinicians, practitioners, and policy makers. As well as reflecting on the achievements of work that has already been conducted, this also outlines an agenda for future research. In keeping with the book's central message, their analysis thus confirms that social identities are not only central, but also the way forward, to *the social cure*.

ACKNOWLEDGMENT

Work on this chapter was supported by a grant from the Economic and Social Research Council (RES-062-23-0135) and a Fellowship from the University of Queensland.

References

Brammer, L. M. (1992). Coping with life transitions. *International Journal for the Advancement of Counselling, 15*, 239–253.

Branscombe, N. R., Schmitt, M. T., & Harvey, R. D. (1999). Perceiving pervasive discrimination among African-Americans: Implications for group identification and well-being. *Journal of Personality and Social Psychology, 77*, 135–149.

Brissette, I., Scheier, M. F., & Carver, C. S. (2002). The role of optimism in social network development, coping, and psychological adjustment during a life transition. *Journal of Personality and Social Psychology, 82*, 102–111.

Cacioppo, J. T., & Patrick, W. (2008). *Loneliness: Human nature and the need for social connection*. New York, NY: W.W. Norton & Company.

Cohen, S., & Wills, T. A. (1985). Stress, social support, and the buffering hypothesis. *Psychological Bulletin, 98*, 310–357.

Cooper, C. (1990). Coping strategies to minimize the stress of transitions. In S. Fisher & C. L. Cooper (Eds.), *On the move: The psychology of change and transition* (pp. 315–327). Chichester, UK: Wiley.

Friedman, M. D., & Rosenman, R. H. (1974). *Type A behavior and your heart*. New York, NY: Knopf.

Haslam, S. A. (2004). *Psychology in organizations: The social identity approach*. London, UK: Sage.

Haslam, S. A., Jetten, J., Postmes, T., & Haslam, C. (2009). Social identity, health and well-being: An emerging agenda for applied psychology. *Applied Psychology: An International Review, 58*, 1–23.

Haslam, S. A., & Reicher, S. D. (2006). Stressing the group: Social identity and the unfolding dynamics of stress. *Journal of Applied Psychology, 91*, 1037–1052.

Holt-Lunstad, J., Smith, T. B., & Layton, J. B. (2010). Social relationships and mortality risk: A meta-analytic review. *PLoS Medicine, 7*(7), e1000316; doi:10.1371/journal.pmed.1000316

House, J. S., Umberson, D., & Landis, K. R. (1988). Structures and processes of social support. *Annual Review of Sociology, 14*, 293–318.

Jetten, J., Branscombe, N. R., Schmitt, M. T., & Spears, R. (2001). Rebels with a cause: Group identification as a response to perceived discrimination from the mainstream. *Personality and Social Psychology Bulletin, 27,* 1204–1213.

Jetten, J., Haslam, C., Haslam, S. A., & Branscombe, N. (2009). The social cure. *Scientific American Mind, 20*(5), 26–33.

Levine R. M., Cassidy, C., Brazier, G., & Reicher, S. D. (2002). Self-categorization and bystander non-intervention: Two experimental studies. *Journal of Applied Social Psychology, 32,* 1452–1463.

Lewin, K. (1951). *Field theory in social science: Selected theoretical papers.* D. Cartwright (Ed.). New York, NY: Harper & Row.

Oakes, P. J., Haslam, S. A., & Turner, J. C. (1994). *Stereotyping and social reality.* Oxford, UK: Blackwell.

Postmes, T., & Branscombe, N. R. (Eds.) (2010). *Rediscovering social identity.* New York, NY: Psychology Press.

Putnam, R. D. (2000). *Bowling alone: The collapse and revival of American community.* New York: Simon and Schuster.

Seligman, M. (2006). *Learned optimism: How to change your mind and your life.* New York, NY: Vintage.

Tajfel, H. (1978). *Differentiation between social groups. Studies in the social psychology of intergroup relations.* London, UK: Academic Press.

Tajfel, H., Billig, M. G., Bundy, R. P., & Flament, C. (1971). Social categorization and intergroup behavior. *European Journal of Social Psychology, 1,* 149–178.

Tajfel, H., & Turner, J. C. (1979). An integrative theory of intergroup conflict. In W. G. Austin & S. Worchel (Eds.), *The social psychology of intergroup relations* (pp. 33–47). Monterey, CA: Brooks/Cole.

Tajfel, H., & Turner, J. C. (1986). The social identity theory of intergroup behavior. In S. Worchel & W. G. Austin (Eds.), *Psychology of intergroup relations* (pp. 7–24). Chicago, IL: Nelson.

Turner, J. C. (1982). Towards a cognitive redefinition of the social group. In H. Tajfel (Ed.), *Social identity and intergroup relations* (pp. 15–40). Cambridge, UK: Cambridge University Press.

Turner, J. C. (1985). Social categorization and the self-concept: A social cognitive theory of group behaviour. In E. J. Lawler (Ed.), *Advances in group processes* (Vol. 2, pp. 77–122) Greenwich, CT: JAI Press.

Turner, J. C. (1991). *Social influence.* Milton Keynes, UK: Open University Press.

Turner, J. C., Hogg, M. A., Oakes, P. J., Reicher, S. D., & Wetherell, M. S. (1987). *Rediscovering the social group.* Oxford, UK: Blackwell.

Turner, J. C., Oakes, P. J., Haslam, S. A., & McGarty, C. A. (1994). Self and collective: Cognition and social context. *Personality and Social Psychology Bulletin, 20,* 454–463.

2 Group identification, social relationships, and health

Fabio Sani
University of Dundee

A vast amount of research conducted within different disciplinary domains, such as sociology, epidemiology, and psychology, has revealed that social relationships are linked to health (Cohen, 2004). The people I see and talk to, work or play with, and love, have an impact on how I feel both mentally and physically; these people get "into my mind" and "under my skin". In general, researchers have found that more intense social relationships and activities lead to better health. However, social ties can be beneficial to health to different degrees, and in some circumstances they can be detrimental even (Rook, 1984). Social relationships that cure are those that are not either conflicting or ambiguous, that are not perceived as burdening and overwhelming, and that are based on cooperation, trust, and mutual support.

What are the factors that determine the quality of social relationships and, therefore, the impact of social relationships on health? In this chapter I will try to answer this question with reference to the "social identity" approach. I will argue that social relationships occur and develop within the context of groups (e.g., families, schools, teams, organizations, communities), and that the way in which one perceives and relates to these groups *as groups* determines the extent to which relationships are curing and beneficial. More specifically, I will contend that group identification (i.e., one's psychological investment in a group, coupled with a sense that the group is self-defining) fosters positive social relationships and, as a result, is a precondition for good health and well-being. For instance, whether my relationship with my spouse, children, siblings, and parents is beneficial or detrimental for my health will depend on the way I experience my family group as a whole. A strong sense of family identification will pave the way for positive relationships with family members and, as a consequence, will enhance my health. On the contrary, feeling estranged and uncommitted to my family group will likely produce negative relationships with family members and will therefore have adverse effects on my health.

In this chapter I will also argue that, while producing compelling evidence about the impact of social relationships on health, current approaches are theoretically ill-equipped and therefore have a limited ability to explain the social psychological mechanisms underlying such impact. The social identity approach can offer the needed theoretical framework, thereby contributing towards a comprehensive and clearer picture of the interplay between social relationships and health.

SOCIAL RELATIONSHIPS AND HEALTH

In a classic sociological study, Durkheim (1897/2007) used census data concerning several European countries and regions to explore the implications of collective life for suicide. He investigated three specific collectives; namely, family, religious, and political groups. Concerning the family, Durkheim found that the larger the family the less likely it was for its members to commit suicide. He therefore contended that the more intense social life afforded by larger families constitutes a shield against suicide. With regards to religious groups, Durkheim observed that Jews and Catholics were much less likely to kill themselves than Protestants all over Europe. For instance, in the period 1869–72, in Prussia the suicide rate for Protestants was about three times higher than that among Catholics and twice the rate of that reported among Jews. Durkheim attributed this difference to the fact that the Protestant faith leaves many questions and areas of enquiry to the judgement of individuals, while Catholics and Jews have clearer prescriptive norms around which their members tightly cohere. Finally, as far as the political community is concerned, Durkheim noted that revolutions and war reduced the number of suicides almost instantaneously, especially when emotion and political passion was particularly high. So, for instance, in 1848 and 1849 – a period of revolution across the whole of Europe – the suicide rate decreased by nearly 10 percent in France, 13 percent in Saxonia, and 18 percent in Prussia, when compared with that reported in the year 1847. Durkheim explained this trend as the product of the sharpening of collective feelings and the concentration of activities towards a unitary purpose, which is typical of political communities in times of great upheaval. Durkheim's observations about suicide rates in domestic, religious, and political aggregates led him to formulate a general proposition – that the likelihood of committing suicide is inversely associated with a person's inclusion and active participation in social aggregates.

While Durkheim focused exclusively on the implications of social relationships for suicide rates, subsequent sociological and epidemiologic research showed that social integration impacts on well-being, health, and mortality rates from all causes of death. For instance, Faris (1934) found that people who were socially isolated were particularly prone to develop schizophrenia, and Holmes, Hawkins, Bowerman, Clarke, and Joffe (1957) found that socially maladjusted individuals were more likely to be diagnosed with tuberculosis. However, for decades there was little research on social relationships and health, and the research that was available relied heavily on cross-sectional and retrospective designs. This made it difficult to establish the direction of these relationships: Is it the case that impoverished social relationships cause people to become ill or die, or that poor health limits socially integration?

Direct and compelling evidence of the causal effects of social relationships on health and mortality has emerged more recently from two large prospective studies of human populations. Berkman and Syme (1979) collected mortality data for a period of 9 years, from 1965 to 1974, in a large sample of adults in Alameda County (California, USA) as part of a survey conducted by the California State Department of Health. It was found that married people had lower mortality rates than the nonmarried (i.e., separated, widowed, single, and divorced); that people who reported stronger ties with friends and relatives had lower mortality than those who were more socially isolated; and that people who belonged to religious or other social groups had lower mortality rates than those belonging to no groups. A "social network" index combining the total number of a person's social ties revealed that people low on the index were twice as likely to die from various causes (i.e., suicide, accident, cancer, or ischemic heart, cerebrovascular, circulatory, digestive, and respiratory disease) as people high on the index. These data are all the more compelling as a range of other potential contributors to mortality, such as socio-economic status, physical health, and health behaviour, were controlled for. In a similar study, House, Robbins, and Metzner (1982) investigated the mortality rates in a large adult sample from the Tecumseh community in Michigan, USA, 10–12 years after they had been interviewed and medically examined. At the time of the interview and medical examination, the participants in this study were between 30 and 69 years of age. Analyses showed that people who led a more solitary life were more likely to die than those with meaningful social relationships (e.g., with their spouse, friends, and relatives) who engaged in social activities (going to meetings of voluntary associations, going to classes or lectures). Again, age and standard biomedical risk factors were partialled out to control for their potential contribution to the findings.

Results from these two pioneering studies were subsequently confirmed in other research and most notably from longitudinal survey studies. For example, a 4-year investigation involving older people free of dementia from the Chicago area revealed that the risk of developing Alzheimer's disease was more than doubled among those with smaller social networks and lower levels of social participation (Wilson et al., 2007). Glass, Mendes de Leon, Bassuk, and Berkman (2006) found that social engagement (e.g., unpaid community work, playing cards, and games) predicted lower levels of depression over time in a large sample of community-dwelling adults aged 65 years and over. Kroenke, Kubzansky, Schernhammer, Holmes, and Kawachi (2006) followed a large sample of US female nurses diagnosed with breast cancer between 1992 and 2002. This research demonstrated that women who were socially isolated before diagnosis had a two-fold increased risk of breast cancer mortality compared to those who were socially integrated.

Compelling and intriguing evidence of the beneficial effects of social relationships on people's lives has also emerged from experimental and quasi-experimental studies. For instance, Baumeister, Twenge, and Nuss (2002) manipulated social exclusion by asking participants to complete a personality inventory and then providing them with false feedback concerning their likely future lives based on their responses. Some participants were told that they would be accident prone, some that they would be surrounded by caring people, and some that they would end up alone. Then the experimenters measured participants' performance on various cognitive and intellectual tests. Analyses showed that performance in complex cognitive tasks such as effortful logic and reasoning was significantly lower among participants who were told they would likely end up alone than among other participants. Taking an even more interventionist approach, Cohen, Doyle, Skoner, Rabin, and Gwaltney (1997) gave nasal drops containing a rhinovirus to a sample of healthy adults from Pittsburgh, USA, after assessing them for participation in 12 types of social relationships (e.g., relationships with a spouse, parents, close neighbours, workmates). These researchers found that participants with more types of relationships were less likely to develop the common cold, and that these effects were robust even when health behaviour was controlled for.

Finally, archival data also support the view that group life reduces mortality. In particular, Pressman and Cohen (2007) selected words related to social ties (e.g., father, sister, neighbour, coworker), as well as words referring to other individuals or interactions with others (e.g., talk, us, friend, group, they) that were included in autobiographies of 96 psychologists and 220 literary writers, for whom biographic and demographic information was available. Statistical analyses revealed that, after controlling for sex, year of birth, and age at the time of writing, a greater use of words that were markers of social ties, other people, and interactions with others, was associated with living longer. For example, among the psychologists, those who mentioned social ties most (highest tertile) lived more than 6 years longer than those who used social ties words the least (lowest tertile).

WHY DO SOCIAL RELATIONSHIPS IMPROVE HEALTH?

Results such as these leave little room for doubt. Social integration has causal effects on mental and physical health outcomes, as well as mortality. But why is this? What are the factors that mediate such effects? Concerning the effects of social integration on suicide, Durkheim referred to our intrinsically social nature. He speculated that an important facet of being human is that we express ourselves through society and serving society, and that only something outside our selves, beyond our mere personal existence, can give meaning and significance to our efforts. When "the individual ego affirms itself excessively over the social ego and at the expense of the latter" (Durkheim, 1897/2007, p. 225) life becomes void and meaningless, thereby paving the way toward the impulse to rid ourselves of it. Durkheim not only considered egotism as a direct factor in suicide, but also as an indirect factor. Egotists, he argued, feel less responsible towards common interests, and are therefore less obstinate about living. Also, egotistic people are deprived of moral support, which essentially makes them weaker and more vulnerable.

Durkheim's speculations on the social causes of suicide have been adopted by contemporary researchers in exploring relationships with health and well-being. For instance, it is argued that social integration fosters well-being and health because it provides people with normative expectations that afford a sense of meaning, belonging, self-worth, and stability (Cassel, 1976; Thoits, 1983), and because it can promote feelings of responsibility for others that enhance motivation to take care of oneself in order to fulfil these responsibilities (Cohen, Underwood, & Gottlieb, 2000). However, most researchers have focused on the importance of the social support that comes from having such ties. It is argued that people with more social ties are healthier because they are the recipients of various types of support. In particular, social ties are thought to secure emotional support (availability of others who can listen sympathetically when one has a problem, and show care and acceptance), instrumental support (availability of practical help and assistance), and informational support (availability of advice, information, and guidance on how to solve problems) (House, 1981). Researchers also believe that social ties lead to the *perceived* availability of social support, that is, the perception that others will provide the resources that may be necessary and appropriate in times of need (Sarason & Sarason, 1986). Perhaps counterintuitively, a substantial body of evidence indicates that perceived availability of support and actually received support are only mildly related (Kaul & Lakey, 2003), and that perceived support has stronger implications for well-being and health than received support (Finch, Okun, Pool, & Ruehlman, 1999; Helgeson, 1993).

How does social support impact on health? Researchers propose that there are both direct and buffering effects (Cohen, 2004). First, receipt of social support has been shown to improve health by reducing blood pressure reactivity (Fritz, Nagurney, & Helgeson, 2003; Lepore, Mata Allen, & Evans, 1993) and by enhancing endocrine and immune system functions (Uchino, Cacioppo, & Kiecolt-Glaser, 1996). Second, social support is believed to buffer the effects of stressful events on both mental and physical health by bolstering one's perceived ability to cope with demands, thus preventing these events from being appraised as highly stressful (Thoits, 1986; Uchino et al., 1996). A prospective study of Swedish men aged 50 years and over conducted by Rosengren, Orth-Gomér, Wedel, and Wilhelmsen (1993) provides clear evidence of the stress buffering function of perceived social support. These researchers found that men with high numbers of stressful life events were at far greater risk of mortality than men with fewer stressful events, but also that these effects were attenuated among those who perceived that emotional support was available to them. In this study it was also found that, among men with few stressful events, the perceived amount of social support did not impact upon mortality.

RELATIONSHIPS THAT DO *NOT* CURE

Clearly, not all forms of social relationships are a source of contentment and positive affect (Rook, 1984). As observed by Cohen (2004), social relationships may prompt conflict, exploitation, humiliation, stress transmission, unwanted help, and many other negative outcomes. A study conducted by Bolger, DeLongis, Kessler, and Schilling (1989) confirmed this observation. Over a 6-week period, these researchers asked a sample of married adults to check how many stressors they were subjected to during the day, out of a list of 21 (e.g., "a lot of work at home", "problem with transportation", "argument with coworker"). It was found that interpersonal conflicts were by far the most upsetting of all daily stressors, and that these were so common as to account for more than 80 percent of the explained variance in daily mood.

If interpersonal conflict is a source of distress, then it can be predicted that negative social relationships will impair physical and mental health. This prediction has been confirmed by a substantial number of studies. Cohen et al. (1998) found that individuals involved in serious and intensive social conflicts were twice as likely to develop a cold as individuals without stressors, following exposure to a virus that can cause a cold. Hooley (2004) conducted research on the type of families that put psychiatric patients at increased risk for relapse, and found that family relationships characterized by high levels of criticism, hostility, and emotional overinvolvement led to increased risk of relapse in patients with schizophrenia and mood disorders, and to less favourable treatment outcomes for patients with anxiety and post-traumatic stress disorder. Other studies have also found that negative social exchanges are linked to negative health outcomes such as depression, worse immune functioning, and increased risk of chronic illness (De Vogli, Chandola, & Marmot, 2007; Umberson, Williams, Powers, Liu, & Needham, 2006). For instance, Holt-Lunstad, Uchino, Smith, and Hicks (2007) examined cardiovascular reactivity in participants who were talking about life events with a friend who was either ambivalent or supportive. Results showed that participants exhibited higher levels of systolic blood pressure reactivity when discussing a negative event with an ambivalent friend compared to a supportive friend.

Even behaviours that are well-intentioned may cause harm. This is particularly the case with social support that is both given and received. For example, concerning social support given, Belle (1982) observed that a carer who provides excessive social support may feel more drained than rewarded. This will produce negative effects on the well-being and health of the carer. Consistent with this observation, Kiecolt-Glaser, Dura, Speicher, Trask, and Glaser (1991) found that elderly carers of a spouse with Alzheimer's disease had lower immune function and were more susceptible to illness than those in a control group. With regards to social support received, it has been noted that this may undermine a person's sense of autonomy and independence, and therefore lead to negative psychological and health outcomes (Thompson & Pitts, 1992). Also, social support received may be unsolicited and unwelcome, thereby prompting negative feelings. For instance, Smith and Goodnow (1999) examined whether older adults differed from younger adults in their experience of different instances of unsolicited support (e.g., support related to health, cognition, finances, or life management). It was found that for participants of all ages, unasked-for support was regarded as more unpleasant than pleasant.

In sum, while the existing literature shows that social relationships tend to improve people's health, it is important to take into account the fact that in some circumstances social relationships may produce deleterious effects. What is more, there is some evidence that these harmful effects of negative aspects of social relationships can sometimes outweigh the beneficial effects of positive aspects (Finch et al., 1999). How, then, do social relationships become *curing* relationships? How might we facilitate relationships that enhance health?

GROUP IDENTIFICATION AND SOCIAL RELATIONSHIPS

The literature on social relationships and health has focused on relationships and interactions that one person may have with other individuals *qua* individuals. For instance, various instruments typically ask participants how often they see or talk to other individuals such as their mother, father, spouse, or child. However, little attention is given to the fact that these individuals are part of a social grouping, the family, which is important *as a collective*, and not merely as a number of individuals. The participant may also be asked if he or she belongs to a group (a church, a class). Then, when the response is affirmative, they are simply asked to specify how many people from the group he or she sees or talks to on a regular basis. Nothing is asked about how he or she relates to the group as a whole, or about the perceived characteristics and properties of the group as a group. Similarly, in some studies the participant has to check the number of social roles that he or she fulfils – for example, as teacher, workmate or church member (e.g., Thoits, 1983). But again, the participant's experience and perceptions of the category of teachers, the work group, or the church group are not assessed. The same logic applies to studies in which participants specify the number of social activities that they are involved in (e.g., Hanson, Isacsson, Janzon, & Lindell, 1989). Here, participants may state, for instance, that they play cards or that they do voluntary work, but they are not asked about their perceptions and feelings regarding the group of people with whom they play cards or about the voluntary work group to which they belong, as groups.

These design features mean that existing literature tends to treat the group as epiphenomenal. Researchers obviously acknowledge the fact that interpersonal relationships and activities may exist within a group frame- work, but the fact that the group *as group* is an object of perceptions, thoughts, and emotions is given scant theoretical and empirical considera- tion. However, as forcefully contended by the social identity approach to group processes and social relations (e.g., Haslam, 2004), the group is not merely an epiphenomenon, it is not just a useful descriptive label used to refer to a collection of individuals. On the contrary, the group is a psycho- logically meaningful entity in its own right. To start with, people have mental representations of the nature, structure, and cohesiveness of their groups (Yzerbyt, Judd, & Corneille, 2004). What is more, people may be *subjectively identified* with a group. Subjective group (or social) identi- fication implies that one is glad to be member of a group, sees the group as important to the sense of who one is, and perceives the self as relatively prototypical of the group (i.e., as similar to other ingroup members on identity-relevant dimensions, and as embodying the norms of the group). The ability to represent the social world in terms of groups, as well as the ability to fuse the self psychologically with a group, is a fundamental and adaptive socio-emotional and cognitive mechanism, as it allows people to function effectively within the social world, a world characterized by com- plex intragroup and intergroup dynamics and relations (Turner & Oakes, 1997). The fact that researchers have neglected group identification and perceptions is unfortunate, because these psychological mechanisms impact upon the quality of social relationships both within and between groups (see Haslam, 2004, for a thorough review). The literature on the influence of group identification on the quality of social relationships is vast, but it is useful to report some illustrative studies.

A team of social identity researchers led by Levine investigated the effects of group identification on helping behaviour in multiple studies using different paradigms (Drury, this volume). They consistently found that whether a person will help another depends on whether the person seeking assistance is categorized as ingroup or outgroup. For instance, Levine, Prosser, Evans, and Reicher (2005) found that a bystander who supported a particular football team was more likely to help an injured stranger in the street when this stranger wore his team's shirt than when the stranger's shirt was either that of a rival team or a nonfootball shirt. Importantly though, when the bystander had been led to identify with the more inclusive group of "football supporters", he or she was more likely to help an injured stranger wearing a team shirt (regardless of whether the team was the one supported by the bystander or a rival team) than one wearing a nonfootball shirt.

Social identity researchers have also explored how perceptions of others as members of either an ingroup or an outgroup affect the way in which a person who is in pain reacts to other people's reassurance. Specifically, research by Platow et al. (2007) found that the level of physiological arousal (measured through Galvanic Skin Response) associated with laboratory-induced pain (immersion of a hand up to wrist into a bath of ice water), following reassurance about the pain-inducing activity, depended on perceptions of the source of reassurance. When reassurance was believed to come from an ingroup member (a student with the same university degree as the participant) arousal was significantly lower than when reassurance was thought to come from an outgroup member (a student with a different university degree).

In a related study, Platow and his colleagues (2005) explored the effects of group identification on the extent to which people found humorous material funny. In the study, a sample of students were asked to listen to some humorous material and associated laughter, after manipulating participants' beliefs about the ingroup or outgroup composition of the laughing audience. It was found that participants laughed and smiled more, laughed longer, and rated humorous material more favourably when laughter was believed to come from other university students (i.e., people sharing the same group identification with the participants) than when it was believed to be produced by members of a political party to which participants did not belong.

Social identity researchers have also investigated the effects of group identification on productivity. Worchel, Rothgerber, Day, Hart, and Butemeyer (1998) conducted an experiment in which small groups of participants were provided with a stack of construction paper, a pair of scissors, and a stapler, and were then instructed to make a paper link chain by cutting one strip of paper at a time off the larger sheets, curling it into a ring, and then stapling it. Participants were told that their individual output could not be identified, but that they should try to make their chain as long as possible. Results revealed that participants were much more productive when the importance of the group was enhanced (by, for instance, asking participants to wear the same uniform, or by telling them that they would work together again in future tasks) than when they worked among unrelated individuals.

This brief review shows that whether or not one identifies with a group has dramatic effects on social relationships. Group identification increases the extent to which one gives help, finds others reassuring when facing a painful situation, is able to have a good time, and is cooperative and productive when performing a group task. Note that these properties of social relationships – help, support, enjoyment, cooperation – coincide with those properties that, according to researchers, exert positive effects on health. Clearly, if shared group identification creates the preconditions for good and curing social relationships, then it can be predicted that group identification is positively associated with health outcomes. This is, indeed, what a growing body of literature is demonstrating.

THE POSITIVE EFFECTS OF GROUP IDENTIFICATION ON HEALTH

The first compelling evidence that group identification has a positive impact on health emerged from the BBC Prison Study, conducted by Reicher and Haslam (1996a, 1996b). These researchers divided 15 participants into a group of prisoners and a group of guards within a purpose-built environment, and then monitored their degree of group identification together with other behavioural, attitudinal, and physiological variables, over a period of 9 days. Data analyses revealed that the guards felt uncomfortable with the exercise of power, and never achieved a shared group identity. The absence of group identification led to disagreement and to lack of leadership and collective coordination that prevented the guards from using their resources effectively. This in turn led to a further drop in group identification and to increased depression, burnout, and physiological stress. On the other hand, the prisoners stuck together as a group in order to challenge the authority of the guards, and in the process came to embrace a sense of shared group identity. This produced clear leadership and strong collective coordination that empowered the prisoners to achieve their goals. As a result of this collective self-realization, the prisoners' level of group identification increased and their degree of depression and physiological stress decreased over time.

These findings are echoed by findings that have emerged from several other studies involving a variety of populations. Much of this research has been conducted in the work and organizational domain. For example, Haslam, O'Brien, Jetten, Vormedal, and Penna (2005) studied groups exposed to high levels of strain, such as bomb-disposal officers and bar staff, and found that group identification was correlated with the support given to, and received from, ingroup members, job/life satisfaction, and perceived stress. Importantly, and in line with the assumption that group identification improves health because, among other things, it facilitates social support, path analysis also showed that social support mediated the effects of social identity on both perceived stress and job/life satisfaction. Along related lines, Wegge, Van Dick, Fisher, Wecking, and Moltzen (2006) found that call centre agents with higher levels of organizational identification were more satisfied with their job, scored higher on organizational citizenship behaviour (e.g., support given, courtesy, altruism), and reported fewer health complaints and emotional exhaustion than agents with lower organizational identification (see van Dick & Haslam, this volume).

In more recent research, Sani, Magrin, Scrignaro, and McCollum (2010) studied a sample of Italian prison guards and found that higher levels of identification with the group of prison guards led to more job satisfaction and lower levels of psychiatric disturbance and perceived stress. Interestingly, this study also revealed that group identification mediated the positive effects of perceived group status (the perceived prestige and status of prison guards when compared with other occupational groups) on well-being and health. In a school context, Bizumic and collegues (2009) studied the effects of organizational identification on well-being and mental health indicators among both students and staff. These researchers found that higher organizational identification was associated with lower levels of depression and higher self-esteem in both the student and staff sample. Among the staff sample, organizational identification was also positively associated with job involvement.

Other researchers have studied people suffering from specific illnesses. For instance, Clare, Rowlands, and Quin (2008) conducted a qualitative 2-year longitudinal study of people with early-stage dementia. These researchers observed that, while at the onset of dementia people felt lost, confused, and hopeless, after joining the self-help network Dementia Advocacy and Support Network International (DASNI) people developed a sense of shared group identity. This implied engaging in mutual support, experiencing a sense of "voice" and collective strength, and gaining a sense of meaning and purpose, which in turn enhanced their well-being. Work also addresses the implications of identification with national and ethnic groups on health. For instance, Kellezi, Reicher, and Cassidy (2009) studied members of identity-affirming groups (i.e., pro-war groups) in Kosovo during the conflict of 1999 (see also Kellezi & Reicher, this volume). Results indicated that members of these groups could discuss the disturbing effects of the war with one another thereby giving and receiving moral support rather than suffering in silence and alone, and that this contributed to good mental health.

My colleagues and I have conducted research on perceived collective continuity, defined as one's sense that the group values, beliefs and attitudes are transmitted across generations (cultural continuity), coupled with a sense that different phases and events marking the group history are inextricably interconnected (historical continuity). In a series of studies focussing on either the regional or the national group (e.g., Valencia, Scotland), we found that higher perceptions of collective continuity predicted stronger group identification and this, in turn, was associated with lower levels of estrangement and higher degrees of social well-being (Sani, Bowe, & Herrera, 2008).

The importance of group identification for health has also emerged from the results of studies focusing on religious institutions and political parties.

For instance, in a study of a schism within the Church of England over the ordination of women to the priesthood, I found that those church members who perceived women priesthood as overthrowing the group identity had lower levels of group identification and higher levels of dejection and agitation-related emotions than those members who saw women priests as maintaining and strengthening the group identity (Sani, 2005). These results were replicated by a study investigating the schism that occurred within Alleanza Nazionale, a right-wing Italian political party, as a consequence of an ideological turn initiated by the party secretary (Sani & Pugliese, 2008). Those party members who perceived the ideological turn as denying the party identity had a lower identification with the party and a higher sense of dejection, agitation, and anger than members who considered the turn as congruent with the party identity.

FAMILY IDENTIFICATION AND HEALTH

More recently, I have started a collaborative research programme concerning the impact of family identification on well-being and health, and the factors that might mediate these effects. The decision to focus specifically on the family group is based on the fact that it is a very important agent of socialization and culture transmission (Cooley, 1909/1992), and is an important basis for self-definition and understanding (Sani & Bennett, 2009). Given its importance, it is not surprising that the family can be either a great source of social support (Uchino et al., 1996) or the origin of major distress and conflict (Elliott & Umberson, 2004). This makes the family an ideal group to study when we aim to investigate the effects of group identification on health and the mediators of these effects.

Results emerging from preliminary analysis of data collected in cross-sectional studies in Scotland and Spain reveal a clear pattern (Sani, Herrera, & Bowe, 2009). In both national contexts, and across both genders and age groups, identification with the family group is associated with a number of well-being and health indicators. For instance, higher degrees of family identification predict greater satisfaction with life, happiness, psychological well-being, physical mobility, and self-reported general health, as well as less depression, loneliness, anxiety, pain, and perceived stress. Intriguingly, we have also found that people who are less identified with the family tend to attribute more human-like traits related with social connectedness (e.g., thoughtful, sympathetic) to pets. This is in line with theory postulating that lack of social relationships leads to attempts to humanize nonhuman agents (Epley, Akalis, Waytz, & Cacioppo, 2008).

Concerning the variables that might mediate the effects of family identification on health, we have assessed the degree of perceived support received from family members (e.g., "I often look to other members of my family for advice and guidance") and the level of perceived collective agency (e.g., "We work together toward the resolution of problems"). Analyses indicate that, overall, these two variables mediate the influence of family identification on health outcomes. Interestingly, perceived support appears to be a particularly important mediator of the effects of family identification on depression, while collective agency seems to be important as a mediator of the effects of family identification on perceived stress. Moreover, all the aforementioned effects (either direct or indirect) remain significant after controlling for factors that are known to affect health, such as health behaviour (smoking, drinking, physical exercise), social status, and extroversion.

In sum, this research supports the argument that subjective identification with a group – the family, in this specific case – exerts a positive influence on our general sense of well-being and health, and that this is because group identification is a precondition for good and curing social relationships among group members. Clearly, it is likely that positive social relationships in turn increase group identification, thereby creating a virtuous circle. However, we also tested an alternative model where group identification was considered as a mediator of the effects of perceived support and collective agency on health, and found no significant mediation effects. Notwithstanding these results, further research – ideally longitudinal and prospective – is needed to investigate the interplay between group identification and within-group social relationships, and the nature of the effects of these variables on health.

CONCLUSIONS

Three decades of research in several disciplinary domains have convincingly demonstrated that our social relationships not only shape the sort of people we are, but also have a substantial impact on our well-being and health. Relationships based on mutual trust, support, and respect, will have positive effects on health. On the contrary, relationships based on mistrust, indifference, and abuse, will have negative repercussions on health. However, to date, researchers have focused almost exclusively on our relationships and exchanges with other individuals *as individuals*. This is a limitation of such research, as people do not always act, think and feel in terms of their unique and idiosyncratic characteristics. As demonstrated by the social identity literature, people subjectively identify with groups and, as a result, they may act, think, and feel in terms of the shared group norms. What is more, group identification will often determine the nature of our relationships with others. In particular, categorizing others as ingroup members will facilitate positive relationships and exchanges. This means that, since positive social relationships are curing and beneficial for health, group identification is an important precondition for health.

For this reason, it is essential that the notion of group identification becomes one of the conceptual tools within the health domain that researchers keep in their theoretical toolbox. This will enrich the field of research on social relationships and health, and enhance researchers' capacity to clarify the complex and multifarious ways in which others influence how we feel both mentally and physically.

References

Baumeister, R. F., Twenge, J. M., & Nuss, C. K. (2002). Effects of social exclusion on cognitive processes: Anticipated aloneness reduces intelligent thought. *Journal of Personality and Social Psychology, 83*, 817–827.

Belle, D. A. (1982). The impact of poverty on social networks and supports. *Marriage & Family Review, 5*, 89–103.

Berkman, L. F., & Syme, L. (1979). Social networks, host resistance, and mortality: A nine-year follow-up study of Alameda County residents. *American Journal of Epidemiology, 109*, 186–204.

Bizumic, B., Reynolds, K. J., Turner, J. C., Bromhead, D., & Subasic, E. (2009). The role of the group in individual functioning: School identification and the psychological well-being of staff and students. *Applied Psychology, 58*, 171–192.

Bolger, N., DeLongis, A., Kessler, R. C., & Schilling, E. A. (1989). Effects of daily stress on negative mood. *Journal of Personality and Social Psychology, 57*, 808–818.

Cassel, J. (1976). Social science in epidemiology: Psychosocial processes and stress theoretical formulation. In E. L. Struening & M. Guttentag (Eds.), *Handbook of evaluation research* (Vol. 1, pp. 537–549). London, UK: Sage.

Clare, L., Rowlands, J. M., & Quin, R. (2008). Collective strength: The impact of developing a shared social identity in early-stage dementia. *Dementia, 7*, 9–30.

Cohen, S. (2004). Social relationships and health. *American Psychologist, 59*, 676–684.

Cohen, S., Doyle, W. J., Skoner, D. P., Rabin, B. S., & Gwaltney, Jr., J. M. (1997). Social ties and susceptibility to the common cold. *Journal of the American Medical Association, 227*, 1940–1944.

Cohen, S., Frank, E., Doyle, W. J., Skoner, D. P., Rabin, B. S., & Gwaltney, Jr., J. M. (1998). Types of stressors that increase susceptibility to the common cold in healthy adults. *Health Psychology, 17*, 214–223.

Cohen, S., Underwood, L., & Gottlieb, B. (2000). *Measuring and intervening in social support.* New York, NY: Oxford University Press.

Cooley, C. H. (1909/1992). *Social organization: A study of the larger mind.* New York, NY: Charles Scribner's Sons.

De Vogli, R., Chandola, T., & Marmot, M. G. (2007). Negative aspects of close relationships and heart disease. *Archives of Internal Medicine, 167*, 1951–1957.

Durkheim, E. (1897/2007). *On suicide.* London, UK: Penguin.

Elliott, S., & Umberson, D. (2004). Recent demographic trends in the US and implications for well-being. In J. Scott, J. Treas, & Richards, M. (Eds.), *The Blackwell companion to the sociology of families* (pp. 34–53). Oxford: Blackwell.

Epley, N., Akalis, S., Waytz, A., & Cacioppo, J. T. (2008). Creating social connection through inferential reproduction: Loneliness and perceived agency in gadgets, Gods, and greyhounds. *Psychological Science, 19*, 114–120.

Faris, R. E. L. (1934). Cultural isolation and the schizophrenic personality. *American Journal of Sociology, 40*, 155–164.

Finch, J. F., Okun, M. A., Pool, G. J., & Ruehlman, L. S. (1999). A comparison of the influence of conflictual and supportive social interactions on psychological distress. *Journal of Personality, 67*, 581–621.

Fritz, H. L., Nagurney, A. J., & Helgeson, V. S. (2003). Social interactions and cardiovascular reactivity during problem disclosure among friends. *Personality and Social Psychology Bulletin, 29*, 713–725.

Glass, T. A., Mendes de Leon, C. F., Bassuk, S. S., & Berkman, L. F. (2006). Social engagement and depressive symptoms in late life. *Journal of Aging and Health, 18*, 604–628.

Hanson, B. S., Isacsson, S.-O., Janzon, L., & Lindell, S.-E. (1989). Social network and social support influence mortality in elderly men. *American Journal of Epidemiology, 130*, 100–111.

Haslam, S. A. (2004). *Psychology in organizations: The social identity approach* (2nd ed.). London, UK: Sage.

Haslam, S. A., O'Brien, A., Jetten, J., Vormedal, K., & Penna, S. (2005). Taking the strain: Social identity, social support, and the experience of stress. *British Journal of Social Psychology, 44*, 355–370.

Helgeson, V. S. (1993). Two important distinctions in social support: Kind of support and perceived versus received. *Journal of Applied Social Psychology, 10*, 825–845.

Holmes, T. H., Hawkins, N. G., Bowerman, C. E., Clarke, E. R., & Joffe, J. R. (1957). Psychosocial and psychophysiologic studies of tuberculosis. *Psychosomatic Medicine, 19*, 134–143.

Holt-Lunstad, J., Uchino, B. N., Smith, T. W., & Hicks, A. (2007). On the importance of relationship quality: The impact of ambivalence in friendships on cardiovascular functioning. *Annals of Behavioral Medicine, 33*, 278–290.

Hooley, J. M. (2004). Do psychiatric patients do better clinically if they live with certain kinds of families? *Current Directions in Psychological Science, 13*, 202–205.

House, J. S. (1981). *Work stress and social support*. Reading, MA: Addison-Wesley.

House, J. S., Robbins, C., & Metzner, H. L. (1982). The association of social relationships and activities with mortality: Prospective evidence from the Tecumseh community health study. *American Journal of Epidemiology, 116*, 123–140.

Kaul, M., & Lakey, B. (2003). Where is the support in perceived support? The role of generic relationship satisfaction and enacted support in perceived support's relation to low distress. *Journal of Social & Clinical Psychology, 22*, 59–78.

Kellezi, B., Reicher, S., & Cassidy, C. (2009). Surviving the Kosovo conflict: A study of social identity, appraisal of extreme events, and mental well-being. *Applied Psychology, 58*, 59–83.

Kiecolt-Glaser, J. K., Dura, J. R., Speicher, C. E., Trask, O. J., & Glaser, R. G. (1991). Spousal caregivers of dementia victims: Longitudinal changes in immunity and health. *Psychosomatic Medicine, 53*, 345–362.

Kroenke, C. H., Kubzansky, L. D., Schernhammer, E. S., Holmes, M. D., & Kawachi, I. (2006). Social networks, social support, and survival after breast cancer diagnosis. *Journal of Clinical Oncology, 24*, 1105–1111.

Lepore, S. J., Mata Allen, K. A., & Evans, G. W. (1993). Social support lowers cardiovascular reactivity to an acute stressor. *Psychosomatic Medicine, 55,* 518–524.

Levine, M., Prosser, A., Evans, D., & Reicher, S. (2005). Identity and emergency intervention: How social group membership and inclusiveness of group boundaries shape helping behaviour. *Personality and Social Psychology Bulletin, 31,* 443–453.

Platow, M. J., Haslam, S. A., Both, A., Chew, I., Cuddon, M., Goharpey, N., et al. (2005). "Its not funny when they're laughing": A self-categorization social influence analysis of canned laughter. *Journal of Experimental Social Psychology, 41,* 542–550.

Platow, M. J., Voudouris, N. J., Coulson, M., Gilford, N., Jamieson, R., Najdovski, L., et al. (2007). In-group reassurance in a pain setting produces lower levels of physiological arousal: Direct support for a self-categorization analysis of social influence. *European Journal of Social Psychology, 37,* 649–660.

Pressman, S. D., & Cohen, S. (2007). Use of social words in autobiographies and longevity. *Psychosomatic Medicine, 69,* 262–269.

Reicher, S., & Haslam, S. A. (1996a). Tyranny revisited: Groups, psychological well-being and the health of societies. *The Psychologist, 19,* 146–151.

Reicher, S., & Haslam, S. A. (1996b). Rethinking the psychology of tyranny: The BBC prison study. *British Journal of Social Psychology, 45,* 1–40.

Rook, K. S. (1984). The negative side of social interaction: Impact on psychological well-being. *Journal of Personality and Social Psychology, 46,* 1097–1108.

Rosengren, A., Orth-Gomér, K., Wedel, H., & Wilhelmsen, L. (1993). Stressful life events, social support, and mortality in men born in 1933. *British Medical Journal, 307,* 1102–1105.

Sani, F. (2005). When subgroups secede: Extending and refining the social psychological model of schisms in groups. *Personality and Social Psychology Bulletin, 31*: 1074–1086.

Sani, F., & Bennett, M. (2009). Children's inclusion of the group in the self: Evidence from a self-ingroup confusion paradigm. *Developmental Psychology, 45,* 503–510.

Sani, F., Bowe, M., & Herrera, M. (2008). Perceived collective continuity and social well-being: Exploring the connections. *European Journal of Social Psychology, 38,* 365–374.

Sani, F., Herrera, M., & Bowe, M. (2009). *Group identification and perceived group cohesion and continuity: Implications for well-being and health.* Paper presented at the APA 117th Annual Convention; Toronto, Canada, 6–9 August.

Sani, F., Magrin, M. E., Scrignaro, M., & McCollum, R. (2010). In-group identification mediates the effects of subjective ingroup status on mental health. *British Journal of Social Psychology, 49,* 883–893.

Sani, F., & Pugliese A. C. (2008). In the name of Mussolini: Explaining the schism in an Italian right-wing political party. *Group Dynamics: Theory, Research, and Practice, 12,* 242–253.

Sarason, I. G., & Sarason, B. R. (1986). Experimentally provided social support. *Journal of Personality and Social Psychology, 50,* 1222–1225.

Smith, J., & Goodnow, J. J. (1999). Unasked-for support and unsolicited advice: Age and the quality of social experience. *Psychology and Aging, 14*: 108–121.

Thoits, P. A. (1983). Multiple identities and psychological well-being: A reformulation and test of the social isolation hypothesis. *American Sociological Review, 48,* 174–187.

Thoits, P. A. (1986). Social support as coping assistance. *Journal of Consulting and Clinical Psychology, 54,* 416–423.

Thompson, S. C., & Pitts, J. S. (1992). In sickness and in health: Chronic illness, marriage, and spousal caregiving. In S. Spacapan & S. Oskamp (Eds.), *Helping and being helped* (pp. 115–151). Newbury Park, CA: Sage.

Turner, J. C., & Oakes, P. J. (1997). The socially structured mind. In C. McGarty & S. A. Haslam (Eds.), *The message of social psychology* (pp. 355–373). Oxford, UK: Blackwell.

Uchino, B. N., Cacioppo, J. T., & Kiecolt-Glaser, J. K. (1996). The relationship between social support and physiological processes: A review with emphasis on underlying mechanisms and implications for health. *Psychological Bulletin, 119,* 488–531.

Umberson, D., Williams, K., Powers, D. A., Liu, H., & Needham, B. (2006). You make me sick: Marital quality and health over the life course. *Journal of Health and Social Behavior, 47,* 1–6.

Wegge, J., Van Dick, R., Fisher, G. K., Wecking, C., & Moltzen, K. (2006). Work motivation, organisational identification, and well-being in call centre work. *Work and Stress, 20,* 60–83.

Wilson, R. S., Krueger, K. R., Arnold, S. E., Schneider, J. A., Kelly, J. F., Barnes, L. L., et al. (2007). Loneliness and risk of Alzheimer disease. *Archives of General Psychiatry, 64,* 234–240.

Worchel, S., Rothgerber, H., Day, E. A., Hart, D., & Butemeyer, J. (1998). Social identity and individual productivity within groups. *British Journal of Social Psychology, 37,* 389–413.

Yzerbyt, V., Judd, C. M., & Corneille, O. (2004). *The psychology of group perception: Perceived variability, entitativity, and essentialism.* New York, NY: Psychology Press.

3   Promoting positive orientation towards health through social identity

Mark Tarrant
University of Exeter

Martin S. Hagger
University of Nottingham

Claire V. Farrow
Loughborough University

How many of us habitually attend a gym class two or three times each week, and monitor the amount of salt and saturated fat we consume in our diets? Hopefully, quite a lot of us. Yet, how many of us also find ourselves quite often – perhaps while in the company of friends – eating more than we should or drinking a few too many glasses of wine? Unfortunately, it seems, quite a lot of people fall into this category as well, as recent statistics on obesity and alcohol-related hospital admissions pay testament (The King's Fund, 2010). How, then, do we explain this apparent inconsistency between making decisions and pursuing behaviours that are beneficial for our health on the one hand and acting in ways that can clearly undermine our health on the other? The current chapter seeks to explain this inconsistency.

People have a considerable amount of control over their long-term health through their volitional behaviour. Clear links exist, for example, between participation in behaviours such as regular exercise and eating a diet low in saturated fat and salt and the prevention of the onset of chronic health conditions such as cardiovascular disease, obesity, and cancer (Byers et al., 2002; Ross, Freeman, & Janssen, 2000; Williams, 2001). Yet the prevalence of such chronic conditions – and our above example – suggests that, actually, many people do not engage in sufficient health-related behaviours (e.g., Activity and Health Research, 1992). Related to this, observed differences between societal groups in levels of participation in health behaviours suggest that "health" does not have the same meaning for all people (Bolam, Murphy, & Gleeson, 2004) and that *social* factors can interfere with or facilitate engagement in health-related behaviours. In the current chapter we elaborate on one such factor – our social identification with others – that can influence people's orientation towards, and decisions concerning, health.

UNDERSTANDING HEALTH BEHAVIOUR: THEORETICAL ACCOUNTS

Traditional psychosocial models of health behaviour have largely empha-sized the influence of personal variables such as individual beliefs con-cerning the health benefits of participating in certain behaviours (e.g., Conner & Armitage, 1998) and have tended to neglect the role of social identity in determining such participation. However, the important role that social identities play in people's decisions about health has recently started to be debated (see Haslam, Jetten, Postmes, & Haslam, 2009). At the heart of this movement is the idea that whether or not people take part in behaviours that are beneficial to health fundamentally depends on the meaning of those behaviours for them, *as group members*. This work will be central to our discussion in this chapter. We very briefly review traditional approaches to the study of health-related behaviour with the theory of planned behaviour (Ajzen, 1991) as an example. Then, after introducing the social identity framework, we present some of our own recent research that has considered the relationship between social identity and health. We do this first in terms of the role of social identity in promoting participation in health-related behaviours, and second in terms of preventing participation in behaviours that are detrimental to health. Finally, we explore the applied implications of this new approach to studying health, outlining some of the ways in which social identity might be practically capitalized upon in order to promote a more positive orientation towards health within society.

Social psychologists have developed psychosocial models to explain the psychological antecedents of those volitional behaviours that can prevent the onset of chronic disease. Such models have three broad aims: (1) to identify the psychological constructs that are implicated in the uptake of, and adherence to, health-related behaviours (such as motivation, intention, and self-efficacy; Conner & Norman, 2005); (2) to understand the mech-anisms through which these constructs influence health-related behaviour (mediation and moderation effects; Hagger, 2009); and (3) to develop interventions that promote increased uptake and adherence to these beha-viours (such as media campaigns, counselling and motivational interview-ing, and online communications; Abraham & Michie, 2008). To date, the majority of these models have been belief-based and have had a social cognitive or motivational form. In addition to the theory of planned beha-viour (Ajzen, 1991), examples of such models include social cognitive theory (Bandura, 2004), the health belief model (Becker, 1974), the theory of reasoned action (Ajzen & Fishbein, 1980), and protection–motivation theory (Rogers, 1975). These models typically view individuals' judgements and expectations of future outcome states as influences on intentions and motivation. A good example is the self-efficacy construct from social cog-nitive theory, which points to the importance of subjective evaluations of capacity and resources to participate in a particular health behaviour in the future (e.g., "I am confident I can participate in physical activity three times per week in the next five weeks").

Central to the theory of planned behaviour is the construct of intention. Intentions are motivational in nature and reflect a person's evaluation of the degree of effort and planning he or she is prepared to invest toward performing a given behaviour. Intention is itself viewed as a function of three sets of beliefs, two of which are personal in conceptualization: *attitudes* reflect beliefs that the behaviour will lead to outcomes that are personally relevant, and *perceived behavioural* control reflects beliefs in one's ability to perform the behaviour. *Subjective norms* represent the social component of intention and are characterized as the perceived extent to which significant others want, or expect one, to perform the target behaviour.

While the theory is generally well-supported empirically (Ajzen, 1991; Armitage & Conner, 2001; Conner & Armitage, 1998), there is substantial variation in the relative contribution of these three sets of beliefs to the prediction of behavioural intentions. Specifically, meta-analyses have identified attitudes and perceived behavioural control as the main predictors of variance in intentions, both in general behavioural contexts (Armitage & Conner, 2001) and also in the study of specific health behaviours such as physical activity and condom use (Albarracín, Johnson, Fishbein, & Muellerleile, 2001; Hagger, Chatzisarantis, & Biddle, 2002). Subjective norms on the other hand have been shown to have a comparatively weak, and sometimes insubstantial, effect in determining intentions and, for this reason, subjective norms have an ancillary role within the theory (Conner & Armitage, 1998).

One acknowledged problem with the normative component of the theory of planned behaviour is that it does not take account of the social context in which each norm referent has influence (Ajzen, 2003). In fact, it has been argued that the way in which this construct is typically understood within the theory may account for its lack of efficacy as a predictor of health-related behaviour (Hagger & Chatzisarantis, 2006). The modification of the theory to account more fully for social contextual influences on behavioural intentions has increased the predictive power of the theory and generally demonstrates the value of social influences within it (Rivis, Sheeran, & Armitage, 2009). Especially noteworthy to the current discussion is work showing that when perceptions of the norms of a specific *social group* are taken into account, a clear role of subjective norms is seen. For example, Terry and Hogg (1996, Study 1) reported that the perceived norms of a salient social group were an important determinant of intentions to exercise, particularly for individuals who identified highly with the group. What is more, those participants who believed that the group norm advocated participation in exercise behaviour were later more likely to report having *actually* exercised than those who did not construe the norm in this way (see also Terry, Hogg, & White, 1999).

These findings are in line with those from other recent studies that have documented the important influence of group norms on people's attitudes and behaviour (e.g., Tarrant, Dazeley, & Cottom, 2009; White, Hogg, & Terry, 2002). But beyond showing that behaviour is predicted better when the normative component is appropriately operationalized, the broader contribution of the above research lies in its highlighting of the fact that people do not make decisions about how they should behave in a "social vacuum". Instead, behavioural decision making is seen as being inextricably linked to people's social group memberships – in terms of how they define themselves *as group members*. This idea builds upon predictions derived from prominent theories of group processes, in particular, *social identity theory* and *self-categorization theory* (Tajfel & Turner, 1986; Turner, Hogg, Oakes, Reicher, & Wetherell, 1987). According to these theories, perception of the self (and others) in terms of social group memberships has a powerful influence on how people interpret and respond to the social world. When a particular social identity is the salient basis for self-definition, individuals define the self with respect to the defining properties of the group and express beliefs that are consistent with those of fellow group members (Tajfel & Turner, 1986). Put another way, when people self-define in terms of a social group membership they internalize and seek to conform to the typical ways of behaving (group norms) and expected roles (e.g., goals, attitudes, and behaviours) of the group (e.g., Turner, 1999).

Recently, social psychologists have built a compelling case for adopting the social identity perspective in the study of health behaviour. Central to this new approach is the idea that social identity provides the framework for individuals to make sense of health issues and, by extension, that this is the basis for their decisions about health (e.g., Levine & Reicher, 1996; St. Claire, Clift, & Dumbelton, 2008; St. Claire & Clucas, this volume). In fact, this is one of the main conclusions to come out of a recent series of studies by Oyserman and colleagues (Oyserman, Fryberg, & Yoder, 2007). According to Oyserman, people engage in health behaviour to the extent that it is congruent with the norms of their social identity; that is, they perform (ill-)health behaviours because those behaviours are *identity-affirming* (Oyserman et al., 2007; see also Terry & Hogg, 1996; Terry et al., 1999). This idea may help explain the paradox that we introduced at the start of this chapter. People who regularly perform health-promoting behaviours (e.g., taking part in an exercise class) may on occasions engage in behaviours that undermine their health (drinking too much alcohol) if such behaviour is consistent with the norms of the social identity that is salient *at that time* (e.g., when socializing with friends).

SOCIAL IDENTITY AND HEALTH PROMOTION

The clear message emerging from the above review is that the way people make sense of, and relate to health and ill-health is fundamentally influenced by their conceptions of themselves in terms of their social identities. Importantly, the evidence points to the conclusion that while some social identities can work against health by inhibiting the psychological processes that underpin health-promoting behaviour, the norms of other social identities are likely to have a positive influence on health behaviour. This observation has influenced some of our own recent work that has employed a social identity perspective to focus on two important questions relevant to the study of health. The first question concerns whether the process of self-categorization can be practically drawn upon to encourage a more positive health orientation amongst members of groups for whom health is not currently normative. The second question focuses on the role of social identity in buffering against the negative health outcomes which can emerge for some people in certain group contexts.

A key insight of self-categorization theory upon which our work is based relates to the context dependency of social identity. Building on the observation that people belong to multiple social groups (e.g., a gender group, national group, and various work and peer groups), the theory holds that which particular social identity is salient for someone at any given point in time depends upon social-contextual cues (Oakes, Haslam, & Turner, 1994; Turner et al., 1987). Thus, whether gender, nationality, or any other social identity forms the basis for self-definition is seen as an outcome of a highly variable and context-dependent process. Crucially, different social identities prescribe different values and beliefs for their members so that what is normative for one social identity will not be normative for another (Haslam, Turner, Oakes, McGarty, & Hayes, 1992). At a practical level, this means that people's stated attitudes about health – and by extension, their health behaviour – can vary according to the norms of the social identity that is salient for them at the time. To press this point a little further, the same individual may report a different health orientation when one particular social identity is salient (e.g., "gym member") compared to when self-categorization is in terms of a different social identity (e.g., "nightclubber"). The dramatic implication of this idea is that by making a social identity salient for which health is normative, or identity-congruent, we should be able to increase people's commitment to health (see Figure 3.1 for a schematic representation of this prediction).

To test this idea, one of us (Tarrant, 2005; Tarrant & Butler, 2011) recently ran a set of studies into the effects of social identity on the health perceptions of university students. Past surveys have revealed the strong group norms that can exist amongst young people at university concerning the performance of health-risk behaviours (e.g., excessive drinking; Haines & Spear, 1996; Wechsler, Molnar, Davenport, & Baer, 1999). For example, researchers have shown that students often describe ill-health behaviours such as excessive drinking as "normal" within the student context, and many have expectations about such norms even before they go to university (Carpenter et al., 2008). Confirming the popular view that young people and

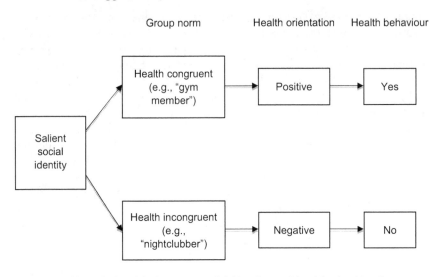

Figure 3.1 The relationship between social identity and health: An identity salience model.

students have a risky attitude towards health, numerous media reports in the UK have recently highlighted a so-called "binge-drinking" culture and have debated the health dangers of student initiation ceremonies that take place in universities and which are often characterized by rapid and excessive alcohol consumption. Such debate is fuelled by research showing that risk-taking – both in the domain of health (e.g., alcohol use, smoking) and in general behaviours – is more marked in 18–24 year olds than in other age groups (Liang, Shediac-Rizkallah, Celentano, & Rohde, 1999).

In our research, we examined the effects on health perceptions of making salient student and youth identity. Because making these identities salient should bring to mind a *health-risk* norm for participants, we expected that orientation towards health would be less positive when they were salient compared to when they did not form the basis for self-definition. We contrasted the effects of making salient student/youth identity with the effects of making an alternative social identity salient, nationality. Information about health is regularly disseminated at a national level and many health promotion campaigns, such as the *Change4Life* campaign in Britain (NHS, 2009), aim to promote the take-up of health promotion behaviours within society in general. We therefore expected that (compared to student and youth identity) national identity would be less closely associated with a risk-taking norm and, as such, our university student participants would be less likely to express a negative orientation towards health when this identity was salient.

An initial study focused on Spanish university students' (*N* = 48) general beliefs about the value of pursuing a healthy lifestyle (Tarrant, 2005). Social identity was manipulated at the outset of the study by giving participants some background information about the research. Participants were told either that the study was concerned with "young people's" or "Spanish people's" lifestyle attitudes. After this, they rated the importance that they personally assigned to each of 14 lifestyle statements. The focal item assessed the importance that participants assigned to the item: "To have a healthy lifestyle". Confirming our expectations, the results showed that participants placed less value on pursuing a healthy lifestyle when their youth identity was salient compared to when their national identity was salient. Reflecting research showing that young people are associated with risk-taking across a range of behavioural domains (Liang et al., 1999), clear differences between the two sets of participants were also observed on several of the other lifestyle values examined, including helping behaviour, environmental behaviour, and choice of vocation. Participants rated these values less highly when their youth identity was salient than when their national identity was salient.

The initial study was followed up with an investigation into the effects of social identity on individual intentions to perform specific health behaviours (reducing alcohol consumption and salt intake; Tarrant & Butler, 2011). Social identity either as "university students" or "British people" was manipulated at the study's outset ($N = 50$ British university students). Two items for each behaviour assessed behavioural intentions (e.g., "I plan to drink alcohol within the recommended safe limits / reduce salt intake during the next two weeks"). As well as examining the effects of social identity on intentions to perform the health behaviours, the study looked more closely at the identity-related meaning of each one. Thus, participants reported their perceptions of the identity congruence of each behaviour (e.g., "I think of students [British people] as the kind of group which would try to reduce salt intake", "Drinking alcohol within the recommended safe limits is important to students [British people]").

The results again confirmed predictions, with participants reporting weaker intentions to engage in the health-promotion behaviours when their student identity was salient than when their national identity was salient. Additionally, and confirming the idea that social identities differ in the degree to which they are associated with health, we found that when student identity was salient ratings of the identity congruence of the behaviours were lower than those produced when national identity was salient.

An important point to make here is that participants in each of these two studies were randomly assigned to one or other of the social identity conditions. That is, *all* of the participants were young people attending university and, by virtue of this group membership, belonged to an "at-risk" group in terms of their health behaviour. But simply by making a different social identity salient – in this case, nationality – these students' health perceptions differed markedly, not just in terms of the general value that they placed on pursuing a healthy lifestyle, but also in terms of their actual commitment to pursue that lifestyle through the performance of specific health-related behaviours. Indeed, in the second study above, participants whose national identity was salient reported a 23 percent increase in intentions to perform the health behaviours over participants whose student identity was salient. According to Cohen's (1992) taxonomy of effect sizes, the size of this effect of social identity was large ($d = 1.14$), meaning that the difference in intentions across the two social identity conditions was greater than one standard deviation unit. In our view, it is this context dependency of social identity salience that has the potential to inform health interventions. By encouraging people to self-categorize in terms of a social identity for which health is normative, or identity-congruent, health promotion campaigns may have a positive impact on people's commitment to developing healthy lifestyles. We return to this idea in the last section of this chapter.

SOCIAL IDENTITY AND ILL-HEALTH PREVENTION

As well as structuring people's orientation towards health and health beha-viours, there is also evidence that social identity processes can influence those health-related cognitions and behaviours that arise in response to the outcomes of specific intergroup encounters. One notable example of this is in the case of people who are overweight and obese, where our recent research has shown that the way people respond to personal experiences of weight-related discrimination is influenced by their perceptions of group norms concerning the treatment of overweight people (Farrow & Tarrant, 2009).

In recent years there has been a wealth of studies documenting the pre-valence of weight bias within society. Such bias, which seems to be increasing (Andreyeva, Puhl, & Brownell, 2008), has been described as one of the last "acceptable" forms of discrimination (Puhl & Brownell, 2001), and there is widespread evidence of it in areas of employment, education, and the health care system (Carr & Friedman, 2005; Greenberg & Worrell, 2005; Puhl & Brownell, 2001). Offensive jokes and degrading portrayals of overweight people are also common in the popular media. Tackling discrimination against overweight people and other stigmatized groups should of course continue to be a priority for social scientists. At the same time, though, it is important to address the negative psychological and behavioural outcomes that are experienced by many victims of discrimination. For overweight people who experience weight bias, such consequences can include depres-sion, psychiatric symptoms, body image disturbance, and lower self-esteem (Friedman et al., 2005), as well as an increased likelihood of engaging in maladaptive eating behaviours such as binge eating and refusal to diet (Puhl, Moss-Racusin, & Schwartz, 2007).

Our research on this topic develops the idea that, in much the same way that social identity can structure people's orientation towards health behaviour, so too can it influence how people deal with those experiences that undermine health (Farrow & Tarrant, 2009). In developing this work, we have drawn on research showing that social group membership can represent an important source of social support for members when they experience stress (Haslam, Jetten, O'Brien, & Jacobs, 2004; Postmes & Branscombe, 2002; see Branscombe, Fernández, Gómez, & Cronin, this volume; Haslam, Reicher, & Levine, this volume). Because experiencing weight bias is also a significant stressor for victims (Ashmore, Friedman, Reichmann, & Musante, 2008), we reasoned that social identity might, in a similar way, present victims of weight bias with a buffer against the negative consequences of those experiences.

Before presenting our research on this topic, it is important to note one major difference between weight bias as a source of stress and other forms of stress that have been the focus of previous research. For example, in Haslam et al.'s (2004) research, bar workers reported the amount of work-related stress they experienced, together with the amount of support they perceived *from their work group*: the source of stress and the source of support were therefore the same. By contrast, people who are overweight may not always define themselves in terms of their weight status but, depending on the social context, may instead define themselves in terms of other social identities (e.g., gender, student, and so on). Building on this observation, we suggested that whether or not a particular social identity will represent a source of support for victims of weight bias will depend upon what these victims believe their fellow group members think of overweight people to be. When one's own group is perceived to consensually oppose the discriminatory treatment of people on the basis of weight, membership of that group should buffer victims against experiences of weight bias. But when one's group does not oppose such discrimination, then that group membership should not help victims deal with their experiences. To test this idea, alongside reporting their past experiences of weight bias, body dissatisfaction, and levels of emotional eating, participants in our study (university students: $N = 168$) reported their perceptions of the student consensus concerning overweight people. That is, they estimated the extent to which university students respected, valued, and liked, overweight people.

The findings provided clear support for the predictions. Mirroring previous research, participants who had experienced weight bias reported higher levels of body dissatisfaction and emotional eating. However, these effects were moderated by their perceptions of their group's consensus concerning the appropriate treatment of overweight people. Specifically, the relationships between experiences of weight bias and body dissatisfaction and emotional eating were found to be weakest amongst participants who believed that the student ingroup opposed the differential treatment of people on the basis of weight. Put another way, victims of weight bias were less likely to report body dissatisfaction and emotional eating when they perceived their ingroup to support group members who were overweight.

PROMOTING HEALTH: LESSONS FROM THE SOCIAL IDENTITY TRADITION

As the research discussed in this chapter has attempted to make clear, the way in which people make sense of and relate to health issues depends upon the meaning of health for social identity. This observation addresses a major limitation of traditional models of health behaviour and helps provide a more complete explanation of intentional behaviour. Moreover, it also lays the foundations for the development of new interventions whereby members of groups in which health is not currently normative can be encouraged to change their orientation towards health and ultimately participate in health-promoting behaviours.

Where health is perceived as relevant for one social identity it is seen as less relevant for another. As Oyserman and colleagues (2007) show, differences in the perceived relevance of health can have important implications for group members' representations of health: perceiving health as incongruent with social identity can undermine cognitions and health knowledge. Our recent investigations (Tarrant, 2005; Tarrant & Butler, 2011) reveal how the context-dependency of social identity salience can be drawn upon to promote a more positive orientation towards health. By encouraging university students (a group that is often associated with behaviour that compromises health) to self-categorize in terms of a social identity for which health is more normative, intentions to perform health-promoting behaviours in the future were strengthened. That such a simple manipulation – a subtle framing of the context of the research study – can yield such powerful effects has important implications for applied interventions.

Developing this idea, one way in which members of "at-risk" groups might be encouraged to change their orientation towards health could be through the deliberate framing of health promotion materials. A good example here is the UK government's recent *Change4Life* campaign (NHS, 2009). In contrast to other health promotion initiatives that are usually directed at the level of the "at-risk" group (such as sexually transmitted infection awareness campaigns that often explicitly target young people), the *Change4Life* campaign targets people at a *societal level*, outlining the various activities that people can take part in to improve their health. A notable feature of the campaign is its use of inclusive language in its publicity documents. The effects of this are likely to be twofold. First, using inclusive language may reduce the defensiveness of recipients when they are exposed to implicit criticisms about their current health behaviour (e.g., "These days, 'modern life' can mean that we're a lot less active . . . none of us are perfect . . . even the best of us can make small changes": NHS, 2009). As research on intergroup communication has established, group members react more positively to critical communications about their group when those communications originate from within the group than when they originate from outside the group; and using inclusive language can act as a cue that communicates shared group membership (Hornsey, Trenbath, & Gunthorpe, 2004). Second, the use of inclusive language may serve to raise the salience of social identity. If people perceive health as being congruent with the norms of a particular social identity, then by making that identity salient, health promotion campaigns have the potential to impact more positively on recipients' health orientation.

This said, a variable that is likely to impact on the effectiveness of health campaigns is the psychological "readiness" of perceivers to self-define in terms of social identities for which health is normative. Thus, even if health campaigns are carefully designed to activate a social identity for which health is normative (e.g., by using inclusive language), they may have limited effectiveness if the social identity is rejected by perceivers. Of relevance here is recent research on the common ingroup identity model (Gaertner & Dovidio, 2000), which has demonstrated that group members who have a strong sense of psychological attachment to their social identity (high group identifiers) sometimes react against attempts to encourage self-definition in terms of a new (superordinate) social identity (Crisp, Stone, & Hall, 2006). In a health context, campaigns which encourage university students to self-define in terms of their national identity rather than their student identity, for example, might inadvertently encourage greater participation in those ill-health behaviours that reflect the student norm, as group members seek to re-establish positive distinctiveness for the student ingroup (e.g., Oyserman et al., 2007; see also Mlicki & Ellemers, 1996). Along these lines, Crisp and colleagues (2006) showed that negative reactions to recategorization can be avoided when group members are encouraged to self-categorize *simultaneously* in terms of their existing identity and the introduced identity. A similar approach in the design of health promotion campaigns may well prove beneficial.

In addition to developing interventions which encourage people to self-categorize in terms of social identities for which health is normative, it might also be beneficial to develop strategies for shaping people's health behaviour that seek to modify their beliefs about the content of particular identities. Our research on responses to weight bias (Farrow & Tarrant, 2009, discussed above) highlighted the relevance of this approach. Following this, reinforcing an ingroup's norms concerning the antidiscriminatory treatment of members of stigmatized groups may well help victims of discrimination cope with their negative experiences and inhibit the maladaptive psychological and behavioural responses that can otherwise present. One factor worth considering, though, relates to *who* has the power to shape a group's norms concerning health. Following Hornsey and colleagues' (2004) work on responses to criticism of groups, appeals to change the norms of a group might be most effective when they emanate from within the group rather than from outside it (see also Haslam et al., 2004). But even when such appeals come from ingroup members it is important to note the position – or authority – of those members to bring about change. While not conducted within a health context, it is worth briefly considering a recent study by Tarrant and Campbell (2007) here. Tarrant and Campbell demonstrated that when a group member criticized their group, the criticism was unlikely to be tolerated if that member had previously undermined the group (see Haslam, Reicher, & Platow, 2010). Criticism was tolerated better – and, by implication, was ultimately more likely to be effective in bringing about change – when it came from a member who had previously upheld the normative values of the ingroup. This study suggests that interventions that aim to modify a group's health behaviour need to pay careful attention to the context in which appeals to change are made; when appeals are perceived to come from outgroup sources or from illegitimate ingroup sources, they may have limited effectiveness.

Finally, it is important to take account of the possibility that the content of social identity can itself change depending on the social context in which that identity is made salient (see e.g., Haslam et al., 1992). Some evidence for this in the domain of health actually comes from one of the lines of research covered earlier in this chapter (Tarrant & Butler, 2011). As in the study reported above, a second study examined the effects of making (British) national identity salient on health behaviour intentions. However, the study also manipulated the *intergroup* context in which that identity was made salient. Half of the participants were presented with information about another nation (Japan) that performed *better* than Britain in terms of health. Thus, for these participants social identity was made salient via an upward intergroup comparison. The other half of participants were presented with information about a nation (USA) that performed *worse* than Britain in terms of health (a downward intergroup comparison). This manipulation had a dramatic effect on participants' health intentions. While the downward comparison had a positive impact on participants' evaluations of Britain's current health status (i.e., it made them feel better about the ingroup), the upward comparison condition was found to have a positive effect on health, with participants in this condition reporting stronger intentions to engage in health behaviour in the future. The perceived norms of the ingroup were not assessed in the study but the effect of the intergroup context manipulation was shown to be partially mediated by participants' attitudes towards the behaviours. Because attitudes reflect group norms, this suggests that perceptions of the norm changed in line with changes in the intergroup context.

CONCLUSIONS

In this chapter, we have argued the case for the modification of models of health-related behaviour such that social identity processes are assigned a more central role in structuring people's orientation towards health. Building on recent work that is grounded within the social identity tradition, our own research has established that the way in which people relate to health and the decisions they make concerning participation in health-related behaviours are fundamentally influenced by self-conceptions at the level of the social group. This research contributes to the emerging debate concerning the interplay between the individual and the group (e.g., Turner, Reynolds, Haslam, & Veenstra, 2006) by revealing that beliefs about health, and related behavioural decisions, whilst on one level appearing to be highly individual processes, are fundamentally products of people's social worlds – and are intrinsically related to who they are *as group members*. Accordingly, interventions which aim to reduce the prevalence of disease by shaping people's beliefs about health must first understand and develop ways of shaping their orientation towards their social identities.

ACKNOWLEDGMENTS

Parts of the research presented in this chapter were funded by a British Academy grant awarded to Mark Tarrant (SG-39260). Time on this project was supported through the Peninsula Collaboration for Leadership in Applied Health Research and Care (PenCLAHRC), funded by the National Institute of Health Research, UK.

References

Abraham, C., & Michie, S. (2008). A taxonomy of behavior change techniques used in interventions. *Health Psychology*, *27*, 379–387.

Activity and Health Research (1992). *Allied Dunbar National Fitness Survey: Summary report*. London, UK: Sports Council and Health Education Authority.

Ajzen, I. (1991). The theory of planned behavior. *Organizational Behavior and Human Decision Processes*, *50*, 179–211.

Ajzen, I. (2003). *Constructing a TPB questionnaire: Conceptual and methodological considerations*. Retrieved 14 April, 2003 from University of Massachusetts, Department of Psychology Web site: http://www-unix.oit.umass.edu/~aizen

Ajzen, I., & Fishbein, M. (1980). *Understanding attitudes and predicting social behavior*. Upper Saddle River, NJ: Prentice Hall.

Albarracín, D., Johnson, B. T., Fishbein, M., & Muellerleile, P. A. (2001). Theories of reasoned action and planned behavior as models of condom use: A meta-analysis. *Psychological Bulletin*, *127*, 142–161.

Andreyeva, T., Puhl, R. M., & Brownell, K. D. (2008). Changes in perceived weight discrimination among Americans, 1995–1996 through 2004–2006. *Obesity*, *16*, 1129–1134.

Armitage, C. J., & Conner, M. (2001). Efficacy of the theory of planned behaviour: A meta-analytic review. *British Journal of Social Psychology*, *40*, 471–499.

Ashmore, J. A., Friedman, K. E., Reichmann, S. K., & Musante, G. J. (2008).

Weight-based stigmatization, psychological distress, and binge eating behavior among obese treatment-seeking adults. *Eating Behaviors, 9*, 203–209.

Bandura, A. (2004). Health promotion by social cognitive means. *Health Education and Behavior, 31*, 143–164.

Becker, M. (1974). The health belief model and sick role behavior. *Health Education Monographs, 2*, 409–419.

Bolam B., Murphy, S., & Gleeson, K. (2004). Individualisation and inequalities in health: A qualitative study of class identity and health. *Social Science & Medicine, 59*, 1355–1365.

Byers, T., Nestle, M., McTiernan, A., Doyle, C., Currie-Williams, A., Gansler, T., et al. (2002). American Cancer Society Guidelines on Nutrition and Physical Activity for Cancer Prevention: Reducing the risk of cancer with healthy food choices and physical activity. *CA – Cancer Journal of Clinicians, 52*, 92–119.

Carpenter, R., Fishlock, A., Mulroy, A., Oxley, B., Russell, K., Salter, C., et al. (2008). After 'Unit 1421': An exploratory study into female students' attitudes and behaviours towards binge drinking at Leeds University. *Journal of Public Health, 30*, 8–13.

Carr, D., & Friedman, M. A. (2005). Is obesity stigmatizing? Body weight, perceived discrimination, and psychological well-being in the United States. *Journal of Health and Social Behavior, 46*, 244–259.

Cohen, J. (1992). A power primer. *Psychological Bulletin, 112*, 155–159.

Conner, M., & Armitage, C. J. (1998). Extending the theory of planned behavior: A review and avenues for further research. *Journal of Applied Social Psychology, 28*, 1429–1464.

Conner, M., & Norman, P. (2005). *Predicting health behaviour: Research and practice with social cognition models.* Buckingham, UK: Open University Press.

Crisp, R. J., Stone, C. H., & Hall, N. R. (2006). Recategorization and subgroup identification: Predicting and preventing threats from common ingroups. *Personality and Social Psychology Bulletin, 32*, 230–243.

Farrow, C. V., & Tarrant, M. (2009). Weight-based discrimination, body dissatisfaction and emotional eating: The role of perceived social consensus. *Psychology and Health, 24*, 1021–1034.

Friedman, K. E., Reichmann, S. K., Costanzo, P. R., Zelli, A., Ashmore, J. A., & Musante, G. J. (2005). Weight stigmatization and ideological beliefs: Relation to psychological functioning in obese adults. *Obesity Research, 13*, 907–916.

Gaertner, S. L., & Dovidio, J. F. (2000). *Reducing intergroup bias: The common ingroup identity model.* Philadelphia, PA: Psychology Press.

Greenberg, B. S., & Worrell, T. R. (2005). The portrayal of weight in the media and its social impact. In K. D. Brownell, R. M. Puhl, M. B. Schwartz, & L. Rudd (Eds.), *Weight bias: nature, consequences, and remedies* (pp. 42–54). New York, NY: Guilford Press.

Hagger, M. S. (2009). Theoretical integration in health psychology: Unifying ideas and complimentary explanations. *British Journal of Health Psychology, 14*, 189–194.

Hagger, M. S., & Chatzisarantis, N. L. D. (2006). Self-identity and the theory of planned behaviour: Between- and within-participants analyses. *British Journal of Social Psychology, 45*, 731–757.

Hagger, M. S., Chatzisarantis, N., & Biddle, S. J. H. (2002). A meta-analytic review of the theories of reasoned action and planned behavior in physical activity:

Predictive validity and the contribution of additional variables. *Journal of Sport and Exercise Psychology*, *24*, 3–32.

Haines, M., & Spear, S. F. (1996). Changing the perception of the norm: A strategy to decrease binge drinking among college students. *Journal of American College Health*, *45*, 134–140.

Haslam, S. A., Jetten, J., O'Brien, A. T., & Jacobs, E. (2004). Social identity, social influence, and reactions to potentially stressful tasks: Support for the self-categorization model of stress. *Stress and Health*, *20*, 3–9.

Haslam, S. A., Jetten, J., Postmes, T., & Haslam, C. (2009). Social identity, health, and well-being: An emerging agenda for applied psychology. *Applied Psychology: An International Review*, *58*, 1–23.

Haslam, S. A., Reicher, S., & Platow, M. J. (2010). *The new psychology of leadership: Identity, influence, and power*. Sussex UK; Psychology Press.

Haslam, S. A., Turner, J. C., Oakes, P. J., McGarty, C., & Hayes, B. K. (1992). Context-dependent variation in social stereotyping 1: The effects of intergroup relations as mediated by social change and frame of reference. *European Journal of Social Psychology*, *22*, 3–20.

Hornsey, M. J., Trenbath, M., & Gunthorpe, S. (2004). 'You can criticize because you care': Identity attachment, constructiveness, and the intergroup sensitivity effect. *European Journal of Social Psychology*, *34*, 499–518.

Levine, M., & Reicher, S. (1996). Making sense of symptoms: Self categorisation and the meaning of illness/injury. *British Journal of Social Psychology*, *35*, 245–256.

Liang, W., Shediac-Rizkallah, M. C., Celentano, D. D., & Rohde, C. (1999). A population-based study of age and gender differences in patterns of health-related behaviors. *American Journal of Preventive Medicine*, *17*, 8–17.

Mlicki, P., & Ellemers, N. (1996). Being different or being better? National stereotypes and identifications of Polish and Dutch students. *European Journal of Social Psychology*, *26*, 97–114.

NHS (2009). *Change4Life Campaign*. Retrieved 17 June 2009 from http://www.nhs.uk/change4life/Pages/MakeChangeUpandAbout.aspx

Oakes, P. J., Haslam, S. A., & Turner, J. C. (1994). *Stereotyping and social reality*. Oxford, UK: Blackwell.

Oyserman, D., Fryberg, S. A., & Yoder, N. (2007). Identity-based motivation and health. *Journal of Personality and Social Psychology*, *93*, 1011–1027.

Postmes, T., & Branscombe, N. R. (2002). Influence of long-term racial environmental composition on subjective well-being in African Americans. *Journal of Personality and Social Psychology*, *83*, 735–751.

Puhl, R., & Brownell, K. D. (2001). Bias, discrimination and obesity. *Obesity Research*, *9*, 788–805.

Puhl, R., Moss-Racusin, C. A., & Schwartz, M. (2007). Internalization of weight bias: Implications for binge eating and emotional well being. *Obesity*, *15*, 19–23.

Rivis, A., Sheeran, P., & Armitage, C. J. (2009). Expanding the affective and normative components of the Theory of Planned Behavior: A meta-analysis of anticipated affect and moral norms. *Journal of Applied Social Psychology*, *39*, 2985–3019.

Rogers, R. W. (1975). A protection motivation theory of fear appeals and attitude change. *Journal of Psychology*, *91*, 93–114.

Ross, R., Freeman, J. A., & Janssen, I. (2000). Exercise alone is an effective strategy for reducing obesity and related comorbidities. *Exercise and Sport Science Review, 28,* 165–170.

St. Claire, L., Clift, A., & Dumbelton, L. (2008). How do I know what I feel? Evidence for the role of self-categorisation in symptom perceptions. *European Journal of Social Psychology, 38,* 173–186.

Tajfel, H., & Turner, J. C. (1986). An integrative theory of intergroup conflict. In S. Worchel & W. G. Austin (Eds.), *Social psychology of intergroup relations* (pp. 2–24). Chicago, IL: Nelson-Hall.

Tarrant, M. (2005). *Social identity effects in the performance of health behaviours during adolescence.* Unpublished data.

Tarrant, M., & Butler, K. (2011). Effects of self-categorization on intentions to perform health behaviours. *British Journal of Social Psychology, 50,* 121–139.

Tarrant, M., & Campbell, E. (2007). Responses to within-group criticism: Does past adherence to group norms matter? *European Journal of Social Psychology, 37,* 1187–1202.

Tarrant, M., Dazeley, S., & Cottom, T. (2009). Social categorization and empathy for outgroup members. *British Journal of Social Psychology, 48,* 427–446.

Terry, D. J., & Hogg, M. A. (1996). Group norms and the attitude–behavior relationship: A role for group identification. *Personality and Social Psychology Bulletin, 22,* 776–793.

Terry, D. J., Hogg, M. A., & White, K. M. (1999). The theory of planned behaviour: Self-identity, social identity and group norms. *British Journal of Social Psychology, 38,* 225–244.

The King's Fund (2010). *A high-performing NHS? A review of progress 1997–2010.* Retrieved 19 April, 2010 from http://www.kingsfund.org.uk/publications/a_high performing_nh.html.

Turner, J. C. (1999). Some current issues in research on social identity and self-categorization theories. In N. Ellemers, R. Spears, & B. Doosje (Eds.), *Social identity: Context, commitment, content* (pp. 6–34). Oxford, UK: Blackwell.

Turner, J. C., Hogg, M. A., Oakes, P. J., Reicher, S. D., & Wetherell, M. S. (1987). *Rediscovering the social group: A self-categorization theory.* Oxford, UK: Blackwell.

Turner, J. C., Reynolds, K. J., Haslam, S. A., & Veenstra, K. E. (2006). Reconceptualizing personality: Producing individuality by defining the personal self. In T. Postmes & J. Jetten (Eds.), *Individuality and the group: Advances in social identity* (pp. 11–36). London, UK: Sage.

Wechsler, H., Molnar, B. E., Davenport, A. E., & Baer, J. S. (1999). College alcohol use: A full or empty glass? *Journal of American College Health, 47,* 247–252.

White, K. M., Hogg, M. A., & Terry, D. J. (2002). Improving attitude–behavior correspondence through exposure to normative support from a salient ingroup. *Basic and Applied Social Psychology, 24,* 91–103.

Williams, P. T. (2001). Physical fitness and activity as separate heart disease risk factors: A meta-analysis. *Medicine and Science in Sports and Exercise, 33,* 754–761.

4 How much is social capital worth?

John F. Helliwell
University of British Columbia
Christopher P. Barrington-Leigh
McGill University

There are many ways in which social engagement can improve physical health and subjective well-being. To move this analysis from the laboratory to the realm of public policy requires two sorts of empirical evidence. The first sort of evidence can be drawn from experimental field trials of promising treatments. The second involves finding comparable values for the results of alternative interventions and policy strategies. Some chapters in this book provide examples of promising "social cures" (e.g., see Haslam, Jetten, Haslam, & Knight, this volume). In this chapter we add a new dimension by using large-scale survey evidence to value different aspects of the social context.

We use large-sample global and Canadian survey data to reveal the powerful effects that social connections and related social identities have on subjective well-being. Our evidence is based on several measures of the extent and frequency of use of social networks, combined with a number of measures of general and domain-specific trust, which are often used to gauge effective social capital. Using these measures we find that trust and social network size and use are all strong predictors of subjective well-being and we demonstrate the size and impact of these effects, by calculating their value in terms of income changes that would produce equivalent levels of life satisfaction.

The second contribution of our chapter is to link our results even more closely to the social identity approach that is central to so many other chapters. We introduce three key measures of social identity – the respondents' sense of belonging to their communities, province, and country – and find that they add significantly to the explanation of life satisfaction among Canadian respondents, and provide important mediating channels whereby social capital is linked to subjective well-being.

HOW CAN THE SOCIAL CONTEXT BE VALUED?

Our conceptualization of "social capital", consistent with that of Putnam (2000), is based on the OECD's definition (2001, p. 41) as "networks together with shared norms, values and understandings that facilitate co-operation within or among groups". Can the importance of social capital be assessed comparably with income support, housing quality, prescription drugs, and other means used by individuals, families, and policy makers to improve the well-being of themselves and others? In epidemiology, the currency of choice has been human lives, with the benefits of medical and social interventions measured in terms of lives saved. Mortality estimates are now frequently supplemented by measures of morbidity, sometimes weighting different sorts of frailty to construct measures of healthy life expectancy. Classic applications of the health-based method to value the social context (e.g., Berkman & Syme, 1979) measured the value of more extensive and happier social relations in terms of longer and healthier lives. An even earlier example is provided by Durkheim's (1897/1952) magisterial analysis, in which suicide was seen as the consequence of hopelessness felt in the face of perceived failures of social relations (Williams, 2001; see Sani, this volume). In the same vein, Helliwell (2007) found that international differences in average social trust had large and significant effects in explaining international differences in both suicides and traffic fatalities.

Linking the social context to mortality and morbidity in these ways remains central to policy evaluation, and deservedly so. Even if the broader objective of the caring professions, and of public policy in general, is to improve the quality of human lives along many dimensions, it will probably always be the case that primary importance is placed on saving lives and restoring health. A life that has been lost cannot be made better, and all of the subjective life evaluations that provide the main evidence reported in this paper show strong linkages to subjective and objective measures of health status. Thus, the traditional measures of better health are not only important in their own right but are important predictors of self-assessed well-being.

However, to assess the overall consequences of the social context requires a broader framework in which good health and other aspects of a good life can be brought together, and their values compared. Many have adopted an a priori approach to such an evaluation. For example, Maslow (1943) argued for a hierarchy of human needs. His pyramidal structure focused first on basic needs and then on "higher order" needs, including those for social companionship. But even if one can measure how well needs and desires at different levels are being met, how are we to compare changes in the degree to which different needs are being met, whether they be at the same or different levels?

Alternatively, Sen (1999) treats capabilities as the fundamental bedrock of human development, represented by some basic set of freedoms from hunger, illness, and fear, and supported by enough education to enable personal and social progress. Yet this also leaves the valuation issue unsolved, as policy makers still need guidance as to the relative values of improving capabilities at different times, and in different contexts.

Utilitarians over several centuries, inspired by Bentham and Mill, among many others, have tackled the valuation issue by presuming some underlying if not-directly-measurable concept of *utility*. Bentham proposed operationalizing utility in terms of a form of hedonic calculus. By this means a balance of pleasure and pain, measured continually and then aggregated through time, would be used to assess each person's experienced utility. In the intervening centuries, many social scientists, and especially economists, have taken a different tack. Assuming that utility could not be directly measured, they instead studied human decisions – believing that these could be used to reveal some features of the underlying utility functions. For example, economists since Adam Smith have used the wages for different jobs (after adjusting as well as possible for differences in skills) to estimate the dis-utility of unpleasant or dangerous jobs, in the process estimating what have been often called "compensating differentials". In the literature, compensating differentials are the wage differences required to offset good or bad characteristics of a job. As will be seen shortly, the same term is now used in the well-being literature to place an income-related value on various features of the social context.

Beyond the indirect revealed preference approach long favoured by economists, Kahneman and colleagues (Kahneman, 1999; Kahneman, Wakker, & Sarin, 1997) have argued for a more direct application of Bentham's hedonic calculus. More precisely, they take the sum of the experienced balance of pain and pleasure to be the underlying measure of utility. Because of the invasiveness and costs of continual monitoring, they have recommended periodic sampling involving relatively short-term memories of moods and emotions.[1] The distinction between experienced and remembered utility has been given especial importance by Kahneman's research. For example, this research shows that the average of moment-by-moment assessments of the painfulness of a colonoscopy is not the same as the remembered pain of the procedure, with the latter best modelled as the average of the peak and final moments of pain (Redelmeier, Katz, & Kahneman, 2003). Similarly, Wirtz, Kruger, Scollon, and Diener (2003) found that moment-by-moment assessments of mid-term break holidays did not closely match the overall memories of the holiday experience. Kahneman has tended to follow Bentham explicitly, and argued that moment-by-moment measures are direct measures of utility and that remembered measures embody cognitive errors (Kahneman & Riis, 2005). Others (including us) argue that the differences between experiences and the memories of them are not errors, but are instead of basic importance. Consistent with this claim, remembered experiences have been found to govern subsequent decisions about holidays and medical procedures, and to represent the long-lasting residual effect underpinning life evaluations. In any event, reports of moods can be used as additional direct measures of utility, and provide an alternative basis for valuing the social context. Our evidence suggests, however, that life circumstances, including income and key elements of social capital, have much more precisely estimated effects on life evaluations than on either current or average moods.

A long time before the utilitarians, however, Aristotle and others made a case for remembered life evaluations, arguing that ethics "gets its grip on the individual at this point of reflection: am I satisfied with my life as a whole, and the way it has developed and promises to develop?" (Annas, 1993, p. 28). Aristotle himself argued that the good life followed a middle course between the Stoics, who put their whole emphasis on the virtuous life, and the Epicureans, who emphasized the importance of pleasures, including the avoidance of pain (Annas, 1993, p. 336). But he was also an early advocate for empirical work on just these issues, and for taking his view of a good life "to the test of the facts of life, and if it harmonizes with the facts we must accept it, but if it clashes with them we must suppose it to be mere theory" (*Nicomachean Ethics*, Book 10, 1179, pp. 20–23).

How should we choose between using the Benthamite U-index (Kahneman & Krueger, 2006) or an Aristotelian life evaluation to provide the raw materials for valuing social capital? There are three main distinctions between the U-index and measures of life satisfaction. First, the U-index is based on moods, which are inherently more changeable during the course of a day and are less subject to changes in life circumstances. Second, the U-index measures the fraction of a day during which bad emotions predominated over good ones, with no further account taken of the strength of the positive or negative feelings. Third, even though both are based on memory rather than current experience, the Daily Reconstruction Method (DRM) underlying the U-index directs and frames recollections in the context of a time-use survey. It therefore provides more information about how specific daily activities (e.g., commuting alone or in company) affect moods during the day.

Life-satisfaction questions, by contrast, ask about "life as a whole these days". It is clear, however, that even these broader assessments are responsive to changes in current circumstances and other mood-affecting patterns of daily life. Thus the U-index and measures of life satisfaction are both found to be correlated with many of the same variables. The two types of data are both useful, but for different purposes, with the former being most appropriate for unravelling the fabric of daily life and the latter for the evaluation of broader and more enduring life circumstances. Thus, as their respective proponents argue, the former can more easily be seen as an application of Bentham's hedonic calculus, and the latter as being truer to Aristotle's advice for evaluating the quality of life as a whole.

It is also worth noting that life-satisfaction evaluations provide evidence supporting Sen's emphasis on capabilities, and Maslow's hierarchy of needs. For example, good health, freedom from hunger, and freedom to make one's own life choices all rank very high as determinants of life satisfaction, and education appears to play a strong mediating role by facilitating better jobs and incomes, better health, and greater trust and social engagement.

Two other practical reasons argue for using life satisfaction, or some similar form of life evaluation (rather than some measure of affect, such as the U-index) as a guide to measuring the value of social capital. The first is that measures of life satisfaction are easier to collect, and have been monitored much more widely, more comparably, and over longer time periods. The second and more fundamental reason is that because measures of life satisfaction are more clearly responsive to basic life circumstances (including both income and the quality of social capital) they provide the basis for much more reliable estimates of the value of social capital.

USING LIFE-SATISFACTION DATA TO VALUE INTERNATIONAL DIFFERENCES IN SOCIAL CAPITAL

In the studies that follow, the basic method used to value social capital involves using large samples of individual measures of life satisfaction (usually ordered responses on a 1 to 10 or 0 to 10 scale) as dependent variables in an estimated utility function for an average individual. In the most general form, we use two-level analysis in which individual utility depends on a set of individual-level circumstances and assessments, plus the same and/or other variables measured to reflect the characteristics of the community or country in which the individual lives. The basic estimation form for two-level analysis of the ordered life-satisfaction responses is:

$$LS_{ij} = \alpha + \delta\ln(y_{ij}) + \mu X_{ij} + \gamma Z_j + \varepsilon_{ij}, \tag{1}$$

where LS_{ij} is some measure of life satisfaction, for respondent i in community or country j, y_{ij} is the level of household income of the respondent, the X_{ij} are other individual- or household-level variables, and the Z_j are community-, state-, or national-level variables, with the same value being used for all individual observations in geographic area j. We use the log form for both household and national average income since most recent evidence suggests, to a first approximation, that life satisfaction rises linearly with the logarithm, and not the level, of household income (e.g., Deaton, 2008; Helliwell, Barrington-Leigh, Harris, & Huang, 2010; Helliwell & Huang, 2010). In some surveys (Helliwell & Putnam, 2004), there is also evidence of an additional tailing off of marginal life satisfaction effects of income at high-income levels, although this is not evident in all surveys. Perhaps this finding reflects the fact that many surveys do not divide income categories finely enough, or do not have large enough samples at the top end of the income distribution. Where there are both individual and societal-level observations on the same social capital variable, the γ coefficients on the societal variables represent contextual effects, or, in other words, the extent of externalities. These contextual effects could

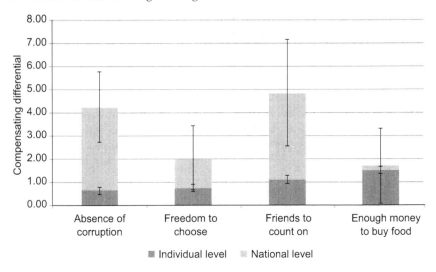

Figure 4.1 Compensating differentials at individual and national levels.

be either positive or negative. In the case of income, the effects of higher neighbourhood average income are usually negative, and often significantly so (Barrington-Leigh & Helliwell, 2008; Helliwell & Huang, 2010; Luttmer, 2005). In the case of social capital variables, the external effects are more generally positive (Helliwell & Putnam, 2004).

Figure 4.1 shows some example estimates of the value of social capital, based on two-level analysis of a global sample of life evaluation data from three waves (between 2006 and 2008) of the Gallup World Poll. The coefficients underlying the compensating differentials of Figure 4.1 are drawn from column 1 of Table 1 of Helliwell et al. (2010). That paper includes comparable estimates for equations using three different life evaluations, each on a scale of 0 to 10: satisfaction with life; the Cantril Self-Anchoring Striving Scale, also known as the ladder of life; and a simple average of each individual's answers to both questions. The Cantril form of life evaluation asks respondents to "Please imagine a ladder with steps numbered zero at the bottom to ten at the top. Suppose we say that the top of the ladder represents the best possible life for you and the bottom of the ladder represents the worst possible. If the top step is 10 and the bottom step is 0, on which step of the ladder do you feel you personally stand at the present time?" The satisfaction with life question (SWL) was: "All things considered, how satisfied are you with life as a whole these days?" (using the same 0 to 10 score; for more details of these measures see the appendix at the end of this volume).

Earlier analysis comparing the first wave of Gallup ladder data with earlier World Values Survey data for life satisfaction showed quite differently shaped distributions, with the ladder data having lower means and more mass at the midpoints than was the case for the World Values Survey data for life satisfaction (Helliwell, 2008). There was also some evidence that the effects of income were greater on the ladder measure. These differences led to the addition of the life satisfaction question to the Gallup World Poll, and to experimental studies designed to see if the framing of the life-satisfaction question could lead to differences in the patterns of responses (Gleibs, Morton, Rabinovich, Haslam, & Helliwell, in press). These experiments showed that increasing the salience of material aspects of life tended to produce subsequent subjective life evaluations that in turn revealed higher correlations with the respondents' actual incomes.

This demonstrated potential sensitivity of coefficients to priming effects made it especially valuable to have matched data for both life satisfaction and the Cantril Scale. Fortunately for our attempts to value the social context in terms of income, we found very similar coefficients using all three dependent variables, thus giving almost identical estimates of compensating differentials (Helliwell et al., 2010). This is quite remarkable, because the distributions of the Cantril Scale and of SWL continue to show significant differences of the sort noted earlier: The national means of the Cantril Scale average about 0.5 points lower than those for life satisfaction, with the difference taking the form of a fuller right-hand shoulder in the life satisfaction distribution. It is encouraging to note that these differences do not lead to conflicting stories from well-being equations estimated from the two different distributions. Indeed, we found that by averaging the two measures we increased the signal-to-noise ratio, as revealed by a significantly higher explained share of total variance. The resulting R^2 of 0.44 is very high for any cross-sectional equation for individual-level measures of subjective well-being, especially an equation that has relatively few structural parameters and no country or region fixed effects. Adding region or country fixed effects raises the explained variance even further, but does not alter the coefficients. Taken together, these results suggest (consistent with Diener, Helliwell, & Kahneman, 2010) that international differences in average values of subjective well-being reflect common responses to international differences in economic and social life circumstances, rather than differences in the way people evaluate their lives. This, coupled with the statistical strength of the key coefficients, helps to provide greater confidence in our estimates of the value of social capital.

We estimate the value of social capital as the ratio of the social capital coefficient to that of income. Following the notation of equation (1), the value of some social capital variable X is $\Delta = \mu/d$, where Δ represents the log change in income that would have for the average respondent the same life-satisfaction effect as a change in some measure of nonfinancial life characteristic, X. These ratios of coefficients are referred to as compensating differentials, since they show how much income could fall and still leave life satisfaction unchanged if there were some improvement in the social context, or vice versa.

To calculate reliable estimates using this method obviously requires secure and reasonably independent estimates of the life-satisfaction effects of an individual's social circumstances and also of income, since the compensating differential is based on the ratio of the sizes of the two effects. If individual-level and societal-level effects are estimated simultaneously, then the error ranges of the two effects can be separately computed. The individual-level effects of social capital are often estimated much more precisely than are the contextual or the societal, in large part because the number of independent observations is invariably much smaller for the contextual effects.

Another important robustness check is to relax the assumption that coefficients are the same in all countries, and to estimate separate well-being equations for each country. Since the sample sizes are now much smaller, and since the social and political contexts shaping well-being differ among nations in many more ways than can be captured by the limited set of explanatory variables, the distributions of national coefficients are quite spread out, as observed by Helliwell et al. (2010). That study shows that the means of the country distributions are almost exactly equal to the global coefficients, once more providing support for the use of the global coefficients for the individual-level effects.

Figure 4.1 shows estimates of compensating differentials for several of the Gallup variables with some connection to social capital. These are based on common global coefficients estimated using two-level modelling of the global sample of individual data. The lower part of each bar shows the individual-level effects, and the vertical line shows the range covered by ±2 standard error. The individual-level effects are thus all highly significant. Consider, for example, the "count on friends" variable. Each individual has been assigned the value 1.0 for this variable (and 0 otherwise) if they answered "yes" to the following question: "If you were in trouble, do you have relatives or friends you can count on to help you whenever you need them, or not?" To be able to answer yes to that question has the same subjective well-being effect as a 1.08 change in the log of household income, which corresponds to almost a trebling of household income. The effects would probably be even larger, and would be more precisely estimated, if a more graduated range of answers had been available. This is especially the case for this variable, because of the very large number of "yes" respondents, who thereby comprise a group too large to have supporting social networks of equivalent quality. For example, almost 82 percent of global respondents answered "yes", and this percentage rises to 92 percent among respondents living in the industrial countries. Since other research has shown that the size and characteristics of one's social networks have important dose-response linkages to subjective well-being, there is obviously significant explanatory power lost by not taking into account the large differences that must exist among the "yes" respondents, all of whom are currently assumed to have equally supporting and engaging social networks.

The upper part of each bar shows the estimated size of the national-level effect, once again accompanied by a vertical line covering the 95 percent confidence region. As noted earlier, the national-level contextual effects for social capital are generally positive. The contextual effects are in some cases significantly positive, although they are always much less precisely estimated than the individual-level effects. Thus to live in a country where others have family and friends to count on has positive well-being effects above and beyond those that result from having one's own supporting network. These spillover effects from social networks are large, even if not very precisely estimated. For example, to live in a country having an Irish level of having friends to count on (97.5 percent) compared to France (at 93.9 percent) would have an income-equivalent value of about 0.175 of log income, about equal to 20 percent of one's income, with one-fifth of this 20 percent due to the average individual effect, and the rest arising from the national-level effect.

Comparing countries much further apart in the international spectrum provides correspondingly larger estimates. If we order the countries in the first three waves of the Gallup Poll in terms of the average percentage of a population having family or friends to count on, the top 10 average just over 96 percent, and the bottom 10 just below 50 percent. The income-equivalent value of this difference is 2.23 (= 0.46(1.08+3.77)), or more than a nine-fold increase in per capita incomes. Put another way, the lack of this type of social capital accounts for a difference of almost a full point (0.95) on the 10-point scale of the Cantril ladder. But this is by no means the whole story, as the total life evaluation gap between these two groups of countries is more than 2.7 points, of which about 1.5 points is explained by their almost 25-fold difference in average per capita incomes. Thus, even though the support of friends is of critical importance, and has huge income-equivalent values, if we look across countries the differences in average incomes are even greater than the differences in the strength of social networks. As we shall now show, this situation may be reversed when we turn to consider differences in incomes, social capital, and well-being within countries.

VALUING SOCIAL CAPITAL DIFFERENCES WITHIN COUNTRIES

In this section we use data from the 17th cycle (2003) of the Canadian General Social Survey (GSS) to value social capital. This survey is especially appropriate for this valuation, since it was designed to measure the extent and quality of social capital. Even without this larger range of social variables, we find that social factors explain a larger proportion of the total variance when the sample is within an industrial nation, since basic wants are largely satisfied.

Table 4.1 shows the standardized betas from several equations explaining cross-sectional differences in life satisfaction among the sample of more

Table 4.1 Weighted ordinary least squares regressions for satisfaction with life

	Equation			
	(1)	*(2)*	*(3)*	*(4)*
Household income (ln)	0.13***	0.12***	0.13***	0.13***
	[9.3]	[8.8]	[9.7]	[9.3]
Social trust	0.028**	0.014	0.013	0.004
	[2.4]	[1.17]	[1.16]	[0.35]
Trust neighbour to	0.072***	0.059***	0.040***	0.034***
return wallet	[6.2]	[5.1]	[3.4]	[2.9]
Trust colleagues	0.25***	0.23***	0.22***	0.20***
	[13.3]	[11.9]	[11.8]	[10.8]
See family (ln)		0.054***		0.033*
		[2.9]		[1.78]
See friends (ln)		0.073***		0.050***
		[4.6]		[3.3]
Have close friends (ln)		0.045***		0.034***
		[3.4]		[2.6]
Have close family (ln)		0.099***		0.079***
		[8.2]		[6.7]
Have other friends (ln)		0.024*		0.012
		[1.87]		[0.97]
Belong in community			0.17***	0.15***
			[13.6]	[11.9]
Belong in province			0.063***	0.059***
			[4.9]	[4.6]
Belong in country			0.074***	0.071***
			[6.1]	[5.9]
R^2	.11	.13	.16	.17

Notes: *$p < .1$. **$p < .05$. ***$p < .01$.
Standardized beta coefficients and, in square brackets, *t*-statistics, are shown.
Detailed definitions of variables, and the coefficients of other variables are in an online appendix.[2]

than 11,000 respondents for whom the full set of variables is available. From this it can be seen that several different measures of the extent, quality, and frequency of use of social capital are significantly correlated with life satisfaction, as are key measures of social identity, especially those relating to the respondent's sense of belonging to his or her local community, province and country. Four equations are modelled in the table, with the most basic [i.e., (1)] on the left and the most complete (4) on the right. The first two equations do not include the social identity variables, while the third and fourth do. The first and third equations do not include variables measuring the size and intensity of use of social networks, while the second and fourth do. Thus it is possible to see the effects of adding social identity and social connections, separately and together.

All of the equations include three measures of trust; a general measure of social trust, assessments of the likelihood of a lost money-bearing wallet being returned intact if found by a neighbour, and a measure of the respondent's trust in his or her workplace colleagues. As analysed in more detail in Helliwell and Wang (2011), all three trust measures are significantly correlated with life satisfaction, with trust in colleagues and in neighbours remaining robustly significant even when the mediating effect of social identity is taken into account, as in the third and fourth equations. The partial SWL correlation of the social trust measure tends to fall with the addition of direct measures of domain trust (as shown earlier in Helliwell & Putnam, 2004), and with the addition of specific measures of social capital and social identity, as shown by the changes in the social trust coefficient when moving from the left to right across the table. Trust in colleagues has the largest explanatory role, with a standardized beta exceeding that for the other two measures combined, and equal to that for income.

The third and fourth equations of Table 4.1 present our first results attempting to measure some direct and indirect effects of social identity on life satisfaction. At this correlational level, we find significant evidence that those who feel a strong sense of belonging are significantly more satisfied with their lives. The sense of belonging to one's local community is especially important, with a beta value slightly exceeding that for income. Thus, if we are seeking to explain the variance across individual respondents to the 2003 Canadian General Social Survey, even more is explained by differences in community-level social identity than by differences in income. Feelings of belonging to country and province are also significant supports for life satisfaction, with the former more important than the latter (except in Quebec); together they explain a slightly smaller share of the variance than does the community-level social identity.

Local social identity appears to mediate about half of the life-satisfaction effects of the neighbourhood trust variable, as the beta coefficient on the latter variable drops in half when the community belonging variable is added. Hence, the life-satisfaction effects of believing that your neighbours would make the effort to return your lost valuables flow substantially through their support for a greater sense of community belonging, as will be shown later in the three parts of Figure 4.2.

We can also use our results to check for parallels with the findings of Haslam, O'Brien, Jetten, Vormedal, and Penna (2005) relating to interactions between social support and social identity. In their regressions, social support and social identity were both strongly predictive of life satisfaction, when entered on their own. The authors then hypothesized that the positive effects of social identity on life satisfaction would be mediated through social support, implying that the estimated effects of social identity on life satisfaction would be significantly less when social support was added to the equation, but not vice versa. Their results supported the hypothesis (see also Sani, this volume).

Our results, shown in Table 4.1, show less of this sort of mediation, and consequentially greater independent roles for both social identity and social support. The estimated coefficients on social support (as measured by the number and frequency of contacts with family and friends) fall when social identity (focusing on the key community belonging variable) is introduced, and vice versa. But the drop is greater for social support [when social identity is introduced, comparing equation (4) with equation (2)] than for social identity [when social support is introduced, comparing equation (4) with equation (3)]. To obtain a closer replication of their tests, we could construct aggregated measures to represent our social support and social identity variables, something lying beyond our current exploratory analysis. As they stand, though, our data seem to admit independent roles for both social identity (especially at the community level) and social support (as measured by the existence and use of larger support networks of family and friends) as simultaneously significant correlates of life satisfaction.

The life-satisfaction results in Table 4.1 also illustrate the claim made earlier, that social variables are more important than economic differences when explaining life-satisfaction differences among respondents living within Canada. For example, the combined social identity variables explain twice as much variance as does income; the trust variables explain more than income, and the social network variables are of roughly similar size. This calculation is based on equation (4), in which all variables are entered simultaneously, so that it is appropriate to add up the standardized betas to a total that is several times as large as that for income. Also noteworthy is the lack of conflict among local, provincial and national identities. Each appears to add to life satisfaction without detracting from the positive effects of the other sorts of belonging. To test this, we defined a variable summing the belonging variables for each individual, and found a slight but nonetheless positive effect. Thus, the benefits of belonging to one's local community do not appear to depend on being less attached to the larger encompassing communities. For any given feeling of belonging at one level, life satisfaction is higher among those who also feel they belong to both more and less encompassing social networks.

Because we found fairly robust correlations between life satisfaction and three different social identities of different but overlapping ambits, we then became curious about what factors might underlie the ways in which individuals identify with their communities, their provinces, and with Canada as a whole. We have therefore done some exploratory analysis using individual and census-tract variables to explain differences among individuals in their sense of belonging in their communities, their provinces, and in Canada as a whole. The main results are shown in Figures 4.2, 4.3, and 4.4, with the regression details reported in the online appendix.[2] All three figures compare the coefficients for each of the three types of social identity. Figure 4.2 shows the effects of different types of trust, while Figure 4.3 shows the effects for different types of social connections, and Figure 4.4

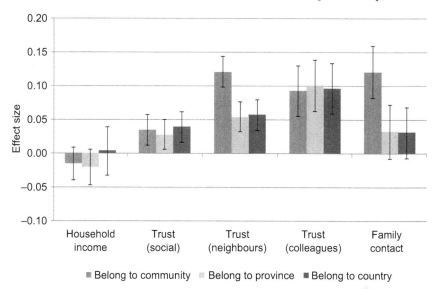

Figure 4.2 Determinants of belonging: Trust.

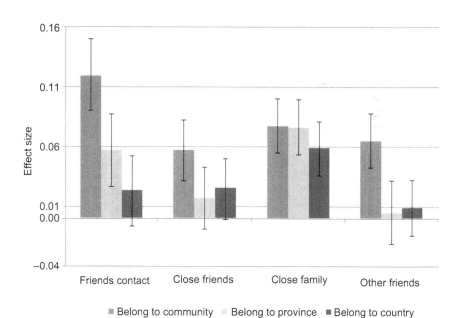

Figure 4.3 Determinants of belonging: Social connections.

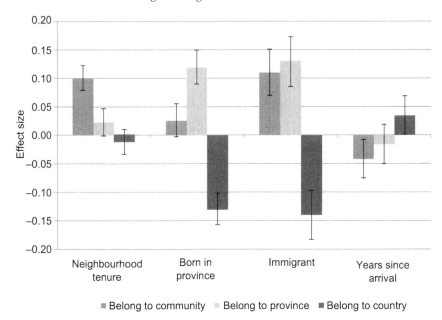

Figure 4.4 Belonging takes time to develop.

contains variables showing that social identities take time to grow. These effects are drawn from equations that include all variables simultaneously, so that they are competing for explanatory power.

The factors explaining the three types of belonging are quite different, in ways that tend to support the validity of all three measures. In particular, community-level belonging, as shown in the first equation, is highly dependent on other local variables, especially neighbourhood trust, social connections with family and friends, and length of time spent in the neighbourhood. A sense of belonging to one's province is higher among francophones, while belonging to Canada is much lower. People who live in the province of their birth identify more with their province, and less with Canada as a whole, than do those who have lived in more than one part of Canada. Immigrants identify significantly more with their local community and province, and less with Canada as a whole, than do those born in Canada. However, all of the immigrant-related effects tend to disappear with increases in the number of years that the immigrant has lived in Canada.

CONCLUSION

Our global and national results both attach high values to several aspects of the social context. Our respondents report significantly higher life satisfaction when they have strong social networks, when they make more frequent use of these supportive networks, when they trust those among whom they live and work, and when they feel a sense of belonging in their communities. Our results are derived from individually based cross-sectional survey data, making it difficult or impossible to derive strict causal interpretations. The economic and social circumstances we have alleged to increase life satisfaction may indeed do so. But there is also the very real possibility that those who are more satisfied with their lives will also reach out to others, form more robust social networks, and be more successful in their economic and social lives.

Because these positive two-way linkages are plausible for both economic and social variables, one can perhaps examine more reliably the relative sizes of economic and social influences. As we have shown, this can be done if both income and social factors are apparently important supports for life satisfaction. If they are, as we found for both the Gallup World Poll data and the data from the Canadian General Social Survey, it is possible to measure the importance of social capital in income-equivalent terms, as we did for the Gallup data, and to compare the overall explanatory power of income and social capital, as we have done using the Canadian GSS data. In both cases we found large values for several different measures of the extent and nature of social engagement and social identity. Our results support the policy relevance of measures of social support and engagement. They also encourage experimental interventions of the sort discussed elsewhere in this volume, since only in such an environment can causality be firmly established.

NOTES

1 Kahneman and Krueger (2006) compare experience sampling and their proposed Daily Reconstruction Method, and discuss their proposed Benthamite U-index, a measure of the preponderance of unpleasant emotions over the previous day.
2 See http://www.nber.org/data-appendix/w16025

References

Annas, J. (1993). *The morality of happiness*. Oxford, UK: Oxford University Press.
Barrington-Leigh, C. P., & Helliwell, J. F. (2008). *Empathy and emulation: Life satisfaction and the urban geography of comparison groups*. (NBER Working Paper 14593). Cambridge, UK: National Bureau of Economic Research.
Berkman, L. F., & Syme, S. L. (1979). Social networks, host resistance, and mortality: A nine-year follow-up study of Almeda county residents. *American Journal of Epidemiology, 109*, 186–204.
Deaton, A. (2008). Income, health and well-being around the world: Evidence from the Gallup World Poll. *Journal of Economic Perspectives, 22*(2), 53–72.
Diener, E., Helliwell, J. F., & Kahneman, D. (2010). *International differences in well-being*. New York, NY: Oxford University Press.

Durkheim, E. (1897). *Le Suicide*. Paris:1[e] edition. First appeared in English as Durkheim, E. (1952). *Suicide: A study in sociology* (Trans. J. A. Spaulding & G. Simpson). London, UK: Routledge & Kegan Paul.

Gleibs, I. H., Haslam, S. A., Morton, T. A., Rabinovich, A., & Helliwell, J. F. (2010). Unpacking the hedonic paradox: A dynamic analysis of the relationships between financial capital, social capital and life satisfaction. *British Journal of Social Psychology*.

Haslam, S. A., O'Brien, A., Jetten, J., Vormedal, K., & Penna, S. (2005). Taking the strain: Social identity, social support and the experience of stress. *British Journal of Social Psychology, 44*, 355–370.

Helliwell, J. F. (2007). Well-being and social capital: Does suicide pose a puzzle? *Social Indicators Research, 81*, 455–496.

Helliwell, J. F. (2008). *Life satisfaction and quality of development* (NBER Working Paper 14507). Cambridge, UK: National Bureau of Economic Research.

Helliwell, J. F., Barrington-Leigh, C. P. Harris, A., & Huang, H. (2010). International evidence on the social context of well-being. In E. Diener, J. F. Helliwell, & D. Kahneman (Eds.), *International differences in well-being* (pp. 291–325). New York, NY: Oxford University Press.

Helliwell, J. F., & Huang, H. (2010). How's the job? Well-being and social capital in the workplace. *Industrial and Labor Relations Review, 63*, 205–228.

Helliwell, J. F., & Putnam, R. D. (2004). The social context of well-being. *Philosophical Transactions of the Royal Society of London, Series B, 359*, 1435–1446. Reprinted in F. A. Huppert, B. Keverne, & N. Baylis (2005, Eds.), *The science of well-being* (pp. 435–459). London, UK: Oxford University Press.

Helliwell, J. F., & Wang, S. (2011). *Trust and well-being*. *International Journal of Wellbeing, 1*, 42–78. www.internationaljournalofwellbeing.org/index.php/ijow/article/view/3/85.

Kahneman, D. (1999). Objective happiness. In E. Diener, D. Kahneman, & N. Schwarz (Eds.), *Well-being: The foundations of hedonic psychology* (pp. 3–25). New York, NY: Russell Sage.

Kahneman, D., & Krueger, A. B. (2006). Developments in the measurement of subjective well-being. *Journal of Economic Perspectives, 20*, 3–24.

Kahneman, D., & Riis, J. (2005). Living, and thinking about it: Two perspectives on life. In F. A. Huppert, N. Baylis, & B. Keverne (Eds.), *The science of well-being* (pp. 435–459). Oxford, UK: Oxford University Press.

Kahneman, D., Wakker, P. P., & Sarin, R. (1997). Back to Bentham? Exploration of experienced utility. *Quarterly Journal of Economics, 112*, 375–405.

Luttmer, E. F. P. (2005). Neighbors as negatives: Relative earnings and well-being. *Quarterly Journal of Economics, 120*, 963–1002.

Maslow, A. H. (1943). A theory of motivation. *Psychological Review, 50*, 370–396.

OECD (2001). *The well-being of nations: The role of human and social capital*. Paris, France: Organization for Economic Cooperation and Development.

Putnam, R. D. (2000). *Bowling alone*. New York, NY: Simon & Schuster.

Redelmeier, D. A., Katz, J., & Kahneman, D. (2003). Memories of colonoscopy: A randomized trial. *Pain, 104*, 187–194.

Sen, A. (1999). *Development as freedom*. New York, NY: Knopf.

Statistics Canada (2003). General Social Survey (GSS), 2003, Cycle 17: Social engagement [user's guide and questionnaire]. Retrieved from http://www.statcan.gc.ca/dli-ild.data-donnees/ftp/gss-esg/gssc-esgc1703-eng.htm

Williams, M. (2001). *Suicide and attempted suicide*. London, UK: Penguin.

Wirtz, D., Kruger, J., Scollon, C. N., & Diener, E. (2003). What to do on spring break? The role of predicted, on-line and remembered experience in future choice. *Psychological Science, 14*, 520–524.

Part II

Social identity, stigma, and coping

5 In sickness and in health

Influences of social categorizations on health-related outcomes

Lindsay St. Claire
Claudine Clucas
University of Bristol

In this chapter we will explore contributions that people's awareness of their group memberships (i.e., social self-categorizations) make to their health-related experiences. How, for example, does a person's knowledge that they are older affect his or her perceptions of illness, and what impact does this have on his or her understanding of any symptoms he or she may have and his or her willingness to seek treatment? How do other people's perceptions that the person is older affect the treatment that the person receives – in society and at the hands of health professionals? In seeking to answer such questions, our perspective reflects a synthesis of social identity theory (Tajfel, 1978, 1981; Tajfel & Turner, 1979), self-categorization theory (Turner, Hogg, Oakes, Reicher, & Wetherell, 1987), and theories of the individual as a source of his or her own development (e.g., Bronfenbrenner, 1979; Dweck, 2000).

To reflect the development of our ideas from their beginning up to the present time, we structure the chapter around five interrelated propositions. Our first proposition is that normative beliefs about health within a culture reflect human history, interests, and purposes. This leads to a second proposition concerning the ways in which normative beliefs determine people's perceptions of others – in particular, those with different forms of illness. Here we argue that the way people categorize others can have detrimental effects on the others' health and well-being – especially when a focus on biological problems leads doctors to perceive individual patients as interchangeable medical cases. Our third proposition focuses on the consequences of applying normative beliefs to oneself through the active process of *self*-categorization. Here we examine the effects that societal beliefs about health and illness can have on people's self-concepts and, through these, on processes of symptom perception. Our fourth proposition relates to the fact that we juggle multiple group memberships or social self-categories (e.g., at the same time as seeing myself as someone with a particular medical condition, I am also a woman and British). Here we argue that interactions between the psychological relevance of these categories can have paradoxical implications for an individual's health and well-being. We bring these various arguments together, in our final proposition that social identity and self-categorization processes provide a basis for social, as opposed to medical, cures.

Proposition 1. **Beliefs about health in a culture reflect human history, interests, and purposes**

In her seminal book, *Labeling the Mentally Retarded*, Jane Mercer (1973) argued that the meaning of diagnostic categories is shaped by normative beliefs that evolve with human interests and purposes. From this perspective, a given medical condition is not solely a matter of pathology, but is also based on shared beliefs and social and political considerations. In support of this argument, Mercer provides the example of children being diagnosed with "minimal brain dysfunction" for the benefit of medical and education systems, even though their "symptomatic" behaviour could easily be explained by social deprivation.

Such beliefs, interests, and purposes are extremely difficult for members of a society to reflect on because they are taken for granted as an aspect of social reality (Wetherell, 1996). Accordingly, it is often easier to see their effects in other cultures and/or times. A fascinating example is provided by the medieval European label "changeling" (see Haffter, 1968), which was used to identify an infant believed to have been left by fairies in exchange for a stolen human baby. Some communities believed that the baby would be returned with gold and hence, the changeling was cherished. Other communities, in which Christianity was followed more closely, believed that the baby had been stolen to punish the mother for sexual activities with the devil (for which she could be burned alive) and the changeling was hidden away, or even murdered. Explanations for the appearance of such babies, expectations about their treatment, and hence, their actual health and well-being, were shaped by differences in prevailing community and religious beliefs. The beliefs represent more than just different contexts for a common condition: from our perspective, they represent different constituents of it. For 21st century Westerners, faith in medical science is a cultural given (e.g., Hardy, 1998) and, on this basis, it is reasonable to reject "changeling" as a diagnostic category and to condemn the consequences that it could have on medieval lives. On the other hand, a prevailing faith in medical science can be seen to underpin the current search for pharmacological cures (e.g., to minimize the effects of premenstrual tension on women's workplace behaviour, or to reduce cardiovascular risk factors or attention deficits), irrespective of cultural beliefs about what behaviours should be performed, how, and by whom (see Golub, 1992; Seale, Pattison, & Davey, 2001). A reasonable question that this raises is whether our faith in medical cures for social ills will one day be seen to be as misguided as our predecessors' view of changelings.

With a view to investigating such processes in action, our early research focused on normative beliefs about people with learning difficulties. In particular, we were interested in identifying differences between groups in their beliefs about people who had been diagnosed with learning difficulties and, whether any such differences could be related to the specific interests and purposes of the groups. To explore these issues, we developed an 81-item measure in which respondents were asked to describe people with learning difficulties on scales with endpoints identified by opposing adjectives (e.g., good – bad; happy – sad). We then surveyed approximately 500 adults.

Many potential groups were represented in this opportunity sample and, amongst other things, we explored differences in beliefs between 400 lay people, 50 psychologists, and 40 teachers. We also explored if, and how, personal acquaintance with someone with learning difficulties affected beliefs. The main findings of the research indicated that all participants shared core normative beliefs that people with learning difficulties have problems in coordinating physical and mental tasks, are childlike, awkward in social situations, and will have trouble in finding a job. However, professionals held additional normative beliefs that seemed aligned with their professional interests. For example, teacher and psychologist groups both believed that people with learning difficulties have problems with coping, with intellectual tasks, and with expressing meaning. Moreover, teachers believed people with learning difficulties are trusting and excitable and psychologists believed people with learning difficulties have limited general knowledge and powers of concentration.

Thirty-five percent of lay participants and fifty-five percent of teachers and psychologists reported that they were personally acquainted with someone with learning difficulties. For lay people and teachers, personal acquaintance introduced more variation into beliefs and more positive, inclusive attitudes, but for psychologists personal acquaintance left normative beliefs unchanged (see St. Claire, 1986). We speculated that psychologists' norms might be underpinned by a detached scientific interest in learning difficulties, in which "personal acquaintance" becomes indistinguishable from "more experience". This speculation was supported by writers who argue that the essence of scientific thinking is that abnormalities in the structure and function of body organs and systems can be systematically identified and reliably diagnosed without distraction from the vagaries of individual experiences (e.g., Bennett, 2003; Helman, 2000).

We developed this speculation into the hypothesis that GPs' (general practitioners') normative beliefs about health should emphasize biomedical definitions of health as an absence of illness and, therefore, that there should be differences between their norms and those of their patients. To explore this hypothesis, St. Claire, Watkins, and Billinghurst (1996) used computerized registers at two general practices to select at random 22 male and 26 female patients with asthma aged 18–55 years who were in receipt of repeat prescriptions for prophylactic medication. For each, a control participant (of matched age, sex, social class, and practice) who was not currently receiving medical treatment was identified. Twenty-seven male and seven female GPs were also selected at random from the local register of GPs.

Table 5.1 Meanings of "health" for general practitioners (GPs), patients with asthma, and control patients

Category of meaning	Example descriptions of health	Patient responses (%)	Control patient responses (%)	GP responses (%)
Biomedical model	an absence of illness or symptoms	5	9	18
Physical well-being	"physically fit", "full of energy", "functioning normally in all bodily activities"	10	10	4
Mental well-being	"feeling happy", "feeling happy with your own body", "feeling good about each day"	6	5	14
Social well-being	"independence", "being independent", "I've got good friends"	2	2	2
General well-being	"trying not to do the things that are bad for you", "not running yourself down", "eating proper foods" and "feeling well"	3	6	11
World Health Organization	1946 definition of health as a state of complete physical, mental and social well-being	0	0	10
Taking action	"looking after yourself"	16	21	2
Being able	"being able to eat normally", "being able to be active if I want", "ability to do things you want with a proper life expectancy"	18	17	6
Value of health	"very important to be healthy"	7	5	1
Unclassified		33	25	32

Each participant was telephoned and asked to provide six descriptions of what "health" meant to them personally. Based on the pool of descriptions they provided, we identified nine categories of meaning. We then assigned each description of health to one of the categories. Table 5.1 presents the percentage of descriptions generated by each participant group that was unanimously assigned by the researchers to each category.

For GPs, the category of meaning into which the highest percentage of descriptions was assigned was "The Biomedical Model", with health being understood primarily as an absence of disease. In contrast, it can be seen that the categories of meaning that best characterized the descriptions of health generated by patients with asthma and control patients focused on being able to do what they wanted in their everyday lives and actively taking care of themselves. In this way, the study confirmed the existence of systematic differences in normative meanings of health. For doctors, health definitions were primarily scientific and medical – focusing on the absence of abnormality in the structure and function of bodily organs and systems – whereas for members of the public they were primarily focused on positive abilities and actions.

Together these two studies provide evidence consistent with *Proposition 1* because differences in beliefs about people with learning difficulties and about health itself were found and could be related to systematic differences in the interests and purposes of the groups of people who held them. The studies also raised a concern and a methodological issue. The concern was that scientific and medical professional norms about health issues imply a focus on abnormalities of body structures and systems and that such a focus might bias perceptions of people with health problems in ways that are disadvantageous to them. The methodological issue was that the groups studied were naturally occurring so we could not be sure that the observed differences between beliefs actually represented active conformity to different normative ways of thinking about health and disease (see Turner, 1995). They could as easily have represented systematic differences in individual characteristics, which predisposed individuals towards membership of particular groups (e.g., people who hold an inclusive attitude are more likely to be personally acquainted with individuals with learning difficulties) or in characteristics resulting from group membership (e.g., people who have been trained in medicine are more likely to focus on health problems). Accordingly, in the next section, we turn our attention to the impact of normative beliefs on perceptions of people and also consider whether the biomedical beliefs held by doctors are socially constructed.

Proposition 2. Social categorization provides a basis for the application of normative beliefs about health and illness to individuals

Tajfel and Wilkes (1963) demonstrated one of the basic characteristics of categorization. In their famous study, participants were presented with eight lines of varying length. In one condition, the four shorter lines were each labelled A and the four longer lines were each labelled B. In a comparison condition, the eight A and B labels were not systematically related to length and in the control condition, there were no labels. When participants were later asked to recall the length of the lines, they (a) increased the perceived similarity of stimuli within classes (i.e., within the set of lines labelled A and within the set of lines labelled B), and (b) increased the perceived differences between the different classes of stimuli (i.e., between A and B) in the first compared with the comparison and control conditions. Based on this study, we examined whether similar accentuation effects were observed when comparing children with and without a diagnosis of learning difficulties. We then considered the implications of any such effects.

We asked 70 psychology students and lecturers to observe slides of eight children, four of whom had been diagnosed with learning difficulties. Slides were presented successively in random order. As each was shown, the child's name and age was read out and participants were asked to rate him or her on 7-point scales (e.g., socially skilled – socially awkward; nice to live with – not nice to live with; sensitive to others – insensitive to others; see St. Claire, 1984). There were two conditions. In the first, "in fact, s/he has received a diagnosis of learning difficulties" or "in fact, s/he has not received any medical diagnoses", as appropriate was added after the name of each child (categorization condition). In the second, no information was added (control condition).

Results showed analogous accentuation effects to those demonstrated by Tajfel and Wilkes (1963). In the categorization condition, ratings were more similar within the set of judgements about the children who had been diagnosed with learning difficulties and also within the set of judgements about the children who had received no such diagnoses. Ratings were also more different between the two sets of judgements about the children who had been diagnosed with learning difficulties and the set of judgements about the children who had received no diagnoses. Relevant to the concern raised at the end of the previous section, we next considered the implications of these accentuation effects. They were most marked on the items previously identified as normative beliefs about learning difficulties, and these were also the items of most relevance to the learning difficulties classification. Because these core items focused on problems in coordinating physical and mental tasks and other difficulties, the net outcome of the accentuation effects for the four children diagnosed with learning difficulties was disadvantageous to them, since perceptions of the children converged towards a more negative mean on each norm.

In a follow-up study, we tested whether analogous accentuation effects would be observed in doctors' perceptions and we also tackled the methodological issue raised at the end of the previous section. Specifically, we examined whether doctors' judgements of children with learning difficulties would be biased under conditions designed to prime categorization. In this study, we randomly assigned 45 doctors and medical students either to a condition designed to enhance the salience of their shared medical identification, or to a control condition designed to enhance the salience of their individual identities (St. Claire, 1993). In the first condition, materials were entitled "Medical diagnosis and beliefs about people with learning difficulties" and the experimenter introduced herself as a psychologist interested in visual cues and medical diagnosis. In the comparison condition, the materials were entitled "Personality and beliefs about people with learning difficulties" and the experimenter introduced herself as someone who needed help with a study of personality differences and person perception. Next, participants performed two tasks. First, they completed 46 7-point scales about children with learning difficulties and, second, they viewed slides of 20 children, 10 of whom had previously received a medical diagnosis of learning difficulties and 10 of whom had not. The slides were presented successively in random order and the doctors were asked to judge which children belonged in which social category, indicating their confidence in each decision.

We predicted that participants whose medical identity was salient would be more likely to conform to scientific and medical professional norms than those in the comparison condition and that this would bias their perceptions of children with learning difficulties in ways that were likely to be disadvantageous to the children. Specifically, doctors and medical students whose medical identity was salient should emphasize abnormality of body structures and systems and therefore endorse more negative beliefs when performing the first task. They should also show a greater tendency to assign children to the "learning disability" category if in doubt when performing the second task. The latter prediction was based on previous findings showing that the direction of errors should be biased towards overexclusion from a positive ingroup category (i.e., in this case, those who do not have learning difficulties; see Tajfel, 1978, 1981).

Results of the first task showed that when participants' medical identity was salient, their normative beliefs about children with learning difficulties emphasized problems with body structures and systems, and their attitudes were more negative. For the second task, signal detection methods were used to assess both accuracy in classification of the children (according to the previous medical diagnoses) and evidence of bias in the direction of errors (see McNicol, 1972). No differences were found between conditions in participants' ability to classify the children, but in line with our second hypothesis, we found that doctors and medical students whose medical identity was salient were more likely than those in the comparison condition to assign children to the learning difficulties category when they were not confident in their decisions.

Both hypotheses were therefore fully supported. Analogous to the case with our nonprofessional sample, the study showed that normative beliefs affected the evaluations made by doctors and medical students. The findings were disturbing because they implied that conformity to medical ways of thinking can entail disadvantages for patients. Other studies that were contemporary at the time, which showed professionals indeed held negative attitudes towards their client and patient groups (e.g., special class teachers towards children with learning difficulties; Kennon & Sandoval, 1978; audiologists towards preschool children with hearing aids; Danhauer, Blood, Blood, & Gomez, 1980), fuelled our concerns as did studies that showed "diagnostic overshadowing" (e.g., such that doctors who categorized patients as having learning difficulties missed non-normative symptoms and, hence, made misdiagnoses; Reiss & Szyszko, 1983). Also consistent with these concerns, a seminal study of more than 2,500 general practice consultations (Byrne & Long, 1976) confirmed that the doctors were oriented towards observable, organic causes of illness. Indeed, many refused to acknowledge the existence of psychosomatic or psychosocial illnesses or to believe that they were responsible for treating them.

With regard to the methodological issue raised at the end of the previous section, *all* participants in this study were doctors or medical students yet a focus on medical norms was only observed in those who had been primed to categorise. This suggests that active social conformity, as opposed to individual characteristics that might predispose people to become doctors (e.g., high social class, intelligence, scientific objectivity) or that result from medical training (e.g., expertise, a focus on health problems) characteristically underpins medical ways of thinking.

We have recently conducted follow-up research on categorization processes in doctors' perceptions, focusing on their implications for patient experiences. A long-standing concern raised by medical patients is that they are treated as interchangeable cases, and not individual people (Bennet, 1979; Gregory, 1979). Related to this, more recent reviews suggest that most complaints relate to doctors' failure to listen to patients and to show them concern and respect (Kumar & Clark, 2005; Morgan, 2003). Because respectful behaviour includes treating people in ways that value their individual humanity (see Dillon, 2003; Lalljee, Laham, & Tam, 2007), we first reasoned that treating patients as interchangeable cases should be perceived by them as disrespectful, and second, that treating patients as interchangeable cases might occur as a result of accentuation effects when doctors categorize individual patients into patient groups.

The first stage in our reasoning was confirmed in a study that we conducted with 220 participants who were asked to reflect on their last medical consultation. Participants generated 203 open-ended responses and thematic analysis showed that "feeling like a unique individual who is understood and cared about" was central to patients' experience of feeling respected. Reasons given for feeling respected included *"Doctor seemed to care, very personal and friendly"* and *"I felt like a person rather than another case or object"* (Clucas, 2008).

For ethical reasons, we were unable directly to test the second stage in our reasoning (i.e., that treating patients as interchangeable cases might occur as a result of accentuation effects, when doctors categorize individual patients into patient groups). However, we tested support for this hypothesis in two subsequent studies, one with doctors and one with medical students, that both included measurement of strength of identification with the medical profession and perceptions of similarity between patients (Clucas, 2008).

In the first study, participants were 35 GPs and 36 hospital consultants; in the second study, participants were 56 medical students. In both, participants were randomly assigned to a condition that either enhanced the salience of their self-categorization as a medical doctor (high-salience condition) or to a condition designed to reduce it (low-salience condition) and were asked to complete a questionnaire. In the high-salience condition, the questionnaire was entitled "Doctors' communication skills" and comprised demographic questions, including place of work (Section A), three scales on which doctors were asked to rate the two last patients they had seen (Section B), and a measure of their identification with the medical profession (Section C; adapted from Doosje, Ellemers, & Spears, 1995). In the low-salience condition, the questionnaire was entitled "Empathy and communication" and the order of Sections A and B was reversed (because we anticipated that answering demographic questions about medical work and training might itself enhance the salience of participants' medical identification).

We predicted that doctors who identified more strongly with their medical identity would perceive individual patients as more similar to each other. To test this hypothesis, we categorized participants into those whose strength of medical identification was "higher" or "lower". Next, we summed the differences between ratings of the last two patients that the participants had seen in order to index perceived patient similarity. Results of both studies indicated that those participants who identified more strongly with the medical profession perceived their patients to be more similar to each other. The results thus supported the hypothesis that the salience of a medical identity increases the perceived interchangeability of patients, and indirectly supported the idea that patients feel treated as interchangeable cases, and hence, disrespected as a result of categorization processes.

Together, the studies in this section provide evidence in support of *Proposition 2*, because they show the powerful role that social categorization can play in medical judgements. They also show that this process can have detrimental consequences for the individuals being perceived, because norms about illness groups lead to a focus on abnormalities and problems and hence, evaluatively biased judgements. More generally, cognitive accentuation of ingroup similarities of patients by doctors might explain why patients often complain that they are treated as interchangeable cases and feel disrespected. The latter is important because feelings associated with disrespectful treatment include injustice, anger and aggression (Miller, 1999) and behaviours include dissatisfaction, lack of adherence to doctors' advice, poor preventive care, and avoidance of treatment-seeking (Beach et al., 2005; Blanchard & Lurie, 2004).

Our discussions thus far have focused on the effects of social categorization processes on others. The role of the individual as a source of his or her own development has not yet been considered. Accordingly, in the next section, we focus on the effects of applying norms to oneself through the process of self-categorization, and we examine whether the experience of illness can itself be socially constructed.

Proposition 3. Social self-categorization provides a basis for the application of normative beliefs about health and illness to oneself

To explore the impact of normative beliefs on self-categorization, we first examined the effects of changes in salient self-categories on the self-perceptions of pupils at a school for children with learning difficulties. The participants were exposed to two conditions that were separated over the period of a week and presented in counterbalanced order. In one condition, school class identification was made salient by emphasizing our interest in "finding out about people at X school and in your class". Questions focused on the length of time at the school, the teacher's and classmates' names, the timetable, and what distinguished participants' class from others in the school. In the second condition, personal identity was made salient by emphasizing that we were interested in "finding out about different people" and questions focused on home, family, personal preferences, and hobbies. After the relevant treatment, participants completed a questionnaire about themselves.

On the basis of self-categorization theory (Turner et al., 1987) we hypothesized that participants' identities would align more closely with those of their classmates and less closely with outsiders under conditions designed to enhance the salience of their shared special school class identification. Results fully supported this hypothesis: The children liked their classmates more, felt more similar to them, were more inclined to help them, and felt more liked and understood by them when their shared school class identification was salient compared to the condition in which their personal identity was salient. When their shared school class identification was salient thay also felt less similarity and liking towards people at their school who were not in their class, and to people outside their school.

We had also hypothesized that school performance would be poorer under conditions designed to enhance the salience of participants' shared special school class identification because poor academic performance is a norm associated with membership of the special school. However, for ethical and practical reasons, we were unable to test this. Nevertheless, indirect support for this hypothesis was found in a study of socially disadvantaged children who had been failing at school (Hartley, 1986). Startling improvements in the children's IQ scores had occurred when they were asked to "imagine that they were the cleverest person they knew" whilst taking their tests. Hartley's study was of particular interest to us because it showed that changes in socially constructed theories about oneself (as opposed to biomedical or scientific interventions) could "cure" the "symptoms" of learning difficulties.

In two recent studies we have tested directly whether changes in salient self-categorization rather than a person's biomedical status can determine concurrent symptom perceptions. Our argument is that illness labels are analogous to group labels and that constellations of symptoms are analogous to norms. Thus, when an individual self-categorizes in terms of a given illness group, his or her symptom perceptions should converge towards those associated with that illness. More formally, we predict conformity to normative symptoms when illness group membership is salient.

Both studies are reported in St. Claire, Clift, and Dumbelton (2008). In the first study, we recruited 22 participants who said they had a cold and 38 who said they did not have a cold. These participants were asked to complete a questionnaire that first manipulated the salience of their self-categorization across one of three conditions. One condition was designed to enhance self-categorization as a member of a group of people with colds. A second condition contained the same facts about colds but did not prime the self-categorization of "cold sufferer" (control). A third condition contained information aimed at enhancing a self-categorization based on exercise status. The questionnaire then measured cold symptoms (Smith, Thomas, Borysiewicz, & Llewelyn, 1995) and symptoms of vitality and fatigue (Smith, Behan, Bell, Millar, & Bakheith, 1993). We expected that participants who reported having a cold would report more intense symptoms than people without colds. Importantly, we predicted that this effect would be qualified by an interaction with the symptom scales and also with participants' salient self-category. Results fully supported our hypotheses. Not only did we find that people with colds had more symptoms than those without colds, but also we found that the difference was more marked on the cold-relevant symptoms than on vitality and fatigue symptoms. Third, self-categorizing as a cold sufferer further increased the experience of cold, but not vitality and fatigue symptoms, so that the difference between the constellations of symptoms experienced was further accentuated.

In the second of the two studies, we recruited people with tinnitus in addition to people with colds: 32 who had a cold but no tinnitus and 32 who had tinnitus but no cold. As in our previous research, the salience of the illness group was manipulated, but this time a tinnitus symptom scale was added (McCombe et al., 2001). The manipulations were successful in that participants identified more strongly with their own illness group under conditions designed to enhance the salience of that self-categorization and the key findings of the first study were replicated. Thus, as expected, people with colds reported more severe cold symptoms than tinnitus symptoms, and people with tinnitus reported more severe tinnitus symptoms than cold symptoms. Critically, however, this contrast was accentuated by salience of illness group membership.

Together, the studies in this section provide evidence in support of *Proposition 3* because they show that health-related outcomes – that are generally understood to be biologically driven – are socially structured by people's self-categorizations. These self-categorizations guide and drive the degree to which we conform to group-relevant expectations. On the positive side, these processes might help us to understand symptom experiences and perhaps increase the likelihood of seeking help for them. On the negative side, however, they are likely to increase the severity of the relevant symptoms and if the illness is embarrassing, stigmatizing, or otherwise negatively evaluated, categorization as a member of such an illness group might also compromise self-esteem. In the next section, we explore this line of reasoning more closely.

Proposition 4. **Individuals actively manage multiple identifications in ways that can have paradoxical implications for their health and well-being**

An extensive literature suggests that illness groups tend to be negatively evaluated. Indeed consistent with the patient reports of depersonalization that we discussed above, becoming a hospital patient may involve giving up jurisdiction of one's own body to the medical system, being stripped of personal possessions and other markers of personal identity, and being assigned to a new devalued identity based on age, organ, or illness (e.g., Lupton, 2003). Given this, it is not surprising that an individual who self-defines as a member of an illness group is also likely to experience a threat to his or her self-esteem. This section explores how people might manage such challenges and the implications of this for symptom perception and other health-related outcomes.

We started from the premise that group members are motivated to make comparisons between their own group and other groups in ways that enhance their positive identity or self-esteem (see Turner, 1981). Social identity theory proposes that perceptions of the broad socio-structural context shape how group members achieve a positive identity. In particular, two perceived features of context have been identified as affecting the way that members of negatively valued groups manage their identity (see Haslam, Jetten, Postmes, & Haslam, 2009; Turner & Brown, 1978). First, when an individual perceives group boundaries as permeable, leaving the group – physically or psychologically – is likely to be an attractive strategy. In such cases a member of an illness group might undertake actions to achieve wellness or might self-categorize in terms of another, more positive identity. Second, when group boundaries are perceived as impermeable, group members' actions depend inter alia on the degree to which they perceive intergroup relations as secure.

If boundaries are perceived as unstable and illegitimate (i.e., insecure), social change strategies based on collective action to challenge the status quo become more likely to be pursued (e.g., as when disability rights groups campaign for equal access). In contrast, if group boundaries are perceived as stable and legitimate (i.e., secure) a series of so-called "social creativity" strategies might be utilized (see Matheson & Anisman, this volume). For example, a member of an illness group might compare his or her group with another group that is worse off (e.g., patients who have colds might compare themselves with patients who have "flu"; see Skevington, 1994). Alternatively, a person might make intragroup comparisons with other ingroup members who are worse off. For example, Taylor (1983) found that breast cancer patients who had lumpectomies were most likely to compare themselves with others who had had mastectomies. Another social creativity strategy might involve members of illness groups reframing or reversing the negative value associated with illness. For example, Viner (1985, cited in Murphy, 1996) reframes the negative experience of suffering from a life-threatening illness – during which time he was helplessly bedridden and hospitalized for 120 days – into a positive experience that helped to make him a better doctor. A final social creativity strategy involves the illness group member making comparisons on selected dimensions, along which he or she will compare more positively. From this we can predict that, under certain conditions, patients are likely to evaluate their health on dimensions that are positive for them, rather than in terms of the signs and symptoms proposed by medical models. The previously reported data from GPs and patients with and without asthma (see Table 5.1) are consistent with this strategy because self-evaluations of health status based on what patients are able to do and how they take care of themselves are likely to be more positive and esteem-enhancing than they would be if based on normative health beliefs of doctors (with their emphasis on biomedical signs and symptoms).

We suggest that social creativity strategies such as this may be an important reason why people with asthma often refuse to carry inhalers. Even though this behaviour may seem irrational from a medical standpoint (to the extent that psychiatric referral may be suggested; Lowenthal, Patterson, Greenberger, & Grammer, 1993), it makes sense if judged with respect to active meanings of health underpinned by salient self-categorizations and motivated to preserve self-esteem. To explore this idea further, we sought to examine these processes more closely in a study of older people who had experienced hearing loss.

Hearing loss is associated with a wide range of symptoms and handicaps, many of which can be ameliorated and sometimes reversed if hearing aids are used (Appollonio, Carabellese, Frattola, & Trabucchi, 1996). Hearing loss is one of the most common conditions affecting older people (National Centre for Health Statistics [NCHS], 1987) and its likelihood increases with age (Davis, 1995). Yet older people typically underestimate their hearing loss and their demand for hearing aids is particularly low (Smeeth, Fletcher, Stirling, Nunes, & Breeze, 2001). These behaviours seem irrational to audiologists because the very people who stand to benefit most from rehabilitation are those who are least likely to seek it.

It is well established that normative beliefs about older age include associations with hearing loss (Walker & Maltby, 1997). Based on our studies of symptom perception, we therefore predicted that older people who self-categorize as older group members would report more hearing-related difficulties than older people who self-categorize in terms of other identities.

In order to test this prediction, St. Claire and He (2009) recruited an opportunity sample of 50 older participants (mean age 63 years) from a university library. On giving consent, participants had their hearing thresholds measured and completed a questionnaire under one of two conditions. The first condition was designed to encourage self-categorization as an "older person", which was made salient by entitling the questionnaire they were asked to complete "Age Groups Study". Participants in this condition were asked to indicate their own age group, list various activities they and other members of their age group commonly do and then complete measures of hearing-related symptoms. This was followed by measures of hearing-related symptoms (Ventry & Weinstein, 1983), identification, and demographic information. The second condition was designed to encourage self-categorization as an individual. Here personal identity was made salient by entitling the questionnaire "How well do you know yourself?" and prefacing it with information about individual differences. Participants in this condition were asked to list various personal activities then complete the symptom, identification, and demographic measures.

As predicted, participants whose self-category as an older person had been made salient reported significantly more hearing-related symptoms and handicaps than those whose individual identity was made salient. Importantly, though, a series of checks confirmed the effectiveness of the identity manipulation and also showed that differences in objective hearing thresholds, age, tinnitus, noise exposure, or personality could not explain the results.

This study showed that self-categorization processes are important – and rational – determinants of older people's subjective reports of their hearing ability. Moreover, since older age is negatively evaluated in the UK (Slater, 2004), there is also a strong likelihood that older people resist self-categorizing as "an older person" in real life (see Jetten & Pachana, this volume). Such resistance should lead older people to perceive less hearing-related difficulties, perhaps explaining the observed underestimation of hearing loss and low demand for hearing rehabilitation. To go forward, a key issue is therefore to examine how best to translate these findings and ideas into rehabilitation strategies that balance the audiometric need for hearing aids with ways to preserve self-esteem of older adults.

Together, the studies in this section provide evidence in support of *Proposition 4*, because they show that social categorization processes can engender health-related disadvantage by increasing symptoms and/or challenging self-esteem. Moreover, strategies designed to protect self-esteem might lead to underestimation of symptoms and failure to take up rehabilitation. In the next and final section of this chapter, we suggest some possible "social cures" to overcome the negative impact of these and other social identity processes.

Proposition 5. **Social identity and self-categorization principles provide a basis for promoting health and well-being through social, not just medical, initiatives**

In Western society, people generally evaluate health problems in terms of underlying biological events. Indeed, statistically and socially defined health problems tend to be seen as medical problems of individuals even though there is no logical connection between the relevant models of normality (Swain, French, & Cameron, 2003). For example, parents of new babies worry that something is wrong with their child if it puts on less than average weight one week, even though the average is a statistical norm, and therefore, by definition calculated with respect to the weights of other children (as opposed to sinister health problems). Similarly, people who have hearing loss often experience difficulties in communication and it is assumed that a biological event, such as cochlear damage is the cause (see Katz, Medwetsky, Burkard, & Hood, 2009) even though such difficulties may be caused by the mumbling of speakers or by self-categorization as "older" and/or "hard of hearing". The consequences of analysing health problems in this way are important because procedures directed at such social aetiologies might cure health-related problems and obviate the need for medical intervention (see also Fielding, 1999). For example, in line with the reasoning and evidence relevant to *Proposition 1* (that beliefs about health in a culture reflect human history, interests, and purposes), a true social cure might one day be achieved by changes in cultural and medical norms about health, away from their focus on professional interests and purposes, and towards values that encourage respect of minority groups, patients, and individuals.

Meanwhile, what might steps towards such a social cure look like? In line with the reasoning and evidence relevant to *Proposition 2* (that social categorization provides a basis for the application of normative beliefs about health and illness to individuals), we concluded that social categorization of patients by doctors increased the perceived interchangeability of patients and also led to conformity to medical norms and hence to more negative evaluations. Patient-centred communication skills training (CST) might present a possible social cure for resultant disadvantages because such training actively works against the depersonalization of individuals as "patients" (see Stewart et al., 1995). To explore the effectiveness of this potential social cure, we performed a secondary analysis of our data on the salience of medical identity and perceived similarity of patients (Clucas & St. Claire, 2011). We classified doctors and clinical year medical students into those who reported that they had received "smaller", "medium" or "greater" amounts of CST and then examined whether this had a bearing on the perceived similarity of patients. Results showed perceived patient similarity was lower for doctors and medical students who had received greater compared with smaller CST. However, further analyses revealed a negative correlation between CST and strength of medical identification for hospital doctors. Thus, even though the effectiveness of CST in reducing perceptions of patient similarity is promising, what is worrying is that it may occur at the cost of reducing doctors' identification with their professional role – potentially threatening conformity to desirable as well as undesirable professional norms. To offer a truly social psychological cure, CST would need to effect positive social change towards more respectful patient-centred medical norms – different from individualistic interventions that mend communication skills of individual doctors or that encourage them psychologically to distance themselves from their professional norms.

Recently, we conducted further studies to examine our idea that facilitating the treatment of patients as individuals, and thereby increasing respect towards them, has the potential to offer social cures (see Clucas & St. Claire, 2010). Specifically, we hypothesized that feeling respected in doctor–patient relations has positive effects on health-related outcomes.

We recruited two opportunity samples, (*n*s = 85 and 54). At random, we gave participants one of two matched booklets describing a doctor–patient scenario. In the first booklet, the doctor behaved in a respectful manner and in the second, the doctor was disrespectful. The booklets began with an Illness Perception Questionnaire (IPQ; Weinman, Petrie, Moss-Morris, & Horne, 1996), and participants were invited to imagine that they were the patient with tinnitus who had completed it. The next section comprised self and collective esteem scales (based on Luhtanen & Crocker, 1992; Rosenberg, 1965) followed by the scenario between the (imagined) tinnitus patient and the respectful/disrespectful doctor. The scenario was interspersed at key points with questions measuring how respected participants felt and followed by further esteem scales and measures of health-related outcomes (including intended adherence to advice, respect felt for the doctor, and a blank IPQ to measure tinnitus representations).

Results of both studies showed that participants felt more respected when playing the role of a patient with a respectful, as opposed to a disrespectful, doctor. Moreover, they reported greater patient satisfaction, trust, and respect, and stronger intentions to adhere to advice, and visit the doctor again. In Study 1, they also reported fewer tinnitus symptoms and milder tinnitus consequences. Respecting patients thus appears not only to enhance the quality of the doctor–patient interaction, but also to improve patients' actual health outcomes. It does this directly by reducing symptoms and indirectly by facilitating healthy behaviours.

In line with *Proposition 3* (that self-categorization provides a basis for the application of normative beliefs about health and illness to oneself), we also explored whether measures of health-related outcomes differed between patients who self-categorized as "traditional" (i.e., cooperative, trusting, obedient, passive, and unquestioning) as opposed to "consumerist" (i.e., a purchaser of services, who does not accept medical paternalism but believes that he or she has the right to medical information, to contribute to medical decision making, and to challenge physician authority). We associated the former self-categorization with greater conformity to depersonalizing medical norms (see Gaard, 2006; Stimson, 1974) and the latter to mobility away from them (see Beisecker, 1990; Lupton, 1997). Therefore, we expected the latter to represent a potential social cure, which should be associated with more positive outcomes. Accordingly, in Study 1 we also manipulated the patient role by asking participants to identify either as a traditional or as a consumerist patient and in Study 2, we measured participants' usual patient role preference. In both studies, participants who self-categorized as consumerist patients reported higher levels of personal self-esteem than participants who self-categorized as traditional patients. In Study 1, they also reported higher levels of collective self-esteem. Moreover, in Study 2, participants who self-categorized as consumerist patients also reported fewer tinnitus symptoms and a stronger belief that tinnitus is curable. On the other hand, they also reported less patient satisfaction, less respect for the doctor, and weaker intentions to adhere to medical advice. Since the patient role in Study 2 was naturally occurring, we cannot infer a causal relationship on the basis of its outcomes. Nevertheless, results of both studies are consistent with the implication of *Proposition 3*, that social cures may be effected when individuals resist self-categorizations that entail conformity to normative beliefs about health and illness. Results of Study 2 are also consistent with *Proposition 4* in suggesting that the benefits to be gained from personal mobility away from patient roles (including increased self-esteem and decreased symptom severity) might be balanced by poorer doctor–patient relationships and health behaviours (see Weinstein, 1987; Wood & Vanderzee, 1997). Future research is therefore needed to pinpoint social identity processes, which promote social cures without creating further barriers for ill or vulnerable people.

FINAL THOUGHTS

In this chapter, we have provided an analysis of the way in which beliefs about health can be socially constructed (*Proposition 1*) and examined the various ways in which categorization processes invoke normative beliefs relevant to an individual's understanding of his or her health (*Propositions 2, 3*, and *4*). Specifically, we observed that people who resist self-categorizing in terms of an illness group experience fewer and less severe symptoms and enhanced self-esteem. At the same time, medical professionals who avoid categorizing their clients as just "another patient", have the power to enhance health outcomes.

It would therefore appear that in order to appreciate – and manage – the complexities of symptom perception and an individual's experience as ill or disabled (*Proposition 5*) we need to advance models that integrate medical factors with those that are both personal and social. Taking this approach also increases the likelihood that the quest for medical cures for illness will be supplemented by social cures. These, we suggest, are every bit as important and can be just as miraculous.

References

Appollonio, I., Carabellese, C., Frattola, L., & Trabucchi, M. (1996). Effects of sensory aids on the quality of life and mortality of elderly people: A multivariate analysis. *Age and Ageing, 5*, 89–96.

Beach, M. C., Sugarman, J., Johnson, R. L., Arbelaez, J. J., Duggan, P. S., & Cooper, L. A. (2005). Do patients treated with dignity report higher satisfaction, adherence and receipt of preventive care? *Annals of Family Medicine, 3*, 331–338.

Beisecker, A. E. (1990). Patient power in doctor–patient communication: What do we know? *Health Communication, 2*, 105–122.

Bennet, G. (1979). *Patients and their doctors: The journey through medical care.* London, UK: Balliere Tindall.

Bennett, P. (2003). *Abnormal and clinical psychology: An introductory textbook* (2nd ed.). Milton Keynes, UK: Open University Press.

Blanchard, J., & Lurie, N. (2004). Respect: Patients' reports of disrespect in the health care setting and its impact on care. *The Journal of Family Practice, 53*, 721–730.

Bronfenbrenner, U. (1979). *The ecology of human development.* Harvard, MA: University Press.

Byrne, P. S., & Long, B. E. (1976). *Doctors talking to patients: A study of the verbal behaviour of general practitioners consulting in their surgeries.* London, UK: Her Majesty's Stationery Office.

Clucas, C. (2008). *Influences on and consequences of patients' experiences of feeling respected in doctor–patient relations.* Doctoral dissertation, University of Bristol, UK.

Clucas, C., & St. Claire, L. (2010). The effect of the patient role and feeling respected on patient health-related outcomes. *Applied Psychology: Health and Well-Being, 2*, 298–322.

Clucas, C., & St. Claire, L. (2011). Relationship between communication skills training and doctors' perceptions of patient similarity. *International Journal of Medical Education, 2*, 30–35.

Danhauer J. L., Blood, G. W., Blood, I. M., & Gomez, N. (1980). Professional and lay observers' impressions of preschoolers wearing hearing aids. *Journal of Speech and Hearing Disorders, 45*, 415–422.

Davis, A. C. (1995). *Hearing in adults.* London, UK: Whurr.

Dillon, R. S. (2003). *Respect.* In E. N. Zalta (Ed.), *Stanford encyclopedia of philosophy.* Available at http://plato.stanford.edu/entries/respect

Doosje, B., Ellemers, N., & Spears, R. (1995). Perceived intragroup variability as a function of group status and identification. *Journal of Experimental Social Psychology, 31*, 410–436.

Dweck, C. S. (2000). *Self-theories: Their role in motivation, personality and development.* Hove, UK: Psychology Press.

Fielding, R. (1999). *How good a doctor will you be? The doctor–patient relationship.*

Retrieved 8 September 2007 from http://www.pitt.edu/~super1/lecture /beh0031/ 001.htm

Gaard, S. (2006). Are we ready for the proactive patient? *Wisconsin Medical Journal, 105,* 50–52.

Golub, S. (1992). *Periods: From menarche to menopause.* Thousand Oaks, CA: Sage.

Gregory, J. (1979). *Patients' attitudes to the hospital service: A survey carried out for the Royal Commission on the NHS to find out about the experiences and attitudes of users of the hospital service.* London, UK: Her Majesty's Stationery Service.

Haffter, C. (1968). The changeling. *Journal of the History of Behavioural Sciences, 2,* 55–61.

Hardy, M. (1998). *The social context of health.* Buckingham, UK: Open University Press.

Hartley, R. (1986). Imagine you're clever. *Journal of Child Psychology and Psychiatry, 27*(3), 383–398.

Haslam, S. A., Jetten, J., Postmes, T., & Haslam, C. (2009). Social identity, health and well-being: An emerging agenda for applied psychology. *Applied Psychology: An International Review, 58*(1), 1–23.

Helman, C. G. (2000). *Culture, health and illness* (4th ed.). London, UK: Hodder Arnold.

Katz, J., Medwetsky, L., Burkard, R., & Hood, L. (2009). *Handbook of clinical audiology* (6th ed.). Philadelphia, PA: Lippincott, Williams and Wilkins.

Kennon, A. F., & Sandoval, J. (1978). Teacher attitudes toward the educable mental retardate. *Education and Training of the Mentally Retarded, 13,* 139–145.

Kumar, P., & Clark, M. (2005). *Clinical medicine* (6th ed.). Edinburgh, UK: Saunders.

Lalljee, M., Laham, S. M., & Tam, T. (2007). Unconditional respect for persons: A social psychological analysis. *Gruppendynamik und Organisationsberatung, 38,* 451–464.

Lowenthal, M., Patterson, R., Greenberger, P. A., & Grammer, L. C. (1993). Malignant potentially fatal asthma: Achievement of remission and the application of an asthma severity index. *Allergy Proceedings, 14,* 333–339.

Luhtanen, R., & Crocker, J. (1992). A collective self-esteem scale: Self-evaluation of one's social identity. *Personality and Social Psychology Bulletin, 18,* 302–318.

Lupton, D. (1997). Consumerism, reflexivity and the medical encounter. *Social Science & Medicine, 45,* 373–381.

Lupton, D. (2003). *Medicine as culture: Illness, disease and the body in Western societies* (2nd ed.). London, UK: Sage.

McCombe, A., Baguley, D., Coles, R., McKenna, L., McKinney, C., & Windle-Taylor, P. (2001). Guidelines for the grading of tinnitus severity: The results of a working group commissioned by the British Association of Otolaryngologists, Head and Neck Surgeons, 1999. *Clinical Otolaryngology, 26,* 388–393.

McNicol, D. (1972). *A primer of signal detection theory.* London, UK: Allen and Unwin.

Mercer, J. (1973). *Labeling the mentally retarded.* Berkeley, CA; London, UK: University of California Press.

Miller, A. G. (1999). Perspectives on evil and violence. *Personality and Social Psychology Review, 3,* 176–178.

Morgan, W. (2003). The doctor–patient relationship. In G. Scambler (Ed.), *Sociology as applied to medicine* (pp. 49–65). London, UK: Saunders.

Murphy, J. (1996). Trigger unit for social psychology: Personal lives, social worlds. *A third level social sciences course*. Buckingham, UK: The Open University.

National Centre for Health Statistics [NCHS]. (1987). *Current estimates from the National Health Interview Survey*. Washington, DC: United States Government Printing Office.

Reiss, S., & Szyszko, J. (1983). Diagnostic overshadowing and professional experience with mentally retarded persons. *American Journal of Mental Deficiency, 87*, 396–402.

Rosenberg, M. (1965). *Society and the adolescent self-image*. Princeton, NJ: Princeton University Press.

Seale, C., Pattison, S., & Davey, B. (2001). *Medical knowledge: Doubt and certainty*. Maidenhead, UK: The Open University Press.

Skevington, S. M. (1994). Social comparisons in cross-cultural QOL assessment. *International Journal of Mental Health, 23*, 29–47.

Slater, R. (2004). Experiencing later life. In B. Davey (Ed.), *Birth to old age: Health in transition* (pp. 211–226). Maidenhead, UK: Open University Press.

Smeeth, L., Fletcher, A. E., Stirling, E., Nunes, M., & Breeze, E. (2001). Reduced hearing, and ownership and use of hearing aids among elderly people in the UK: Findings from MRC trial of the assessment and management of older people in the community. *British Medical Journal, 323*, 1403–1407.

Smith, A. P., Behan, P., Bell, W., Millar, K., & Bakheith, M. (1993). Behavioural problems associated with chronic fatigue syndrome. *British Journal of Psychology, 84*, 411–423.

Smith, A. P., Thomas, M., Borysiewicz, L., & Llewelyn, M. (1995). A comparison of the acute effects of a low dose of alcohol on mood and performance of healthy volunteers and subjects with upper respiratory tract illnesses. *Journal of Psychopharmacology, 9*, 267–272.

St. Claire, L. (1984). *An application of social categorisation and social identity theory to mental retardation*. Doctoral dissertation, Bristol University, UK.

St. Claire, L. (1986). Mental retardation: Impairment or handicap? *Disability, Handicap and Society, 1*, 233–243.

St. Claire, L. (1993). Does medics' social identification increase handicap for mentally retarded patients? *Journal of Community and Applied Social Psychology, 3*, 183–195.

St. Claire, L. (2003). *Rival truths: Common sense and social psychological explanations in health and illness*. Hove, UK: Psychology Press.

St. Claire, L., Clift, A., & Dumbelton, L. (2008). How do I know what I feel? Evidence for the role of self-categorisation in symptom perceptions. *European Journal of Social Psychology, 38*, 173–186.

St. Claire, L., & He, Y. (2009). How do I know if I need a hearing aid? Using self-categorisation theory to understand symptoms of hearing loss in older people. *Journal of Applied Psychology, 58*, 24–41.

St. Claire, L., Watkins, C. J., & Billinghurst, B. (1996). Differences in meanings of health. A preliminary study of doctors and their patients. *Family Practice, 13*, 511–516.

Stewart, M., Brown, J. B., Weston, W. W., McWhinney, I. R., McWilliam, C., & Freeman, T. R. (1995). *Patient-centered medicine: Transforming the clinical method*. Thousand Oaks, CA: Sage.

Stimson, G. V. (1974). Obeying doctor's orders: A view from the other side. *Social Science & Medicine, 8,* 97–104.

Swain, J., French, S., & Cameron, C. (2003). *Controversial issues in a disabling society.* Buckingham, UK: Open University Press.

Tajfel, H. (1978). *Differentiation between social groups: Studies in the social psychology of intergroup relations.* London, UK: Academic Press.

Tajfel, H. (1981). *Human groups and social categories: Studies in social psychology.* Cambridge, UK: Cambridge University Press.

Tajfel, H., & Turner J. C. (1979). An integrative theory of intergroup conflict. In W. G. Austin & S. Worchel (Eds.), *The social psychology of intergroup relations* (pp. 33–48). Monterey, CA: Brooks/Cole.

Tajfel, H., & Wilkes, A. L. (1963). Classification and quantitative judgement. *British Journal of Psychology, 54,* 101–114.

Taylor, S. E. (1983). Adjustment to threatening events: A theory of cognitive adaption. *American Psychologist, 817,* 1161–1173.

Turner, B. S. (1995). *Medical power and social knowledge* (2nd ed.). London, UK: Sage.

Turner, J. C. (1981). Towards a cognitive redefinition of the social group. *Cahiers de Psychologie Cognitive, 1,* 93–118.

Turner J. C., & Brown, R. J. (1978). Social status, cognitive alternatives and intergroup relations. In H. Tajfel (Ed.), *Differentiation between social groups* (pp. 201–234). London, UK: Academic Press.

Turner, J. C., Hogg, M. A., Oakes, P. J., Reicher, S. D., & Wetherell, M. S. (1987). *Rediscovering the social group: A self-categorization theory.* New York, NY: Basil Blackwell.

Ventry, I., & Weinstein, B. (1983). Identification of elderly people with hearing problems. *American Speech and Hearing Association, 25,* 37–42.

Walker, A., & Maltby, T. (1997). *Ageing Europe.* Buckingham, UK: Open University Press.

Weinman, J., Petrie, K. J., Moss-Morris, R., & Horne, R. (1996). The illness perception questionnaire: A new method for assessing the cognitive representation of illness. *Psychology & Health, 11,* 431–445.

Weinstein, N. D. (1987). Unrealistic optimism about susceptibility to health problems: Conclusions from a community-wide sample. *Journal of Behavioural Medicine, 10,* 481–500.

Wetherell, M. (1996). Life histories and social histories. In M. Wetherell (Ed.), *Identities, groups and social issues* (pp. 229–361). London, UK: Sage and the Open University Press.

Wood, J. V., & Vanderzee, K. (1997). Social comparisons among cancer patients: Under what conditions are comparisons upward and downward? In B. P. Buunk & F. X. Gibson (Eds.), *Health, coping and wellbeing* (pp. 299–328). Mahwah, NJ: Lawrence Erlbaum Associates.

6   Not wanting to grow old

A Social Identity Model of Identity Change (SIMIC) analysis of driving cessation among older adults

Jolanda Jetten
University of Queensland
University of Exeter

Nancy A. Pachana
University of Queensland

Old age is not considered either attractive or indeed of value in many Western societies and seniors are consequently ascribed low status (Bugental & Hehman, 2007). Given the stigma associated with ageing, and the perceived legitimacy of expressing these stereotypical beliefs, it is not surprising that many older adults resist self-defining as old (Jetten, Schmitt, Branscombe, Garza, & Mewse, 2011). However, circumstances rarely allow individuals to escape from the realities of growing older. Retirement, illness, decreasing cognitive abilities, and failing bodily strength conspire to force us to face our own ageing. Indeed, physical and mental decline are perceived as markers of age and this undermines individuals' ability to successfully ward off old age as "something that does not apply yet but will happen in the future". That is, there are limits to the extent to which one can maintain like Bernard Baruch that "old age is always 15 years older than I am".

Regardless of whether declines are gradual or sudden, their impact on lifestyle and independence can bring increasing age and its attendant concerns into sharper focus. We propose that driving cessation in older adults is one such important milestone that makes ageing salient to the individual and those around him or her. Accordingly, having to give up driving not only involves having to find alternative ways of transportation and losing independence, it also signifies for many that "old age" can no longer be denied.

In this chapter we focus on the topic of driving cessation among older adults and propose that it signifies ageing in both concrete and symbolic ways. Being unable to drive results in objective changes to one's routine, but may also trigger a subjective shift in self-perception – as a milestone marking the transition from younger-old to older-old. When older adults hand in their driving licence, for whatever reason, the symbolic change of group membership becomes very salient. Importantly too, because old age is viewed negatively in Western society, giving up one's licence may constitute a particularly important and threatening form of identity change.

In this chapter we develop our reasoning on why driving cessation can be thought of as an identity change process and outline how the impact of this change is rather similar to that of other important life-changes that people encounter in the course of their life. In particular, we do this by exploring the usefulness of a social identity model of identity change in the context of older adults who give up driving. Here we will argue that part of the reason why driving cessation is perceived as highly stressful is that it implies irreversible identity change into the stigmatized category of "old".

A SOCIAL IDENTITY MODEL OF IDENTITY CHANGE

To date, research into coping with identity change has adopted approaches that focus on individuals' ability to cope with change *as individuals*. These approaches have focused on individual differences (i.e., suggesting that personality traits like "hardiness" help to buffer against change), concentrated on the importance of interpersonal support (Underwood, 2000), or applied transactional models of stress to explain coping with identity change (e.g., Lazarus & Folkman, 1984; see van Dick & Haslam, this volume for a review). Even though these approaches are valuable in helping to understand the personality traits that help individuals to cope best with identity change, the explanatory power of most of these models is limited because they only focus on the individual and not on the broader social context in which life transitions take place. That is, these changes not only affect the way we perceive ourselves, but also how we define ourselves in relation to others. Importantly, the latter aspect of change is not captured by these models. And because life transitions typically affect both the *personal* and *social* self, individualistic models of identity change can, at best, only explain part of the identity change process.

In our recently developed Social Identity Model of Identity Change (SIMIC; Iyer, Jetten, & Tsivrikos, 2008; Jetten, Haslam, Iyer, & Haslam, 2009), we define identity change quite broadly and include anticipated life changes (e.g., the transition from secondary school to university, starting a new job), but also more sudden changes to one's identity (e.g., changes as a result of illness). We include positive as well as negative changes and have examined our model in a range of organizational (Jetten, O'Brien, & Trindall, 2002), educational (Iyer, Jetten, Tsivrikos, Postmes, & Haslam, 2009), and clinical contexts (Haslam et al., 2008). We start this chapter with an overview of the recently developed SIMIC, and point to ways in which social identities (present and past) are implicated in important life transitions. A schematic representation of SIMIC is presented in Figure 6.1.

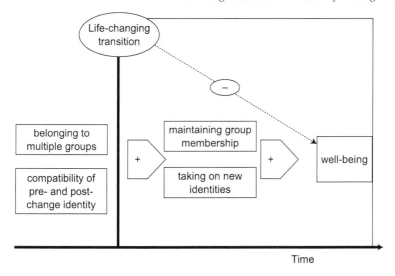

Figure 6.1 A schematic representation of the Social Identity Model of Identity Change (SIMIC).

Central to the SIMIC reasoning is the idea that our self-concept is largely determined by the social groups we belong to (Tajfel & Turner, 1979). Groups provide us with grounding and connectedness to others. The more an individual identifies with a group, the more self-definitions become intertwined with group definitions. Indeed, people use both personal and group memberships to define who they are. For example, when people are asked to describe themselves, they often list group memberships or social categories to answer this question (e.g., "I'm a woman, Australian" etc.). And given that our self-definition is bound up with these social identities, it is hardly surprising that breaking with groups or joining new groups can affect us deeply.

The fact that both personal and social identity are implicated in important life changes explains why life transitions are often difficult and unsettling (see Jetten et al., 2009). Lewin (1948) – one of the first to emphasize this point – states: "the high sensitivity persons show to any change which may possibly affect their security can to some extent be ascribed to fear of being unable to earn a living, yet this sensitivity is probably connected with something even more fundamental than the fear of hunger" (p. 145). Lewin continues by arguing that this more fundamental reason for negative responses to change relates to the fact that individuals lose their grounding, continuity, and stability in times of change. This grounding is mainly pro-vided by social groups and it is therefore, in the words of Lewin, "the primary reason why (s)he is extremely affected the moment this ground begins to give way" (p. 145).

Losing one's grounding is stressful in part because it is associated with discontinuity and a break with that which we know best. That is, the connection between the past and the present becomes interrupted and this in itself presents a threat to individuals' well-being. Indeed, research in a range of contexts has shown that the more individuals experience temporal discontinuity in their life, the more their mental well-being is compromised (Bluck & Alea, 2008; Landau, Greenberg, & Solomon, 2008; Sani, 2008; see also Haslam, Jetten, Haslam, & Knight, this volume). This explains why, regardless of whether changes are positive or negative, changes themselves are often perceived as unsettling (see Figure 6.1).

However, despite the (temporary) negative effects of identity change on well-being, this does not necessarily mean that we go out of our way to avoid life transitions. It does mean, however, that individuals are often more vulnerable in times of transition because changes force them to reorient not just the personal self but also their connections to others (i.e., the social self). Rituals often help to make this process more transparent and force individuals to consider the way that changes impact on their life. Indeed, rites of passage aim to prepare us for the upcoming change and to provide us with all the necessary resources, social support, and skills to do well in the next phase of our life (e.g., weddings, baby showers).

Not surprisingly, however, our culture has far fewer rites of passage when the life transition involves a negative change. For instance, losing one's job, getting a divorce, or being diagnosed with a life-threatening illness are changes that occur largely outside the public domain. In a similar vein, whereas changes from adolescence to adulthood are highly ritualized in many cultures (e.g., involving barmitzvahs and significant birthday parties), the transition from younger-older adult to older-older adult is a life transition that typically goes unnoticed and unheralded. In societies that value youth, stereotypes of older adults are typically negative, and attributions that the old are frail, dependent, incompetent, and slow are commonplace (Cuddy, Norton, & Fiske, 2005; Hummert, Garstka, Shaner, & Strahm, 1994). It is therefore not surprising that ageing is a change that most individuals do not want to draw attention to.

Transition rituals are also typically lacking when life change is unexpected. For example, expected changes such as retirement may be negative for many people, but they are nevertheless anticipated. Similarly, death is extremely negative, but it is expected and people know it is unavoidable. As a result, there are rituals to help people to make the transition. However, as most people assume that there is no point in time at which they will be forced to give up driving, no rituals are available to facilitate the transition. What this also means is that – because the life transition is negative and unexpected – individuals often cope with these transitions without help or appropriate social support from others. This in turn is likely to have negative consequences for well-being (Haslam, O'Brien, Jetten, Vormedal, & Penna, 2005).

WHEN ARE LIFE TRANSITIONS DIFFICULT?

Aside from the observation that transition from younger-old to older-old involves changing from a more positive social category to a more devalued category, this life transition may be stressful for a number of other reasons. In the SIMIC model, we identify a number of processes that may hinder adjustment following identity change of this nature (Jetten et al., 2009).

First, individuals may not be able to maintain their old identity and change requires them to give up or move away from old group memberships ("unfreezing"; Lewin, 1948). This is not an easy process because people are often unwilling to give up identities that have been important in defining themselves in the past. People may be particularly reluctant to relinquish a positive identity (e.g., as no longer healthy when acquiring disability after stroke; Haslam et al., 2008). It has also been found that resistance to change is higher among those who identify strongly with the old identity than among those whose commitment was lower (Jetten et al., 2002).

Second, even if people are willing to relinquish an old identity, or if they are able to integrate the old identity in the new context, adjustment also depends on individuals' ability and willingness to take on a new identity. This is important, as the main assumption of SIMIC is that stress resulting from identity loss can be countered when people are willing to take on a new identity (to replace an old identity). Taking on a new identity not only provides grounding and a new sense of belonging, it also forms the basis for receiving and benefiting from new sources of social support (Haslam et al., 2005; Iyer et al., 2009; see also Haslam, Reicher, & Levine, this volume). Taking on a new identity indicates that people are able to respond to their new environment – they become more involved and are better able to deal with the demands imposed by their new environment. Those who are unable or unwilling to take on a new identity are more likely to remain "frozen" in time, and thereby run the danger of "living in the past" (Iyer & Jetten, 2011). In sum, we suggest that taking on new identities following important life transitions can protect, buffer, and reverse the negative effects of change and, when individuals effectively draw upon new identities as a basis for self-definition, they can protect and enhance their well-being (see Haslam, Jetten, Postmes, & Haslam, 2009, for an overview).

The experience of entering a new phase in life is likely to be perceived as less stressful and associated with fewer negative consequences when a new identity is readily available – for instance, if there is employment after losing a job, or if there is recovery from illness. However, at times, new identities are not available or they are unattractive. If we take the example of people who have lost their job, the new identity as an unemployed person is a stigmatized identity and implies a loss of social status.

In SIMIC, we propose that features of the broader social context in which change occurs determine an individual's ability to break from their "frozen" state and take on a new identity. Specifically, identity change does not take place in isolation, but rather within the context of a broader network of identities (Iyer et al., 2008). Change affects relationships between all identities, the centrality of identities to self-definition, and the extent to which social identity forms the basis for social support.

Our previous research has shown that two aspects of the identity network are particularly important in determining the way that identities promote successful adjustment to important life transitions (see Figure 6.1). First, the number of group memberships before the life transitions is an important predictor of successful coping with identity change. We argued that multiple identities protected well-being in times of change because, when people belong to multiple groups before the transition and maintain membership in these groups, (1) the old identity network continues to form a basis for drawing social support, and (2) this provides a good platform for people to build new identities that are compatible and integrated with old identities, thereby enhancing identity continuity.

The negative impact of disrupted continuity on well-being was observed in a study among patients recovering from a stroke (Haslam et al., 2008). We found that life satisfaction *after* the stroke was higher for those who had experienced the least amount of discontinuity in terms of losing social groups that they belonged to *before* their stroke. Further analysis of the data suggested that this was because the more groups stroke sufferers belonged to before their stroke, the more groups that remained for them to fall back on *after* their stroke and this protected their life satisfaction. One further interesting feature of this study was that continuity in group membership also mediated the relationship between stroke sufferers' perceptions of everyday cognitive failures – such as problems with directions, forgetting names, having trouble making up one's mind – and their life satisfaction. Unsurprisingly, the more failures reported by stroke sufferers, the greater the reduction in quality of life. More interesting was the finding that those who experienced failures found it harder to retain their social relationships and it was this disruption to social identity continuity that was an important contributor to the observed reduction in life quality. It thus appears that it was not cognitive failures alone that were the problem. In large part, these failures were damaging because they restricted access to ongoing group life and the support that it provided.

Second, we argue that, when predicting adjustment to change, it is not just the number of identities that matters, but also the relationships among them. Identity change can strain relationships when the old identity and new identity are not compatible. In such situations, it is likely that tensions between past and present identities undermine the extent to which identities are a useful source of social support. That is, in such contexts, identities will have lost their ability to serve as a buffer and resource, helping individuals to adjust to present stressors – primarily because these identities fail to provide self-continuity and stability over time. That is, if pre- and post-transition identities are incompatible, it is less likely that individuals can maintain the pre-transition identities in the new context, and less likely that they can successfully adopt new identities (see Figure 6.1).

Evidence for the important role of compatibility of old and new identities was obtained in a study where we examined students' transition to university. In this study, we monitored first-year university students over a period of 4 months – 2 months before through to 2 months after they commenced their study (Iyer et al., 2009). While there was some excitement associated with going to university, we found that levels of depression were higher among students who had lived away from home for a couple of months. Clearly, and in line with our reasoning that even positive changes require adjustment, these data suggest that the first months at university were challenging. Importantly, though, the more the participants had taken on their new student identity, the more resilient they became over time and the higher their well-being.

A key question for us then was whether we could predict which of these students was most likely to embrace their new identity. As the study among stroke sufferers indicated (Haslam et al., 2008), a good predictor appeared to be the number of groups that students belonged to before they came to university: the more groups they belonged to before commencing study, the more likely they were to take on the new student identity and this was in turn associated with lower depression. However, in line with the above reasoning, the compatibility of old and new identities was also an important predictor. The more the identity before entering university was compatible with being a university student, the easier it was for individuals to take on the new student identity and, in turn, this protected well-being. These effects held even after accounting for other factors relevant to the transition such as uncertainty about entering university, available social support, and awareness of academic obstacles.

When we examined the long-term consequences of compatibility perceptions among students entering university we found that perceived incompatibilities do not go away, but continue to provide a stumbling block when taking on new identities (Jetten, Iyer, Tsivrikos, & Young, 2008). Specifically, we found that individuals identified not only more highly with the university when their social background was compatible with the new context that they were entering in the short term (i.e., after having been at university for 3 months), but also in the longer term (i.e., after having been at university for 9 months). This confirms the importance of seeking out new identities that are compatible with old identities. Compatibility allows maintenance of old identities which enhances continuity perceptions and thereby facilitates adjustment to change.

In sum, our studies among students entering university and among individuals recovering from a stroke suggest that (new or maintained) social identities can buffer against the negative consequences of change. In this, being a member of multiple social groups that are compatible with the new identity is an important resource because it makes it easier to take on new identities and because this allows an individual to maintain identities despite the life transition (see Figure 6.1).

THE CASE OF DRIVING CESSATION AMONG OLDER ADULTS

So can we better understand the psychological consequences of driving cessation among older adults if we explore this as an identity change process with implications for both personal and social identity? In considering this question, we start with a brief review of the existing literature on driving cessation after which we examine whether the processes identified in SIMIC apply to this specific life transition. We also present preliminary data that examine driving cessation as identity change and suggest ways in which social identities can help to buffer against the negative effects of having to give up driving.

Aside from the practical convenience of having a driving licence, driving is culturally also symbolically associated with competence, independence, freedom, and mobility. Not surprisingly therefore, when older adults are forced to give up driving either through ill health or age-related changes, this is typically associated with negative emotions and a deterioration in well-being (Fonda, Wallace, & Herzog, 2001; Ragland, Satariano, & MacLeod, 2005). Evidence for the negative well-being consequences of driving cessation among older adults is now well-established, and is provided by both cross-sectional (e.g., Siren, Hakamies-Blomqvist, & Lindeman, 2004) and longitudinal (see Ragland et al., 2005; Windsor, Anstey, Butterworth, Luszcz, & Andrews, 2007) studies. To date, though, attempts to explain the negative effects of driving cessation on well-being have focused mainly on issues of social isolation and reduced participation in community life, as well as the practical hassles associated with not being able to drive to places (e.g., Glasgow & Blakely, 2000).

Yet despite the importance of reduced control and reliance on other modes of transport, it is clear that these processes only provide a partial explanation for the negative relationship that has been observed. For example, in a study of older adults, Fonda and colleagues (2001) found that those who stopped driving experienced increased depressive symptoms. However, the negative impact of driving cessation on well-being was not reduced if the person had a spouse who was able to drive. This suggests that the negative impact of driving cessation reflects more than just difficulties associated with the availability of, and access to, alternative modes of transportation. This point is crucial because it suggests that interventions for those who have ceased driving may not be particularly effective if they focus solely on facilitating access to alternative transportation (e.g., by providing information about public transport).

The perceived loss of control and self-efficacy (Windsor et al., 2007), and the loss of independence among older adults who stop driving (Yassuda, Wilson, & von Mering, 1997) are two factors that have received most attention in previous research that examines the negative effect of driving cessation on well-being. Qualitative data indeed suggest that concerns about control and dependency on others are important concerns that older adults spontaneously voice when thinking about driving cessation (e.g., Siren & Hakamies-Blomqvist, 2005). But despite the importance of these issues, desire for research that leads to a better understanding of a broader range of factors that affect the consequences of driving cessation has been voiced by a number of researchers in the field (e.g., Laliberte Rudman, Friedland, Chipman, & Sciortino, 2006). As we will outline below, we propose that a factor that has been ignored in much of the research to date is that driving cessation also implies a changed relationship with others. That is, it may not only practically be hard to maintain some relationships when people stop driving, it is also likely that older adults do not feel they belong anymore or fit groups once they have lost their licence. This is particularly likely when driving allowed them to be members of activity groups where independence and mobility was key (e.g., bush walking).

Interestingly, qualitative studies also point to narratives that driving cessation is perceived as an identity change process. In particular, given the importance of driving as an identity marker (i.e., being independent, free), not being able to identify as a driver is perceived as a loss of identity (Yassuda et al., 1997). Other researchers have elaborated on older adults' reluctance to give up their driving licence and suggested that holding a driving licence may be an effective way of "warding off old age" (Eisenhandler, 1990; Gardezi et al., 2006; Laliberte Rudman et al., 2006; Siren & Hakamies-Blomqvist, 2005). Indeed, driving cessation is perceived as a negative rite of passage where the driver moves from membership of a relatively positively valued group (i.e., older adults who are independent and mobile) to a group that is less valued in society. The latter identity is more stigmatized than the former and dependent older adults face discrimination in many areas of life (Pasupathi & Löckenhoff, 2002). This is likely to make the transition from a driver to an ex-driver all the more painful: it marks the transition from young-old to old-old and is associated with exclusion from mainstream society.

Important too is the fact that the transition in the case of driving cessation is usually permanent. Few older adults who have given up their driving licence for health reasons regain their licence once they have successfully recovered. Interestingly, though, older adults who lost their licence often hold onto the belief that driving cessation is reversible. In our research we found that many older adults who stopped driving reported hanging onto their licence because they were hoping to resume driving one day (Pachana & Jetten, 2010; see also Eisenhandler, 1990).

The perception that the new identity as ex-driver is permanent may be daunting not only because it highlights that one has been unsuccessful in warding off old age but also because it is an undeniable marker for others that one is getting old. In this regard, a licence is more than a document – it is a symbol that one may be an older adult, but not so old that one cannot drive anymore. The symbolic value of a licence may become all the more important in combination with the fact that age is a category with flexible boundaries such that it is not necessarily clear who is "old" and who is "young". Driving cessation may make salient the fact there are sub-categories of older adults, whereby those who are forced to stop driving find themselves categorized on the unattractive side of the boundary. This also means that when older adults have to stop driving, the flexibility of defining oneself as "younger than I really am" becomes constrained. In that sense, driving cessation may represent a categorization threat whereby individuals are categorized by others into a social category that they would rather not belong to (Branscombe, Ellemers, Spears, & Doosje, 1999). For other older adults, it may also mean that they feel they are no longer able to pass as something they are not (Eisenhandler, 1990; Hornsey & Jetten, 2003).

To sum up, if we examine driving cessation as an identity change process (not unlike other important life transitions), it becomes apparent that it often involves all the factors identified in SIMIC that make it difficult to adjust to change. Specifically, driving cessation involves giving up a valued identity – the identity as a driver. It also involves taking on a new identity that is unattractive because it involves joining a new age group that is stigmatized (Eisenhandler, 1990), and one that the older person is typically unable to leave (i.e., implying that boundaries are impermeable; Garstka, Schmitt, Branscombe, & Hummert, 2004; Tajfel & Turner, 1979). Moreover, and as specified in SIMIC, effects of driving cessation are not restricted to loss of the driver identity, but affect individuals' broader identity network. That is, driving cessation also affects the extent to which older adults can maintain membership in social groups and the extent to which they can engage actively in group life. The social isolation that occurs and the loss of group membership as a result of driving cessation is therefore likely to impoverish individual's social identity and, by extension, his or her personal identity (Jetten, Haslam, Pugliese, Tonks, & Haslam, 2010).

DRIVING CESSATION AS MARKER OF IDENTITY CHANGE AND AGEING

We examined some of these processes in a study among older adults who had stopped driving ($N = 47$) and a control sample consisting of older adults who were still driving ($N = 161$; Pachana & Jetten, 2010). Respondents were recruited in Queensland (Australia) from both rural and more urban areas. The sample that had stopped driving consisted of 13 males (17.7 percent) and 33 females (70.2 percent, with 1 missing value) whose average age was 78 years. The sample of older adults who were still driving consisted of 44 males (27.2 percent) and 115 females (71 percent, with 3 missing values), whose average age was 72 years.

In the research we focused on three key issues: (1) the extent to which driving cessation was considered a major life stressor compared to other important life stressors (e.g., moving into a care home); (2) the narratives of older adults when thinking about driving cessation and considering whether driving cessation was perceived as ageing; and (3) whether anticipated practical problems (e.g., the unavailability of public transport) were more or less important than the identity change associated with driving cessation. We compared responses of ex-drivers to those who were still driving. We were particularly interested in whether the anticipation of driving cessation among those still driving was more stressful and perceived as a stronger marker of ageing than amongst those who had given up driving.

In relation to the first question, we presented respondents with a list of important life stressors and asked them to rate how stressful they felt certain events would be (scale from 0 = "not at all stressful" to 100 = "as stressful as it can be"). Severely disabling conditions such as "having loss of eyesight", "having loss of hearing", "having dementia", "having poor health", and "having loss of memory" were rated as highly stressful with average responses between 73 (in the case of hearing loss) and 94 (in the case of loss of eyesight). Among these older adults who still lived independently, moving into a nursing home was also rated as highly stressful ($M = 78$). Interestingly, "stopping driving" was rated as equally stressful as "death of a close friend" ($Ms = 65$ and 67, respectively). Moreover, these ratings were much higher than those for other important life transitions such as "retiring from paid work" ($M = 28$). Examination of responses by ex-drivers and drivers did not reveal any differences.

These findings were further contextualized by responses to some open-ended questions. In particular, we asked respondents to "tell us what it would mean or means to you to have to give up driving". Only a small minority of respondents said they would not mind giving up driving. The vast majority emphasized the change this would entail and their negative response to it. Some telling responses were that people told us they would be "devastated" and they would "hate it". Respondents also highlighted explicitly that they saw driving cessation as entering the final stage of life:

> This would be a major paradigm shift which I assume I will have to face up to one day. I think the psychological transition would be great, marking a transition to the last phase of my life. It is likely it would make me feel handicapped and much older.

Another respondent reflected:

> I have a driving licence until February 2010. It is important for me to have this as I feel unhappy about having lost things due to age. I even keep my RACQ [Australian motoring club] subscription.

A number of respondents briefly mentioned it would mean the "acceptance of 'I am old'" and "another feeling of getting old". These responses provide some initial evidence that driving cessation is perceived as a milestone that is a strong indicator of ageing.

In addition to the fear of losing the independence that driving cessation would signify, we also found that many respondents indicated that driving cessation would make it more difficult to maintain membership in their current groups and remain connected with friends and family. For example, when asked to imagine what driving cessation would mean, respondents mentioned:

> My independence would be horribly compromised. I would be severely restricted in contact with my children and grandchildren, with my religious faith community, and all my friends,

> I would be house-bound. No bridge, toast masters, etc.

or

> Being unable to participate in current activities easily, especially functions/club meetings held at night venues not easily accessible by public transport.

We also found some evidence for the importance of compatibility perceptions: that is, whether driving cessation was compatible with one's current identity as a driver. Only some participants mentioned that driving cessation would not be incompatible with their current life and would therefore not be life changing (e.g., "I would accept it as I do not enjoy driving. My living costs would be less"). Most respondents emphasized the incompatibility of their life as an ex-driver with their current life (e.g., "Devastating, would alter my whole lifestyle"). For some, the incompatibility was felt quite strongly and driving appeared to be a central part of their life. For example, one participant wrote:

> I was a driver in the army, drove semi-trailers out west QLD [Queensland] after army life, operated earthmoving plant equipment for many years and visited jobsites as a supervisor. Now in retirement I've travelled extensively through Alice Springs and West Coast, up to the Kimberlies, Darwin, across the NT [Northern Territory] up to Cape York down through Daintree and want to continue to do many more trips.

In sum, the majority of respondents were highly attuned to the fact that driving was an important enabler of group life – it allowed them to engage actively in groups and remain connected to friends, family, and social groups. Having to give up driving would force them to lead a life that was so incompatible with their current life that it evoked powerful negative emotions. There was also some evidence that belonging to many groups was an important predictor of how participants felt about the prospect of having to give up driving. Specifically, it was those who belonged to groups that varied in their activities that mentioned spontaneously that they could easily focus more on activities and social groups that were in close proximity to their house or that did not involve them having to leave their house. Having some group memberships or social ties in close proximity to fall back on in case they would lose their licence may have made it easier for these individuals to accept giving up driving.

Further evidence that driving cessation was perceived as ageing was obtained from two questions asking respondents to indicate how they thought they would feel *before* they stopped driving and how they thought they would feel *after* they stopped driving. Response categories ranged from (1) "much younger than I really am", (2) "a bit younger than I really am", (3) "my real age", (4) "a bit older than I really am", (5) "much older than I really am". While respondents indicated that on average they would feel slightly younger than their real age when considering how they would feel before stopping driving, they indicated that they would feel a bit older than their real age when considering their lives after stopping driving. Interestingly too, these ageing effects were more pronounced for those who were still driving than for those who had already given up. It thus appears that the *anticipation* of driving cessation is perceived as particularly stressful. For in many cases those who had given up driving had successfully rebuilt their lives and adjusted to the change.

A final question we addressed in our research was the perceived impact of the practical hassles associated with giving up driving relative to identity loss. As a measure of practical problems we asked respondents to indicate to what extent driving cessation would mean that they would worry about being able to get to places, worry about relying on others, and worry about knowing how to use public transport. Whether driving cessation was associated with identity change was assessed with items tapping the extent to which driving cessation involved entering a new life phase, closing a chapter of their life, and whether life would change quite a bit. We found that while respondents agreed that driving cessation would involve practical hassles, they were more concerned that driving cessation would involve an important life change. Again, we found that those who were still driving were particularly concerned about the extent to which driving cessation would result in life change.

One of the findings that deserves particular attention relates to evidence that those who were still driving were more likely to see its cessation as ageing and were more likely to perceive it as an important life transition than those who had stopped driving. As intimated above, this finding is consistent with the observation that the anticipation of loss is more stressful among older adults than the actual loss (Yassuda et al., 1997). This also explains the finding by Yassuda and colleagues that older adults are reluctant to plan for driving cessation. This is not surprising if driving cessation is perceived as irreversible ageing. We also found that those who had given up driving minimized the difference between the group that was still driving and the group that was not. Ex-drivers presumably used a social creativity strategy (Tajfel & Turner, 1979) whereby they turned the negative experience of driving cessation into a positive one. In other words, they no longer appeared to define driving as an older adult as an indicator of "successful ageing". Some of those who had given up driving even mentioned feeling relieved that they no longer had a licence and that their life had become less stressful as a result.

FINAL REMARKS

In this chapter, we have developed the argument that identity change, even the most personal type of change, typically involves a change of group membership. Like Lewin (1948), we argue that it is important to understand the social nature of identity change in order to understand how individuals experience change and how they adjust to the change. In the case of driving cessation, stress associated with the change largely relates to having to give up a valued identity, resistance to the new identity which signifies ageing, and the disruption of social networks that driving cessation would entail. Our initial evidence suggests that these processes, as identified within SIMIC, affected whether the prospect of driving cessation caused stress and compromised well-being.

From these findings, we conclude that in addition to the practical difficulties associated with driving cessation, respondents were certainly thinking of identity loss when asked about driving cessation. In any programme preparing older adults for a life without a licence, it may therefore be important to focus not only on dealing with practical problems that older adults are likely to face when they can no longer drive, but also on driving cessation as an important life transition involving identity change. Along the lines of previous research that points to the importance of belonging to multiple groups due to the greater likelihood of maintaining some of those groups after a life-changing event (Haslam et al., 2008), we predict that any intervention that is aimed at maintaining continuity in people's social life after driving cessation would have positive well-being effects. Indeed, continuity of group membership before and after driving cessation may buffer individuals against the threats to well-being by increasing the likelihood that they will be able to retain some connection with past sources of social support.

It thus appears that the *social cure* offered by continued group membership would do its protective work without the individual even being aware of the potential health problem. That is, driving cessation may not even be perceived as a life transition at all if one's social network remains intact despite having to stop driving. What is more, positive side effects of this social cure would be that stopping driving may not be perceived as a sign of ageing. Indeed, for those individuals benefiting from continued group membership, driving cessation would primarily involve changing modes of transport – and this is likely to be far less troublesome than changing social identity.

References

Bluck, S., & Alea, N. (2008). Remembering being me: The self-continuity function of autobiographical memory in younger and older adults. In F. Sani (Ed.), *Self continuity; Individual and collective perspectives* (pp. 55–70). New York, NY: Psychology Press.

Branscombe, N. R., Ellemers, N., Spears, R., & Doosje, B. (1999). The context and content of social identity threat. In N. Ellemers, R. Spears, & B. Doosje (Eds.), *Social identity: Context, commitment, content* (pp. 35–58). Oxford, UK: Blackwell Science.

Bugental, D. B., & Hehman, J. A. (2007). Ageism: A review of research and policy implications. *Social Issues and Policy Review, 1*, 173–216.

Cuddy, A. J. C., Norton, M. I., & Fiske, S. T. (2005). This old stereotype: The pervasiveness and persistence of the elderly stereotype. *Journal of Social Issues, 61*, 267–285.

Eisenhandler, S. A. (1990). The asphalt identikit: Old age and the driver's license. *International Journal of Aging and Human Development, 30*, 1–14.

Fonda, S. J., Wallace, R. B., & Herzog, A. R. (2001). Changes in driving patterns and worsening depressive symptoms among older adults. *Journal of Gerontology, Social Sciences, 56B*, 343–351.

Gardezi, F., Wilson, K. G., Man-Son-Hing, M., Marshall, S. C., Molnar, F. J., Dobbs, B., et al. (2006). Qualitative research on older drivers. *Clinical Gerontologist, 30*, 5–22.

Garstka, T. A., Schmitt, M. T., Branscombe, N. R., & Hummert, M. L. (2004). How young and older adults differ in their responses to perceived age discrimination. *Psychology and Aging, 19*, 326–335.

Glasgow, N., & Blakely, R. M. (2000). Older nonmetropolitan residents' evaluation of their transportation arrangements. *Journal of Applied Gerontology, 19*, 95–116.

Haslam, C., Holme, A., Haslam, S. A., Iyer, A., Jetten, J., & Williams, W. H. (2008). Maintaining group memberships: Social identity continuity predicts well-being after stroke. *Neuropsychological Rehabilitation, 18*, 671–691.

Haslam, S. A., Jetten, J., Postmes, T., & Haslam, C. (2009). Social identity, health and well-being: An emerging agenda for applied psychology. *Applied Psychology: An International Review, 58*, 1–23.

Haslam, S. A., O'Brien, A., Jetten, J., Vormedal, K., & Penna, S. (2005). Taking the strain: Social identity, social support and the experience of stress. *British Journal of Social Psychology*, *44*, 355–370.

Hornsey, M. J., & Jetten, J. (2003). Not being what you claim to be: Impostors as sources of group threat. *European Journal of Social Psychology*, *33*, 639–657.

Hummert, M. L., Garstka, T. A., Shaner, J. L., & Strahm, S. (1994). Stereotypes of the elderly held by young, middle-ages and elderly adults. *Journal of Gerontology: Psychological Sciences*, *49*, 240–249.

Iyer, A., & Jetten, J. (in press). What's left behind: Identity continuity moderates the effect of nostalgia on well-being and life choices. *Journal of Personality and Social Psychology*. doi:10.1037/a0022496.

Iyer, A., Jetten, J., & Tsivrikos, D. (2008). Torn between identities: Predictors of adjustment to identity change. In Sani, F. (Ed.), *Self-continuity: Individual and collective perspectives* (pp. 187–197). New York, NY: Psychology Press.

Iyer, A., Jetten, J., Tsivrikos, D., Postmes, T., & Haslam, S. A. (2009). The more (and the more compatible) the merrier: Multiple group memberships and identity compatibility as predictors of adjustment after life transitions. *British Journal of Social Psychology*, *48*, 707–733.

Jetten, J., Haslam, S. A., Iyer, A., & Haslam, C. (2009). Turning to others in times of change: Shared identity and coping with stress. In S. Stürmer & M. Snyder (Eds.), *New directions in the study of helping: Group-level perspectives on motivations, consequences and interventions* (pp. 139–156). Chichester, UK: Wiley-Blackwell.

Jetten, J., Haslam, C., Pugliese, C., Tonks, J., & Haslam, S. A. (2010). Declining autobiographical memory and the loss of identity: Effects on well-being. *Journal of Clinical and Experimental Neuropsychology*, *32*, 408–416.

Jetten, J., Iyer, A., Tsivrikos, D., & Young, B. M. (2008). When is individual mobility costly? The role of economic and social identity factors. *European Journal of Social Psychology*, *38*, 866–879.

Jetten, J., O'Brien, A., & Trindall, N. (2002).Changing identity: Predicting adjustment to organisational restructure as a function of subgroup and superordinate identification. *British Journal of Social Psychology*, *41*, 281–297.

Jetten, J., Schmitt, M. T., Branscombe, N. R., Garza, A. A., & Mewse, A. J. (2011). Group commitment in the face of discrimination: The role of legitimacy appraisals. *European Journal of Social Psychology*, *41*, 116–126.

Laliberte Rudman, D., Friedland, J., Chipman, M., & Sciortino, P. (2006). Holding on and letting go: The perspectives of pre-seniors and seniors on driving self-regulation in later life. *Canadian Journal on Aging*, *25*, 65–76.

Landau, M. J., Greenberg, J., & Solomon, S. (2008). The never-ending story: A terror management perspective on the psychological functions of self-continuity. In F. Sani (Ed.), *Self-continuity: Individual and collective perspectives* (pp. 87–100). New York, NY: Psychology Press.

Lazarus, R. S., & Folkman, S. (1984). *Stress, appraisal, and coping*. New York, NY: Springer.

Lewin, K. (1948). *Field theory in social science*. New York, NY: Harper & Row.

Pachana, N., & Jetten, J. (2010). *Driving cessation as aging*. Unpublished data, University of Queensland, Australia.

Pasupathi, M., & Löckenhoff, C. E. (2002). Ageist behavior. In T. D. Nelson (Ed.), *Ageism: Stereotyping and prejudice against older persons* (pp. 201–246). Cambridge, MA: The MIT Press.

Ragland, D. R., Satariano, W. A., MacLeod, K. A. (2005). Driving cessation and increased depressive symptoms. *Journal of Gerontology: Medical Sciences, 60A*, 399–403.

Sani, F. (Ed.) (2008). *Self-continuity: Individual and collective perspectives.* New York, NY: Psychology Press.

Siren, A., & Hakamies-Blomqvist, L. (2005). Sense and sensibility: A narrative study of older women's car driving. *Transportation Research, F8*, 213–228.

Siren, A., Hakamies-Blomqvist, L., & Lindeman, M. (2004). Driving cessation and health in older women. *The Journal of Applied Gerontology, 23*, 58–69.

Tajfel, H., & Turner, J. C. (1979). An integrative theory of intergroup conflict. In W. G. Austin & S. Worchel (Eds.), *The social psychology of intergroup relations* (pp. 33–47). Monterey, CA: Brooks/Cole.

Underwood, P. W. (2000). Social support: The promise and reality. In B. H. Rice (Ed.), *Handbook of stress, coping and health* (pp. 367–391). Newbury Park, CA: Sage.

Windsor, T. D., Anstey, K. J., Butterworth, P., Luszcz, M. A., & Andrews, G. R. (2007). The role of perceived control in explaining depressive symptoms associated with driving cessation in a longitudinal study. *The Gerontologist, 2*, 215–223.

Yassuda, M. S., Wilson, J. J., & Mering, O. von (1997). Driving cessation: The perspective of senior drivers. *Educational Gerontology, 23*, 525–538.

7 Moving toward or away from a group identity

Different strategies for coping with pervasive discrimination

Nyla R. Branscombe
University of Kansas

Saulo Fernández
Angel Gómez
UNED, Madrid

Tracey Cronin
University of Kansas

Being a member of a socially stigmatized group can entail considerable negative treatment and result in harm to well-being. Those who are stigmatized can find themselves overtly, or more subtly, rejected from a variety of important life domains, and experience discrimination in employment, housing, education, and outcomes received from the legal system, to name just a few. In some cases, those who are stigmatized may even be on the receiving end of public humiliation and disparaging media depictions that indicate that they are considered by others to be barely human. In this chapter we identify strategies that members of ethnic minority groups, women, the elderly, and people with physical disabilities employ in their efforts to cope with systematic discrimination. We also illustrate how the social context can influence which strategy is most likely to be favoured by such targets of discrimination, and consider the implications of these different strategies for the psychological well-being of the individual and the group as a whole.

Considerable evidence has accumulated that shows that the more pervasive across time and contexts discriminatory treatment is, the greater the toll on the psychological and physical health of stigmatized group members (see Clark, Anderson, Clark, & Williams, 1999; Schmitt & Branscombe, 2002a). The devaluation that such discrimination reflects is an important stressor, which may help explain differences between stigmatized and non-stigmatized groups in a host of health outcomes (Clark et al., 1999; Contrada et al., 2000; Herek, Gillis, & Cogan, 1999; Krieger, 1990; Matheson & Anisman, 2009, this volume). Perceptions of the severity and frequency of discrimination have been linked with lower psychological well-being on measures of self-directed negative affect such as depression and self-esteem in a wide variety of social groups including: women (Dambrun, 2007; Klonoff, Landrine, & Campbell, 2000; Schmitt, Branscombe, Kobrynowicz, & Owen, 2002), African Americans (Branscombe, Schmitt, & Harvey, 1999; Williams, Neighbors, & Jackson, 2003), Latino Americans (Armenta & Hunt, 2009), Jewish Canadians (Dion & Earn, 1975), gays and lesbians (Herek et al., 1999), international students (Schmitt, Spears, & Branscombe, 2003b), and immigrants in several different national contexts (Bourguignon, Seron, Yzerbyt, & Herman, 2006; Jasinskaja-Lahti, Liebkind, & Perhoniemi, 2006).

In addition to such correlational evidence, experiments in which stigmatized individuals are exposed to a single discriminatory outcome from another individual who is prejudiced against their group also demonstrate that this can undermine psychological well-being, with the degree of harm depending on the extent to which the experience is seen as reflecting social conditions that are likely to be encountered again in the future (see Schmitt, Branscombe, & Postmes, 2003a). So, for example, not only do women who experience more pervasive discrimination report worse negative affect following a discriminatory outcome than men who experience gender discrimination infrequently (Schmitt & Branscombe, 2002b), but when women attribute a single negative outcome to pervasive discrimination their self-esteem suffers more than when they attribute that same negative outcome to an isolated instance of discrimination (Schmitt et al., 2003a). Thus, the evidence is clear that experiencing discrimination that is perceived as pervasive harms self-directed affect (i.e., people's positive feelings about themselves) – and this is the case regardless of whether that perception stems from a single discriminatory event or it represents a summary of the perceiver's past experiences and expectations of future discriminatory treatment.

INDIVIDUALISTIC AND COLLECTIVE COPING STRATEGIES

In this chapter we examine different strategies for coping with discrimination and devaluation that members of socially stigmatized groups employ – both individualistic and collective means – and their consequences for psychological well-being. We define individualistic strategies as those primarily aimed at protecting the stigmatized individual's personal self, which can be accomplished by either figuratively or literally leaving the stigmatized group. Such abandonment of one's stigmatized group can be personally protective of well-being by minimizing the likelihood of future discrimination based on that identity. To the extent that the individual successfully dissociates the self from an identity that elicits discrimination, and thereby avoids the source of suffering, the individual's well-being may be protected, even though the stigmatized group as a whole continues to be a target of discrimination. In contrast, collective strategies do not minimize the likelihood of future painful discrimination. Rather, reliance on one's group identity – indeed, taking pride in one's fellow groups members' ability to cope with and potentially overcome the discrimination directed toward the group – can protect well-being when discrimination is experienced. We describe evidence supporting the "adaptive" value of both individualistic and collective strategies, in terms of helping to alleviate the harm of experiencing discrimination, and illustrate how the means by which that protection is achieved can differ.

The consequences for the stigmatized group as a whole depends on whether its members systematically favour one strategy over the other. As Tajfel (1978) noted some time ago, in contrast to the "self-hatred hypothesis" (Allport, 1954; Fanon, 1952; Lewin, 1948), members of stigmatized groups, even those facing severe devaluation, rarely simply internalize the dominant group's view of their group (see also Crocker & Major, 1989). Rather, those who are stigmatized can cope with their predicament in a range of ways, with different strategies being preferred depending on whether an alternative to the existing status relations can be envisioned or not. When stigmatized group members cannot imagine their group's position improving, individual stigmatized group members may be tempted to cope as individuals. In contrast, when members of the stigmatized group can imagine different relations existing between the groups, then stigmatized group members will be more likely to join forces with others with whom they share a common fate and attempt to work collectively to improve the position of their group as a whole.

The individualistic strategy that we consider – that of social mobility – involves attempting literally to leave the stigmatized group or, at a minimum, hide one's true group membership and "pass" as a nonstigmatized group member. By definition, this strategy for coping with stigma involves moving away from one's devalued group and, often, entails seeking acceptance among the majority. In contrast, the collective strategy for coping with discrimination that we consider involves increasingly moving toward and identifying with the stigmatized group, which is frequently reflected in greater contact with other members of the stigmatized group.

Using social identity theory (Tajfel & Turner, 1986) and the appraisal theory of stress and coping (Lazarus & Folkman, 1984) we argue that favouring an individualistic option in terms of attempting to leave the stigmatized group depends, in part, on appraisals of whether doing so will limit the individual's exposure to further harmful discrimination. When the option of leaving the group is not feasible or desired, stigmatized group members can cope with the discrimination they encounter by moving closer to their group – by increasingly identifying with other stigmatized group members. Thus, when faced with pervasive discrimination, psychological well-being can be protected in either of two ways – by moving toward or away from a stigmatized group identity, with social structural conditions affecting which option is likely to be chosen.

Use of these two different strategies is not without consequences for the group as a whole. Branscombe and Ellemers (1998) described ways in which individualistic coping strategies can improve the individual's personal status and well-being, but do little to change the overall conditions of the devalued group. In contrast, employing a collective coping strategy has the potential to elevate the status of the group as a whole and ultimately change the existing relations between groups; but it too is not without risks. By increasingly moving toward the stigmatized group identity, there is the risk of being further marginalized from the mainstream and only feeling "safe" in the presence of other ingroup members (see Tatum, 1997). In other words, "seeking separatism" may limit the contexts in which discrimination is experienced *and* provide valued group members to rely on for solace when discrimination is encountered, but this strategy may also involve giving up rewards and opportunities that come from navigating and living within the mainstream world (see Postmes & Branscombe, 2002). Furthermore, when stigmatized group members give public indications that their stigmatized group identity is valued, there is an implied willingness to confront the dominant group's higher status position, and this may result in even more hostile reactions on the part of dominant group members. When stigmatized group members seek equality through social change, they frequently encounter resistance and increased oppression from the dominant group, at least initially.

Although some researchers have suggested that devalued group members prefer individualistic coping strategies such as disengaging from the lower status group and attempting to gain entrance into the higher status group (Miller & Kaiser, 2001; Wright & Tropp, 2002), this may be most likely for those whose stigma can be easily hidden, and by those who experience discrimination infrequently, or in a limited set of contexts in which the exclusion may even be perceived as somewhat legitimate (e.g., young people being ineligible for certain age-based privileges and therefore attempting to "pass" as older than they are). Stigmatized group members are most likely to prefer collective coping strategies when the group's subordinate position and the discrimination experienced is perceived as illegitimate, pervasive, difficult to avoid, and when disadvantaged group members believe their group's status can be improved by direct competition with the dominant group for social value (i.e., when the existing status relations are unstable) (Tajfel & Turner, 1986). In this chapter we will identify how additional aspects of the existing social structural context can affect which of these two distinct types of strategies are most likely to be employed by members of stigmatized groups in response to the stress of devaluation and discrimination.

IMPORTANCE OF THE SOCIAL STRUCTURAL CONTEXT

The social context that different stigmatized groups find themselves in has important implications for the coping strategy used – individualistic or collective – when confronted with discrimination. Some theorists argue that disadvantaged groups only identify with their group and seek social change on behalf of their group when individual mobility is almost completely impossible (Taylor & McKirnan, 1984). Certainly pervasive discrimination when *imposed* on a stigmatized group – in terms of physical and social segregation – is likely to result in greater minority group identification and perception of the relations between the groups in hostile intergroup terms. Consistent with this hypothesis, research has revealed that African Americans who have had to contend with racially segregated schooling and housing, and whose social relationships are also relatively segregated, report perceiving White Americans in intergroup terms, feeling greater hostility toward Whites, and experiencing more discrimination than those who have spent their lives in more racially integrated life contexts (Branscombe et al., 1999; Postmes & Branscombe, 2002).

In fact, a different psychological risk is faced by African Americans attempting to navigate their lives in primarily White worlds. Minorities attempting to assimilate or at least navigate within White worlds, or who otherwise find themselves in contexts in which they are few in numbers (sometimes tokens) risk feeling (and being) rejected by members of their own group. Such rejection – reflecting the perception that the individual is insufficiently loyal to his or her minority ingroup – is no less painful than rejection by the dominant group (Postmes & Branscombe, 2002). Indeed, perceived ingroup rejection might have even more negative psychological consequences than discrimination on the part of the dominant group because it blocks the individual's ability to cope in terms of increased minority group identification. When people feel rejected by their ingroup, they are unlikely to respond with greater ingroup identification; feeling rejected by one's minority group is, instead, likely to encourage greater movement toward and identification with the dominant group. Thus, perceived ingroup rejection can block an important coping option for devalued group members, and encourage greater use of individualistic strategies.

Pervasive discrimination

Perceiving pervasive discrimination can encourage greater alignment with the minority group because unfair treatment based on group membership represents rejection from the dominant society and means that the individual is unable to exert control over current and future outcomes. Increasing identification with one's stigmatized group represents an adaptive strategy in the face of pervasive discrimination because those who share one's stigma can be counted on to not reject the individual on that basis. A number of correlational and experimental studies have illustrated the "rejection-identification-well-being protection" process (see Branscombe et al., 1999; Schmitt & Branscombe, 2002a). For example, when people are led to believe that they will be discriminated against in the future because of their sub-cultural group membership (i.e., having visible body piercings), they identify more strongly with others who share their category membership compared to when little discrimination in the future is expected (Jetten, Branscombe, Schmitt, & Spears, 2001). Likewise, when women in gender-segregated workplaces consider the negative treatment they experience at work to arise because they are women, they report greater identification with their gender group than when they do not consider discrimination as the reason for their negative experience or are in gender-integrated workplaces (Redersdorff, Martinot, & Branscombe, 2004). Thus, social conditions reflecting pervasive discrimination can certainly push disadvantaged group members toward a more collective psychological response – in part by blocking any perceived chance of individual mobility or the possibility of avoiding future painful discrimination.

Time course of discrimination experiences

There are additional social structural factors, besides the degree to which discrimination is pervasive, that can affect people's likelihood of coping via increased identification with their stigmatized group. Even if discrimination is a relatively frequent occurrence in the present, if it is also seen as likely to be minimal in the future, greater identification with the stigmatized group may be unlikely to develop. Consider the responses exhibited by young and elderly people, both of whom report experiencing discrimination based on their age group membership (Garstka, Schmitt, Branscombe, & Hummert, 2004). A key factor for understanding why these two age groups respond differently to the discrimination that they experience is that these groups differ in the permanence of their membership in their devalued age group. For young people, the group boundaries are relatively permeable, but they are relatively impermeable for the elderly. Indeed, individual upward mobility to the higher status middle-aged group is effortless and inevitable for young adults, whereas movement back in age to the higher status middle-aged group is impossible for the elderly (see also Jetten & Pachana, this volume).

Given that the discrimination experienced by the elderly is likely to be seen as unavoidable and a negative consequence of a group membership they have little chance of leaving, the elderly should favour group identification as a means of coping. In contrast, among young adults, who can look forward to the cessation of the forms of discrimination they report experiencing (e.g., age restrictions on voting, alcohol use, driving, and marriage rights) when certain chronological age markers are attained (e.g., reaching 18 or 21 years), they should favour individual mobility and not respond to discrimination with greater age group identification. This is precisely the pattern of effects that was obtained in research with young and elderly adults (Garstka et al., 2004). Perceived discrimination did not predict group identification in young adults, but it did do so for elderly adults. In fact, overall, the elderly showed greater identification with their group than did young adults, and group identification was more strongly predictive of positive psychological well-being among the elderly than it was among young adults.

This research with different age groups provides clear evidence that being a member of a stigmatized or low status group does not alone determine whether group identification will serve as a way of coping with discrimination. The young and the elderly reported having similar low status compared to middle-aged adults, and experiencing similar levels of age discrimination. Yet it was primarily among the elderly that the negative psychological well-being effects of that discrimination were observed, and only among the elderly did group identification increase in response to perceived rejection based on their age. Thus, permanent group memberships – where individual mobility is completely blocked – are particularly likely to evoke collective responses. Moreover, when such stigma inescapability is coupled with a sense of collective efficacy to achieve social change, it is likely to be reflected in changes in the group identity itself (e.g., shifts from "the elderly" to "grey panthers").

Changing contexts and acquiring a group identity across time

When stigmatized groups expect to assimilate into the mainstream, as do Latino Americans who attend college (Deaux & Ethier, 1998; Sears, 2008), discrimination may be perceived as something that can be avoided in the future by conforming to mainstream social norms. Yet over time, as Latino Americans enter primarily White worlds – such as prestigious universities – they may come to realize that assimilation is more difficult than they previously thought. Moreover, as these minority group members increasingly perceive discrimination as pervasive across contexts, regardless of individual efforts to assimilate to mainstream norms, perceived discrimination may come to be experienced as a critical barrier to their ability to move upward. Ultimately perception that their ethnic minority group membership cannot be overcome and will prevent assimilation, can result in the strengthening of a minority group identity, and, for some, a politicized minority group identity may develop over time (Simon & Klandermans, 2001).

To explore these ideas, we conducted a study with Latino students from Los Angeles County (Cronin, Levin, Branscombe, Van Laar, & Tropp, 2010). Although these students have primarily spent their early schooling in Latino-majority environments, they had just entered University of California at Los Angeles (UCLA) where they were a numerical minority. Among these students, perceived discrimination based on their ethnicity predicted greater minority group identification, which in turn positively predicted these Latino students' well-being during both their first and fourth years. Perceived discrimination also had a direct negative effect on Latino students' well-being during their fourth year, but not during their first year. Ethnic identification was a mediator of the relationship between perceived discrimination and well-being in the fourth year. By their fourth year in a White university environment, these Latino students exhibited all the components of the rejection–identification model, where greater perceived discrimination resulted in poorer well-being, but this negative effect of discrimination was partially alleviated to the extent that their Latino identification had strengthened. These findings with Latino students, navigating in a White institution for the first time, are consistent with other recent longitudinal research (Ramos, Cassidy, Reicher, & Haslam, in press) that found that international students at Scottish universities who similarly began by favouring an assimilation acculturation strategy displayed the rejection–identification pattern in response to perceived discrimination over time.

According to Taylor and McKirnan (1984), it is largely failed attempts at gaining entrance into the higher status group that lead to collective strategies as a response to disadvantage. Consistent with this idea, we found that for Latino students in the UCLA sample, it did take some time for these students to recognize the negative implications of discrimination for their future and for it to harm their self-esteem. When these negative effects were recognized, the rejection experienced on the basis of their ethnic group membership during their earlier years of study resulted in greater identification with their minority group and this served to protect their subsequent well-being. Perhaps after having expended futile energy in attempts to fully assimilate – toward the end of their educational experience they realized that complete acceptance was unlikely and that it was not possible to individually overcome discrimination in such White-dominated settings. As a result, across time they developed an adaptive response to perceived pervasive discrimination and turned toward their ethnic group as a means of alleviating the harm sustained to their well-being.

Structural conditions can affect coping strategy use within a single stigmatized group

The case of people with skeletal dysplasias that cause disproportionate short stature (dwarfism) is an interesting example of how structural factors in a given social context can influence the coping strategies of groups with a physical disability stigma. In a multi-nation study we investigated how people with skeletal dysplasias – a rare genetic condition affecting the development of the long bones – cope with the severe discrimination that they experience (Fernández, Branscombe, Gómez, & Morales, 2011).

The most common type of skeletal dysplasia that causes dwarfism is achondroplasia, with an estimated prevalence in the population of 1 in 26,000 births (Thompson, Shakespeare, & Wright, 2008). People with achondroplasia have abnormally short stature; their limbs are short in contrast to relatively normal-sized heads and trunks. Although there are several physical and medical difficulties associated with the condition, affected individuals are mobile on their own, score average on intelligence tests, and have an average life span (Gollust, Thompson, Gooding, & Biesecker, 2003; Trotter & Hall, 2005). Nonetheless, dwarfism is a socially stigmatized condition that tends to evoke particularly high levels of intergroup anxiety and social distancing in majority group members (Fernández, 2009).

Several factors make this group an interesting one in which to investigate the role of contextual factors that might influence the process of coping with social stigmatization. Due to the low prevalence of the condition and the absence of other affected individuals in the family – more than 80 percent of cases are due to a spontaneous genetic mutation that appears in families with no history of skeletal dysplasias – people with dwarfism are geographically widely dispersed. As a result, individuals with dwarfism are usually the only person with that physical condition in their near environment (i.e., the only affected person in their school, neighborhood, or town). Because of this isolation from others who share their condition, and the severe social stigma associated with it, for people with dwarfism rejection is often an individualistic experience. In this sense, it is easy for people with dwarfism to feel more like a *deviant* (i.e., individuals who are rejected by members of their own group) rather than as members of a *classical minority* (i.e., groups that experience rejection from outgroup members) (see Jetten, Branscombe, & Spears, 2006).

Another reason why people with dwarfism are especially informative for studying the processes involved in coping with devaluation is that within this population there is the possibility for young people with achondroplasia to undergo limb-lengthening surgery (LLS) and gain up to 30 cm extra length in their lower limbs and 14 cm in their upper limbs. LLS therefore, to some extent, can permit people with dwarfism to conceal their stigmatized condition, which could be considered an individualistic strategy for coping with severe and pervasive discrimination. However, LLS is a controversial issue within the community of people with achondroplasia, and not all those with the condition decide to undergo LLS.

One reason for the controversy is that the lengthening process is intensive and requires several surgical interventions and long rehabilitation periods during which serious complications can arise. Moreover, because the process must begin at a young age – usually before 10 years old – the decision to undergo LLS is strongly influenced by the parents of an affected individual. Consequently, surgery may be seen as an attempt by parents to protect themselves and their child from the harmful effects of anticipated discrimination based on this stigma, as much as a coping strategy selected by the actual recipients of the discrimination. In addition, the fact that LLS can be seen as an attempt to conceal the condition is probably another important reason why it is controversial within the dwarfism community. Although it is by no means certain that LLS fully enables "successful passing" for those with dwarfism (because there are other subtle physical cues to the condition), it is almost certain that attempting to conceal the condition will make it more difficult to form a positive social identity based on this group membership.

It is particularly noteworthy that LLS is a *less* popular practice in the USA than in many other countries (Trotter & Hall, 2005). Given that the USA is typically seen to be characterized by its extreme individualism (e.g., Triandis, 1994), it might seem ironic that the individualistic strategy of LLS is least likely to be employed by those with dwarfism in the USA. In contrast, in Spain, which has been described as a relatively collectivist country, LLS is now almost uniformly performed on children with achondroplasia (Alonso-Álvarez, 2007).

There are several economic and identity-relevant reasons why use of LLS by people with dwarfism differs across these two national contexts. The different health care systems – a publicly funded national one in Spain vs. a private system in the USA – is undoubtedly an important factor. However, there are other important social psychological factors that influence the prevailing attitudes toward dwarfism in each country and that contribute to the differential use of LLS in these two national contexts. We argue that one of the crucial factors is the presence of different norms in relevant institutions. That is, in the USA since 1957 there has been a large and active organization of people with dwarfism (e.g., "Little People of America" or LPA). LPA is an organization whose mission is to "improve the quality of life for people with dwarfism *while celebrating with great pride Little People's contribution to social diversity*" (from LPA's mission statement; emphasis added). A close examination of the LPA website shows that, in fact, their activities, their statements and positions about issues related to dwarfism, and even the motifs used on their website (e.g., lively photos of non-enlarged people with dwarfism communicating positive feelings about their bodies) reflect a transformation of identity from "those with a genetic mutation causing dwarfism" to "Little People". Furthermore, and at least as important, the existence of LPA has facilitated contact between adults with dwarfism in the USA.

In Spain, on the other hand, the comparison organization of people with dwarfism (ALPE-Achondroplasia Foundation) was created relatively recently, in 2000. ALPE's agenda is to assist and support the families and people with dwarfism. ALPE, like LPA, aims to improve the quality of life of people with dwarfism and it also provides information and services to affected individuals and their families. However, consistent with our hypothesis that institutional norms can affect coping strategy preferences, there are some subtle but important differences between ALPE and LPA that parallel the differential use of individualistic versus group-based strategies among people with dwarfism in each country. For example, one interesting difference between these organizations is the support that ALPE provides for genetic research, which is aimed at ensuring that people who are born with the genetic mutation that produces skeletal dysplasias are provided with available treatments to develop and lengthen their bones. Indeed, such genetic and medical research projects *have as their goal the elimination of dwarfism*. In contrast, such research is neither publicized, nor is it officially supported, by LPA. Moreover, while the position of ALPE toward LLS is clearly favourable, LPA spends little time on the issue and when it is mentioned, the organization is considerably more skeptical about the value of this surgery. We think these visibly observable differential approaches within each of these national organizations are good indicators of two rather different norms for how the stigma of dwarfism is best coped with.

In order to investigate the extent to which these organizational and structural differences observed between Spain and the USA are reflected in how people with dwarfism cope with the social stigma of the condition, coping and well-being data were collected from people with dwarfism in both countries (Fernández et al., 2011). The results illustrate important differences in the coping strategies that prevail in each of these national contexts. In the Spanish sample of people with dwarfism, there was significantly more use of LLS than in the American sample. Interestingly, in Spain height predicted the extent to which people with dwarfism reported feeling socially excluded, ostracized, and derogated by others due to their physical condition – with those who were taller reporting lower levels of such treatment than those who were shorter. In other words, in Spain, those who did have LLS to increase their height, reported experiencing less discrimination than those who did not do so, whereas in the USA this path between height and lower discrimination was absent because very few people had chosen to have such surgery to gain greater height. In both countries, the extent to which participants reported experiencing discrimination based on their physical condition negatively predicted quality of life. However, in the American sample, having positive contact with other members of the ingroup (i.e., other people with dwarfism) buffered the negative effect of discrimination experiences on quality of life, although this was not the case in Spain.

These results suggest that in Spain a more individualistic coping strategy based on LLS prevails, while in the USA a collective strategy involving greater positive contact with other ingroup members is preferred. It is interesting to note that the study revealed no overall difference in the quality of life reported in the Spanish and American samples, suggesting that both strategies can be effective at protecting psychological well-being. Individual social mobility – favoured in Spain – protects well-being by decreasing the likelihood of the individual experiencing discrimination, whereas group-based strategies protect well-being – and are favoured in the USA – because they provide solace when discrimination that is difficult to avoid is encountered.

Thus, social structural conditions can afford people the opportunity to cope with stigma by either moving toward the group or away from the group. The group that officially represents people with dwarfism (LPA) in the USA has not only been in existence for some time, it is organized by adults with dwarfism rather than the parents of children with dwarfism as is the case in Spain. LPA facilitates long-distance contact among its members, and has clear norms that are supportive of strong identification with others who share the stigmatized condition. For these reasons alone, it is not surprising that formation of a positive identity as a "little person" in the American sample proved to be an important means of coping with discrimination. In addition, in the US case, there is little ability to leave the stigmatized group – because LLS is not supported by the group and is not affordable or widely available within the American health care system. In Spain, where it is possible to leave the stigmatized group via LLS – because it is both financially feasible and is favoured by the affected individual's own family and the national organization representing the group – people with dwarfism appear to cope with discrimination by attempting to avoid the discrimination by masking their stigmatized condition. Both of these strategies – individualistic and collective – appear to be adaptive for individual members of stigmatized groups in terms of protecting their well-being – with strategy preference depending on the structural conditions in which the stigmatized find themselves.

DISADVANTAGES OF INDIVIDUALISTIC VERSUS COLLECTIVE COPING STRATEGIES

While attempting to leave one's stigmatized group, even through extreme measures such as surgery, has the potential virtue of lessening the personal experience of discrimination, it continues to make clear that one's stigmatized group membership is fundamentally devalued in the wider society. To the extent that exiting the stigmatized group is successful, those individuals who do engage in social mobility may suffer less from discriminatory outcomes. Nevertheless, they may continue to be exposed to others' derogatory attitudes toward their stigmatized group. Consider the plight of gay and lesbian members of the American military under the current policy of "don't ask, don't tell". Although concealing one's homosexual identity can prevent what is ostensibly the worst outcome from occurring – losing one's job and being dismissed from a valued institution – it also undermines the formation of a positive group identity. Furthermore, there is evidence that individuals who attempt to conceal a devalued group membership have lower self-confidence and report more guilt and shame than participants who do not conceal their devalued group membership (Barreto, Ellemers, & Banal, 2006). Indeed, attempting to conceal one's stigmatized group identity (e.g., having AIDS) predicts more rapid HIV disease progression and death (Cole, Kemeny, Taylor, Visscher, & Fahey, 1996). Thus, although avoiding discrimination may have some immediate benefits, even among people with HIV disease (Molero, Fuster, Jetten, & Moriano, 2011), failure to identify with and reach out to members of one's own group can also have critical and negative health consequences.

As we suggested earlier, coping with devaluation by moving toward a stigmatized identity and increasing one's investment in that group identity is not without potential disadvantages. Doing so could be seen as the pathway to separatism, which can entail both economic and social costs for stigmatized group members. But it is also – through constructive engagement with the dominant group's values – a critical step toward changing the status relations between groups. Certainly the ability to conceal one's group membership will not be feasible for all devalued groups, nor will it be deemed desirable, even if available. For many members of disadvantaged groups, despite the potential costs of identifying with and acting collectively on behalf of their group, abandoning or disengaging from it is simply inconceivable.

CONCLUSIONS

Across diverse stigmatized groups – from women, who constitute a numerical majority, to people with a specific physical stigma such as dwarfism who constitute a small minority – perceiving and experiencing pervasive discrimination has negative implications for psychological well-being. How the threat stemming from group-based devaluation is most likely to be managed – in terms of moving toward or away from the devalued identity – depends on aspects of the social structural context. We presented evidence that both individualistic and group-based responses in the face of discrimination can be adaptive *in the sense of protecting the individual's well-being*. But, how that protection is achieved – by either moving toward or away from a group identity – reflects different strategies that have implications for the likelihood of change occurring in terms of the status position of the devalued group as a whole.

Each of the following conditions are likely to *tempt* stigmatized group members to move away from their group identity: (1) when discrimination is seen as limited to particular contexts or period in the life of the individual, (2) when the differential treatment is seen as having some legitimacy, (3) when there is little contact with other ingroup members who share the stigma, or (4) when existing social conditions are perceived as impossible to change but the stigma itself can be concealed. In such circumstances, people may be inclined to perceive the group identity as the problem and therefore focus on minimizing their exposure to discrimination based on it. This can be accomplished by attempting to figuratively or literally change group memberships in order to prevent the discrimination itself, and its painful implications. Thus, by moving away from their stigmatized group identity, individuals may lessen the likelihood that they will continue to experience discrimination on that basis. By pursuing this strategy, however, the situation of the group as a whole will go unchanged.

On the other hand, when a stigmatized group membership cannot be hidden and pervasive discrimination cannot be avoided, research has revealed that the primary means by which members of a host of devalued groups protect their well-being is by increasingly moving toward their stigmatized group identity. Indeed, doing so is the critical means by which the devalued can convert their "mark of shame" into a "badge of honor". We consider movement toward stigmatized group identities as consistent with the "social cure" for two reasons. First, others who share one's stigmatized group identity serve as a coping resource when the stressor of discrimination and devaluation are experienced. As a result, psychologically, the individual is no longer alone. Indeed, research has thus far revealed this to be the *only replicable mechanism by which the psychological harm stemming from discrimination can be alleviated.* Second, it is through identification with one's stigmatized group and taking pride in one's group (including its ability to withstand the injustice of discrimination) that hope for a more just future can be achieved. Coupled with a sense of efficacy to bring about such social change, group identities – even those that are devalued in the broader society – can lead to actions aimed at improving the position of the group as a whole.

ACKNOWLEDGMENTS

Preparation of this chapter was facilitated by an award to Nyla Branscombe from the Canadian Institute for Advanced Research: Social Interactions, Identity, and Well-Being Program.

References

Allport, G. (1954). *The nature of prejudice.* Reading, MA: Addison-Wesley.

Alonso-Álvarez, C. (2007). *A new horizon: Guide to Achondroplasia* [*Un nuevo horizonte. Guía de la acondroplasia*]. Madrid, Spain: The Royal Board on Disability [Real Patronato Sobre Discapacidad].

Armenta, B. E., & Hunt, J. S. (2009). Responding to societal devaluation: Effects of perceived personal and group discrimination on the ethnic group identification and personal self-esteem of Latino/Latina adolescents. *Group Processes and Intergroup Relations, 12,* 23–39.

Barreto, M., Ellemers, N., & Banal, S. (2006). Working under cover: Performance-related self-confidence among members of contextually devalued groups who try to pass. *European Journal of Social Psychology, 36,* 337–352.

Bourguignon, D., Seron, E., Yzerbyt, V., & Herman, G. (2006). Perceived group and personal discrimination: Differential effects on personal self-esteem. *European Journal of Social Psychology, 36,* 773–789.

Branscombe, N. R., & Ellemers, N. (1998). Coping with group-based discrimination: Individualistic versus group-level strategies. In J. K. Swim & C. Stangor

(Eds.), *Prejudice: The target's perspective* (pp. 243–266). New York, NY: Academic Press.

Branscombe, N. R., Schmitt, M. T., & Harvey, R. D. (1999). Perceiving pervasive discrimination among African Americans: Implications for group identification and well-being. *Journal of Personality and Social Psychology*, *77*, 135–149.

Clark, R., Anderson, N. B., Clark, V. R., & Williams, D. R. (1999). Racism as a stressor for African Americans: A biopsychosocial model. *American Psychologist*, *54*, 805–816.

Cole, S. W., Kemeny, M. E., Taylor, S. E., Visscher, B. R., & Fahey, J. L. (1996). Accelerated course of human immunodeficiency virus infection in gay men who conceal their homosexual identity. *Psychosomatic Medicine*, *58*, 219–231.

Contrada, R. J., Ashmore, R. D., Gary, M. L., Coups, E., Egeth, J. D., Sewell, A., et al. (2000). Ethnicity-related sources of stress and their effects on well-being. *Current Directions in Psychological Science*, *9*, 136–139.

Crocker, J., & Major, B. (1989). Social stigma and self-esteem: The self-protective properties of stigma. *Psychological Review*, *96*, 608–630.

Cronin, T. J., Levin, S., Branscombe, N. R., Van Laar, C., & Tropp, L. R. (2011). *Ethnic identification in response to perceived discrimination protects well-being and promotes activism: A longitudinal study of Latino college students*. Manuscript submitted for publication.

Dambrun, M. (2007). Gender differences in mental health: The mediating role of perceived discrimination. *Journal of Applied Social Psychology*, *37*, 1118–1129.

Deaux, K., & Ethier, K. A. (1998). Negotiating social identity. In J. K. Swim & C. Stangor (Eds.), *Prejudice: The target's perspective* (pp. 302–323). San Diego, CA: Academic Press.

Dion, K. L., & Earn, B. M. (1975). The phenomenology of being the target of prejudice. *Journal of Personality and Social Psychology*, *32*, 944–950.

Fanon, F. (1952). *Black skins, white masks*. New York, NY: Grove Press.

Fernández, S. (2009). *El estigma social del enanismo óseo. Consecuencias y estrategias de afrontamiento* [*The social stigmatization of dwarfism: Consequences and coping strategies*]. PhD Dissertation, UNED, Madrid, Spain.

Fernández, S., Branscombe, N. R., Gómez, A., & Morales, J. F. (2011). *Influence of the social context on use of individualistic and collective coping strategies among people with dwarfism*. Manuscript submitted for publication. Unpublished manuscript, UNED, Madrid, Spain.

Garstka, T. A., Schmitt, M. T., Branscombe, N. R., & Hummert, M. L. (2004). How young and older adults differ in their responses to perceived age discrimination. *Psychology and Aging*, *19*, 326–335.

Gollust, S. E., Thompson, R. E., Gooding, H. C., & Biesecker, B. B. (2003). Living with achondroplasia in an average-sized world: An assessment of quality of life. *American Journal of Medical Genetics*, *120*, 447–458.

Herek, G. M., Gillis, J. R., & Cogan, J. C. (1999). Psychological sequelae of hate-crime victimization among lesbian, gay, and bisexual adults. *Journal of Consulting and Clinical Psychology*, *67*, 945–951.

Jasinskaja-Lahti, I., Liebkind, K., & Perhoniemi, R. (2006). Perceived discrimination and well-being: A victim study of different immigrant groups. *Journal of Community and Applied Social Psychology*, *16*, 267–284.

Jetten, J., Branscombe, N. R., Schmitt, M. T., & Spears, R. (2001). Rebels with a cause: Group identification as a response to perceived discrimination from the mainstream. *Personality and Social Psychology Bulletin, 27,* 1204–1213.

Jetten, J., Branscombe, N. R., & Spears, R. (2006). Living on the edge: Dynamics of intragroup and intergroup rejection experiences. In R. Brown & D. Capozza (Eds.), *Social identities: Motivational, emotional and cultural influences* (pp. 91–107). London, UK: Sage.

Klonoff, E. A., Landrine, H., & Campbell, R. (2000). Sexist discrimination may account for well-known gender differences in psychiatric symptoms. *Psychology of Women Quarterly, 24,* 93–99.

Krieger, N. (1990). Racial and gender discrimination: Risk factors for high blood pressure? *Social Science Medicine, 12,* 1273–1281.

Lazarus, R. S., & Folkman, S. (1984). *Stress, appraisal, and coping.* New York, NY: Springer.

Lewin, K. L. (1948). *Resolving social conflicts: Selected papers on group dynamics.* New York, NY: Harper.

Matheson, K., & Anisman, H. (2009). Anger and shame elicited by discrimination: Moderating role of coping on action endorsements and salivary cortisol. *European Journal of Social Psychology, 39,* 163–185.

Miller, C. T., & Kaiser, C. R. (2001). A theoretical perspective on coping with stigma. *Journal of Social Issues, 57,* 73–92.

Molero, F., Fuster, M. J., Jetten, J., & Moriano, J. A. (2011). Living with HIV/AIDS: A psychosocial perspective on coping with prejudice and discrimination. *Journal of Applied Social Psychology, 41,* 609–626.

Postmes, T., & Branscombe, N. R. (2002). Influence of long-term racial environmental composition on subjective well-being in African Americans. *Journal of Personality and Social Psychology, 83,* 735–751.

Ramos, M., Cassidy, C., Reicher, S., & Haslam, S. A. (in press). A longitudinal investigation of the rejection–identification hypothesis. *British Journal of Social Psychology.*

Redersdorff, S., Martinot, D., & Branscombe, N. R. (2004). The impact of thinking about group-based disadvantages or advantages on women's well-being: An experimental test of the rejection-identification model. *Current Psychology of Cognition, 22,* 203–222.

Schmitt, M. T., & Branscombe, N. R. (2002a). The meaning and consequences of perceived discrimination in disadvantaged and privileged social groups. *European Review of Social Psychology, 12,* 167–199.

Schmitt, M. T., & Branscombe, N. R. (2002b). The internal and external causal loci of attributions to prejudice. *Personality and Social Psychology Bulletin, 28,* 484–492.

Schmitt, M. T., Branscombe, N. R., Kobrynowicz, D., & Owen, S. (2002). Perceiving discrimination against one's gender group has difficult implications for well-being in women and men. *Personality and Social Psychology Bulletin, 28,* 197–210.

Schmitt, M. T., Branscombe, N. R., & Postmes, T. (2003a). Women's emtional responses to the pervasiveness of gender discrimination. *European Journal of Social Psychology, 33,* 297–312.

Schmitt, M. T., Spears, R., & Branscombe, N. R. (2003b). Constructing a minority group identity out of shared rejection: bThe case of international students. *European Journal of Social Psychology, 33,* 1–12.

Sears, D. O. (2008). The American color line 50 years after Brown v. Board: Many "Peoples of Color" or Black exceptionalism? In G. Adams, M. Biernat, N. R. Branscombe, C. S. Crandall, & L. S. Wrightsman (Eds.), *Commemorating Brown: The social psychology of racism and discrimination* (pp. 133–152). Washington, DC: American Psychological Association.

Simon, B., & Klandermans, B. (2001). Politicized collective identity: A social psychological analysis. *American Psychologist, 56,* 319–331.

Tajfel, H. (1978). *The social psychology of minorities.* New York, NY: Minority Rights Group.

Tajfel, H., & Turner, J. C. (1986). The social identity theory of intergroup behavior. In S. Worchel & W. Austin (Eds.), *Psychology of intergroup relations* (pp. 7–24). Chicago, IL: Nelson-Hall.

Tatum, B. D. (1997). *Why are the black kids sitting together in the cafeteria?* New York, NY: Basic Books.

Taylor, D. M., & McKirnan, D. J. (1984). A five-stage model of intergroup relations. *British Journal of Social Psychology, 23,* 291–300.

Thompson, S., Shakespeare, T., & Wright, M. J. (2008). Medical and social aspects of the life course of adults with skeletal dysplasia: A review of current knowledge. *Disability and Rehabilitation, 30,* 1–12.

Triandis, H. C. (1994). *Culture and behavior.* New York, NY: McGraw-Hill.

Trotter, T. L., & Hall, J. G. (2005). Health supervision for children with achondroplasia. *Pediatrics, 116,* 774–783.

Williams, D. R., Neighbors, H. W., & Jackson, J. S. (2003). Racial/ethnic discrimination and health: Findings from community studies. *American Journal of Public Health, 93,* 200–208.

Wright, S. C., & Tropp, L. R. (2002). Collective action in response to disadvantage: Intergroup perceptions, social identification, and social change. In I. Walker & H. J. Smith (Eds.), *Relative deprivation: Specification, development, and integration* (pp. 200–236). New York, NY: Cambridge University Press.

8 Biological and psychosocial responses to discrimination

Kimberly Matheson
Hymie Anisman
Carleton University

- An Aboriginal youth, picked up by police, is then dropped off in an isolated rural area in sub-Arctic winter temperatures.
- A gunman comes into a classroom, and shoots the women shouting that he hates feminists.
- A child watches from his hiding spot, as his family is lined up and shot because they are Jews.

There is little argument that these incidents, targeted at individuals merely for belonging to a social category, are experienced as traumatic, rendering affected individuals vulnerable to subsequent psychological and physical pathologies. But what about the everyday events that do not seem particularly serious, yet happen time and again, day after day?

- A gay man going through the morning paper reads a politician's statement that his sexual proclivities are so sick they ought to be outlawed.
- On a routine business trip to the USA, a Black man is profiled at customs and immigration, and subjected to a 2-hour search and questioning about possible terrorist connections.
- A Muslim girl wearing a hijab is banned from a soccer tournament in which she is playing, allegedly because the headwear makes the game unsafe for her.

Though undoubtedly distressing, these latter experiences appear to be relatively mild and innocuous. However, their repetitive, intermittent, and unpredictable nature, coupled with the emotional responses elicited (e.g., anger, distress, shame), are hallmark characteristics of stressors that are likely to result in the psychological and physical wear and tear that undermine individuals' health and well-being. Indeed, even if the everyday experiences of discrimination do not result in pathology, they may serve as a powerful backdrop that sensitizes the individual to the adverse impacts of subsequent stressors.

Belonging to a social group is important to individuals' sense of self (Tajfel & Turner, 1979). Identification with a group, particularly one that is socially devalued, can play a protective role against stigma and rejection, as well as a strategic function, facilitating a response to collective disadvantage (Branscombe, Schmitt, & Harvey, 1999; Jetten, Branscombe, Schmitt, & Spears, 2001; Louis & Taylor, 1999). Yet, even as individuals derive some benefit from group membership, the discriminatory actions of others represent a source of daily and even traumatic stressors (Allison, 1998). Such events tend to occur on an intermittent and unpredictable basis, and in an atmosphere of political correctness, the underlying discriminatory intent is frequently ambiguous ("was that person's reaction to me because of my group membership?"). This stressor profile makes it difficult for individuals to anticipate, interpret, or even decide on appropriate responses.

Despite the fact that stressful events, ranging from severe traumas to everyday hassles, are known to promote or exacerbate numerous physical and psychological disturbances, there has been limited attention devoted to pathophysiological consequences of discrimination (or other identity threats), and the factors that moderate such outcomes. Members of socially devalued groups (e.g., women, blacks, gays, Aboriginals) suffer disproportionately from adverse psychological (depression, post-traumatic stress disorder [PTSD]) and physiological (immune disturbances, diabetes, cardiovascular problems, physical disabilities, infant mortality) disturbances, even after adjusting for age or socioeconomic status (Bombay, Matheson, & Anisman, 2009; Klonoff, Landrine, & Campbell, 2000; Walsemann, Gee, & Geronimus, 2009). In fact, as presented in Table 8.1, we found that traumatic experiences of discrimination were more strongly related to symptoms of psychological disturbances than most other traumatic events, and had a similar impact to having been physically or sexually assaulted as an adult.

Of course, not all members of disadvantaged groups demonstrate signs of mental or physical pathology. Such variation stems from differences among group members regarding their objective experiences of discrimination, along with their subjective appraisals, coping strategies, and resources available to contend with the threat. Variation of health outcomes also exists across groups, likely emanating from some combination of genetic, cultural, and environmental factors (e.g., diet, activity, environmental pollutants) that exacerbate or alleviate particular stress reactions. For example, although suicide rates are particularly high among Aboriginals (Bombay et al., 2009), they are notably low among African Americans (Gibbs, 1997), who are more likely to present with cardiovascular disturbances (Wyatt et al., 2003). In effect, stressors may elicit heterogeneous physiological responses across individuals (and groups) leading to different functional outcomes (Anisman, Merali, & Hayley, 2008).

In this chapter, we set out to describe how social identity threats, particularly discrimination experiences, instigate biological changes that might render individuals vulnerable to stress-related psychological and physical

Table 8.1 Pearson correlations between the frequency of trauma types (experiences that elicited "fear, helplessness, or horror") and psychological symptoms for women and for racial minorities

	n	IES-R	BDI	BAI
Women	72			
Shock (car accident)	37	$-.22^+$	$-.06$	.04
Death of a loved one	38	.01	.05	.08
Trauma to other	30	.14	.16	$.21^+$
Assault	44	.14	.15	.28*
Discrimination	17	.24*	.28*	.34**
Visible minorities	39			
Shock (car accident)	24	.02	.13	$.29^+$
Death of a loved one	19	.05	.26	.12
Trauma to other	16	.11	.17	.25
Assault	24	$.28^+$	.44**	.38**
Discrimination	16	.47**	.48**	.48**

$^+ p < .10;$ * $p < .05;$ ** $p < .01.$

Note: n is the number of participants who reported at least one experience of this trauma type. Psychological symptoms were assessed using the Impact of Events Scale–Revised (IES-R) for the post-traumatic stress disorder; the Beck Depression Inventory (BDI); and the Beck Anxiety Inventory (BAI).

disorders, as well as the appraisal-coping process and social support resources that might serve as buffers against negative outcomes. To illustrate some of the links between social stressors and the emergence of pathology, we will present the findings of several survey and laboratory studies that we have conducted with Canadian university students, as well as with community samples of women, visible minorities, Aboriginals, religious groups, and refugee immigrants.

THE STRESS PROCESS

All of us encounter day-to-day annoyances, and at times we may have to deal with serious threats to our well-being. Many stressful events, or the consequences stemming from such events, are chronic in nature, including interpersonal problems (family disputes, divorce), illness, financial, or work-related issues, to name a few. In addition, we may encounter acute or ongoing threats associated with the social categories to which we belong (based on religion, sex, ethnicity, socioeconomic status, age). These threats can take the form of personal or collective challenges (our group is negatively stereotyped, is expected to assimilate with the dominant group, or is disadvantaged or discriminated against).

In response to stressors or potential stressors (threats), individuals appraise the situation, and then engage coping strategies to deal with it

(Lazarus & Folkman, 1984). Concurrently, several physiological changes occur that serve multiple functions essential to the individual's well-being. These biological changes are influenced by psychosocial factors and appraisal-coping processes, and conversely, they may influence the way individuals deal with stressors. Under most conditions, the combination of emotional, behavioural, and biological methods of dealing with stressful circumstances are relatively effective, and as a result, the threat subsides and well-being is maintained. However, if the stressor continues unabated, then our biological coping systems may become overly taxed (referred to as allostatic overload; McEwen, 2000), rendering the individual more vulnerable to the development of pathology. In this regard, stressful experiences have not just been associated with psychological illnesses, such as depression, burnout, anxiety, and PTSD, but also with numerous physical disorders. These include Type II diabetes, heart disease, various immunologically related disorders (e.g., susceptibility to virally related illnesses, autoimmune disorders), as well as neurodegenerative processes (e.g., Alzheimer's, Parkinson's disease). Interestingly, many of these illnesses are comorbid with depression, and it has been suggested that they involve common stressor-provoked underlying mechanisms (Anisman et al., 2008).

Even if we escape from a stressful encounter unscathed does not mean that the event has not had a profound and lasting impact. Potent stressors provoke the "sensitization" of several neurochemical systems, so that upon later encounters with stressors (even if they differ from the original event), exaggerated neurochemical responses are elicited (Anisman, Hayley, & Merali, 2003). These sensitized responses may be pivotal in the provocation of depression and in illness recurrence (Post, 1992).

Biological sequelae of stressors

In response to a stressor, several biological changes are instigated that serve to preserve the individual's well-being. Of these, the best known and most widely studied system is the hypothalamic–pituitary–adrenal (HPA) axis, whose end product, cortisol, serves to facilitate or permit other stress responses, acts in preparatory capacity to deal with further or impending stressors, or limits responses that might otherwise be harmful or counterproductive (Sapolsky, Romero, & Munck, 2000). Cortisol and other hormones interact with one another, as well as with central neuronal processes, and thus affect numerous behavioural and biological outputs (e.g., eating and metabolic processes, cognitive processes). In addition, stressors influence brain neurotransmitters and growth factors that have been implicated in mood states, cognitive functioning, and coping efforts (Anisman et al., 2008).

Two basic approaches have been used to assess cortisol changes in relation to stressors. The first, a laboratory procedure, assesses cortisol levels in response to a challenge that may or may not include reminders of previous stressor experiences (oral or visual representations, or written scripts). A common paradigm involves public speaking to a small panel of judges coupled with a verbal arithmetic test (the Trier Social Stress Test; Kirschbaum, Pirke, & Hellhammer, 1993). Such laboratory stressors typically promote an increase of cortisol that is evident in blood or saliva within 15 min and returns to basal levels at about 1 h. A meta-analysis indicated that uncontrollable social-evaluative threats were particularly effective in provoking cortisol elevations in laboratory contexts (Dickerson & Kemeny, 2004).

The second approach used to assess cortisol responses in relation to stressful events entails the analysis of diurnal changes. Circulating cortisol levels ordinarily rise markedly over the first 30 min following awakening (40 percent is typically measured in saliva) and then begin a precipitous decline (Schmidt-Reinwald et al., 1999). By late afternoon the rate of decline diminishes, and the cortisol nadir is reached near midnight. A meta-analyses revealed that, in naturalistic settings, chronic stressors were particularly effective in promoting the exaggerated morning cortisol elevation, but as chronicity was often confounded by controllability and the type of stressor experienced, the relative contributions of these stressor features could not be dissociated from one another (Michaud, Matheson, Kelly, & Anisman, 2008). Other analyses have similarly reported that the morning cortisol rise was positively associated with job stress and general life stress, but negatively related to burnout, fatigue, and exhaustion (Chida & Steptoe, 2009).

Although the acute cortisol rise associated with stressors has multiple adaptive effects, sustained cortisol release may have adverse consequences. However, compensatory processes may be instigated to limit such outcomes (McEwen, 2000) through HPA down-regulation, including blunted cortisol reactivity. For example, in response to a stressor, cortisol may vary as an inverted U-shaped function in relation to PTSD symptoms. As trauma symptoms increase, so do cortisol elevations; however, with relatively pronounced PTSD symptoms cortisol levels are comparable to, and even fall below those of individuals who show no symptoms (Yehuda, 2002). In addition to the cortisol variations associated with PTSD, under conditions of excessive or prolonged strain, the diurnal cortisol profile may become flattened (i.e., morning cortisol levels are lower, and evening cortisol levels elevated) (Michaud et al., 2008). Inasmuch as excessive cortisol release over extended periods could have adverse physiological effects, including hippocampal cell loss that could promote pathology (McEwen, 2000), the down-regulated HPA response might be adaptive, limiting adverse effects that might otherwise occur.

Despite the down-regulated HPA response among previously traumatized individuals, when depressed women who had previously been abused were placed in a situation that elicited social evaluative threat (the Trier test), the HPA response was exaggerated (Heim, Owens, Plotsky, & Nemeroff, 1997). Likewise, as shown in Figure 8.1, we observed that among women in abusive

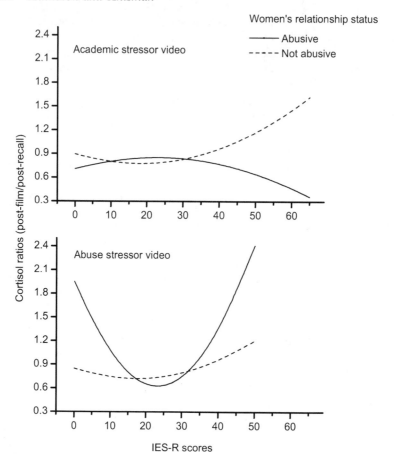

Figure 8.1 Relations between symptoms of PTSD (IES-R) and cortisol reactions to irrelevant (academic; upper panel) or relevant (abuse; lower panel) stressor video challenges among women who were or were not currently in an abusive (physically or psychologically) dating relationship.

Note: Abused women showing high PTSD scores exhibited a blunted cortisol response to an academic stressor, but the cortisol response was greatly exaggerated to the more meaningful ongoing trauma (abuse). PTSD = post-traumatic stress disorder; IES-R = Impact of Events Scale–Revised.

dating relationships who exhibited high PTSD scores, basal cortisol levels were diminished. But, when these women were presented with abuse reminder cues, cortisol levels increased markedly (Matheson, 2003). It seems that *relevant* stressor cues might still instigate exaggerated HPA activity, possibly by activating brain regions (e.g., prefrontal cortex or amygdala) involved in stressor-appraisal processes, which would then influence HPA functioning. It would, after all, be counterproductive for HPA functioning

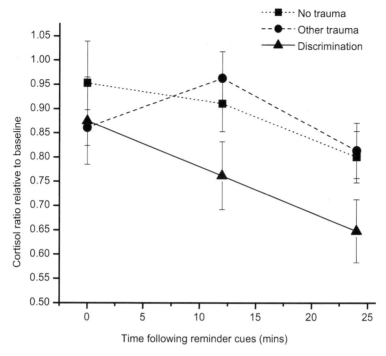

Figure 8.2 Cortisol reactivity of students following reminder cues of prior trauma (e.g., death of a loved one, assault, car accident, life-threatening illness) or traumatic discrimination.

Note: Ratios were calculated by dividing cortisol levels at baseline (i.e., when participants arrived at the laboratory) into levels evident in saliva samples immediately following reminder cues (Time 0), and again approximately 12 and 24 mins following reminder cues.

to be down-regulated in response to all external stimuli, particularly when the threat is still present. Hence, this selective HPA activation might also be viewed as highly adaptive.

We examined the cortisol response to reminder cues associated with prior trauma involving discrimination, relative to cues associated with other traumatic experiences (e.g., assault, death of a loved one). As seen in Figure 8.2, the normal diurnal cortisol decline over the course of the session was evident in participants who had never experienced trauma. In contrast, among participants reminded of prior trauma (other than discrimination) there was a significant increase of salivary cortisol following stressor exposure, followed by the normal decline. However, those participants who were reminded of a traumatic discrimination experience did not show such an increase, but instead showed a relatively precipitous cortisol decline over time (Figure 8.2). In effect, among these participants, discrimination reminders appeared to suppress cortisol reactivity, and precipitated its decline. Like abusive dating relationships, discrimination may entail both traumatic, as well as chronic repeated exposure to less severe experiences, and so one might have expected hyper-reactivity. However, the two stressors might differ in the extent to which individuals remain vigilant to their social environment. Whereas abuse comes from a trusted close other and is personal, discrimination is perpetrated by outgroup members, is an experience shared by others, and was less persistent in these participants' cultural environments. In this instance, the blunted response may have been the most adaptive reaction; had the sample comprised a more vulnerable population (e.g., a target of ethnic genocide), then HPA hyper-responsivity might be more functionally useful.

BUFFERS AGAINST PATHOLOGICAL OUTCOMES

Individual difference factors (self-esteem, coping skills, group identification), experiential factors (trauma history, past discrimination, intergroup contact), and organismic variables (genetics, sex, race) interact to determine the impact of stressors on neuroendocrine disturbances (Anisman & Matheson, 2005). As noted earlier, not all members of social categories under threat demonstrate disturbed health outcomes. Indeed, individuals who report high identification with a devalued social group experience the *least* depression or loss of esteem when their identity is threatened (Branscombe et al., 1999; Mossakowski, 2003). Group identification may form the basis of a cognitive framework that facilitates effective coping with discrimination, along with the social support resources that buffer the individual from negative outcomes.

Appraisals and coping resources

According to Social Identity Theory (Tajfel & Turner, 1979), when individuals' membership in a devalued group is salient, they assess their cognitive alternatives in order to identify an appropriate course of action to enhance their identity. In effect, group members appraise their disadvantaged situation, and then adopt strategies to cope with it. This process is reminiscent of Lazarus and Folkman's (1984) transactional model of stress and coping. When confronted with a stressor, including threats to a social identity, individuals appraise or interpret the event, and then evaluate their ability to cope with it. Appraisals comprise a constellation of evaluative dimensions, including the meaning of the event ("is it discrimination?"), the potential to harm or benefit the individual, its severity, controllability, and predictability. However, appraisals of discrimination are often encumbered by the ambiguity inherent in such events, and indeed, group members frequently do not define such experiences as discrimination, even when independent confirmation exists (Crosby, 1982; Major, Quinton, & McCoy, 2002). Individuals who identify strongly with the group are more likely to acknowledge discrimination (Operario & Fiske, 2001; Sellers & Shelton, 2003) and appraise it as threatening, but may also perceive greater resources (ingroup support) to contend with it. In this respect, both the capacity to cope with the experience, as well as perceptions that social support exists, may influence appraisal outcomes.

Coping is often simplified to refer to the family of strategies that comprise problem- and emotion-focused efforts. Yet, a broad range of methods can be used to deal with stressors, including cognitive restructuring, social support seeking, active distraction, religion, humor, and rumination (Matheson & Anisman, 2003). Several of these dimensions subsume other strategies; emotion-focused coping may comprise expression, containment, blame, denial, or passive resignation. Likewise, a given strategy may be expressed through various actions (problem-solving might occur through tangible action or thoughtful planning), have multiple functions that can vary across situations (social support seeking in an effort to distract oneself, as a component of problem-solving, or a form of emotional expression), and the efficacy of a given strategy may be situation-specific (DeLongis & Holtzman, 2005).

The relation between appraisal and coping processes is reciprocal and dynamic (Lazarus & Folkman, 1984). When the stressor is perceived as controllable, problem-focused strategies may prevail, although such an appraisal may be more likely among individuals who typically adopt a problem-solving orientation. If the stressor is perceived as one that must be endured, emotion-focused coping strategies might dominate, although the reverse may also be true, in that an emotion-focused orientation may entail greater sensitivity to subsequent threats and their potential consequences (Stanton, Kirk, Cameron, & Danoff-Burg, 2000). Moreover, coping in response to an event at one point in time might influence subsequent coping efforts. For example, when an individual initially encounters discrimination, emotion-focused strategies might be used to manage emotions (e.g., to contain anger), thereby facilitating subsequent problem-focused efforts. Indeed, we found that anger responses to discrimination activated a broad range of problem- and emotion-focused coping efforts (Matheson & Anisman, 2009). However, initial strategies might also work at cross-purposes with later strategies; avoidant coping (perhaps linked to feelings of shame or humiliation) might diminish the likelihood that the individual will take further actions to alter his or her situation (Snyder & Pulvers, 2001).

In a national survey we conducted examining the coping styles of women and visible minorities, certain methods were commonly used. The most effective methods for diminishing distress associated with discrimination were problem-solving (trying to plan a response), cognitive restructuring (looking for what can be learned by the experience), active distractions (e.g., going to the gym), and seeking support from others. In addition, discrimination evoked responses that served to increase distress, including ruminating about the situation, blaming one's self for the experience, and wishful thinking (believing that if the problem was ignored, it would just go away).

The buffering effects of various coping efforts can depend on their co-occurrence with other strategies. For example, when rumination was combined with other emotion-focused strategies (such as emotional containment, blame), it was associated with greater depression; however, if linked to problem-focused coping, levels of depression were reduced (Kelly, Matheson, Ravindrun, Merali, & Anisman, 2007). In this regard, the role of cognitive restructuring as a coping response to discrimination is particularly interesting. Cognitive restructuring corresponds to one of the actions taken by members of a disadvantaged group, namely that of "social creativity". This coping strategy entails redefining a negative situation in such a way as to derive some benefit either in the present or for future encounters (i.e., finding the silver lining). We found that the buffering effects of cognitive restructuring depended on its co-occurrence with other strategies. Specifically, although cognitive restructuring consistently co-occurred with problem-solving, among group members who did not appraise an event as constituting discrimination, it was also associated with humor and other-blame, (*"they were just being dopey"*; *"you can't teach an old dog new tricks"*). Among those group members who actually perceived that discrimination had occurred, but did *not* report distress, cognitive restructuring was associated with emotional expression (*"this was upsetting, but I'll know better next time"*). In contrast, among group members who encountered discrimination and were distressed, cognitive restructuring was highly related to self-blame. This, combined with the endorsement of problem-solving, suggests that the latter group members were appraising the experience as one that they ought to be able to control, *"if only I was a more capable person, this might not have happened"*. Based on these findings, we concluded that the combination of coping strategies that individuals adopt appear to be linked to how they interpret the situation, and subsequently, the levels of psychological distress they experience.

The coping strategies adopted, and their effectiveness in buffering against negative health consequences, might vary depending on the social identity that is under threat. For example, both Euro-Caucasian and visible minority women who experienced sex discrimination used similar coping strategies (problem-solving, cognitive restructuring, and social support seeking). When visible minority women reported their coping strategies in the context of race discrimination, in addition to these problem-focused efforts, they were more likely to endorse avoidant strategies, such as trying not to think about the issue and trying to keep their emotions to themselves. Although we did not assess whether women's emotional reactions to sex versus racial discrimination differed, in other laboratory-based studies, we found that when women were angered about their situation, a broader range of coping responses was elicited, including both problem- and emotion-focused efforts. The tendency to use problem-focused coping when angered was associated with a greater inclination to confront the perpetrator. But both problem-focused and avoidant coping styles were associated with lower feelings of shame and diminished cortisol reactions following discrimination (Matheson & Anisman, 2009). In effect, when women were angered by a discrimination event, they adopted a range of coping efforts to deal with multiple aspects of the situation, including actions to alter it, as well as to manage their emotional responses.

Inherent to some identities is a system of beliefs or social norms that may influence appraisals and coping strategies. For example, emotional expression is more common among women than men, and to the extent that effective social support buffers exist, such a strategy may allow the individual to confront his or her feelings and to move on, rather than keeping everything bottled up (Stanton et al., 2000). We asked community participants to describe a time when they had encountered discrimination that targeted either their religious or ethnic group membership, and then asked how they appraised it, how they coped, and their emotional outcomes. Among highly identified group members (religious or ethnic), the discrimination they encountered was appraised as threatening, and they felt distress. Responses to a religious threat, however, were unique, in that this form of discrimination was appraised as a challenge (i.e., it was a test that they felt motivated to overcome) and was more likely to elicit problem-focused coping efforts. Such an appraisal and coping orientation, in turn, elicited greater feelings of personal strength. In addition, those who belonged to a religious minority were more likely to endorse support-seeking actions. In effect, the appraisals and coping responses associated with a religious identity threat may have evoked a belief system that embraced "the power of the righteous", as threats to a religious identity not only targeted a social category, but as well, made salient a system of beliefs and a shared social network (Ysseldyk, Matheson, & Anisman, 2010).

Finally, coping strategies have implications for biological responses to stressors that, as noted earlier, may render individuals more resilient or vulnerable to health problems. For example, when participants were discriminated against in a laboratory context, those with a propensity to problem-solve reported greater appraisals of control, a more optimistic mood, and limited cortisol reactivity following the discrimination challenge. In contrast, individuals who distanced themselves from their group identity following discrimination (a form of avoidant coping) showed higher cortisol reactivity (Matheson & Cole, 2004). It is possible that the latter individuals found the situation especially aversive, and distancing themselves from the group alleviated such feelings. Alternatively, individuals who did not feel connected to the group may not have perceived the availability of social resources to cope effectively with the situation, and hence experienced it as more stressful.

As noted earlier, threats to one's social category do not happen in isolation, and are often superimposed on a backdrop of other experiences. For example, in a sample of Somali refugee immigrants (who reported ongoing discrimination encounters), we found that problem-focused efforts did little to buffer against compromised psychological or physical health, but such coping strategies were associated with a lower rise of morning cortisol (Matheson, Jorden, & Anisman, 2008). In contrast, emotion-focused and avoidant coping strategies were associated with a greater morning cortisol rise and with poorer self-reported health. However, when these same participants were exposed to reminder cues of their traumatic experiences (including an extreme form of discrimination, namely ethnic genocide), avoidant coping (especially passive resignation) was associated with reduced cortisol reactivity. It will be recalled that blunted cortisol reactions are characteristic of chronic stress and PTSD. In effect, the diminished cortisol reactivity of Somali immigrants following a challenge may have reflected an adaptive response that was essential to limit adverse effects associated with protracted HPA activation.

Social support resources

Membership within a social category may provide individuals with an ingroup support network that is integral to maintaining well-being in the face of discrimination (Jetten et al., 2001; Postmes & Branscombe, 2002). Social support generally buffers against stress-related psychological disturbances (Cohen, 2004), and support from others who have had the same types of experiences may be particularly effective in alleviating distress (Frable, Platt, & Hoey, 1998). Indeed, when we test participants individually in the laboratory, cortisol levels are higher than when participants are accompanied by a friend. This said, distinctions need to be made when assessing the effectiveness of social support, including the source of the support, whether the support is enacted or rather individuals simply trust that it will be enacted (perceived availability), and the quality of the support when it is sought.

Although there has been considerable research regarding the role of social support in numerous health-related contexts, to a great extent, this research has not been applied to understanding responses to discrimination. In this regard, it is important to distinguish between support from the ingroup versus outgroup. Ingroup support may buffer individuals from being the distinct target of negative stereotypes (Brewer, 1991), minimize feelings of rejection (Schmitt, Spears, & Branscombe, 2002), and facilitate a collective response (Louis & Taylor, 1999). Support from members of an ideological ingroup might also affirm a system of beliefs that facilitates coping (Ysseldyk et al., 2010).

Outgroup support may be most effective when social categories are strongly integrated and overlapping (groups based on sex, age). For example, males and females are often in intimate relationships, work in common environments, and so on. In this case, male recognition of women's disadvantaged situation might elicit greater support. However, given their different group contexts, such support may be limited, as acknowledging discrimination may entail holding the outgroup accountable, and may elicit feelings of collective guilt among outgroup members (Branscombe, Doosje, & McGarty, 2002). The effectiveness of the source of support might also depend on the individual's goals within a given context. For example, immigrants trying to adapt to a new culture might benefit as much from outgroup support as they do from support from other immigrants (Jorden, Matheson, & Anisman, 2009).

Much of the research demonstrating the benefits of social support relies on individuals' perceptions that support is available. Indeed, there is considerable evidence for the notion that *perceived* support is critical to respond effectively to stressors. Yet, it has been argued that actually receiving support might be counterproductive (Rook, 1992). Several possible explanations have been suggested for this negative relation, including (1) those who receive support are under more stress than those who do not; (2) receiving support may have negative effects on self-esteem, as the individual may feel incompetent to contend with the situation; (3) individuals might feel indebted to the support provider, which may serve as an additional stressor for an already stressed individual; and (4) social support attempts may cause more harm than good, in that they sometimes promote an ineffective response, sometimes involve inaccurate advice, and so on.

This brings us to an important, but often overlooked aspect of social support, namely, *unsupportive* interactions. These refer to occasions when others are unwilling to provide support when it is sought, are insensitive to the individual's needs, or simply say the wrong things. Such encounters may result in adverse consequences beyond those engendered when support was simply perceived as unavailable in the first place. Unsupportive interactions have been linked to reduced psychological well-being, over and above the perceived unavailability of social support, or the effects of the stressor experience itself (e.g., diagnosis of HIV/AIDS) (Song & Ingram, 2002). In our sample of Somali refugee immigrants, as seen in Table 8.2, encountering unsupportive interactions with either ingroup or outgroup members was associated with symptoms of depression and anxiety, and indeed, unsupportive encounters (particularly from ingroup members) mediated the relation between trauma experiences and pathological symptoms (Jorden et al., 2009). Moreover, greater encounters of unsupportive interactions, particularly with other ingroup members, were associated with higher morning cortisol levels. Similarly, Aboriginals who encountered unsupportive reactions from either other Aboriginals or non-Aboriginals in relation to discrimination, exhibited greater depressive and anxiety symptoms and reduced well-being (Bombay, Matheson, & Anisman, 2008). Finally, unsupportive social interactions were particularly detrimental to group members (refugee immigrants, Aboriginals) who turned to emotion-focused coping strategies

Table 8.2 Pearson correlations between frequency of unsupportive encounters from other ingroup and from outgroup members with indices of physical and mental health, and cortisol levels among Somali refugee immigrants to Canada

	Unsupportive encounters from	
	ingroup	outgroup
Self-report		
Health quality of life	$-.33^{***}$	$-.30^{***}$
Depressive symptoms	$.41^{***}$	$.44^{***}$
PTSD symptoms	$.44^{***}$	$.44^{***}$
Cortisol elevations		
Reminder reactivity	$-.04$	$-.07$
Morning rise	$.27^*$	$.21$

$^* p < .05; ^{***} p < .001.$

Note: The sample size for the self-report measures was 90. Due to exclusion criteria, the sample sizes for the cortisol outcomes were $n = 42$ (morning rise) and $n = 84$ (reminder reactivity). PTSD = post-traumatic stress disorder.

(e.g., emotional expression), as the relation between such coping efforts and psychological symptoms were exacerbated under these conditions.

Anticipating what kind of interactions will be experienced as unsupportive is not always clear. Interpretations of support may be determined by the social and cultural norms of the group. For example, Asians were more likely to interpret explicit support negatively, in comparison to Americans, who felt less supported when only implicit support was offered (Kim, Sherman, & Taylor, 2008). In our survey of Aboriginal participants, perceptions that others *blamed* them for their experiences were especially related to compromised well-being. Yet, in a laboratory study in which women were discriminated against, we had a female stooge convey what we thought to be an unsupportive response by blaming the victim for not confronting the perpetrator, and suggesting that this passive response was why women continue to experience discrimination. Contrary to expectations, rather than being upset by this "unsupportive" reaction, women appeared to find it affirming – they had a right to be upset, even if they did not react as they themselves wished they might have. Thus, the extent to which a response will be experienced as unsupportive may be dependent on features of the situation.

The relations between the support giver and recipient are not unidirectional, but reflect a dynamic process wherein the individual encountering the threat, by virtue of his or her own responses might determine the nature of support that is forthcoming. For example, angered victims of discrimination are viewed as overly sensitive, complainers, trouble-makers, and rude (Kaiser & Miller, 2001). Indeed, in a laboratory study in which participants listened to a victim of sex discrimination recounting her experiences, males (outgroup members) who perceived her to be feeling ashamed (but not angry) indicated a greater willingness to provide her with support (Matheson, Raspopow, & Anisman, 2011). In contrast, women appeared to be annoyed by the victim when she expressed any emotion (feelings of shame or anger), perhaps because they were concerned that an emotional response would serve to further threaten or diminish the status of the group as a whole (Garcia, Horstman Reser, Amo, Redersdorff, & Branscombe, 2005).

Just as support may be sought to attenuate emotional reactions, it may influence biological stress responses. In this regard, perceived support was inversely related to cortisol levels (Rosal, King, Ma, & Reed, 2004), and women with metastatic breast cancer who had a high quality of social support generally had lower cortisol levels than those with lower quality support (Turner-Cobb, Sephton, Koopman, Blake-Mortimer, & Spiegel, 2000). Likewise, based on a meta-analysis, it was concluded that social support diminished the cortisol response elicited by laboratory stressors (Thorsteinsson & James, 1999), and such effects appeared to be augmented by elevated oxytocin, a hormone that has been implicated in social attachment and prosocial behaviours (Heinrichs, Baumgartner, Kirschbaum, & Ehlert, 2003). However, the social norms associated with some groups might moderate the effectiveness of support. For example, although men and women both reported that support from their partner reduced distress associated with the Trier test, reduced cortisol was only evident among men. In fact, among women, the presence of their partner acted to increase cortisol levels (Kirschbaum, Klauer, Filipp, & Hellhammer, 1995). Thus, the efficacy of social support may be sex or group dependent, and under some circumstances support may not be experienced positively. In line with the preceding studies, based on an analysis that involved functional magnetic resonance imaging (fMRI), it was suggested that a blunted cortisol response might emanate from social support inhibiting threat appraisals (reflected by amygdala activation), rather than from diminished threat sensitivity (Taylor et al., 2008).

CONCLUSIONS

As should now be evident, the relation between encountering a stressor and a biological response culminating in mental or physical health disturbances is not a simple one. Specific characteristics of the stressor (severity, chronicity, controllability) alter the biological response, and the superimposition of additional stressors, or the co-occurrence of multiple consequences associated with a given stressor, can fundamentally alter the biological response from one that is hyper- to one that is hypo-reactive.

Threats to an individual based on their social category membership, including discrimination, can similarly vary. We noted that discrimination can elicit both stronger and blunted cortisol reactions, depending on features of the event (severe vs. ambiguous), the group that is targeted (visible minorities vs. women), and characteristics of the individual (coping and social resources). Given such variability, one is led to wonder whether we can identify the circumstances under which a particular response will be elicited, and when this response can be considered adaptive or maladaptive? To this end, we might ask the following questions.

Is the stressor chronic or severe? If the event is acute and not especially severe, the stress response will probably entail a heightened cortisol reaction that is likely adaptive. If, however, the stressor is part of a broader profile of adversities (e.g., ethnic genocide, followed by immigration, which may give rise to family conflicts, loss of status, language difficulties), then responses that protect the individual might involve blunting of cortisol reactivity to further stressors. This said, systems might still be sensitized, and exposure to more severe or persistent uncontrollable stressors may culminate in a hyper-reaction that may overtax biological systems, resulting in mental or physical health disorders.

Is the situation ambiguous or does it create uncertainty? Appraisals of the situation are critical to the individual's ability to identify an appropriate coping response. When ambiguity exists about the intent of the situation, or uncertainty regarding its implications, it is difficult to mount a clear or effective coping response. Individuals may become hyper-vigilant to alternative cues that might convey meaning, they may "relive" the experience, or anticipate further negative consequences, all of which increase the reactivity of biological systems, and render individuals more vulnerable to negative health outcomes.

Is the situation perceived as uncontrollable? Although ambiguity and uncertainty leave the individual unable to identify an appropriate course of action, a lack of perceived control means that the individual does not believe that any course of action will alter the situation. This has been found to result in hyper-reactivity of biological systems. If the event persists, then these systems may become overly taxed rendering the individual vulnerable to pathology. However, some coping strategies may diminish negative impacts by altering emotional reactions (emotion-engagement or avoidance), or by altering the framing of the situation as one that the individual can learn from or adapt to (cognitive restructuring). Indeed, although problem-focused efforts in response to controllable aspects of the situation may be effective, they may be counterproductive if they are, in fact, fruitless endeavours, resulting in greater frustration and stress. In this regard, perhaps emotion-focused efforts are viewed as maladaptive because the situations in which they are typically evoked in are ones that the individual must find ways of enduring. Yet, under these circumstances they might be the best possible strategies, at least until alternatives can be found.

Are there social norms that support particular ways of coping? Effective coping strategies vary as a function of individuals' salient social categorization, in part because groups provide us with guiding norms and beliefs. Although these norms might not necessarily evoke effective responses (e.g., religious groups who do not believe in medical intervention), they might elicit forms of ingroup support that enhance coping effectiveness. For example, avoidant strategies combined with social support may allow individuals to distance themselves from an experience that they feel that they cannot change, and to refocus their priorities on more beneficial aspects of their lives. As a result, the longer term health challenges may not be evident. Moreover, adopting strategies that are inconsistent with the norms of the group may be counterproductive, particularly if they alienate others, hence limiting support. Thus, although some strategies are often found to be more effective than others, the social context in which they are adopted may ultimately determine whether they serve as a buffer against stress.

Is the ingroup sufficiently cohesive to provide effective support? Although perceived support from others who share a given experience is often an effective buffer against distress, if support is not proffered when it is sought, the individual may be especially vulnerable. Encountering unsupportive interactions undermines the individual's coping efforts, and may create further distress, as the individual's faith in others is undermined. For various reasons, ingroup members may not be willing to provide one another with support. For example, refugee immigrants who are trying to assimilate may wish to distance themselves from the sometimes all-too-similar woes of other refugees. Women may downplay the reactions of another woman encountering discrimination, as she might identify more strongly with groups (e.g., professional) or interpersonal dyads (spousal relationships) in which men and women are highly integrated. Though enacted support from other ingroup members may not be necessary to buffer against negative outcomes associated with an identity threat, unsupportive responses when such support is sought could be especially detrimental.

Clearly the confluence of multiple factors, at the individual and social group level, coupled with biological processes, determine how individuals deal with stressful experiences, and whether coping strategies will be effective. Understandably, these processes are largely determined by previous experiences that affect the way stressors are appraised, as well as the coping strategies that are at hand. This constellation of factors ultimately determines psychological and physical well-being.

ACKNOWLEDGMENTS

This research was supported by the Canadian Institutes for Health Research and the Social Sciences and Humanities Research Council of Canada.

References

Allison, K. W. (1998). Stress and oppressed social category membership. In J. K. Swim & C. Stangor (Eds.), *Prejudice: The target's perspective* (pp. 145–170). San Diego, CA: Academic Press.

Anisman, H., Hayley, S., & Merali, Z. (2003). Sensitization associated with stressors and cytokine treatments. *Brain, Behavior, and Immunity, 17,* 86–93.

Anisman, H., & Matheson, K. (2005). Anhedonia and depression: Caveats of animal models. *Neuroscience Biobehavioral Review, 29,* 525–546.

Anisman, H., Merali, Z., & Hayley, S. (2008). Neurotransmitter, peptide and cytokine processes in relation to depressive disorder: Comorbidity of depression with neurodegenerative disorders. *Progress in Neurobiology, 85,* 1–74.

Bombay, A., Matheson, K., & Anisman, H. (2008). *Perceived discrimination, in-group rejection and depressive symptoms among offspring of Indian Residential School survivors in Canada.* Poster presented at the CPA Annual Meeting, Halifax, Canada.

Bombay, A., Matheson, K., & Anisman, H. (2009). Intergenerational trauma: Convergence of multiple processes among First Nations peoples in Canada. *Journal of Aboriginal Health, 5*(3), 6–47.

Branscombe, N. R., Doosje, B., & McGarty, C. (2002). Antecedents and consequences of collective guilt. In D. M. Mackie & E. R. Smith (Eds.), *From prejudice to intergroup emotions: Differentiated reactions to social groups* (pp. 49–66). Philadelphia, PA: Psychology Press.

Branscombe, N. R., Schmitt, M. T., & Harvey, R. D. (1999). Perceiving pervasive discrimination among African Americans: Implications for group identification and well-being. *Journal of Personality and Social Psychology, 77,* 125–149.

Brewer, M. (1991). The social self: On being the same and different at the same time. *Personality and Social Psychology Bulletin, 17,* 475–482.

Chida, Y., & Steptoe, A. (2009). Cortisol awakening response and psychosocial factors: A systematic review and meta-analysis. *Biological Psychology, 80,* 265–278.

Cohen, S. (2004). Social relationships and health. *American Psychologist, 59,* 676–684.

Crosby, F. (1982). *Relative deprivation and working women.* New York, NY: Oxford University Press.

DeLongis, A., & Holtzman, S. (2005). Coping in context: The role of stress, social support, and personality in coping. *Journal of Personality, 73,* 1–24.

Dickerson, S., & Kemeny, M. (2004). Acute stressors and cortisol responses: A theoretical integration and synthesis of laboratory research. *Psychological Bulletin, 130,* 355–391.

Frable, D., Platt, L., & Hoey, S. (1998). Concealable stigmas and positive self-perceptions: Feeling better around similar others. *Journal of Personality and Social Psychology, 74,* 909–922.

Garcia, D. M., Horstman Reser, A., Amo, R. B., Redersdorff, S., & Branscombe, N. R. (2005). Perceivers' responses to in-group and out-group members who blame a negative outcome on discrimination. *Personality and Social Psychology Bulletin, 31,* 769–780.

Gibbs, J. T. (1997). African-American suicide: A cultural paradox. *Suicide and Life-Threatening Behavior, 27,* 68–79.

Heim, C., Owens, M., Plotsky, P., & Nemeroff, C. (1997). Persistent changes in corticotropin-releasing factor systems due to early life stress: Relationship to the pathophysiology of major depression and post-traumatic stress disorder. *Psychopharmacology Bulletin, 33*, 185–192.

Heinrichs, M., Baumgartner, T., Kirschbaum, C., & Ehlert, U. (2003). Social support and oxytocin interact to suppress cortisol and subjective responses to psychosocial stress. *Biological Psychiatry, 54*, 1389–1398.

Jetten, J., Branscombe, N. R., Schmitt, M., & Spears, R. (2001). Rebels with a cause: Functions of identification with a self-selected socially devalued group. *Personality and Social Psychology Bulletin, 27*, 1204–1213.

Jorden, S., Matheson, K., & Anisman, H. (2009). Supportive and unsupportive social interactions in relation to cultural adaptation and psychological symptoms among Somali refugees. *Journal of Cross-Cultural Psychology, 40*, 853–874.

Kaiser, C. R., & Miller, C. (2001). Stop complaining! The social costs of making attributions to discrimination. *Personality and Social Psychology Bulletin, 27*, 254–263.

Kelly, O., Matheson, K., Ravindrun, A., Merali, Z., & Anisman, H. (2007). Ruminative coping and dysthymia. *Depression and Anxiety, 24*, 233–234.

Kim, H. S., Sherman, D. K., & Taylor, S. (2008). Culture and social support. *American Psychologist, 63*, 518–526.

Kirschbaum, C., Klauer, T., Filipp, S., & Hellhammer D. (1995). Sex-specific effects of social support on cortisol and subjective responses to acute psychological stress. *Psychosomatic Medicine, 57*, 23–31.

Kirschbaum, C., Pirke, K. M., & Hellhammer, D. H. (1993). The 'Trier Social Stress Test' – a tool for investigating psychobiological stress responses in a laboratory setting. *Neuropsychobiology, 28*, 76–81.

Klonoff, E. A., Landrine, H., & Campbell, R. (2000). Sexist discrimination may account for well-known gender differences in psychiatric symptoms. *Psychology of Women Quarterly, 24*, 93–99.

Lazarus, R. S., & Folkman, S. (1984). *Stress, appraisal, and coping*. New York, NY: Springer.

Louis, W. R., & Taylor, D. M. (1999). From passive acceptance to social disruption: Towards an understanding of behavioural responses to discrimination. *Canadian Journal of Behavioural Science, 31*, 19–28.

Major, B., Quinton, W. J., & McCoy, S. K. (2002). Antecedents and consequences of attribution to discrimination: Theoretical and empirical advances. In M. Zanna (Ed.), *Advances in experimental social psychology* (Vol. 34, pp. 251–330). San Diego, CA: Academic Press.

Matheson, K. (June, 2003). *The (in)capacity to define when "Enough is enough": Behavioral and neuroendocrine coping responses of women in abusive dating relationships*. Paper presented at the CPA Preconference, Hamilton, ON.

Matheson, K., & Anisman, H. (2003). Systems of coping associated with dysphoria, anxiety, and depressive illness: A multivariate profile perspective. *Stress, 6*, 223–234.

Matheson, K., & Anisman, H. (2009). Anger and shame elicited by discrimination: Moderating role of coping on action endorsements and salivary cortisol. *European Journal of Social Psychology, 39*, 163–185.

Matheson, K., & Cole, B. (2004). Coping with a threatened group identity:

Psychological and neuroendocrine responses. *Journal of Experimental Social Psychology, 40,* 777–786.

Matheson, K., Jorden, S., & Anisman, H. (2008). Relations between trauma experiences and psychological, physical and neuroendocrine functioning among Somali refugees: Mediating role of coping with acculturation stressors. *Journal of Immigrant and Minority Health, 10,* 291–304.

Matheson, K., Raspopow, K., & Anisman, H. (in press). Bearing witness: Social support responses to sex discrimination as a function of the emotions conveyed by the victim. *Social Psychology.*

McEwen, B. S. (2000). Allostasis and allostatic load: Implications for neuro-psychopharmacology. *Neuropsychopharmacology, 22,* 108–124.

Michaud, K., Matheson, K., Kelly, O., & Anisman, H. (2008). Impact of stressors in a natural context on release of cortisol in healthy adult humans: A meta-analysis. *Stress, 11,* 177–197.

Mossakowski, K. N. (2003). Coping with perceived discrimination: Does ethnic identity protect mental health? *Journal of Health & Social Behavior, 44,* 318–331.

Operario, D., & Fiske, S. T. (2001). Ethnic identity moderates perceptions of prejudice: Judgments of personal versus group discrimination and subtle versus blatant bias. *Personality and Social Psychology Bulletin, 27,* 550–561.

Post, R. M. (1992). Transduction of psychosocial stress into the neurobiology of recurrent affective disorder. *American Journal of Psychiatry, 149,* 999–1010.

Postmes, T., & Branscombe, N. R. (2002). Influence of long-term racial environ-mental composition on subjective well-being in African Americans. *Journal of Personality and Social Psychology, 83,* 735–751.

Rook, K. (1992). Detrimental aspects of social relationships: Taking stock of an emerging literature. In H. Veiel & U. Baumann (Eds.), *The meaning and measurement of social support* (pp. 157–169). New York, NY: Hemisphere.

Rosal, M. C., King, J., Ma, Y., & Reed, G. (2004). Stress, social support, and cortisol: Inverse associations? *Behavioral Medicine, 30,* 11–21.

Sapolsky, R. M., Romero, L. M., & Munck, A. U. (2000). How do glucocorticoids influence the stress response? Integrating permissive, suppressive, stimulatory, and preparative actions. *Endocrinology Review, 21,* 55–89.

Schmidt-Reinwald, A., Pruessner, J., Hellhammer, D. H., Federenko, I., Rohleder, N., Schurmeyer, T. H., et al. (1999). The cortisol response to awakening in relation to different challenge tests and a 12-hour cortisol rhythm. *Life Science, 64,* 1653–1660.

Schmitt, M., Spears, R., & Branscombe, N. (2002). Constructing a minority group identity out of shared rejection: The case of international students. *European Journal of Social Psychology, 33,* 1–12.

Sellers, R. M., & Shelton, J. N. (2003). The role of racial identity in perceived racial discrimination. *Journal of Personality and Social Psychology, 84,* 1079–1092.

Snyder, C. R., & Pulvers, K. M. (2001). Dr. Seuss, the coping machine, and "Oh, the places you'll go". In C. R. Snyder (Ed.), *Coping with stress: Effective people and processes* (pp. 3–29). Oxford, UK: Oxford University Press.

Song, Y., & Ingram, K. (2002). Unsupportive social interactions, availability of social support, and coping: Their relationship to mood disturbance among African Americans living with HIV. *Journal of Social and Personal Relationships, 19,* 67–85.

Stanton, A. L., Kirk, S. B., Cameron, C., & Danoff-Burg, S. (2000). Coping through emotional approach: Scale construction and validation. *Journal of Personality and Social Psychology, 78*, 1150–1169.

Tajfel, H., & Turner, J. C. (1979). An integrative theory of intergroup conflict. In W. G. Austin & S. Worchel (Eds.), *The social psychology of intergroup relations* (pp. 33–47). Monterey, CA: Brooks/Cole.

Taylor, S. E., Burklund, L. J., Eisenberger, N., Lehman, B., Hilmert, C., & Lieberman, M. D. (2008). Neural bases of moderation of cortisol stress responses by psychosocial resources. *Journal of Personality and Social Psychology, 95*, 197–211.

Thorsteinsson, E., & James, J. (1999). A meta-analysis of the effects of experimental manipulations of social support during laboratory stress. *Psychological Health, 14*, 869–886.

Turner-Cobb, J. Sephton, S., Koopman, C., Blake-Mortimer, J., & Spiegel, D. (2000). Social support and salivary cortisol in women with metastatic breast cancer. *Psychosomatic Medicine, 62*, 337–345.

Walsemann, K. M., Gee, G. C., & Geronimus, A. T. (2009). Ethnic differences in trajectories of depressive symptoms: Disadvantage in family background, high school experiences, and adult characteristics. *Journal of Health & Social Behavior, 50*, 82–98.

Wyatt, S. B., Williams, D. R., Calvin, R., Henderson, F. C., Walker, E. R., & Winters, K. (2003). Racism and cardiovascular disease in African Americans. *American Journal of Medical Science, 325*, 315–331.

Yehuda, R. (2002). Current status of cortisol findings in post-traumatic stress disorder. *Psychiatric Clinical North America, 25*, 341–368.

Ysseldyk, R., Matheson, K., & Anisman, H. (2010). Religiosity as identity: Toward an understanding of religion from a social identity theory perspective. *Personality and Social Psychology Review, 14*, 60–71.

Part III

Social identity, stress, and trauma

9　When other people are heaven, when other people are hell

How social identity determines the nature and impact of social support

S. Alexander Haslam
University of Exeter

Stephen D. Reicher
University of St Andrews

Mark Levine
University of Lancaster

In the 2009 movie *Up in the Air* George Clooney plays the part of Ryan Bingham, a corporate consultant who is hired to fly around the United States firing company employees whose bosses "don't have the balls" to do this themselves (Reitman & Turner, 2009, p. 13). The film opens with scenes of Bingham reeling off a tried and trusted patter that takes a steady stream of workers through the process of being "let go". They all react differently (with tears, anger, shock, horror) but in every case their distress is palpable. Bingham by contrast, is measured and unflappable. He is in control and above it all. The scenes are all the more arresting because many of the people seen in the film are not professional actors but ordinary people reliving recent personal experiences of being fired.[1]

We are given some insight into the philosophical basis for Bingham's equanimity through work he does on the side as a sought-after motivational speaker. In this role his trademark presentation "What's in your backpack?" invites the audience to set themselves free from the material trappings of domestic life (the contents of the metaphorical backpack) in order to make way for a life of unencumbered freedom:

> Imagine for a second that you're carrying a backpack. I want you to *feel* the straps on your shoulders . . . You feel them? Now I want you to pack it with all the stuff you have in your life. . . . This is what we do to ourselves on a daily basis. We weigh ourselves down until we can't even move . . . Now I'm going to set your backpack on fire. . . . Let everything burn and imagine waking up tomorrow with nothing. It's kind of exhilarating isn't it? That is how I approach everyday.
>
> (Reitman & Turner, 2009, pp. 1–2)

As the film progresses, so does Bingham's philosophy – to the point where he identifies life's core problem to be people rather than possessions:

> Okay. This is where it starts to get a little difficult, but stay with me. You have a new backpack, but this time, I want you to fill it with people. Start with casual acquaintances . . . and work your way to the people you trust with your most intimate secrets. Now move on to family members . . . And finally your husband or wife or boyfriend or girlfriend. Get them in there too. . . . Feel the weight of that bag. Make no mistake, your relationships are the heaviest components of your life. Feel the straps cutting into your shoulders. All those negotiations and arguments and secrets and compromises. Now set that bag down. You don't need to carry all that weight. Some animals were meant to carry each other, to live symbiotically over a life time. . . . We are not one of those animals.
>
> (Reitman & Turner, pp. 54–55)

This rather depressing analysis is taken one step further by Jean Paul Sartre in his play *Huis Clos* (*In Camera*), written at the height of Nazi tyranny in Europe. Sartre, it seems, is suggesting not only that we have no need for others, not only that others drag us down, but also that others are the definitive source of misery in our lives. The three key characters in the play have all recently died and gone to hell. On arrival, they search in vain for the instruments of torture that they anticipate being subjected to. Over time, however, the characters become tormenters of each other. At the very end of the play, one of the triad, Joseph Garcin, thus comes to the realization that it is not "the torture-chambers, the fire and brimstone, 'the burning marl'" they have to fear. No, "hell is . . . other people" ("l'enfer . . . c'est les autres"; Sartre, 1944, p. 191).

But surely these claims are overblown. It may be possible to find cases where people compound rather than relieve our misery (see, for instance, Kellezi & Reicher, this volume), where they fail to give us support, where the support they do give is unwanted or even corrosive, or else where the process of providing support is factious and fraught with misunderstanding. But is it not still fundamentally the case that we are social animals who require and revel in interactions with others? If we are looking for an accurate expression of this in our culture, is it not found less in Ryan Bingham or Joseph Garcin than in lines from the famous Civil Rights song "Eyes on the Prize"?

> The only chain that a man can stand
> Is the chain of hand in hand!

So are other people heaven or hell? In more sober, scientific, and specific terms, do others generally improve or harm our well-being? What does the evidence tell us?

To assess such issues systematically, Schwarzer and Leppin (1991) conducted a meta-analysis looking at the relationship between social support and measures of health and coping in 88 studies involving more than 60,000 participants. The majority of studies revealed positive correlations between these variables ($0 < r < .43$), suggesting that support is associated with improved health. However, as Ryan Bingham might have predicted, a sizeable minority (16 percent) also uncovered negative correlations, suggesting the opposite ($0 < r < -.17$). This analysis also revealed two further facts: first, that the mean effect size was only quite small ($r = .07$) and second, that the majority of effects were close to zero (only 21 percent were stronger than $\pm.10$).

Schwarzer and Leppin also note that even in the most influential and highly cited studies that investigate this relationship, the strength of statistical association between support and health tends only to be weak. This is true, for example, of Berkman and Syme's (1979; see Sani, this volume) well-known epidemiological study of the relationship between social support and mortality (in which it is estimated that $r = -.07$). On the basis of another careful review, Cohen and Syme (1985, p. 9) thus conclude:

> One of the attractive aspects of studying the role of social support in health and health maintenance is its seemingly magic-bullet-like quality. Unfortunately, but unsurprisingly, this simplicity is more illusion than reality.

For the purposes of the present volume, this might appear to be something of a blow. One interpretation of the findings is that other people are neither heaven or hell; they simply do not matter very much to our well-being. But another, more interesting, possibility is that they do matter very much, but sometimes positively and sometimes negatively – so that, when different people in different circumstances are lumped together, many positives are cancelled out by negatives thereby concealing their contribution. It is this latter possibility that we explore in this chapter. But such a position does little to clarify our understanding unless we are also in a position to specify what conditions are responsible for these different outcomes. That is, what are the variables that moderate the effect of others on our own well-being?

In attempting to answer this question, our analysis will draw heavily on principles of social identity and self-categorization theories (Tajfel & Turner, 1979; Turner, Hogg, Oakes, Reicher, & Wetherell, 1987; Turner, Oakes, Haslam, & McGarty, 1994) and on recent theorizing that applies their insights to issues of health and well-being (e.g., Haslam, Jetten, Postmes, & Haslam, 2009a, 2009b; Reicher & Haslam, 2006). A key point that this approach alerts us to is that the dynamics of support – i.e., giving, receiving, and interpreting help of various forms – are always structured by the identity-based relationships between those who give and receive it.

When (and to the extent that) these relationships are grounded in, or help to build, a mutual sense of common group membership (i.e., shared social identity) then support has a greater chance both of being provided and of being effective. Indeed, when parties to the support process share (or come to share) identity, the process can be almost heavenly. However, when they do not – as Bingham and Garcin both anecdotally attest – life can be positively hellish.

SOCIAL IDENTITY AND SOCIAL SUPPORT: THEORETICAL EXPOSITION

Definitions and core concepts

Social identity refers to that part of a person's sense of self that is associated with his or her membership in a given social group (Tajfel, 1972). One's social identity as an academic, for example, is constituted by an internalized sense that one is part of a community of academics, and it is a basis for seeing other academics not as "them" but as "us" (i.e., as part of a psychological *ingroup* or *social self-category*). The notion of internalization is important here, and serves to differentiate the psychological group from sociological notions of a person's reference group. In sociological terms, a person might be deemed to be a member of a group (e.g., an academic, an Australian) by virtue of externally defined properties (e.g., the fact that he or she works as a lecturer in a university; the fact that he or she is born or lives in Australia). Psychologically, though, what is important is that the person *categorizes themselves* in these terms, so that the group serves as a basis for perceiving, thinking and acting in the world (Turner, 1982).

Social support refers to acts in which individuals and groups provide resources to others. Those who provide support are often "significant others" (e.g., family, friends, coworkers; House & Kahn, 1985), but they can also be unknown to the recipients (e.g., as happens in the case of victims of natural disasters, or when help is provided by passing "bystanders"). Resources can take a range of forms (House, 1981) – including material (e.g., giving money or goods), emotional (e.g., being sympathetic), and informational (e.g., giving advice). Where successful, this results in an individual or group feeling that they are cared for and valued by others, and that they are "part of a network of mutual assistance and obligations" (Taylor, 2007, p. 145; see also Wills, 1991). Nevertheless, it is far from the case that social support achieves positive ends simply by virtue of being provided. As we will explore further below, one reason for this is that its impact depends (a) on the motives and goals of providers, and (b) on the interpretation and experience of recipients. These in turn depend upon the nature of the relationship between donors and recipients as well as features of the broader social context within which they are embedded.

On the basis of the above definitions, one might be forgiven for thinking that social identity and social support have little to do with each other. Moreover, for the most part, this conclusion would also be reached by surveying the relevant literatures to which these concepts are central. For researchers who have been interested in the dynamics of social support (particularly those that determine its effectiveness) have tended to stress the importance of sociological variables (e.g., demographic factors such as a person's age, gender and social class; see Thoits, 1995, for a review). And where they have considered psychological factors these have tended to be individual-level variables (e.g., the personality of support recipients; Delongis & Holtzman, 2005).

However, the links between the two start to become apparent once one recognizes, as the above definition implies, that social support is always an aspect of a *relationship* between two (or more) parties, and that its *meaning* – for both provider and recipient – will always depend on the nature of this relationship. Importantly too, social identity theorizing provides a basis for understanding the psychological nature of this relationship and its implications for the experience of giving and receiving social support. In particular, this is because self-categorization theory suggests that one of the critical factors that defines the relationship between any two parties – and their motivations towards each other – is the degree to which they perceive each other as members of the same social category (Turner et al., 1987).

Theoretical elaboration and core hypotheses

To understand why and how the nature and experience of social support is structured by patterns of shared social identity, it is necessary to flesh out the underpinnings of the social identity approach in a little more detail. In this regard, two fundamental assumptions of social identity theory (Tajfel & Turner, 1979) are (a) that people are motivated to define the self positively and (b) that there are many contexts in which the self is defined, not in personal terms (as "I" and "me"), but in collective terms (as "us" and "we"). Self-categorization theorists have sought to specify the nature of these contexts through a formal analysis of *social identity salience* (Oakes, Haslam, & Turner, 1994). Broadly speaking, their research supports claims that individuals come to define themselves in terms of a given social identity (e.g., as "us Manchester United supporters"; "us Americans") to the extent that this identity has both historical importance for them (e.g., because they have been members of a given group for a long time) and it is an appropriate way of understanding the self in the situation at hand (e.g., because the identity has been primed, or the environment is one in which there are striking differences between ingroup and outgroup members). Putting these assumptions together, it follows that in those contexts where people do self-categorize, and act, in terms of a particular social identity then (a) they will be interested in enhancing the group's overall well-being, and (b) they

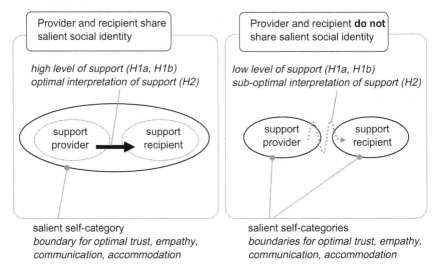

Figure 9.1 The role of shared social identity (salient self-categories) in determining the level (H1) and interpretation (H2) of social support.

will understand other ingroup members – who are not now external to self, but who are defined as *part of the self* – as having an important role to play in this process.

These arguments can in turn be fleshed out in terms of two hypotheses that are central to the present chapter (see also Haslam, 2004) and that are represented schematically in Figure 9.1. The first is that, when (and to the extent that) a given social identity is salient for perceivers, the process of seeking to advance the interests of their ingroup will motivate them to *provide support* to fellow ingroup members (H1a). Under these conditions they will want to help those recipients in whatever ways they can because by doing so they are promoting the interests of the collective self ("us"; Turner et al., 1987). As a corollary of this, it follows that individuals are more likely to *be given support* by others with whom they share social identity (H1b).

Significant as these outcomes are, bearing in mind that *perceptions* are so central to the support process (e.g., Lazarus & Folkman, 1984; Taylor, 2007), a second, equally important hypothesis is that shared social identity should provide a basis for providers and recipients to *interpret support* in ways that are mutually beneficial (H2). This is the case for a wide range of reasons. One is that a sense of shared social identity provides parties to the support process with a common interpretative framework that facilitates processes of communication and co-ordination (Haslam, 2004; Postmes, 2003). In effect, this means that those parties have a sense of "coming from the same place" or "singing from the same song sheet". In this way too, shared social identity provides a basis for shared expectations (e.g., as to what level and form of support is appropriate and reasonable) and shared emotion (i.e., empathy), as well as for mutual trust, respect, and accommodation (Foddy, Platow, & Yamagishi, 2009; Tyler & Blader, 2000).

A wealth of previous research suggests that these various elements of social relationships – expectation, empathy, communication, trust, accommodation – are all vital to the success of support efforts. Without them it is all too easy for the process to be derailed (e.g., see Taylor, 2007). Accordingly, it is the fact that these elements are all contingent upon the self-categorization process that makes this process so central to the dynamics of social support. This, then, is the theory, but is there any evidence to support it?

SOCIAL IDENTITY AND SOCIAL SUPPORT: EMPIRICAL EVIDENCE

Experimental evidence

Imagine that you are in a hurry. You are running along, but you trip and fall awkwardly to the ground. You clutch your ankle in agony, and let out a cry of anguish. In this situation, it would certainly be helpful if any passers by were to stop and take the time to see if you were alright and needed any assistance. But would they? This is a question that Levine, Prosser, Evans, and Reicher (2005) addressed in a series of experiments that involved precisely this scenario. Critically, though, in order to examine whether people's willingness to provide support to another person varied as a function of that person's status as an ingroup or outgroup member (i.e., H1), this was something that was manipulated experimentally.

The first stage of this process involved selecting as participants individuals who were fans of Manchester United football club and making this social identity salient by asking them questions about their support for the club. After this, for every participant in turn an accident was staged in which a male actor ran in front of them and then tripped, seeming to fall to the ground in agony. The manipulation of shared social identity was then achieved by having this actor wear either a Manchester United shirt, the shirt of a rival team (Liverpool), or a plain shirt. As predicted, the actor's shirt had considerable impact on the level of help that participants extended towards him. When he was wearing a Manchester United shirt (i.e., when he was an ingroup member), the typical response (shown by 92 percent of participants) involved stopping to ask if he needed help or directly helping him. However, when he was in a Liverpool shirt or a plain shirt, the typical response involved either "not noticing" the accident or merely glancing in his direction. On average, across these two conditions, only 32 percent of participants offered any form of help. The level of support that was provided in this situation was thus very much dependent on the extent to which the two parties to this process shared a salient social identity.

One of the important assertions of self-categorization theory, however, is that the nature of the social identities that inform perception and action are not fixed. As noted above, social identity salience is partly deter-mined by historical factors, but also varies as a function of context (Oakes et al., 1994). This means that sometimes self-categories are defined narrowly and exclusively, but sometimes they are defined more broadly and more inclusively.

To explore this point, and its implications for social support, Levine and colleagues conducted a second experiment, again involving Manchester United fans. This was similar to their first study, but here, prior to being exposed to the person in distress, the experimenters asked participants questions that made their social identity as *football fans* salient (rather than their identity as fans of a particular club). When the actor wore a Manchester United shirt or a plain shirt, responses were very similar to those in the first experiment (80 percent of participants offered help in the former case, but only 22 percent did in the latter). Now, though, the support given to the actor in a Liverpool shirt was elevated to the same level as that given to the one wearing the Manchester United shirt. Thus, where in Experiment 1 only 30 percent of participants had offered him help, now 70 percent did. Here, then, because participants' social identity as a football fan was salient, support was given to all other football fans not just those who supported their own team.

These findings are also consistent with those from programmatic experi-mental work conducted by Dovidio, Gaertner and colleagues (for a review, see Dovidio, Gaertner, Schnabel, Saguy, & Johnson, 2010). To the extent that ingroup social identity is narrowly defined, help will be provided to a relatively select subset of people; however, assistance will be offered more widely when identity is more inclusively defined (i.e., to the extent that people self-categorize at a higher, more abstract level; Turner et al., 1987; see also Haslam, Reicher, & Platow, 2011).

One might object, however, that in Levine et al.'s studies and in other work, the forms of assistance and support that are provided are not those that really matter in society. They are relatively trivial and demand little of those providing support. So do the same processes apply to the forms of social support which (at least potentially) involve serious costs to the donor?

To address this question, Levine and Thompson (2004) looked at British students' intentions to provide financial and political support to victims of floods and earthquakes in Europe and South America. These students were generally more willing to provide support for those victims who were closer to home (i.e., in Europe rather than South America). However, the researchers also showed that this depended upon the specific social identity that was salient for the students. In particular, when the researchers had made respondents' European (rather than British) identity salient, then the tendency to give more support to Europeans than to South Americans was much more pronounced (for related findings, see Drury, this volume; Drury, Cocking, & Reicher, 2009).

Experimental evidence thus supports the idea that people are more likely to give support to, and be given support by, those with whom they share common group identity (i.e., H1a, H1b). But is there any evidence that self-categorization affects the perceptions that surround the support process (i.e., H2)? Levine and Thompson provide some additional data that begin to address this question. This arose from looking not just at how much aid people indicated they would donate in response to disasters, but also measuring participants' emotional reaction to the disasters in question. So, amongst other things, they asked participants to what extent they were moved, sympathetic, upset, and distressed. Responses on these measures followed the same pattern as did those on primary measures of support. The overall pattern of findings thus indicated that people's greater willingness to support members of their (contextually defined) ingroup is associated with greater emotional empathy for their plight, and thus reflects genuine concern to look after and protect them. Extrapolating from this, it suggests that people might also see the help that they receive from fellow group members as deriving from a genuine sense of care and hence respond to it more favourably.

Haslam, Jetten, O'Brien, and Jacobs (2004) conducted a study that speaks more directly to this point. This built upon a paradigm previously used by Lazarus and colleagues to show that the experience of stress depends very much upon the way that people *appraise* – and are encouraged to appraise – a given stressor (a point that is central to the transactional model of stress; Lazarus & Folkman, 1984; see also van Dick & Haslam, this volume). However, in line with H2, we reasoned that the positive impact of such informational support might be attenuated if the person who provided it was a member of an outgroup rather than an ingroup.

To test this idea, undergraduate students were asked to perform a task that involved performing a number of demanding mathematical exercises in a limited amount of time. Before doing these exercises, they watched a video-recoded interview in which a woman who had supposedly performed the task previously recounted her experiences for the camera – focusing on how stressful she had found it. In one version of the video she described experiencing a high degree of physical and mental discomfort, and her comments thus primed a negative appraisal of the exercises; however, in a second version her reactions encouraged participants to construe the tasks much more positively (as character-building and challenging).

In addition to this manipulation of informational support, we also manipulated the identity of the person providing that support. Specifically, half of the students who watched the video were led to believe that the woman providing the feedback was a fellow student (an ingroup member), while the other half were led to believe she was someone suffering from a stress disorder (an outgroup member). In a subsequent study the support provider's ingroup–outgroup status was manipulated by making the informational source either another woman (an ingroup member) or a man (an outgroup member; see Jetten, Haslam, Iyer, & Haslam, 2010).

After they had watched the video and performed the tasks themselves, participants then indicated how anxious and stressed the tasks had made them. As expected, and consistent with previous work informed by the transactional model of stress, the students reported having been much less stressed when they had found out from the person on the video that the exercises were nothing to worry about. Importantly, though, this was only true when the person providing these words of comfort was understood to be a fellow ingroup member. If support was provided by an outgroup member, the message had no impact – presumably because it was no longer trusted or taken at face value.

Archival evidence

Experimental research of the form discussed in the previous section is useful because it allows us to examine the role that social identity plays in the provision of support in controlled settings and thereby isolate the distinctive impact of this variable. The findings consistently show, not only that there is an effect of the level of shared identity between support provider and support recipient but also that these effects tend to be large (e.g., in the two experiments by Levine et al., 2005, the effect sizes were $r = .59$ and .51). Nevertheless, the rational sceptic might ask whether these effects hold up, or are quite so impressive, when they are tested in less contrived settings.

As a starting point for deliberating on this point, it is instructive to reflect on the way in which funding for disaster relief is conditioned by the geographical location of victims relative to donors. At a policy level, it is clearly the case that governments devote a far greater proportion of their budgets to dealing with disasters that occur inside rather than outside their borders.[2] Of course, one might argue that this is to some extent mandated by law, but the pattern is no less evident when aid is discretionary. For example, Muller and Whiteman (2009) recently investigated patterns of philanthropic response to three major disasters amongst the world's top 500 companies. Their analysis showed that companies were more likely to give money, and gave more money, if disasters occurred on "home" soil. For example, 61 percent of 214 North American firms gave aid to victims of Hurricane Katrina, but only 23 percent gave aid to victims of the Kashmiri earthquake; while for 170 European firms corresponding figures were 29 percent and 16 percent. This effect was also conditioned by whether the companies in question had a local presence in the affected country: if they did, philanthropy was far more apparent.

Overall, then, it appears that although charity may not end at home, it certainly begins there – noting of course, along with Levine and Thompson (2004), that "home" varies with identity. It could be our town, our region, our country – and it could be still narrower or still wider – depending upon how we define ourselves. But, by the same token, exactly who we help at home depends upon who we see as belonging to our neighbourhood, town, region, or country. In Nazi Germany, for instance, Jewish people were explicitly rejected from the Nazi's definition of the national ingroup and hence could be treated as legitimate targets for persecution. By contrast, in those countries under Nazi occupation where a definition of national identity which excluded Jews was not widely accepted (e.g., Denmark; see Oliner & Oliner, 1988), Jewish people were much more likely to be protected. Within different countries too, people's willingness to help Jews varied as a function of their own acceptance of particular definitions of national identity.

Reicher, Cassidy, Wolpert, Hopkins, and Levine (2006) use the example of Bulgaria to drive home this point that there is a link between ingroup inclusion and solidarity. Twice in the history of that country, mass movements thwarted plans to deport the Jewish population to the extermination camps. Analysis of the key texts that were used to mobilize people (see Todorov, 2001) suggests that a key factor that motivated and made possible these courageous acts of support was the success of efforts to define Jews, not as an outgroup, but instead as an essential part of the national ingroup. Indeed, for the most part, this involved avoiding all references to Jews as a distinct social category (i.e., as "them") – with political mobilizers preferring instead to identify them as "Bulgaria's Jews" or "Bulgarian citizens of Jewish origin" or "a national minority" (Reicher et al., 2006, p. 58; see also Haslam, Reicher, & Platow, 2011).

In this, the gravest of circumstances, we thus see again that the dynamics of support are bound up with, and predicated upon, perceptions that those who will receive it are not "other" but rather are contained within the boundaries of the psychological ingroup, "us". Where this is the case, advancing the cause of one's neighbour never comes at cost to self – for the simple reason that *they are self*.

SUPPORTING THE OUTGROUP

Up to this point, our theoretical and empirical considerations have focused largely on the ingroup – showing that there is a greater likelihood that social support will be given, received and taken on board if those who are party to the process perceive themselves to share social identity. As a corollary of this point, in several of the studies we have reviewed it is also clear that those who fall outside the boundaries of the ingroup tend to receive less support and that the interpretation of support across social category boundaries tends to be complicated by lower levels of empathy and trust.

Nevertheless, one might object to these claims by pointing to a range of social contexts in which people *do* provide support to outgroups, and argue that this undermines our general argument. In this regard, the first point to make is that while we assert that shared social identity provides a cognitive and motivational basis for successful support efforts, we are not suggesting that support will only ever be offered to ingroup members. There are at least two reasons for this. The first is that there may be a range of *strategic* reasons why ingroups will want to support outgroups. In particular, this may be a way of increasing ingroup influence and of demonstrating the ingroup's power over outgroups (van Leeuwen & Tauber, 2010). It may also be a way of repairing the reputation of the ingroup in the eyes of outgroups. Proof of this point comes from a study that Hopkins, Reicher, Harrison, Cassidy, Bull, and Levine (2007) conducted with Scottish students. They asked students to provide financial support for an outgroup cause (buying raffle tickets to support victims of crime in Wales), but made some of the participants aware that English people endorsed a stereotype of the Scots as mean. In the condition where this negative stereotype was made salient, the participants went out of their way to give more support to the outgroup than they had to the Scottish ingroup as a way of discon- firming the negative stereotype – leading them to buy more than twice as many tickets as they did otherwise and more than twice as many as they did to support the ingroup.

A second reason why support is sometimes given to outgroups is that, while social identification always provides a basis for supporting fellow ingroup members, it does not necessarily dictate a failure to support others (Turner, 1999).[3] Amongst other things, this is because a group's orientation towards any outgroup will always be structured by both the context of intergroup relations and the *content* of the ingroup's social identity (Livingstone & Haslam, 2008). This means, for example, that if the ingroup has norms (e.g., of charity or solidarity) such that it prides itself on helping those who are in distress, then the conformity to ingroup norms that is associated with identification with that ingroup will tend to be translated into motivations to support outgroups. Indeed, within such groups (e.g., medical practitioners, aid workers), codes of conduct, ethical guidelines, and other normative frameworks (e.g., the Hippocratic oath, religious commandments) will often *prescribe* outgroup helping as an aspect of idealized ingroup behaviour.

Nevertheless, even though there may be a range of reasons why support is offered across intergroup boundaries, there are still dangers that this will lead to suboptimal outcomes. To help us consider some of the issues involved, it is interesting to look at patterns that emerged from classic research by Pendleton and Bochner (1980) that looked at patterns of patient consultation among General Practitioners (GPs). Despite the fact that GPs' code of practice instructs them to deliver health care impartially, analysis revealed (a) that GPs spend more time in consultation with patients who have high socio-economic status (SES) than with those who have low SES (on average, the former patients were seen for 7.3 min the latter for 5.3

min), and that this reflected the fact (b) that GPs give high-SES patients more information than those who are low-SES (3.2 vs. 1.6 units), and (c) that GPs get more information back from high-SES than low-SES patients (2.5 vs. 0.7 units).

What this research shows is that patients have very different experiences as a function of their identity. Low-SES patients not only receive less attention and less information from doctors, but it is clear that this increases the potential for misunderstanding and hence for recrimination. The obvious question is what lies at the root of these problems? There are several possibilities, of course. One has to do with shared social stereotypes of working class people as less intellectually able and hence less worth talking to. But another, that speaks to the topic of this chapter, is that it derives from a sense of shared identity between doctors (high-SES professionals) and their high-SES patients (see also St. Claire & Clucas, this volume).

The data provided by Pendleton and Bochner themselves do not allow us to settle the matter. So we can do no more than advance the level of shared identification as a plausible contributor to the success or breakdown of communication in clinical settings. However, much clearer and stronger evidence of this link comes from programmes of research conducted by Nadler and his colleagues (e.g., Nadler, 2010), and Stürmer and Snyder (e.g., 2010). Nadler's work examines instances of outgroup helping in situations of intergroup conflict (e.g., between Israelis and Palestinians; between conservative men and feminists), and shows that rather than ameliorating difficulties, attempts to provide support can often exacerbate them. Amongst other things, this is because – in line with the strategic reasons for support being given (see above) – those who receive support often interpret this as an attempt to manoeuvre them into a position of weakness and dependency that serves to consolidate the donor's privileged status. This failure to respond in ways that the donor expects can then be used to justify discrimination in the future and thereby set in train a vicious spiral of increased intergroup hostility.

In a related vein, the work of Stürmer and Snyder looks at subtle differences in the ways in which help is given to "them" rather than "us". This suggests that, whereas support for ingroup members is generally underpinned by high levels of empathy, that which is provided to outgroups is much more likely to be based on a strategic analysis of costs and benefits. In this way, it appears that people help outgroups "as long as they feel they get something out of it" (Stürmer & Snyder, 2010, p. 55). Unsurprisingly, support of this form tends to be seen by recipients as relatively insincere, and rather than simply saying "thank you" they may be motivated to look the gift horse in the mouth (i.e., to interrogate the donors' motives as well as the quality of their gifts). In situations where short-term material outcomes are all that matter, this may not be a problem. However, because it lends itself to support that is more fragile, more conditional, and less enduring, in the long run it has a far greater chance of breaking down.

Amongst other things, this is because such support (and the process of monitoring the costs and benefits that it entails) will generally be seen as "very hard work".

CONCLUSION

We started this chapter by observing that there are a range of contexts in which other people – and the social support they provide – prove to be more hellish than healing. Because it is so central to the purposes of this book, our goal in the remainder of the chapter has been to provide a theoretical framework that provides insight into some of the reasons for this. In this regard, our central conclusion is that the dynamics of social support are always conditioned by the social identities that inform this process (in ways specified by both social identity and self-categorization theories). This means that where parties to the support process perceive themselves to share social identity (i.e., where they define themselves in terms of the same social self-category) then, generally speaking, not only will more support be more forthcoming but it will also tend to be interpreted in ways that allow it to achieve its intended effect. However, in the absence of this shared identity, this is less likely to be the case. This is because here those elements that contribute to successful support – shared expectations, empathy, communication, trust, and accommodation – will all tend to be in relatively short supply.

In this way, the impact – and the curative potential – of social support is heavily conditioned by its psychological partnership with social identity. This does not mean, of course, that all support that is founded on shared identity is "good" or even desirable. If the social identity in question is in some sense toxic then support may take forms and sustain activities that ultimately compromise the health and well-being of both outgroup *and* ingroup (see Tarrant et al., this volume). For example, this might be the case if the content of the identity leads people to provide damaging forms of support (e.g., by encouraging drug dependency) or if the identity that is advanced has destructive objectives (e.g., promoting violence; Cordon, Haslam, Williams, Haslam, & Rabinovich, 2010). It is also the case that these negative aspects of the support process will generally be less apparent to ingroup members than to outgroup observers, and may prove difficult for members of that ingroup to acknowledge.

Returning to the examples that we started with, one of the key implications of our analysis is that providing people share identity with others then they are not routinely condemned to finding their company – and the process of supporting them – onerous, burdensome, or tiring. Indeed, quite the opposite. In *Up in the Air* this is seen once Ryan Bingham is induced out of his cocoon of personal self-absorption and allows others to become part of his self-definition. At this point, he loses faith in his "What's in your backpack?" routine, and starts to aspire to the various things that group life can bring: companionship, a sense of "home", love. Likewise, we see that it is these same things that provide those who have been victims of the corporate axe (that he and others wield) with a basis for support that allows them to rebuild their lives.

Although these victims are not actors, one might, nonetheless, be forgiven for dismissing this as just another Hollywood ending. So let us return to the altogether more erudite *Huis Clos*. As we intimated earlier, this play (and much of Sartre's existential philosophy) is generally remembered for its stark four-word conclusion. It is notable, however, that Sartre himself spent much of his life trying (largely in vain) to challenge popular interpretations of this text. Thus, 20 years after writing it, he complained:

> "Hell is other people" has always been misunderstood. People thought that what I meant by it is that our relations with others are always rotten or illicit. But I mean something entirely different. I mean that if our relations with others are twisted or corrupted, then others have to be hell. Fundamentally, others are what is important in us for our understanding of ourselves.
>
> (Sartre, 1965; cited in Contat & Rybalka, 1974, p. 99)

Ultimately, then, whether we find the company and support of others to be a source of torment or of solace depends to a considerable extent on the way that we relate to them social psychologically. More importantly, though, understanding how we regard others also tells us a lot about ourselves (Reicher & Haslam, 2010). In this respect, possibly the most fundamental benefit of supportive relations with others is not that it allows us to help them (important as this may be), but that it allows human beings to formulate an understanding of "us" that has the potential to be better in every sense.

ACKNOWLEDGMENT

Work on this chapter was supported by a grant from the Economic and Social Research Council (RES-062-23-0135).

NOTES

1 Full transcript retrieved from: http://www.script-o-rama.com/movie_scripts/u/up-in-the-air-script-transcript.html
2 For a discussion, see http://www.prospectmagazine.co.uk/2006/06/national anxieties
3 Sometimes too, this effect will be predicted by the fact that erstwhile outgroups come to be recategorized as part of a very broadly defined ingroup (e.g., all humans).

References

Berkman, L. F., & Syme, L. (1979). Social networks, host resistance, and mortality: A nine-year follow-up study of Alameda County residents. *American Journal of Epidemiology, 109*, 186–204.

Cohen, S., & Syme, S. L. (1985). Issues in the study and application of social support. In S. Cohen & S. L. Syme (Eds.), *Social support and health* (pp. 3–21). San Francisco, CA: Academic Press.

Contat, M., & Rybalka, M. A. (1974). *The writings of Jean-Paul Sartre* (Vol. 1). Evanston, IL: Northwestern University Press.

Cordon, G., Haslam, S. A., Williams, W. H., Haslam, C., & Rabinovich, A. (2010). *Exploring the contribution of gang identification, gang violence and head injury to offending behaviour and mental health in young offenders.* Unpublished manuscript, University of Exeter, UK.

DeLongis, A., & Holtzman, S. (2005). Coping in context: The role of stress, social support and personality in coping. *Journal of Personality, 73*, 1–24.

Dovidio, J. F., Gaertner, S. L., Schnabel, N., Saguy, T., & Johnson, J. (2010). Recategorization and prosocial behavior. In S. Stürmer & M. Snyder (Eds.), *The psychology of pro-social behavior: Group processes, intergroup relations, and helping* (pp. 289–309). Oxford, UK: Blackwell.

Drury, J., Cocking, C., & Reicher, S. D. (2009). Everyone for themselves? A comparative study of crowd solidarity among emergency survivors. *British Journal of Social Psychology, 48*, 487–506.

Foddy, M., Platow, M. J., & Yamagishi, T. (2009). Group-based trust in strangers. *Psychological Science, 20*, 419–422.

Haslam, S. A. (2004). *Psychology in organizations: The social identity approach* (2nd ed.). London, UK: Sage.

Haslam, S. A., Jetten, J., O'Brien, A., & Jacobs, E. (2004). Social identity, social influence, and reactions to potentially stressful tasks: Support for the self-categorization model of stress. *Stress and Health, 20*, 3–9.

Haslam, S. A., Jetten, J., Postmes, T., & Haslam, C. (2009a). Social identity, health and well-being: An emerging agenda for applied psychology. *Applied Psychology: An International Review, 58*, 1–23.

Haslam, S. A., Jetten, J., Postmes, T., & Haslam, C. (Eds.) (2009b). Social identity, health and well-being. Special Issue of *Applied Psychology: An International Review, 58*, 1–192.

Haslam, S. A., Reicher, S. D., & Platow, M. (2011). *The new psychology of leadership*. Hove, UK and New York, NY: Psychology Press.

Hopkins, N., Reicher, S. D., Harrison, K., Cassidy, C., Bull, R., & Levine, M. (2007). Helping to improve the group stereotype: On the strategic dimension of pro-social behavior. *Personality and Social Psychology Bulletin, 33*, 776–788.

House, J. S. (1981). *Work stress and social support*. Reading, MA: Addison-Wesley.

House, J. S., & Kahn, R. L. (1985). Measures and concepts of social support. In S. Cohen & S. L. Syme (Eds.), *Social support and health* (pp. 83–108). San Francisco, CA: Academic Press.

Jetten, J., Haslam, S. A., Iyer, A., & Haslam, C. (2010). Turning to others in times of change: Social identity and coping with stress. In S. Stürmer & M. Snyder (Eds.), *The psychology of pro-social behavior: Group processes, intergroup relations, and helping* (pp. 139–156). Oxford, UK: Blackwell.

Lazarus, R. S., & Folkman, S. (1984). *Stress, appraisal and coping*. New York, NY. Springer.

Levine, R. M., Prosser, A., Evans, D., & Reicher, S. D. (2005). Identity and emergency intervention: How social group membership and inclusiveness of group boundaries shapes helping behavior. *Personality and Social Psychology Bulletin, 31*, 443–453.

Levine R. M., & Thompson, K. (2004). Identity, place and bystander intervention: Social categories and helping after natural disasters. *Journal of Social Psychology, 144*, 229–245.

Livingstone, A., & Haslam, S. A. (2008). The importance of social identity content in a setting of chronic social conflict: The case of intergroup relations in Northern Ireland. *British Journal of Social Psychology, 47*, 1–21.

Muller, A., & Whiteman, G. (2009). Exploring the geography of corporate disaster response: A study of Fortune Global 500 firms. *Journal of Business Ethics, 84*, 589–603.

Nadler, A. (2010). Interpersonal and intergroup helping relations as power relations: Implications for real-world helping. In S. Stürmer & M. Snyder (Eds.), *The psychology of pro-social behavior: Group processes, intergroup relations, and helping* (pp. 269–287). Oxford, UK: Blackwell.

Oakes, P. J., Haslam, S. A., & Turner, J. C. (1994). *Stereotyping and social reality*. Oxford, UK: Blackwell.

Oliner, S. P., & Oliner, P. M. (1988). *The altruistic personality – Rescuers of Jews in Nazi Europe: What led ordinary men and women to risk their lives on behalf of others?* New York, NY: The Free Press.

Pendleton, D. A., & Bochner, S. (1980). Communication of medical information in general practice consultations as a function of patients' social class. *Social Science & Medicine, 14*, 669–673.

Postmes, T. (2003). A social identity approach to communication in organizations. In S. A. Haslam, D. van Knippenberg, M. J. Platow, & N. Ellemers (Eds.), *Social identity at work: Developing theory for organizational practice* (pp. 81–97). Philadelphia, PA: Psychology Press.

Reicher, S. D., Cassidy, C., Wolpert, I., Hopkins, N., & Levine, M. (2006). Saving Bulgaria's Jews: An analysis of social identity and the mobilisation of social solidarity. *European Journal of Social Psychology, 36*, 49–72.

Reicher, S. D., & Haslam, S. A. (2006). Tyranny revisited: Groups, psychological well-being and the health of societies. *The Psychologist, 19*, 146–150.

Reicher, S. D., & Haslam, S. A. (2010). Beyond help: A social psychology of collective solidarity and social cohesion. In S. Stürmer & M. Snyder (Eds.), *The psychology of pro-social behavior: Group processes, intergroup relations, and helping* (pp. 289–309). Oxford, UK: Blackwell.

Reitman, J., & Turner, S. (2009). *Up in the air* [screenplay from the novel by W. Kim]. Downloaded from http://www.imsdb.com

Sartre, J.-P. (1944). *In camera and other plays* (trans. S. Gilbert, 1958). Harmondsworth, UK: Penguin.

Schwarzer, R., & Leppin, A. (1991). Social support and health: A theoretical and empirical overview. *Journal of Personal and Social Relationships, 8*, 99–127.

Stürmer, S., & Snyder, M. (2010). Helping "us" versus "them": Towards a group-level theory of helping and altruism across group boundaries. In S. Stürmer & M.

Snyder (Eds.), *The psychology of pro-social behavior: Group processes, intergroup relations, and helping* (pp. 33–58). Oxford, UK: Blackwell.

Tajfel, H. (1972). La catégorisation sociale (English trans.). In S. Moscovici (Ed.), *Introduction à la psychologie sociale* (Vol. 1, pp. 272–302). Paris, France: Larousse.

Tajfel, H., & Turner J. C. (1979). An integrative theory of intergroup conflict. In W. G. Austin & S. Worchel (Eds.), *The social psychology of intergroup relations* (pp. 33–48). Monterey, CA: Brooks/Cole.

Taylor, S. E. (2007). Social support. In H. S. Friedman & R. C. Silver (Eds.), *Foundations of health psychology* (pp. 145–171). New York, NY: Oxford University Press.

Thoits, P. A., (1995). Stress, coping and social support processes: Where are we? What next? *Journal of Health and Social Behavior, 35*, 53–79.

Todorov, T. (2001). *The fragility of goodness*. London, UK: Weidenfeld & Nicolson.

Turner, J. C. (1982). Towards a cognitive redefinition of the social group. In H. Tajfel (Ed.), *Social identity and intergroup relations* (pp. 15–40). Cambridge, UK: Cambridge University Press.

Turner, J. C. (1999). Some current issues in research on social identity and self-categorization theories. In N. Ellemers, R. Spears, & B. Doosje (Eds.), *Social identity: Context, commitment, content* (pp. 6–34). Oxford, UK: Blackwell.

Turner, J. C., Hogg, M. A., Oakes, P. J., Reicher, S. D., & Wetherell, M. S. (1987). *Rediscovering the social group: A self-categorization theory*. Oxford, UK and New York, NY: Blackwell.

Turner, J. C., Oakes, P. J., Haslam, S. A., & McGarty, C. A. (1994). Self and collective: Cognition and social context. *Personality and Social Psychology Bulletin, 20*, 454–463.

Tyler, T. R., & Blader, S. (2000). *Co-operation in groups: Procedural justice, social identity and behavioral engagement*. Philadelphia, PA: Psychology Press.

van Leeuwen, E., & Tauber, S. (2010). The strategic side of out-group helping. In S. Stürmer & M. Snyder (Eds.), *The psychology of pro-social behavior: Group processes, intergroup relations, and helping* (pp. 81–99). Oxford, UK: Blackwell.

Wills, T. A. (1991). Social support and interpersonal relationships. In M. S. Clark (Ed.), *Prosocial behavior* (pp. 265–289). Newbury Park, CA: Sage.

10 Stress and well-being in the workplace

Support for key propositions from the social identity approach

Rolf van Dick
Goethe University Frankfurt

S. Alexander Haslam
University of Exeter

Of all the domains in which issues of well-being rear their head, the workplace is one of the most prominent. Apart from anything else, this is because it is apparent that an unhealthy workforce is an unproductive one. In recognition of this point, the financial costs of mismanaging well-being are of considerable interest to labour economists and organizational policy makers. For example, a recent report by the UK's National Director for Health and Work, Dame Carol Black (2008), estimated that in Britain around 175 million working days were lost to sickness in 2006 (around 7 per employee), and that work-related ill health costs the country in excess of £100 bn a year – more than the entire health budget of the National Health Service and around £4,000 for every employee. Black's report laid much of the blame for this on the fact that nearly half of all UK organizations had no policy for managing issues of health and sickness in the workplace, and, accordingly, had taken no proactive steps to try to minimize this impact. While at an economic level this would seem to be a major oversight, at a human one it would seem to be catastrophic. For, as Black's report highlights, by failing to tackle these issues directly, organizations are not only being financially negligent, they are also greatly increasing the sum of human distress and misery – impacting not just on individuals, but also on their families and on society as a whole.

The aim of this chapter is to make two contributions to the analysis of well-being in the workplace. First, it seeks to provide a conceptual analysis of how and why issues of social identity are important for understanding well-being in organizational contexts – with a particular emphasis on the dynamics of workplace *stress*. Second, we present empirical evidence that provides support for this conceptual analysis. On this basis we also make practical recommendations about strategies for managing and promoting well-being at work. A key conclusion here is that while it is common for theorists and practitioners to conceptualize, and treat, well-being in the workplace as if it were largely a personal matter that is best addressed through medical pathways, there is a need to complement such analysis with an appreciation of the role that groups and group dynamics play both in compromising health and in promoting it. Our claim here is not that groups are a universal cure (nor, for that matter, that they constitute an insurmountable curse). Rather, we suggest that groups play a key role in shaping both the severity and the trajectory of health-related problems, and that without attending to this role organizations are unlikely to achieve optimal outcomes – in terms of either health or performance.

STRESS AND WELL-BEING IN THE WORKPLACE

Stress is an established but still very "hot" topic in psychology as a whole. In recent years it has come to occupy a particularly prominent position in the domain of organizational psychology. Here, the topic has proved important because it has enormous implications both for individual welfare and for organizational effectiveness. Indeed, when it comes to this issue, the individual and the organization are clearly yoked together because if an individual reacts negatively to stress (e.g., as evidenced through absenteeism or burnout) then this will impact directly on organizational functioning (Cartwright & Cooper, 2009). To back this point up with some more alarming statistics, according to the UK's Health and Safety Executive (HSE), in 2009 around 17 percent of all employees thought that their job was highly stressful. Work-related anxiety, stress and depression were also the second most prevalent cause of lost working days (estimated to account for 11.4 m; HSE, 2009, p. 6).

Yet despite its importance, the management of stress in the workplace proves to be a complex challenge. A key reason for this is that while there is some consensus about those features of work that can be stress-inducing, it is apparent that whether or not these are translated into the actual experience of stress is no straightforward matter. More specifically, Cooper, Dewe, and O'Driscoll (2001) have identified six major categories of workplace stressors (high demands, low control, poor support, confused roles, poor relationships, and organizational change), but just as these can all lead to chronic stress, so too they can stimulate a range of positive personal and organizational outcomes. Organizational change, for example, can be a source of uncertainty, frustration, and confusion, but it can also provide novelty, stimulation, and opportunities for growth. This complexity has led many organizations either to place problems of stress in the "too-hard basket" (something that potentially accounts for the lack of policy in this area, as remarked upon by Black, 2008) or to claim that the significance of these problems is wildly overstated and that concerns about stress simply mask the indolence of lazy employees (Patmore, 2006).

Nevertheless, in helping researchers and practitioners come to grips with this complexity, one analytical framework that has been enormously influential is the *transactional model* developed by Lazarus and colleagues (e.g., Lazarus, 1991; Lazarus & Folkman, 1984). In particular, this is helpful when it comes to understanding the psychological dimensions of the relationship between potential stressors and outcomes such as strain and chronic stress (i.e., burnout). The model suggests that two interdependent phases of appraisal are responsible for translating exposure to stressors into the experience of stress. First, *primary appraisal*, involves individuals evaluating the situation that they confront and asking whether or not it is relevant to them, and, more specifically, whether it involves the potential for harm, loss, or threat to the self. Here a situation is considered potentially stressful only if it is appraised as having negative implications for self. In a further stage of *secondary appraisal*, individuals evaluate whether or not they can successfully deal with the stressor. This involves appraisal of the coping resources that are at their disposal. Most importantly for our present discussion, these include the potential to receive and benefit from the social support of others.

If an individual either does not perceive a stressor to be potentially harmful or does perceive this harm as not exceeding his or her capacity to cope, then he or she is unlikely to experience stress, and the situation would not be expected to have negative consequences for health and well-being. Indeed, in this case, the stressor may be appraised as presenting a positive challenge and therefore serve as a stimulus for positive forms of personal development and growth. By way of example, if a female lawyer has a very demanding case to manage, but does not see this as harmful and is given a lot of support by colleagues, then she may construe the experience as a positive one that promotes her professional advancement. However, if the case is seen as potentially harmful and she senses that she lacks support, then management of the case may prove very stressful and have a range of negative consequences (e.g., encouraging her to disengage from her profession altogether; Ryan, Haslam, Hersby, Kulich, & Atkins, 2007).

Notwithstanding its importance and influence, one limitation of the transactional model is that its approach to the psychology of stress is highly *personal* – seeing the appraisal of stressors largely as a matter for the individual *as an individual* (Is this threatening to *me*? Can *I* cope?). Yet evidence suggests that such appraisals and the overall experience of stress also have a very significant *social* dimension (Haslam, 2004). Amongst other things, this means that groups of people working in the same work environment or culture often come to *share* complaints relating to their work experience, and hence it is at a group (not just an individual) level that such processes need to be understood and tackled.

THE SOCIAL IDENTITY APPROACH

It is largely to accommodate evidence of the social dimensions of stress appraisal that in recent years a number of researchers have advocated a *social identity approach* to the study of stress (e.g., Haslam, 2004; Haslam & Reicher, 2006; Jetten, Haslam, Iyer, & Haslam, 2009). However, before going into the details of this, it is useful to provide a brief overview of the social identity approach more generally. As noted in earlier chapters in this book (e.g., Jetten, Haslam, & Haslam, this volume), the social identity approach is comprised of two closely related theories: social identity theory (SIT; Tajfel & Turner, 1979) and self-categorization theory (SCT; Turner, Hogg, Oakes, Reicher, & Wetherell, 1987). Both theories emphasize the potential for individuals to derive a sense of self from their membership of social groups – that is, from *social identity*. A key idea here is that in order to understand behaviour in a range of significant social contexts (e.g., those in which there is conflict, prejudice, and discrimination), it is necessary to recognize that individuals can – and often do – define the self ("who they think they are") in social not just personal terms (as "us" and "we", not just "I" and "me").

Self-categorization theorists, in particular, have delved forensically into the social psychological dynamics of the self with a view to understanding both the determinants and the consequences of self-definition in group-based terms. In this regard, one core insight of SCT is that shared social identity is the basis for mutual *social influence* (Turner, 1991). This means that when people perceive themselves to share group membership with others in a given context they are motivated to strive actively to reach agreement with them and to coordinate their behaviour in relation to activities that are relevant to that identity. A female employee who defines herself as a woman should seek out other women in order both to validate her understanding of issues that relate to this social identity (e.g., instances of sexism in the workplace) and to develop a coordinated response to those issues (Hersby, Ryan, & Jetten, 2009). This occurs because here it is the group that defines the individuals' sense of self. Accordingly, in advancing the group (and its members), he or she is actually promoting the self – even though this may involve some level of personal self-sacrifice (e.g., taking time out of one's own busy schedule to help others).

In recent years the social identity approach has provided a range of fresh insights into the nature of organizational behaviour. The first researchers to explicitly recognize the approach's potential in this regard were Ashforth and Mael (1989). In a highly influential *Academy of Management Review* article they noted that social identity has considerable capacity to provide a self-definitional and self-referential basis for people's behaviour in the workplace in light of the important role that various forms of group (e.g., teams, departments, divisions, and the organization itself) play in organizational dynamics. Indeed, Ashforth and Mael observed that if the social identity of employees is defined in terms of their membership of a particular organizational unit then they are likely to strive with relevant workmates to achieve positive outcomes for that unit and to perceive the successes (and failures) of that unit as their own. In line with this idea, subsequent research (e.g., Mael & Ashforth, 1992; see also van Knippenberg & Ellemers, 2003) showed that just as high organizational identification is a powerful predictor of individuals' willingness to commit themselves to a specific organization (or organizational unit), so low identification is a strong predictor of their desire to disengage from and exit the organization – if not physically then psychologically (e.g., as revealed by turnover intentions; Abrams, Ando, & Hinkle, 1998; Randsley de Moura, Abrams, Retter, Gunnarsdottir, & Ando, 2009; van Dick et al., 2004).

A SOCIAL IDENTITY APPROACH TO STRESS AND WELL-BEING IN THE WORKPLACE

The ideas outlined in the forgoing section provide some preliminary insights into the way in which the social identity approach can feed in to the analysis of health-related issues in the workplace. In particular, this is because the processes of cooperation, support, and engagement (vs. conflict, isolation, and disillusionment) that we have been discussing are ones that clearly have a bearing on workplace health and well-being (vs. sickness and stress). It is useful, however, to elaborate on these ideas in terms of a series of propositions, before drawing these propositions together within an integrated model.

Proposition 1

To the extent that members of an organization (or organizational unit) identify strongly with that organization (or unit) they will tend to be more satisfied with organizational life and to report higher levels of well-being.

There are several reasons for believing that organizational identification will impact directly on well-being. In particular, this proposition follows from Pratt's (1998, 2001) assertion that group-based identification satisfies a range of important human needs – specifically those for safety, belonging, self-enhancement, and for a sense of identity and meaning (in terms of one's holistic worldview). In general terms, social identification should help to satisfy all these needs. It follows that organizational members whose needs are satisfied can in turn be expected to report a stronger sense of well-being than those who (for whatever reason) find it hard to identify with groups in the workplace.

Importantly though, whereas traditional approaches to these issues have tended to regard such needs as personal (e.g., Maslow, 1943) and relatively free-floating (e.g., Baumeister & Leary, 1995) the social identity approach suggests that they are underpinned by a desire for meaningful social identifications that help the individual to make sense of his or her environment and to function effectively within it. In organizational contexts, then, employees will not be satisfied by membership of "any old group" but rather should seek out, and aspire to, membership of groups that contribute to a positive and distinctive sense of self. Amongst other things, this means that they should tend to report greater well-being to the extent that they can claim membership either in high-status organizations, or in high-status units within those organizations (Veenstra, Haslam, & Reynolds, 2004). As Haslam, Powell and Turner (2000) observe, this is one reason why even when it is financially more rewarding to work for a low-status organization than a high-status one, people will often prefer to work for the latter than the former.

It also follows that to the extent that individuals sense that they share social identity with fellow organizational members then this should lead them to be more disposed to those colleagues (e.g., to like and trust them more; Kramer & Tyler, 1996; Platow, Haslam, Foddy, & Grace, 2003) and to find the process of interacting with them more pleasant and more rewarding. At a higher level of abstraction, this should also lead them to be more positively disposed and attracted both to the organization as a whole (Highhouse, Thornbury, & Little, 2007) and to those who act on its behalf (in particular, those in leadership roles; Ellemers, De Gilder, & Haslam, 2004; Haslam, Reicher, & Platow, 2011).

Support for this general proposition comes from a large number of organizational studies. For example, in a study of German schoolteachers, van Dick and Wagner (2002) observed a moderate correlation ($r = -.30$) between occupational identification and measures of the frequency with which they had suffered from eight different physical symptoms (e.g., headaches, neck-and-shoulder pain, weariness). This pattern was then replicated in a follow-up study with a different group of teachers that assessed both occupational identification and team identification. Here both forms of identification were found to be related to reports of physical symptoms ($rs = -.43$ and $-.28$, respectively). In another school context, this time in Australia, Bizumic, Reynolds, Turner, Bromhead, and Subasic (2009) found weak but reliable associations between school identification and a range of clinical conditions, including chronic anxiety ($r = -.14$) and depression ($r = -.13$).

Speaking to more general issues of well-being, in a study of bar staff and bomb disposal experts, Haslam, O'Brien, Jetten, Vormedal, and Penna (2005) observed a moderate correlation ($r = .49$) between identification with one's workteam and a global measure of work satisfaction. Along similar lines, in a more extensive study of four different organizational samples (1,135 employees of two German banks, call centre agents, and hospital workers), van Dick and colleagues (2004) observed zero-order correlations between organizational identification and job satisfaction that were, on average, of moderate strength (mean $r = .40$) but that ranged from being relatively weak (in the case of hospital employees; $r = .21$) to being quite strong (in the case of one of the banks; $r = .52$). More recently, very similar patterns were reported by Randsley de Moura and her colleagues (2009) in a study of 1,392 employees drawn from seven different organizational samples. Here zero-order correlations between organizational identification and job satisfaction were again typically of moderate strength (mean r = .36) and they ranged from those that were weak (in the case of hospital employees; r = .28) to those that were very strong (in the case of a UK commercial organization; r = .62).

The reliability of such relationships is also confirmed in meta-analyses which have examined the capacity for different forms of organizational identification to predict well-being in the workplace. Specifically, in a statistical summary of 38 studies, Riketta (2005) observed a strong relationship between organizational identification and job satisfaction (r = .54), and in a comparison of 19 studies Riketta and Van Dick (2005) also observed a moderate correlation between team attachment and job satisfaction (r = .38).

Proposition 2

To the extent that members of an organization (or organizational unit) identify strongly with that organization (or unit) they will tend to experience and report lower levels of stress.

In many ways, this proposition can be seen as a straightforward corollary of Proposition 1. In particular, if a sense of shared identity tends to be a basis for positive interactions between members of an organization, then this should mean that those individuals find the day-to-day business of organizational life less fraught and less threatening to self. In part too, this inclination to make more positive primary appraisals will reflect the fact that shared organizational identity leads to an alignment of perspective such that employees feel that they are working *with* rather than *against* each other. Moreover, this should have implications at both personal and social levels, such that shared identity leads to workplace experiences being seen as less problematic both for organizational members as individuals (i.e., this stressor is less threatening to *me*) and for the organizational unit with which they identify (i.e., this stressor is less threatening to *us*).

Consistent with this proposition, in the study of bar staff and bomb disposal experts alluded to above, Haslam and colleagues (2005) observed moderate-sized negative correlations between workteam identification and workplace stress (r = −.49). In a study of staff from four airlines in Thailand, Peters and colleagues reported a strong negative correlation between identification with the organization as a whole and work-related stress (r = −.61; Peters, Tevichapong, Haslam, & Postmes, 2010). Likewise, in two studies of call centre workers, Wegge and Van Dick (2006; Wegge, Van Dick, Fisher, Wecking, & Moltzen, 2006) found that organizational identification was a moderately strong predictor of the three distinct components of burnout previously identified by Jackson, Schwab and Schuler (1986; see also Maslach, Jackson, & Leiter, 1996): emotional exhaustion ($r = -.28$), lack of accomplishment: ($r = -.48$), and callousness ($r = -.40$).

Speaking to the capacity for organizational identification to predict stress prospectively, in a longitudinal study of staff working on different theatre productions Haslam, Jetten, and Waghorn (2009) also found that participants' identification with their workteam at the start of a production (i.e., during auditions) was a moderately-sized negative predictor ($r = -.39$) of reports of burnout during the production's critical phases (i.e., from dress rehearsal to final performance). Evidence of the physiological substrates of such effects also emerged from an experimental study conducted by Wegge, Schuh, and Van Dick (in press) in which call centre workers participated in a task designed to simulate the demands of call centre work. Here, when exposed to rude customers, call centre employees who were highly identified with their organization evinced lower levels of stress (as revealed by levels of cortisol in their saliva) than their counterparts who were less strongly identified.

Proposition 3

The capacity for an organizational stressor to induce stress will vary as a function of its relevance to an organizational identity that is currently salient.

Proposition 2 concerns the capacity for shared organizational identity to engender positive primary appraisals of workplace stressors through its tendency to promote positive forms of intra-organizational interaction. Independent of these dynamics, though, it should also be the case that the implications of any given stressor for the self will depend upon its *relevance* for the organizational identity that defines an individual's sense of self in any given organizational context. In other words, the impact of a given stressor will generally be moderated by the relevance of that stressor for a salient social identity.

Evidence that this is the case emerges from a programme of research conducted by Levine and Reicher (1996; Levine, 1999; see also St. Claire & Clucas, this volume). These researchers conducted an initial study with female sports scientists in which they found that when the women's gender identity was salient they perceived the stress of a threat to their attractiveness (e.g., a facial scar) to be much more serious than they did when their identity as sports scientists was made salient. On the other hand, when participants' identity as sports scientists was made salient, they found the stress of a threat to their fitness (e.g., a knee injury) much more serious than when their gender identity was salient. Very similar patterns also emerged from a follow-up study of female secretaries in which threats (e.g., a facial scar vs. repetitive strain injury) related either to the participants' gender identity (as women) or their professional identity (as secretaries; Levine, 1999).

It is not the case, however, that simply because a stressor is perceived as more relevant to an organizational identity that is salient for an individual in a particular context that it will necessarily lead to more stress. In particular, this is because the group itself can be a powerful mechanism for helping people to cope with, neutralize, and sometimes counteract, that stressor. Again, support for this suggestion emerged from the study of bomb disposal officers and bar staff that we have already discussed (Haslam et al., 2005). Here, as well as rating their organizational identification, job satisfaction, and stress, the participants were also asked to evaluate the stressfulness of handling bombs and serving in a bar. As one might expect, pretesting among the general population indicated that the job of handling bombs was perceived to be much more stressful than that of working in a bar, and indeed this was the pattern revealed by the responses of bar staff in the study. Bomb disposal officers, however, reported the opposite pattern. While bar staff were thus relatively untroubled by the stresses of bar work, bomb handlers were equally unfazed by the stresses of handling bombs. This would tend to suggest that individuals' experiences as members of these different groups had allowed them to *normalize* aspects of work that might be quite abnormal and threatening to the uninitiated (Ashforth & Johnson, 2001). This possibility brings us to our next proposition that concerns the capacity for social identity to play a key role in determining individuals' capacity to cope with organizational stressors by drawing upon the support of fellow group members.

Proposition 4

To the extent that members of an organization (or organizational unit) identify strongly with that organization (or unit), they will tend to receive and report greater levels of social support, and the support they receive will have more positive impact.

Whereas Propositions 2 and 3 relate largely to organizational members' primary appraisal of stressors in the workplace, Proposition 4 suggests that organizational identity should also have a bearing on the experience of stress and well-being through its capacity to impact upon *secondary* appraisal (Haslam, 2004). More specifically, in assessing their ability to cope with any potential threat to the self, individuals who perceive themselves to share organizational identity with their work colleagues are more likely to see themselves, and be, in a position to benefit from those colleagues' *social support*. At least three factors are important here. First, to the extent that individuals perceive themselves to share identity in any given context, then it follows from self-categorization theory that they should be both more motivated and more likely to help each other out (i.e., to cooperate; Turner et al., 1987).

Second, by the same token, a sense of shared identity should also incline individuals to make more positive secondary appraisals of any organizational challenges they confront because this should engender a sense that "we are in this together" rather than that "I must deal with this alone" (Haslam & Reicher, 2006). And because these perceptions of shared identity will generally bear a close relation to organizational reality, organizational members are also likely to be protected from those workplace stressors that are targeted specifically at isolated individuals – the most significant of which is probably workplace *bullying* (O'Brien & Haslam, 2003).

Third, because social identity provides individuals with the basis for a shared cognitive framework, this means that any help which they offer each other is likely to be interpreted in the spirit in which it is intended. In contrast, if individuals do not perceive themselves to share identity – because they are acting in terms of opposed (us–them) or lower-level (me–you) self-categorizations – then not only are they less likely to support each other, but any support that they do provide is liable to be misinterpreted.

Support for the first of these ideas comes from a large number of studies which show that organizational identification is an extremely powerful predictor of employees' willingness to engage in acts of *organizational citizenship* (Organ, 1988, 1997). This work attests to the fact that – when it comes to making personal sacrifices in order to advance the organization as whole (e.g., by helping out new employees, or contributing to mentoring programmes) – individuals' identification with a relevant organizational unit is a far better predictor of their behaviour than a range of alternative candidate variables, including the rewards they receive and their personal goals and preferences (Ouwerkerk, Ellemers, & De Gilder, 1999; Tyler, 1999; Tyler & Blader, 2000).

Within the social identity literature more generally, a great deal of experimental and survey evidence speaks to the fact that people's willingness to help others is enhanced to the extent that they perceive themselves and those others to be members of the same social category (e.g., Stürmer & Snyder, 2010; Van Dick, Grojean, Christ, & Wieseke, 2006; see also Haslam, Reicher, & Levine, this volume). By the same token, people are also found to respond more positively to the advice and input of others, and are much more likely to take it on board, if they see those others as members of an ingroup rather than an outgroup (Haslam, Jetten, O'Brien, & Jacobs, 2004). Importantly though, experimental research has supported SCT's assertion that these processes are context-sensitive and change meaningfully as a function of factors that serve to make particular group memberships salient (Levine, Prosser, Evans, & Reicher, 2005). Accordingly, the member of Team X who at one point in time is offered little or no help by a person who defines themselves as a member of Team Y, may be given, and benefit from, generous support from the very same person in another context where these employees recategorize themselves in terms of a shared higher-order organizational identity (e.g., as members of the same department).

Proposition 5

To the extent that members of an organization (or organizational unit) identify strongly with that organization (or unit), their responses to stressors will influence, and will be influenced by, the responses of others who are representative of that identity. This will increase the likelihood of the organization (or unit) developing a collective response to those stressors.

As well as potentially helping individuals to cope with various stressors that they face in the workplace, it is also the case that the process of mutual support that is facilitated by a sense of shared organizational identity provides organizational members with a basis, and a motivation, for developing a shared understanding of their stress-related experiences. This follows from SCT's assertion that shared social identity is a basis for *social influence* that allows people to move beyond essentially idiosyncratic views of the world and work towards collective understandings of it. Moreover, whereas the views that they alone hold (on the basis of their personal experiences and identity) will tend to be perceived by individuals as matters of *opinion*, those that they ultimately come to share with fellow ingroup members are more likely to be seen as matters of *fact* – and hence to be held with greater conviction and certainty.

Although these ideas have been tested extensively in the field of social psychology (e.g., see Haslam, Turner, Oakes, McGarty, & Reynolds, 1998), they have been comparatively underexplored in the organizational domain. Nevertheless, there is some evidence from the stress literature that speaks to this point. Most particularly, it is clear that "stress epidemics" (e.g., mass sociogenic illnesses such as Sick Building Syndrome and Repetitive Strain Injury) tend to reflect the contours of shared group membership rather than simply commonalities of physical experience. In the first instance, these complaints are typically associated with workers (generally women; Sternberg & Wall, 1995) perceiving that they do *not* share identity with their (generally male) managers and are not supported by them (Macfarlane, Hunt, & Silman, 2000). Yet, at the same time, the organizational contexts in which these complaints tend to become most pronounced are those in which employees can validate their experiences through interaction with fellow group members. Indeed, this is one reason why employers (who will often want to downplay the significance of such experiences) are frequently observed to personalize such complaints and to isolate those who make them from their peers (Haslam, 2004).

As a corollary of this, if workers are unable to act in terms of shared identity then their capacity to mount a collective response to particular stressors is likely to be limited. Evidence to this effect is provided by James (1997) in a study which looked at the work experience and health-related outcomes of Black and White Americans. This study found that Black workers were less likely than Whites to develop a sense of shared identity in the workplace (particularly with their supervisors) and, as a result, were less likely to develop organized, mutually supportive, responses to the stressors that they faced (e.g., those associated with prejudice and discrimination). This in turn was associated with their having more health-related problems as measured by absence from work, visits to the doctor, use of prescription medicines, and hospitalization.

An integrative proposition

The proposed relationships between organizational identification and (a) stress and (b) well-being are partly mediated by effective social support and collective responses to stressors.

Our discussion of empirical evidence in the previous sections might appear to suggest that the five propositions we have outlined have been independently developed and tested by those various social identity researchers who are interested in issues of stress and well-being in the workplace (and elsewhere). In fact, though, most previous studies have sought to provide an integrated analysis of these propositions. In part, this reflects researchers' desire to develop parsimonious models of well-being and stress processes, but it also arises from the fact that the principles that inform this research are already quite well integrated within the social identity tradition.

The greatest part of that work that has specified and tested such integrations has been concerned to examine the capacity for social support to mediate relationships between organizational identification and both well-being and stress. In addition to the direct paths specified by Propositions 1 and 2, an indirect path thus suggests that organizational identification can both enhance well-being and minimize stress because it is a basis for employees to provide each other with beneficial forms of social support (as specified by Proposition 4). Consistent with this model, Haslam and colleagues' (2005) study of bomb disposal experts and bar staff provided statistical evidence that social support was a partial mediator of relationships between workteam identification and both stress and well-being. This pattern was also replicated by O'Brien and Haslam (2003) in a much larger study of over 1,000 hospital workers. Outside the organizational domain, the capacity for identification to increase feelings of social support and thereby minimize the negative impact of identity-related stressors (e.g., exposure to prejudice) on well-being has also been demonstrated in a large number of studies (Branscombe, Schmitt, & Harvey, 1999; see also Branscombe, Fernández, Gómez, & Cronin, this volume).

Yet just as social support can mediate the direct relationship between identification and well-being (and stress), so too the development of a collective response to stress can mediate the relationship between support and well-being. As we noted above, this is because, where it is effective, the experience of social support can reduce individuals' sense that the challenges of work life must be confronted alone and also give them a practical, embodied sense of the group as a positive force. Whereas individually, employees' coping strategies are likely to involve attempting to avoid or deny the impact of particular stressors, as members of a functioning group they can work together to try to *resist* those stressors (see Haslam & Reicher, 2006).

To date, relatively little work has been conducted to test this proposition. In large part this is a reflection of the tendency for researchers to conceptualize – and hence study – stress and well-being as individual-level issues, rather than as processes that have a collective dimension. Nevertheless, research that has explored issues of *collective protest* does provide some evidence that is consistent with this point. In the first instance, this work shows clearly that workplace social identification (in particular, with a trade union) is a very good predictor (e.g., $r = .62$; Kelly & Kelly, 1994) of individuals' willingness to participate in industrial protest (and that it is a far better predictor than other candidate variables such as a sense of political efficacy or a collectivist orientation; Kelly, 1993; Veenstra & Haslam, 2000). Yet, having participated in such action, individuals also tend to report greater levels of intragroup trust and an enhanced sense of collective efficacy (Klandermans & Oegema, 1992). This in turn feeds into a sense of collective empowerment and self-positivity (even if, in objective terms, the industrial action is actually unsuccessful; Drury, Cocking, Beale, Hanson, & Rapley, 2005; see also Cocking & Drury, 2004).

Much more work needs to be done to clarify the nature of this pathway, but what evidence there is points to the fact that the experience of standing shoulder-to-shoulder with one's workmates is bound up with processes of mutual identification (both deriving from shared identity but also helping to build it) and can be an effective way both of tackling stress and enhancing a sense of collective purpose and well-being. As Haslam and Reicher (2006) observe, a key reason for this is that such experiences encourage people to look beyond the ways in which stressors are changing them (for the worse) and to focus instead on ways in which they can change those stressors (for the better).

CONCLUSION: CAVEATS, COMPLICATIONS, AND CHOICES

In this chapter we have identified five key propositions related to the impact of social identity processes on stress and well-being in the workplace. As well as providing a concise review of evidence which supports these propositions, we have also shown how they lend themselves to relatively parsimonious integration, along the lines illustrated in Figure 10.1. As this figure suggests, the one-sentence summary of our argument is that identification with an organization (or a lower-level organizational unit) is predicted to have positive effects on health and well-being, some of which

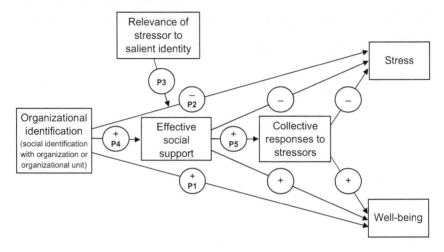

Figure 10.1 Pathways from organizational identification to stress and well-being (integrating propositions 1 to 5; P1 to P5).

are direct but others of which are mediated by both social support and collective responses to self-threatening stressors. Expressed slightly differently, our claim is that feeling, and being, part of a group is good for organizational members because this allows them to capitalize (psychologically and materially) on resources and power that only groups can provide. In even simpler terms, we would claim that organizational group memberships have positive effects because they allow individuals to fulfil their potential to be social beings (Haslam et al., 2009).

It is clearly the case, however, that a great deal of work needs to be done in order to test and elaborate upon these arguments – not least because, in the form presented here, they are relatively unnuanced. In particular, there is a need to explore the implications of the fact that many (if not most) employees have *multiple* sources of social identification in the workplace (e.g., Ashforth & Johnson, 2001). The interrelationships between these identities will clearly have implications for well-being – most obviously because, where they are unaligned or incompatible, their management can itself be a source of stress (Iyer, Jetten, Tsivrikos, Postmes, & Haslam, 2009; Van Dick, Van Knippenberg, Kerschreiter, Hertel, & Wieseke, 2008). Relatedly, *over*-identification with a single organization (or organizational unit) may ultimately compromise well-being because it encourages individuals to invest heavily in that one group membership, but to neglect others that might provide them with greater balance and breath (Johnson, 2002; Van Steenbergen, Ellemers, Haslam, & Urlings, 2008). Highly identified employees may also be particularly prone to suffering from burnout if an organization fails or if they are forced to relinquish their group membership (Van Dick et al., 2004).

Yet bearing the significance of such issues in mind, what is perhaps most surprising about the literature on stress and well-being in the workplace is how little attention this has hitherto paid to questions of groups and identity. As testament to this fact, between us, on our bookshelves we have around a dozen leading books on stress in the workplace (e.g., Cooper et al., 2001; Cooper & Robertson, 2001; Firth-Cozens & Paine, 1999). Excellent as these volumes are, not one includes mention of "groups" or "(social or organizational) identity" in its index (or appreciable treatment of the topics in the text). Moreover, in the plethora of reports and brochures that discuss ways of tackling stress, few discuss the palliative power of the organizational group.

There are many reasons for this. The most basic is simply that much of the previous research in this field has been informed by clinical models that tend to be highly individualistic (Folkman & Moskowitz, 2004). A somewhat darker reason, however, may be that the paymasters of researchers in this area are reluctant to explore and expose the capacity for organizational subgroups to allow their members to combat stress through collective endeavour (Haslam, 2004). For if groups allow employees not only to cope with stressors in the workplace (e.g., high demands, low control, lack of support) but also to challenge and remove them (e.g., through collective action), then it is clear that they can do much more than simply enhance well-being and reduce stress – they can also produce organizational *change* (Tajfel & Turner, 1979).

In the end, then, it may be the reluctance of organizational leaders to countenance real change (of a form that they themselves have not engineered and do not tightly control) that encourages them to prefer an asocial curse to a social cure. Yet as we saw at the start of this chapter, this strategy comes with a very high price tag. How long can we continue to pay?

References

Abrams, D., Ando, K., & Hinkle, S. (1998). Psychological attachment to the group: Cross-cultural differences in organizational identification and subjective norms as predictors of workers' turnover intentions. *Personality and Social Psychology Bulletin, 24,* 1027–1039.

Ashforth, B. E., & Johnson, S. A. (2001). Which hat to wear? The relative salience of multiple identities in organizational contexts. In M. A. Hogg & D. J. Terry (Eds.), *Social identity processes in organizational contexts* (pp. 31–48). Philadelphia, PA: Psychology Press.

Ashforth, B. E., & Mael, F. (1989). Social Identity Theory and the organization. *Academy of Management Review, 14,* 20–39.

Baumeister, R. F., & Leary, M. R. (1995). The need to belong: Desire for interpersonal attachments as a fundamental human motivation. *Psychological Bulletin, 117,* 497–529.

Bizumic, B., Reynolds, K. J., Turner, J. C., Bromhead, D., & Subasic, E. (2009). The role of the group in individual functioning: School identification and the psychological well-being of staff and students. *Applied Psychology: An International Review, 58,* 171–192.

Black, C. (2008). *Working for a healthier tomorrow.* Colegate, Norwich: UK Cabinet Office.

Branscombe, N. R., Schmitt, M. T., & Harvey, R. D. (1999). Perceiving pervasive discrimination among African-Americans: Implications for group identification and well-being. *Journal of Personality and Social Psychology, 77,* 135–149.

Cartwright, S., & Cooper, C. L. (Eds.) (2009). *The Oxford handbook of organizational well-being.* Oxford, UK: Oxford University Press.

Cocking, C., & Drury, J. (2004). Generalization of efficacy as a function of collective action and intergroup relations: Involvement in an anti-roads struggle. *Journal of Applied Social Psychology, 34,* 417–444.

Cooper, C. L., Dewe, P. J., & O'Driscoll, M. P. (2001). *Organizational stress: A review and critique of theory, research and applications.* London, UK: Sage.

Cooper, C., & Robertson, I., (Eds.) (2001). *Well-being in organizations.* Chichester, UK: Wiley.

Drury, J., Cocking, C., Beale, J., Hanson, C., & Rapley, F. (2005). The phenomenology of empowerment in collective action. *British Journal of Social Psychology, 44,* 309–328.

Ellemers, N., De Gilder, D., & Haslam, S. A. (2004). Motivating individuals and groups at work: A social identity perspective on leadership and group performance. *Academy of Management Review, 29,* 459–478.

Firth-Cozens, J., & Paine, R. (1999). *Stress in health professionals.* Chichester, UK: Wiley.

Folkman, S., & Moskowitz, J. T. (2004). Coping: Pitfalls and promise. *Annual Review of Psychology, 55,* 745–774.

Haslam, S. A. (2004). *Psychology in organizations: The social identity approach.* London, UK: Sage.

Haslam, S. A., Jetten, J., O'Brien, A. T., & Jacobs, E. (2004). Social identity, social influence, and reactions to potentially stressful tasks: Support for the self-categorization model of stress. *Stress and Health, 20,* 3–9.

Haslam, S. A., Jetten, J., & Waghorn, C. (2009). Social identification, stress, and citizenship in teams: A five-phase longitudinal study. *Stress and Health, 25,* 21–30.

Haslam, S. A., O'Brien, A. T., Jetten, J., Vormedal, K., & Penna, S. (2005). Taking the strain: Social identity, social support and the experience of stress. *British Journal of Social Psychology, 44,* 355–370.

Haslam, S. A., Powell, C., & Turner, J. C. (2000). Social identity, self-categorization, and work motivation: Rethinking the contribution of the group to positive and sustainable organizational outcomes. *Applied Psychology: An International Review, 49,* 319–339.

Haslam, S. A., & Reicher, S. D. (2006). Stressing the group: Social identity and the unfolding dynamics of responses to stress. *Journal of Applied Psychology, 91,* 1037–1052.

Haslam, S. A., Reicher, S. D., & Platow, M. (2011). *The new psychology of leadership. Identity, influence and power.* Hove, UK: Psychology Press.

Haslam, S. A., Turner, J. C., Oakes, P. J., McGarty, C., & Reynolds, K. J. (1998). The group as a basis for emergent stereotype consensus. *European Review of Social Psychology, 8,* 203–239.

Health and Safety Executive (2009). *Health and safety statistics 2008/09*. London, UK: National Statistics Office, London.

Hersby, M. D., Ryan, M. K., & Jetten, J. (2009). Getting together to get ahead: The role of social structure on women's networking. *British Journal of Management, 20*, 415–430.

Highhouse, S., Thornbury, E. E., & Little, I. S. (2007). Social identity functions of attraction to organizations. *Organizational Behavior and Human Decision Processes, 103*, 134–146.

Iyer, A., Jetten, J., Tsivrikos, D., Postmes, T., & Haslam, S. A. (2009). The more (and the more compatible) the merrier: Multiple group memberships and identity compatibility as predictors of adjustment after life transitions. *British Journal of Social Psychology, 48*, 707–733.

Jackson, S. E., Schwab, R. L., & Schuler, R. S. (1986). Toward an understanding of the burnout phenomenon. *Journal of Applied Psychology, 71*, 630–640.

James, K. (1997). Worker social identity and health-related costs for organizations: A comparative study between ethnic groups. *Journal of Occupational Health Psychology, 2*, 108–117.

Jetten, J., Haslam, S. A., Iyer, A., & Haslam, C. (2009). Turning to others in times of change: Shared identity and coping with stress. In S. Stürmer & M. Snyder (Eds.), *The psychology of prosocial behavior: Group processes, intergroup relations, and helping* (pp. 139–156). Oxford, UK: Wiley-Blackwell.

Johnson, S. (2002). *Management by stress: The influence of social identification in empowered teams on occupational stress and performance*. Unpublished thesis, The Australian National University, Australia.

Kelly, C. (1993). Group identification, intergroup perceptions and collective action. *European Review of Social Psychology, 4*, 59–83.

Kelly, C., & Kelly, J. (1994). Who gets involved in collective action? Social psychological determinants of individual participation in trade unions. *Human Relations, 47*, 63–88.

Klandermans, B., & Oegema, D. (1992). Potentials, networks, motivations and barriers: Steps toward participation in social movements. *American Sociological Review, 52*, 519–531.

Kramer, R. M., & Tyler, T. R. (Eds.) (1996). *Trust in organizations: Frontiers of theory and research*. Thousand Oaks, CA: Sage.

Lazarus, R. S. (1991). *Emotion and adaptation*. New York, NY: Oxford University Press.

Lazarus, R. S., & Folkman, S. (1984). *Stress, appraisal, and coping*. New York, NY: Springer.

Levine, M., Prosser, A., Evans, D., & Reicher, S. (2005). Identity and emergency intervention: How social group membership and inclusiveness of group boundaries shapes helping behavior. *Personality and Social Psychology Bulletin, 31*, 443–453.

Levine, M., & Reicher, S. (1996). Making sense of symptoms: Self-categorisation and the meaning of illness and injury. *British Journal of Social Psychology, 35*, 245–256.

Levine, R. M. (1999). Identity and illness: The effects of identity salience and frame of reference on evaluation of illness and injury. *British Journal of Health Psychology, 4*, 63–80.

Macfarlane, G. J., Hunt, I. M., & Silman, A. J. (2000). Role of mechanical and psychosocial factors in the onset of forearm pain: Prospective population-based study. *British Medical Journal, 321,* 676–679.

Mael, F., & Ashforth, B. E. (1992). Alumni and their alma mater: A partial test of the reformulated model of organizational identification. *Journal of Organizational Behavior, 13,* 103–123.

Maslach, C., Jackson, S. E., & Leiter, M. P. (1996). *Maslach Burnout Inventory manual* (3rd ed.). Palo Alto, CA: Consulting Psychologists Press.

Maslow, A. H. (1943). A theory of motivation. *Psychological Review, 50,* 370–396.

O'Brien, A. T., & Haslam, S. A. (2003). *Shaping the future (Report in response to the issuing of a Stress Improvement Notice from the UK Health and Safety Executive).* Exeter, UK: School of Psychology, University of Exeter, UK.

Organ, D. W. (1988). *Organizational citizenship behavior: The good soldier syndrome.* Lexington, MA: Lexington.

Organ, D. W. (1997). Organizational citizenship behavior: Its construct clean-up time. *Human Performance, 10,* 85–97.

Ouwerkerk, J. W., Ellemers, N., & De Gilder, D. (1999). Group commitment and individual effort in experimental and organizational contexts. In N. Ellemers, R. Spears, & B. J. Doosje (Eds.), *Social identity: Context, commitment, content* (pp. 184–204). Oxford, UK: Blackwell.

Patmore, A. (2006). *The truth about stress.* London, UK: Atlantic Books.

Peters, K., Tevichapong, P., Haslam, S. A., & Postmes, T. (2010). Making the organization fly: Organizational identification and citizenship in full-service and low-cost airlines. *Journal of Personnel Psychology, 9,* 145–148.

Platow, M. J., Haslam, S. A., Foddy, M., & Grace, D. M. (2003). Leadership as the outcome of self-categorization processes. In D. van Knippenberg & M. A. Hogg (Eds.), *Leadership and power: Identity processes in groups and organizations* (pp. 34–47). London, UK: Sage.

Pratt, M. G. (1998). To be or not to be? Central questions in organizational identification. In D. A. Whetten & P. C. Godfrey (Eds.), *Identity in organizations. Building theory through conversations* (pp. 171–207). Thousand Oaks, CA: Sage.

Pratt, M. G. (2001). Social identity dynamics in modern organizations: An organizational psychology/organizational behavior perspective. In M. A. Hogg & D. J. Terry (Eds.), *Social identity processes in organizational contexts* (pp. 13–30). Philadelphia, PA: Psychology Press.

Randsley de Moura, G., Abrams, D., Retter, C., Gunnarsdottir, S., & Ando, K. (2009). Identification as an organizational anchor: How identification and job satisfaction combine to predict turnover intention. *European Journal of Social Psychology, 11,* 129–149.

Riketta, M. (2005). Organizational identification: A meta-analysis. *Journal of Vocational Behavior, 66,* 358–384.

Riketta, M., & Van Dick, R. (2005). Foci of attachment in organizations: A meta-analysis comparison of the strength and correlates of work-group versus organizational commitment and identification. *Journal of Vocational Behavior, 67,* 490–510.

Ryan, M. K., Haslam, S. A., Hersby, M. D., Kulich, C., & Atkins, C. (2007). Opting out or pushed off the edge? The glass cliff and the precariousness of women's leadership positions. *Social and Personality Psychology Compass, 1,* 266–279.

Sternberg, B., & Wall, S. (1995). Why do women report sick building symptoms more often than men? *Social Science & Medicine, 40*, 491–502.

Stürmer, S., & Snyder, M. (2010). *The psychology of prosocial behavior: group processes, intergroup relations, and helping*. Chichester, UK: Blackwell.

Tajfel, H., & Turner, J. C. (1979). An integrative theory of intergroup conflict. In W. G. Austin & S. Worchel (Eds.), *The social psychology of intergroup relations* (pp. 33–47). Monterey, CA: Brooks/Cole.

Turner, J. C. (1991). *Social influence*. Milton Keynes, UK: Open University Press.

Turner, J. C., Hogg, M. A., Oakes, P. J., Reicher, S. D., & Wetherell, M. S. (1987). *Rediscovering the social group*. Oxford, UK: Blackwell.

Tyler, T. R. (1999). Why people co-operate with organizations: An identity-based perspective. In B. M. Staw & R. Sutton (Eds.), *Research in organizational behaviour* (Vol. 21, pp. 201–246). Greenwich, CT: JAI Press.

Tyler, T. R., & Blader, S. (2000). *Co-operation in groups: Procedural justice, social identity and behavioral engagement*. Philadelphia, PA: Psychology Press.

Van Dick, R., Christ, O., Stellmacher, J., Wagner, U., Ahlswede, O., Grubba, C., et al. (2004). Should I stay or should I go? Explaining turnover intentions with organizational identification and job satisfaction. *British Journal of Management, 15*, 351–360.

Van Dick, R., Grojean, M. W., Christ, O., & Wieseke, J. (2006). Identity and the extra-mile: Relationships between organizational identification and organizational citizenship behaviour. *British Journal of Management, 17*, 283–301.

Van Dick, R., Van Knippenberg, D., Kerschreiter, R., Hertel, G., & Wieseke, J. (2008). Interactive effects of work group and organizational identification on job satisfaction and extra-role behavior. *Journal of Vocational Behavior, 72*, 388–399.

Van Dick, R., & Wagner, U. (2002). Social identification among school teachers: Dimensions, foci, and correlates. *European Journal of Work and Organizational Psychology, 11*, 129–149.

Van Knippenberg, D., & Ellemers, N. (2003). Social identity and group performance: Identification as the key to collective effort. In S. A. Haslam, D. van Knippenberg, M. J. Platow, & N. Ellemers (Eds.), *Social identity at work: Developing theory for organizational practice* (pp. 29–42). Philadelphia, PA: Psychology Press.

Van Steenbergen, E. F., Ellemers, N., Haslam, S. A., & Urlings, F. (2008). There is nothing either good or bad but thinking makes it so: Informational support and cognitive appraisal of the work–family interface. *Journal of Occupational and Organizational Psychology, 81*, 349–367. (Special Issue on 'Innovations in the study of the work–family interface'.)

Veenstra, K., & Haslam, S. A. (2000). Willingness to participate in industrial protest: Exploring social identification in context. *British Journal of Social Psychology, 39*, 153–172.

Veenstra, K., Haslam, S. A., & Reynolds, K. J. (2004). The psychology of casualization: Evidence for the mediating roles of security, status and social identification. *British Journal of Social Psychology, 43*, 499–514.

Wegge, J., Schuh, S. C., & Van Dick, R. (in press). I feel bad – We feel good!? Emotions as a driver for identity and identity as a buffer against stress. *Stress and Health*.

Wegge, J., & Van Dick, R. (2006). Arbeitszufriedenheit, Emotionen bei der Arbeit und berufliche Identifikation [Job satisfaction, emotions at work and organizational identification]. In L. Fischer (Hrsg.), *Arbeitszufriedenheit* (pp. 11–36) [Job satisfaction]. Göttingen, Germany: Verlag für Angewandte Psychologie.

Wegge, J., Van Dick, R., Fisher, G. K., Wecking, C., & Moltzen, K. (2006). Work motivation, organisational identification, and well-being in call centre work. *Work and Stress, 20*, 60–83.

11 Collective resilience in mass emergencies and disasters

A social identity model

John Drury
University of Sussex

Following the 9-11 attacks in the United States in 2001, the concept of "resilience" increased in prominence among policy makers and organizations concerned with national security. In the same period the United Kingdom has not only faced the global terrorist threat, but also a fuel crisis, an outbreak of foot-and-mouth disease, serious flooding, and fears of pandemic flu. These events were seen as sufficiently damaging to the national infrastructure to warrant greater coordination in emergency planning and response. Hence among the provisions of the 2004 Civil Contingencies Act is the requirement for the emergency services, local authorities, and National Health Service bodies jointly to assess the risk of particular emergencies occurring, and to produce plans for local "resilience" – that is, adaptive response and recovery from such emergencies.

This chapter argues that *crowds* can provide the mutual support, coordinated activity and other features of resilience that enable people to cope psychologically with mass emergencies and disasters. I begin by showing how the practices and policies that flow from the concept of "resilience" stand in stark opposition to policies based on an assumption of (psycho-social) *vulnerability*. These competing assumptions of "vulnerability" and "resilience" are evident in the various theories of mass emergency behaviour. The most well-known of these theories – "mass panic", with its implication of pathological overreaction and reversion to primitive "instincts" in the face of danger – has largely been discredited by the research evidence. Contemporary theories of both mass emergency behaviour and "collective resilience" refer instead to the influence of existing social bonds. Ties of family relationships, affiliation, social roles and networks would appear to explain why most emergencies and disasters are characterized by social, adaptive behaviour, and indeed why helping among survivors is so widespread.

However, I will show that there is another, crucial, source of collective resilience in emergencies and disasters, over and above pre-existing social bonds. Specifically, people in a crowd tend to *come together*, both psychologically and behaviourally, simply by virtue of sharing a "common fate" in relation to the emergency or disaster. This spontaneous "togetherness" can be understood psychologically as the shift from a personal to a shared social identity that occurs when the context itself shifts to being structured in terms of intergroup rather than interpersonal relations (Turner, 1982). This is explained in the Social Identity (SI) model of collective resilience that can be used to develop a set of predictions concerning the antecedents and consequences of shared social identity in mass emergencies and disasters. In this chapter, I consider the evidence that supports these predictions before drawing out the practical and policy implications of the SI model. While the crowd has traditionally been seen as a "social problem", this chapter shows how crowd psychology can be the "social solution" that enables us to cope with the most catastrophic of crises.

"RESILIENCE" VERSUS "VULNERABILITY"

In psychology, the term "resilience" usually means *personal* resilience. The concept emerged in the 1970s in response to the (over)emphasis on the effects of psychological damage suffered in early life (Masten & Gewirtz, 2006). Here, resilience refers to "a person's capacity for adapting psychologically, emotionally and physically reasonably well and without lasting detriment to self, relationships or personal development in the face of adversity, threat or challenge" (Williams, 2007, p. 268). Such resilience may be conceptualized and measured as a given individual "trait" (e.g., Bonanno, 2004; Fredrickson, Tugade, Waugh, & Larkin, 2003). However, it is also argued to be a dynamic psychosocial *process* of forming, maintaining and drawing upon ongoing relationships (Williams, 2007; Williams & Drury, 2010, in press).

In social-organizational contexts, resilience refers to the recovery and continued functioning of infrastructure – including public services, governing and administrative bodies, business and commerce, transport systems, and power supplies – in the face of natural disaster or terrorist attack. In common with the psychological account, resilience is understood as an adaptive response to challenge, stress, or trauma, leading to recovery (see Masten & Gewirtz, 2006). Further, in both psychology and social-organizational contexts, resilience is conceptualized as an inherent potential. Resilience is therefore a positive concept in that it suggests hope for the future prospects of the individual or collective entity; even the most serious damage is repairable.

Furedi (2007) argues that much current security policy supposedly aimed at furthering resilience is actually informed, and hence undermined, by assumptions of "*vulnerability*".[1] The "vulnerability" framework emphasizes the inherent psychological and social frailties of, and risks to, the public. An example that reflects the assumption of vulnerability is the claim that, since people are collectively prone to over-react, they cannot be trusted with information about the extent of any danger they face (Drury, 2002).

Communication as a strategy in emergency preparedness and response is therefore downgraded, to avoid irrational panic among members of the public (Ripley, 2008). Instead, sensitive information is restricted to the establishment elite and their functionaries, who not only "know best", but are somehow immune to the pathology that befalls the rest of the population (Drury, 2004).

The vulnerability framework is also used to support the claim that collective reactions to disasters will take the form of widespread "disorderly" rioting and criminal, acquisitive "looting", as the delicate veneer of civilized values gives way to an underlying barbarism (Tierney, Bevc, & Kuligowski, 2006). Once the inherently volatile masses have descended to this primitive psychological state, it is thought to be pointless trying to reason with them about their civic obligations – let alone attempting to involve them as active partners in disaster response. Instead, greater legal powers for government, and even coercive force, should be used to restore social order. Examples include the centralized and mistrustful policies of "Homeland Security" in the United States post 9-11 (Dynes, 2003; Tierney, 2003), and the dehumanizing discourses and treatment of the (black working class) survivors of Hurricane Katrina (Dynes & Rodriguez, 2006; Tierney et al., 2006). Expert and elite control is reinforced, for our own good.

Furthermore, in terms of "cures" for "ills", the vulnerability framework medicalizes experiences of distress in response to mass emergencies and disasters as forms of serious mental disorder ("trauma") that require specialized psychiatric intervention (Wessely, 2004, 2005).

Working backwards through each of these points, critics argue, first, that *distress* in response to disasters is "normal", not a *disorder*. Distress eases with time, and with practical assistance. In the aftermath of an emergency or disaster, only a tiny minority will need psychiatric treatment (Williams & Drury, 2010, in press). Second, the prevalence of looting following disasters is exaggerated by the mass media (Tierney et al., 2006). More importantly, what is at issue are the reasons for and definitions of the behaviour that outsiders label as "looting". In the aftermath of Hurricane Hugo (1989) and Hurricane Katrina (2005), the taking of necessities from abandoned shops was widely supported; the goods were socially shared and the action was socially necessary (Rodriguez, Trainor, & Quarantelli, 2006). The authorities need to facilitate such adaptive popular initiatives; containing and controlling communities affected by disasters could mean depriving them of the independence and agency they need for survival. Finally, far from resulting in panic, provision of practical information in fact enables preparation, effective action, and coping (Glass & Schoch-Spana, 2002; Proulx & Sime, 1991). It is the *lack* of information that causes dysfunctional emotions, such as anxiety (Wessely, 2005). We can go further, however, and show that "mass panic" has been discredited as an account of crowd behaviour in emergencies and disasters.

FROM "MASS PANIC" TO "SOCIAL BONDS" IN EMERGENCIES AND DISASTERS

Mass panic is both an image in popular culture and a family of academic theories. As an explanation for behaviour in emergencies and disasters, mass panic is emblematic of the vulnerability framework, for it suggests that the social group is a conduit for inherent tendencies to psychological frailty, pathology, and maladaptive behaviour when faced with stress. However, research has demonstrated that the social bonds that mass panic theories suggest are eclipsed by "instincts" for personal survival are in fact extremely durable.

Mass panic

The necessary conditions for mass panic to occur are said to be threefold: (i) life-threatening danger; (ii) limited opportunity for escape; (iii) and, crucially, the presence of a crowd (Quarantelli, 2001). Some or all of the following are said to be its defining features: (a) fears that are disproportionate to the actual danger, since emotions overwhelm reasoning; (b) primitive instincts ("fight or flight") that supersede socialized, civilized values and rules; (c) the shedding of social obligations and the loss of behavioural control, which together mean that individualistic ("selfish") competition between people predominates; and (d) the absence of collective coordination (for reviews of the various panic theories, see Chertkoff & Kushigian, 1999; Mawson, 2007). Accordingly, mass panic poses a serious public health and safety concern, since it suggests that human reactions to emergencies – especially *collective* human reactions – lead to more problems (e.g., fatalities) than the danger that people are trying to escape from.

The Cocoanut Grove theatre fire of 1942 is one of the "classic" textbook examples of supposed mass panic (e.g., Schultz, 1964). During a performance at the theatre, fire quickly spread through the whole building, resulting in 492 deaths among those trapped inside. However, a close inspection of the event would seem to absolve the crowd of accusations of "selfishness" or irrationality. There were no fire exit signs; staff tried to lead people to safety, but had no knowledge of fire exits; and the revolving doors at the entrance malfunctioned. Indeed, it was the nightclub owners who were held responsible for the deaths, and they were successfully prosecuted for negligence (Chertkoff & Kushigian, 1999).

Mass panic might provide a convenient warrant for blaming crowds for tragedies (Ripley, 2008). But reviews suggest that it is rare (Fritz, 1961/1996) or even mythical (Keating, 1982; Sime, 1990). Most flight behaviour in mass emergencies cannot be assumed to be irrational and is not antisocial (Quarantelli, 1960). Detailed case studies concur. The World Trade Center attack (9-11) is the most well-researched disaster in history. Despite the extreme danger, density, and urgency of the situation, "panic" was displayed by only a tiny minority of individuals, not by the crowd (e.g., Blake, Galea, Westeng, & Dixon, 2004; Connell, 2001; Proulx & Fahy, 2003).

Social bonds

The overwhelming conclusion of numerous case studies and reviews is that socially structured and orderly behaviour, and in particular helping, is far more common in mass emergencies and disasters than individualistic mass panic (e.g., Barton, 1969).

The Beverly Hills Supper Club fire of 1977, at which 164 people died, has been the subject of numerous analyses and is a good illustration of this point. Up to 2,800 people were present in the building when the fire broke out. During the evacuation of the dinner theatre and other public rooms in the building, routine, everyday patterns of social behaviour were maintained, including queuing, helping each other up, expressions of courtesy (such as the greater assistance offered to the elderly and infirm than the able bodied), and role conformity (e.g., men helping women more than vice versa). Even at the point of greatest pressure to escape the fire and fumes, social bonds held. People strove to support and remain with their friends and loved ones (Johnson, 1988). Indeed, patterns of helping and subgroup clustering, as well as variations in exit times, survival, and mortality rates are consistent with the view that "normal" social micro-organization – existing rules, roles and relationships – structured evacuation behaviour. In particular, people tried to remain in their affiliation groups during evacuation, even if it delayed their own exit (Cornwell, 2003; Feinberg & Johnson, 2001). Contemporary psychological accounts (e.g., Donald & Canter, 1992) agree in crucial respects with sociologists that everyday roles, rules, and relationships are not dissolved through panic but continue to govern behaviour in emergencies. Similarly, in Mawson's (2005, 2007) affiliation theory, the "familiar" reduces our fear and "panic reactions"; hence our first impulse in an emergency is not personal escape but to seek out and stay close to familiar others (Sime, 1983).

Pre-existing social bonds are also central in recent accounts of *collective resilience*. Descriptively, the term has been used to refer to a community's coping processes (e.g., Hernández, 2002). More substantively, collective resilience has been explained in terms of the relational bonds and networks that hold communities together, provide support and protection, and facilitate recovery in times of extreme stress and during the process of resettlement (Fielding & Anderson, 2008).

There is widespread agreement, therefore, that pre-existing social bonds are enduring and protective in situations of extreme collective stress. However, there are both empirical and conceptual reasons for believing that such social bonds are neither necessary nor always sufficient to explain collectively resilient behaviour in emergencies and disasters. Social bonds are not necessary because, in many major incidents, the crowds that are affected are made up of many people who are strangers to each other, yet still there is evidence of widespread helping and other forms of social coordination. An example is the 2005 London terrorist bombings on public transport, discussed below. Social bonds are also insufficient in the sense that, since everyday life makes available a multitude of sometimes conflicting social bonds and norms, greater specification is required to understand why in an emergency people act on the basis of one social bond rather than another.

While the evidence of patterns of family and affiliate loyalty in mass emergencies is undeniable, there is another important source of collectively resilient and survival-oriented behaviours: the psychological togetherness, or "we-feeling", that arises within such events and which extends across the crowd as a whole. Proponents of "social bonds" theories of mass emergency behaviour acknowledge the prevalence of this spontaneous togetherness in emergency crowds (e.g., Aguirre, 2005; Aguirre, Torres, Gill, & Hotchkiss, 2011; Jacob, Mawson, Payton, & Guignard, 2008; Mawson, 2007). But, crucially, as they cannot explain such widespread togetherness in terms of pre-existing relationships, they neglect it as a source of resilience. While supposedly describing crowd events, social bonds accounts deny the explanatory role of the *crowd* as a dynamic, psychological entity in its own right. What is required, then, is a model of collective resilience in emergencies and disasters based on a notion of *mass emergent* sociality.

A SOCIAL IDENTITY MODEL OF COLLECTIVE RESILIENCE

The Social Identity (SI) model of collective resilience (Drury, Cocking, & Reicher, 2009b; Williams & Drury, 2009, 2010) is an application of the SI model of crowd psychology (Reicher & Drury, 2010; Reicher, in press). It is therefore grounded in the core concepts of self-categorization theory (SCT; Turner, Hogg, Oakes, Reicher, & Wetherell, 1987) and the wider SI approach (Tajfel & Turner, 1979).

The model has two parts: (i) antecedents (how do ad hoc crowds that are affected by emergencies come to share a social identity?), and (ii) consequences (how does this shared social identity affect participants' perceptions, expectations, motivations, and behaviours in ways that can contribute to collective survival, recovery, and well-being?; for a schematic representation see Figure 11.1).

ANTECEDENTS OF SHARED SOCIAL IDENTITY IN MASS EMERGENCIES

The SI model of crowd psychology makes a fundamental distinction between *physical* crowds (individuals who are simply co-located in space),

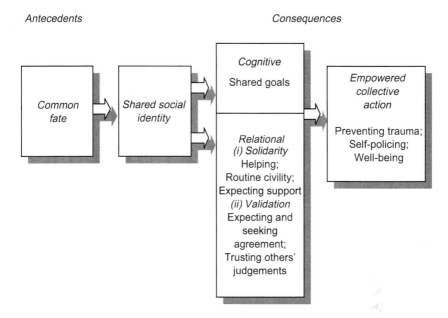

Antecedents   Consequences

Figure 11.1 The Social Identity model of collective resilience.

and *psychological* crowds (people who feel and act "as one"; Reicher & Drury, 2010). People *shift* from seeing themselves as unique individuals amongst other individuals to seeing themselves as fellow members of a crowd where a group-based self-definition is seen to best *fit* their social reality (Turner et al., 1987). Turner et al. (1987) cite a number of criteria for such fit and hence collective self-categorization, one of which is "common fate" (see also Campbell, 1958).

SI analyses of crowd conflict – including studies of anti-tax demonstrations, environmental direct actions, and football "hooliganism" – provide vivid illustrations of the way that common fate creates psychological group membership (for reviews, see Drury, Reicher, & Stott, in press). In each of the crowd events studied, members of an initially fragmented physical crowd came to share a social identity and hence act as one, but only in response to an external threat to them *as* crowd members. Specifically, the experience of indiscriminate police action (e.g., mounted and baton charges) brought people together, against the police as an outgroup.

In accounts of mass emergencies and disasters, it has likewise been suggested that an experience of common threat creates a sense of "we-ness" among survivors (Clarke, 2002; Fritz & Williams, 1957; Kaniasty & Norris, 1999; Solnit, 2009). Thus, based on evidence from over 144 studies of disasters, the sociologist Fritz (1961/1996, p. 58) offers this rich description of social and psychological transformation:

Since . . . the dangers in disasters . . . indiscriminately affect persons of all groups and statuses, there is a temporary breakdown in social class, ethnic group, and other hierarchical status distinctions, and a general democratization of the social structure. The reference changes from "only I have suffered" to "all of us have suffered; we are all in it together." This is the basis for the widespread feeling of community and equality of suffering found in disasters.

In cognitive terms, the social "figure and ground" shifts from "me in contrast to others", to "us in contrast to the emergency". In self-categorization terms, all those who perceive themselves equally (or "inter-changeably") threatened thereby come to categorize themselves as a psychological unit, in relation to that threat. The seriousness (salience) of the threat overrides other possible categorizations of those involved, thereby creating (or in some cases enhancing) a *shared social identity*.

We have recently tested the hypothesis that emergencies create a common fate among survivors, which in turn gives rise to a shared social identity, in three different research designs: a case study, a comparative event interview study, and an innovative role-play experiment. The limitations of each method are offset by the strengths of the others to provide convergent evidence in support of the hypothesis. We now describe each of these studies in turn.

On 7 July 2005, in a coordinated terrorist attack, four bomb blasts hit London's public transport system during the morning rush hour. The explosions on three Underground trains and a bus killed 56 people (including the four bombers) and injured over 700. Those in the bombed trains were left for some time literally in the dark, among the dying and dead, with few announcements, and with no way of knowing whether they would survive. As part of a case study of the event (Drury et al., 2009b), we took statements from 17 survivors.

Eleven respondents were explicit that there was a strong feeling of togetherness in the crowd in the period immediately after the explosions; only one denied that there was togetherness. Some contrasted this positive togetherness during the emergency with the (unpleasant) interpersonal competition and separateness they normally experienced travelling by Underground. We take this as evidence that a shared social identity arose among many survivors during the events. Most also said that they and others in the crowd felt in "danger of death"; where they (spontaneously) offered an explanation for the togetherness they perceived in the crowd, they attributed it to this shared danger.

In our comparative event study, we interviewed 21 survivors of 11 emergencies (see Drury, Cocking, & Reicher, 2009a). Almost all referred to emergent feelings of togetherness in the crowd. However, those independently judged to have experienced *high* crowd-unity were more likely to refer to "common fate" than those who experienced relatively *low* crowd-unity.

Our role-play experiment used Virtual Reality visualization to enhance engagement (Drury et al., 2009c, Study 1). The scenario was a busy underground rail station from which participants were asked to exit "as quickly as possible". Participants reported greater identification with the crowd when the reason they were given for the urgency was a fire threatening all passengers ("common fate") than when they were told it was in order to get to the sales ("individual competition").

In sum, the results of these three studies, which vary in their degree of control, and which employ different types of measures, converge on support for the predicted relationship between common fate and shared social identity.

CONSEQUENCES OF SHARED SOCIAL IDENTITY IN MASS EMERGENCIES

Becoming psychologically part of a crowd – seeing people as part of (collective) "self" rather than as "other" – entails two crucial psychological transformations: "cognitive" and "relational" (Reicher & Drury, 2010; Reicher, in press).

A cognitive transformation

The shift from "me" to "we" means that "self-interest" becomes interpreted in terms of *"our* interest". This is a profoundly practical, and future-oriented transformation, as it ties one's goals for action to those of the crowd. Collective survival may require immediate consensus over aims (e.g., whether and which route to evacuate). If group-normative actions are internalized as one's own, there is a sense of duty or motivation such that, even without discussion, people want to act in the collective interest – a process equivalent to "organizational citizenship" in formal groups (Haslam, 2004).

A relational transformation

While the cognitive transformation concerns values and goals, the relational transformation concerns how people act to and with each other. It comprises two aspects: social *solidarity* and social *validation.*

Solidarity

Within a psychological crowd, solidarity translates into the following consequences that can contribute towards survival and recovery: (i) helping; (ii) routine civility; and (iii) expectations of support.

In the case of helping, the dissolving of the psychological boundaries between "me" and "we" as a psychological group means that I will experience your distress as *"ours"*. Therefore I am motivated to help you (or, at least, I will not automatically put my personal needs first). Enhanced intervention to assist others when there is a shared social identity is well established in both experimental studies of individual reactions to distress (Levine, Prosser, Evans, & Reicher, 2005; see Haslam, Reicher, & Levine, this volume) and in interview studies of conflictual collective action (Drury & Reicher, 1999). However, helping someone in a mass emergency may involve a serious personal risk or cost to the helper. Such a situation therefore presents a much sterner test of this basic tenet of SCT than the scenarios employed in most research on altruism.

A preliminary experimental investigation of the hypothesis that shared social identity increases helping behaviours in a mass emergency was carried out using our Virtual Reality paradigm, as described above (Drury et al., 2009c). The visualization included four injured characters requiring help. Stopping to give help delayed the participant's exit time and increased their "danger of death" score, whereas ignoring these "victims" and pushing other characters aside – our measure of personal selfishness – meant a quicker exit time. Across two versions of the basic experimental design (Drury et al., 2009c, Studies 2 and 3), there was a consistent positive relationship between identification with the crowd and the amount of help given, and a negative relationship between such identification and personal selfishness.

In our London bombs study, the total dataset comprised accounts from over 90 survivors and 56 witnesses (see Drury et al., 2009b). Reports of personally selfish acts were rare, while helping was common. In the initial absence of the emergency services, survivors themselves acted as "first responders": applying makeshift bandages and tourniquets, sharing water, talking to keep each others' spirits up, physically supporting each other, and thus contributing to each others' survival and recovery as far as they were physically able. Crucially, the vast majority of reported helping behaviours were between strangers. Of all those ($n = 84$) who gave information on who they were with at the time, only 12 were with people they knew.

Our multi-event interview study combined the ecological validity of the London bombs analysis with a comparative design, enabling us to make stronger claims about the relationship between shared social identity and helping (see Drury et al., 2009a). Reported behaviours coded as "help" included physically supporting others, sharing water, and giving encouragement and advice. Personally selfish behaviours included ignoring others in need and trying to step in ahead of others. In line with the majority of previous research, evidence of helping far outweighed reports of personal selfishness. However, in line with the SI model specifically, reports of helping (whether given, received, or observed) were far more numerous for the "high" than the "low" crowd-unity survivors.

While "helping" reflects an asymmetry of need and ability in the relationship between giver and receiver, and may carry a cost or risk for the helper, there are many mundane forms of social coordination, cooperation, or "orderliness" – such as giving way to others, waiting one's turn, and so on – that involve "giving" between equals (Reicher & Haslam, 2010). This second aspect of solidarity, *routine civility*, is a vital part of the social cohesion of everyday life. In mass emergencies, such routine civility is also vital. Indeed, it is more important than helping. For example, the overwhelming majority of those evacuating the World Trade Center towers during the 9-11 attacks did not need assistance. They simply needed others to coordinate with them – to move at the same tempo, and to give them space to join the dense crowd – as they might do in a busy shopping street (Connell, 2001).

The basis of this routine civility is again a shared social identity. We tested this proposition in our comparative interview study of 11 different emergencies (Drury et al., 2009a) by coding all references to mundane social "orderliness" (including references to order and calm, being in control of one's emotions, adherence to everyday norms such as queuing, maintenance of social roles, and courtesy) versus "disorderliness" (discourtesy). As expected, reports of mundane orderliness and supposedly generic norms – queuing, maintenance of social roles – were more likely to be observed for high crowd-unity participants. This finding takes us beyond merely positing a "normative" explanation for behaviour in emergencies (e.g., Johnson, 1988), by suggesting the conditions under which particular norms will be instantiated. Specifically, a shared social identity enhances adherence to the acts of routine civility that bind "us" together.

Finally, shared social identity leads to at least three different forms of *expectations of support* that can contribute to resilience in and through the crowd. First, there is the expectation that I will be helped by others if I am in need of such help. If I am injured or fallen, others will take care of me, not ignore me; I will survive and recover to the extent that I feel that I am "one" with others. Second, and relatedly, I will seek out that help and support from others if I need it; and I will do so in the expectation that my request will meet with a positive response. Third, and finally, is the expectation that I will be backed up and encouraged if I take group-normative action. Again, given that most survivors may be able-bodied, and therefore that successful evacuation may be more a matter of coordination among the majority than help for the minority, this may be the most important expectation of support. As Mintz (1951) showed in his classic analogue study, if we trust others to act with social responsibility (e.g., queuing and coordinating over limited exits, acting normatively, and helping us if necessary), then we are more likely to behave in an orderly, socially structured way ourselves.

Expectations of support have been shown to be important in well-being. Anxious responses during mass emergencies may inhibit adaptive evacuation response, and can increase the stress of the situation, both at the time and subsequently. Field and experimental research on the integrated social identity model of stress (ISIS; Haslam, O'Brien, Jetten, Vormedal, & Penna, 2005; Haslam & Reicher, 2006) shows that shared social identity can reduce stress and anxiety reactions in difficult situations via greater expectations of social support and greater support-seeking from fellow ingroup members (see also Haslam, Reicher, & Levine, this volume).

Validation

Social validation is the second aspect of the relational transformation that occurs when "I" becomes "we". A shared social identity provides a consensual definition of social reality, such that we expect agreement from fellow ingroup members (Turner et al., 1987). Moreover, it is because we expect to agree with those in our group that we will work towards consensus if necessary; we would not bother engaging in discussion if we expect the other to be committed to a different view of reality (Haslam, Turner, Oakes, McGarty, & Reynolds, 1998). Further, the expectation of agreement means that we trust our fellows' judgements; our fellows' accounts are definitions of reality, whereas those of outgroup members are mere opinion (Turner et al., 1987).

The importance of validation for collective resilience becomes clear when the cognitive and relational transformations outlined above are considered in combination.

Empowered collective action

Shared social identity provides not only shared goals and understandings, but also the means to translate our understandings into practice. Shared social identity is therefore the basis of all collective behaviour (Turner et al., 1987; Reicher, in press). Put differently, the combination of (i) shared values and (ii) shared perceptions of the world and expectations of support is the basis of *empowered collective action* in a crowd. The role of shared social identity in empowering a crowd to act as one in a novel and relatively unstructured situation is well established in the literature on crowd conflict (see Drury & Reicher, 2009). We delineate here the particular consequences of such empowerment for collective resilience in mass emergencies and disasters. There are at least three consequences.

First, a shared social identity enables groups of survivors to organize the world to *prevent or minimize the risk of further trauma* (Williams & Drury, 2009). For example, a shared understanding that there was danger in remaining in the bombed out London Underground trains, and the expectation that certain acts would be supported, was the basis of coordinated attempts to remove the doors.

Second, if unity is necessary, then individuals who fail to show solidarity undermine the achievement of collective goals and hence threaten collective well-being. Pressuring deviants to comply – *crowd self-policing* (Stott & Pearson, 2007) – is possible when the crowd is sufficiently empowered. In the 9-11 evacuation, those who tried to cut across the rest of the exiting crowd were collectively forced into line by a chorus of disapproval (Connell, 2001).

Third, empowerment is considered positive for *well-being*. The pathways to well-being are both direct (empowered action itself) and indirect (the positive emotions associated with empowerment; Drury, Cocking, Beale, Hanson, & Rapley, 2005; Drury & Reicher, 2009). Being part of a successful collective evacuation can be associated with positive emotions of relief, exhilaration, pride, and joy (Drury et al., 2009b). Corresponding to the direct route, increased public participation, responsibility, and autonomy in civil defence has been shown to be associated with greater public morale and reduced mental health admissions (Jones, Woolven, Durodié, & Wessely, 2006).

IMPLICATIONS OF THE SI MODEL OF COLLECTIVE RESILIENCE

The emphasis in the SI model of collective resilience, in line with accounts of resilience in other contexts, is on the inherent potential of the crowd itself, or the endogenous origins, of such resilience. Nevertheless, there are clear practical implications to be drawn from the theory and research outlined here for those who manage emergency preparedness and response. We outline these implications, and add a word of caution on the limits of resilience.

Enabling participation and facilitating resilience

Our finding that those trapped in the bombed London Underground trains acted as "first responders" is of much more than theoretical interest. This research study, and the conclusions on resilience we drew from it, contributed to the evidence base in the recent NATO (2009) guidelines. Our SI model also featured as part of the guidance in the recent Cabinet Office/Emergency Planning College (2009) document *Understanding crowd behaviours*. In these documents and elsewhere, the practical implications of the SI model of collective resilience for practice and policy fall into three areas: public empowerment; prioritization of communication and trust; and finally the language used in mass communication.

Public empowerment

The desire of survivors to help in an emergency is virtually inevitable, as is the impulse of the wider public to come to the scene to offer assistance (Fritz, 1968). This tendency should therefore not only be catered for and harnessed (Cocking, Drury, & Reicher, 2009), but also allowed some autonomy by emergency planners and the emergency services (Williams & Drury, 2010). Given that adaptive behaviour is more likely than panic, centralized control should give way to wider public participation (Jones et al., 2006). The involvement of the crowd and the public represents a vital opportunity that needs to be recognized as such. In many, if not most, cases, the emergency services simply cannot get to the needy in time or in sufficient numbers. A *"mass democratization"* of emergency response is required, we argue, for these practical reasons. Moreover, as we have seen, enhanced public involvement can in turn enhance public morale and trust, at a time when these qualities are most needed (Jones et al., 2006).

Arguably, in both current Civil Contingencies planning and in the policing initiative Project Griffin,[2] the public are encouraged and expected to take increased responsibility for preventing and preparing for emergencies. The argument here is that this "public empowerment" needs to go further and deeper in strategic planning. It needs to be integral rather than an "add on".

One of the best ways that experts, officials, and leaders can be of service is to facilitate survivors' natural resilience. A swift return to everyday routines and to their normal capabilities to attend to their own needs is the best "social cure" for many survivors (Williams & Drury, 2010, in press). In the first instance, survivors may need the provision of resources (food, shelter, communications technologies). They will also benefit from practical information. They may need to know their family's whereabouts, for example. They will need contact and location details for the appropriate services, so that they can approach them themselves. Information that allows survivors to act enhances their agency, in contrast to those strategies of expert care that assume and reproduce a relation of passive dependency (Wessely, 2005).

Communication and trust

If information empowers, then communication strategies should have top priority, at both the highest level (government announcements) right down to the principles informing the training of professional first responders. However, "information" only counts as valid if it comes from a trusted source. In self-categorization theory terms, where the source is seen as "outgroup" ("them"), then the information is more likely to be seen as partial. In contemporary British society, the discredited Iraq war and a host of other recent controversies mean that it will take time to reverse the mistrust widely held towards the political classes, the police, and others in (legal) authority (O'Connor, 2009). In the meantime, consideration should be given to making more use of medical and scientific authority, which is more trusted than political and legal authority, to communicate information in times of emergency. It is also possible that this strategy would avoid possible crowd conflicts around issues of legitimacy (e.g., to move away from an incident or to be contained if there is a possibility of spreading infection), since in this case the "rights" would be understood as those of (public) health rather than free movement.

The language of mass communications

It is a commonplace now to observe (at least among social psychologists) that language has the power to construct the world in different ways with differing (positive or negative) outcomes. The most effective mobilizers of masses pay special attention to the words they use in public (Reicher, Haslam, & Platow, 2007). Thus we need to ask: What are the social category terms used in mass emergency communications? Do they highlight people's social separateness (e.g., "customers", stressing the individualizing money-nexus) or their collectivity (e.g., "passengers", stressing a common relationship to transport)? Who is the "we" in "our" emergency? How is the relationship between the public and the government referred to? Is it one of "shared fate", service, "partnership", or authority (benevolent or otherwise)?

Further, there are issues around how the emergency event itself and the advice surrounding it are constructed. If the situation is described as panic, then those who hear (and believe) this might rationally assume that everyone else is behaving "selfishly"; therefore they will do so themselves (cf. Mintz, 1951). Trust in others' commitment to the wider social good is undermined by the discourse of panic.

Moreover, if the public are advised "don't panic", this may be taken as evidence that there is indeed something to be anxious about. Again, at both the highest level and in terms of the training of first responders, there needs to be reflexivity in formulating the wording of warnings, advice and other mass emergency communications. Language can be used both to facilitate or to undermine the natural tendency to psychological collectivity that contributes so vitally to survival, recovery and well-being in mass emergencies and disasters.

The politics of "resilience"

Mass emergencies can reveal the strength of people's propensity for sociality and quest for community in an everyday world where these qualities are frequently lacking (Fritz, 1961/1996; Solnit, 2009). However, it would be naïve and dangerous to think that arguments for inherent collective resilience can only be an unalloyed good. For example, the motif of the "Blitz spirit", which embodies many of the themes that make up our conception of collective resilience, is not simply a *description* of positive wartime spirit; it is also a rhetorical device used to try to promote unity and endurance of deprivation among citizens who might actually be better off protesting about a war rather than rallying behind it.

In his powerful critique of the disempowering politics of the "vulnerability" framework, Furedi (2007) nevertheless acknowledges that a discourse of resilience can easily be used to minimize government and corporate responsibility by downplaying structural inequalities and hardships. For example, the discourse might be used to argue for a greater reliance on charity and personal resourcefulness, and against the duty of society itself to organize support for all citizens equally.

Related to this point, in a nuanced review of the evidence, Kaniasty and Norris (1999) point out that both suffering and assistance are often distributed inequitably – reflecting structured inequality in resources (by class, age, and ethnic group). The shared experience of disaster may contain the basis for empowerment and even "utopian" social change (cf. Solnit, 2009); but "therapeutic communities" (cf. Barton, 1969) eventually wither away (Fritz, 1961/1996). Governmental pressure (or "support") on the "new community" for a "return to normal" characteristically means the reimposition of structural disadvantage.

FINAL THOUGHTS

In line with the emerging agenda for applied psychology (Haslam, Jetten, Postmes, & Haslam, 2009), the argument and evidence of this chapter points to the positive role of the "social dimension". Shared social identity based on group membership can explain social support and hence coping, survival and well-being in even the most extreme events. Specifically, the SI model suggests that membership of a psychological crowd can be beneficial in emergencies. Rather than being part of the "problem" in mass emergencies and disasters (to be "remedied" by more centralized control and more stifling security practices), the crowd can be understood as part of a "social cure" – to both the disaster and its (mis)management. Facilitating collective resilience, through empowering the wider public and hence the emergency crowd, is not only politically desirable, it is a practical necessity. The SI model and the evidence described here can therefore be seen as one contribution to the broader research project of "rediscovering" the crowd and indeed celebrating its positive role in the social world.

ACKNOWLEDGMENTS

Some of the research described in this paper was made possible through funding from the Economic and Social Research Council to John Drury, Steve Reicher, Damian Schofield, and Paul Langston (RES-000-23-0446).

NOTES

1 In the field of disaster research, the term "vulnerability" can describe structural susceptibilities of some populations to hazards such as floods, hurricanes and

earthquakes (e.g., Comfort, 1990). In the present account, however, we are concerned only with the (more controversial) concept of *psychological vulnerability*.

2 http://www.projectgriffin.org.uk/

References

Aguirre, B. E. (2005). Commentary on 'Understanding mass panic and other collective responses to threat and disaster': Emergency evacuations, panic, and social psychology. *Psychiatry, 68,* 121–129.

Aguirre, B. E.. Torres, M. R., Gill, K. B., & Hotchkiss, H. L. (2011). Normative collective behavior in the Station building fire. *Social Science Quarterly, 92,* 100–118.

Barton, A. H. (1969). *Communities in disaster: A sociological analysis of collective stress situations.* New York, NY: Doubleday.

Blake, S. J., Galea, E. R., Westeng, H., & Dixon, A. J. P. (2004). An analysis of human behaviour during the World Trade Center disaster of 11 September 2001 based on published survivor accounts. *Proceedings of Third International Symposium on Human Behaviour in Fire*, Belfast, September. Available online at: http://fseg2.gre.ac.uk/HEED/participants_area/work_area/resource_documents/oug_wtc_human_behaviour_iafss_final_4b.pdf

Bonanno, G. A. (2004). Loss, trauma and human resilience: Have we underestimated the human capacity to thrive after extremely aversive events? *American Psychologist, 59,* 20–28.

Cabinet Office/Emergency Planning College (2009). *Understanding crowd behaviours.* London, UK: Cabinet Office/Emergency Planning College.

Campbell, D. T. (1958). Common fate, similarity and other indices of the status of aggregates of persons as social entities. *Behavioral Science, 3,* 14–25.

Chertkoff, J. M., & Kushigian, R. H. (1999). *Don't panic: The psychology of emergency egress and ingress.* Westport, CT: Praeger.

Clarke, L. (2002). Panic: Myth or reality? *Contexts, 1,* 21–26.

Cocking, C., Drury, J., & Reicher, S. (2009). The psychology of crowd behaviour in emergency evacuations: Results from two interview studies and implications for the Fire & Rescue Services. *Irish Journal of Psychology, 30,* 59–73.

Comfort, L. (1990). Turning conflict into cooperation: Organizational designs for community responses in disasters. *International Journal of Mental Health, 19,* 89–108.

Connell, R. (2001). *Collective Behavior in the September 11, 2001 Evacuation of the World Trade Center.* Preliminary paper #313. University of Delaware, Disaster Research Center.

Cornwell, B. (2003). Bonded fatalities: Relational and ecological dimensions of a fire evacuation. *The Sociological Quarterly, 44,* 617–638.

Donald, I., & Canter, D. (1992). Intentionality and fatality during the King's Cross underground fire. *European Journal of Social Psychology, 7,* 203–218.

Drury, J. (2002). 'When the mobs are looking for witches to burn, nobody's safe': Talking about the reactionary crowd. *Discourse & Society, 13,* 41–73.

Drury, J. (2004). No need to panic. *The Psychologist, 17,* 118–119.

Drury, J., Cocking, C., Beale, J., Hanson, C., & Rapley, F. (2005). The phenomenology of empowerment in collective action. *British Journal of Social Psychology*, *44*, 309–328.

Drury, J., Cocking, C., & Reicher, S. (2009a). Everyone for themselves? A comparative study of crowd solidarity among emergency survivors. *British Journal of Social Psychology*, *48*, 487–506.

Drury, J., Cocking, C., & Reicher, S. (2009b). The nature of collective resilience: Survivor reactions to the 2005 London bombings. *International Journal of Mass Emergencies and Disasters*, *27*, 66–95.

Drury, J., Cocking, C., Reicher, S., Burton, A., Schofield, D., Hardwick, A., et al. (2009c). Cooperation versus competition in a mass emergency evacuation: A new laboratory simulation and a new theoretical model. *Behavior Research Methods*, *41*, 957–970.

Drury, J., & Reicher, S. (1999). The intergroup dynamics of collective empowerment: Substantiating the social identity model. *Group Processes and Intergroup Relations*, *2*, 381–402.

Drury, J., & Reicher, S. (2009). Collective psychological empowerment as a model of social change: Researching crowds and power. *Journal of Social Issues*, *65*, 707–725.

Drury, J., Reicher, S., & Stott, C. (in press). The psychology of collective action: Crowds and change. In B. Wagoner, E. Jensen, & J. Oldmeadow (Eds.), *Culture and social change: Transforming society through the power of ideas*. London, UK: Routledge.

Dynes, R. R. (2003). Finding order in disorder: Continuities in the 9-11 response. *International Journal of Mass Emergencies and Disasters*, *21*, 9–23.

Dynes, R. R., & Rodriguez, H. (2006). *Finding and framing Katrina: The social construction of a disaster*. Understanding Katrina: Perspectives from the Social Sciences. Available online at: http://understandingkatrina.ssrc.org/Dynes_Rodriguez/

Feinberg, W., & Johnson, N. R. (2001). The ties that bind: A macro-level approach to panic. *International Journal of Mass Emergencies and Disasters*, *19*, 269–295.

Fielding, A., & Anderson, J. (2008). *Working with refugee communities to build collective resilience*. Occasional paper 2. Association for Services to Torture and Trauma Survivors, Perth, Australia.

Fredrickson, B. L., Tugade, M. M., Waugh, C. E., & Larkin, G. R. (2003). What good are positive emotions in crises? A prospective study of resilience and emotions following the terrorist attacks on the United States on September 11th, 2001. *Journal of Personality and Social Psychology*, *84*, 365–376.

Fritz, C. E. (1996). *Disasters and mental health: Therapeutic principles drawn from disaster studies*. Historical and comparative disaster series #10. University of Delaware, Disaster Research Center, USA. (Original work published 1961)

Fritz, C. E. (1968). Disasters. In D. Sills (Ed.), *International encyclopedia of the social sciences* (Vol. 4, pp. 200–207). New York, NY: Macmillan and Free Press.

Fritz, C. E., & Williams, H. B. (1957). The human being in disasters: A research perspective. *The ANNALS of the American Academy of Political and Social Science*, *309*, 42–51.

Furedi, F. (2007). *Invitation to terror*. London, UK: Continuum Press.

Glass, T. A., & Schoch-Spana, M. (2002). Bioterrorism and the people: How to vaccinate a city against panic. *Clinical Infectious Diseases*, *34*, 217–223.

Haslam, S. A. (2004). *Social psychology in organizations: The social identity approach* (2nd ed.). London, UK: Sage.

Haslam, S. A., Jetten, J., Postmes, T., & Haslam, C. (2009). Social identity, health and well-being: An emerging agenda for applied psychology. *Applied Psychology: An International Review, 58*, 1–23.

Haslam, S. A., O'Brien, A., Jetten, J., Vormedal, K., & Penna, S. (2005). Taking the strain: Social identity, social support and the experience of stress. *British Journal of Social Psychology, 44*, 355–370.

Haslam, S. A., & Reicher, S. D. (2006). Stressing the group: Social identity and the unfolding dynamics of stress. *Journal of Applied Psychology, 91*, 1037–1052.

Haslam, S. A., Turner, J. C., Oakes, P., McGarty, C., & Reynolds, K. (1998). The group as a basis for emergent stereotype consensus. *European Review of Social Psychology, 28*, 203–239.

Hernández, P. (2002). Resilience in families and communities: Latin American contributions from the psychology of liberation. *The Family Journal, 10*, 334–343.

Jacob, B., Mawson, M. A., Payton, M. D., & Guignard, J. C. (2008). Disaster mythology and fact: Hurricane Katrina and social attachment. *Public Health Reports, 123*, 555–566.

Johnson, N. R. (1988). Fire in a crowded theatre: A descriptive investigation of the emergence of panic. *International Journal of Mass Emergencies and Disasters, 6*, 7–26.

Jones, E., Woolven, R., Durodié, B., & Wessely, S. (2006). Public panic and morale: Second world war civilian responses re-examined in the light of the current anti-terrorist campaign. *Journal of Risk Research, 9*, 57–93.

Kaniasty, K., & Norris, F. (1999). The experience of disaster: Individuals and communities sharing trauma. In R. Gist & B. Lubin (Eds.), *Response to disaster: Psychosocial, community and ecological approaches* (pp. 25–61). Philadelphia, PA: Brunner/Mazel.

Keating, J. P. (1982). The myth of panic. *Fire Journal, 147*, 56–61.

Levine, M., Prosser, A., Evans, D., & Reicher, S. (2005). Identity and emergency intervention. How social group membership and inclusiveness of group boundaries shape helping behavior. *Personality and Social Psychology Bulletin, 31*, 443–453.

Masten, A. S., & Gewirtz, A. H. (2006). Resilience in development: The importance of early childhood. In R. E. Tremblay, R. G. Barr, & R. De V. Peters (Eds.), *Encyclopedia on early childhood development* (pp. 1–6). Montreal, Quebec: Centre of Excellence for Early Childhood Development [online]. Available online at http://www.child-encyclopedia.com/documents/Masten-GewirtzANGxp.pdf

Mawson, A. R. (2005). Understanding mass panic and other collective responses to threat and disaster. *Psychiatry, 68*, 95–113.

Mawson, A. (2007). *Mass panic and social attachment: The dynamics of human behavior.* Aldershot, UK: Ashgate.

Mintz, A. (1951). Non-adaptive group behavior. *Journal of Abnormal & Social Psychology, 46*, 150–159.

NATO (2009). *Psychosocial care for people affected by disasters and major incidents.* Brussels, Belgium: NATO.

O'Connor, D. (2009). *Adapting to protest: Nurturing the British model of policing.* London, UK: Her Majesty's Inspectorate of Constabulary.

Proulx, G., & Fahy, R. F. (2003). Evacuation of the World Trade Center: What went right? In *Proceedings of the CIB-CTBUH International Conference on Tall Buildings* (CIB Publication No. 290, pp. 27–34) October 20–23, Malaysia. Available online at http://nparc.cisti-icist.nrc-cnrc.gc.ca/npsi/ctrl?action=rtdoc&an=5755429&article-0&lang=en

Proulx, G., & Sime, J. D. (1991). To prevent 'panic' in an underground emergency: Why not tell people the truth? In G. Cox & B. Langford (Eds.), *Fire safety science: Proceedings of the third international symposium* (pp. 843–852). London, UK: Elsevier Applied Science.

Quarantelli, E. L. (1960). Images of withdrawal behaviour in disasters: Some basic misconceptions. *Social Problems, 8,* 68–79.

Quarantelli, E. L. (2001). Panic, sociology of. In N. J. Smelser & P. B. Baltes (Eds.), *International encyclopedia of the social and behavioural sciences* (pp. 11020–11023). New York, NY: Pergamon Press.

Reicher, S. (in press). Crowd psychology. In V. S. Ramanchandran (Ed.), *The encyclopedia of human behaviour* (2nd ed.). Amsterdam: Elsevier.

Reicher, S., & Drury, J. (2010). Collective identity, political participation and the making of the social self. In A. Azzi, X. Chryssochoou, B. Klandermans, & B. Simon (Eds.), *Identity and participation in culturally diverse societies: A multidisciplinary perspective.* Oxford, UK: Blackwell/Wiley.

Reicher, S., & Haslam, S. A. (2010). Beyond help: A social psychology of collective solidarity and social cohesion. In M. Snyder & S. Stürmer (Eds.), *The psychology of helping: New directions in the study of intergroup prosocial behavior* (pp. 289–309). Oxford, UK: Blackwell.

Reicher, S., Haslam, S. A., & Platow, M. (2007). The new psychology of leadership. *Scientific American Mind,* August/September, 22–29.

Ripley, A. (2008). *The unthinkable: Who survives when disaster strikes – and why.* London, UK: Random House.

Rodriguez, H., Trainor, J., & Quarantelli, E. (2006). Rising to the challenges of a catastrophe: The emergent and prosocial behavior following Hurricane Katrina. *ANNALS of the American Academy of Political and Social Science, 604,* 82–101.

Schultz, D. P. (Ed.) (1964). *Panic behavior: Discussion and readings.* New York, NY: Random House.

Sime, J. D. (1983). Affiliative behavior during escape to building exits. *Journal of Environmental Psychology, 3,* 21–41.

Sime, J. D. (1990). The concept of 'panic'. In D. Canter (Ed.), *Fires and human behaviour* (2nd ed., pp. 63–81). London, UK: David Fulton.

Solnit, R. (2009). *A paradise built in hell: The extraordinary communities that arise in disaster.* New York, NY: Viking.

Stott, C., & Pearson, G. (2007). *Football hooliganism: Policing and the war on the English Disease.* London, UK: Pennant Books.

Tajfel, H., & Turner, J. C. (1979). An integrative theory of intergroup relatons. In S. Worchel & W. G. Austin (Eds.), *Psychology of intergroup relations* (pp. 33–47). Monterey, CA: Brooks-Cole.

Tierney, K. (2003). Disaster beliefs and institutional interests: Recycling disaster myths in the aftermath of 9-11. In L. Clarke (Ed.), *Research in social problems and public policy. Terrorism and disaster: New threats, new ideas* (Vol. 11, pp. 33–51). Burlington, MA: Elsevier Science.

Tierney, K., Bevc, C., & Kuligowski, E. (2006). Metaphors matter: Disaster myths, media frames and their consequences in Hurricane Katrina. *ANNALS of the American Academy of Political and Social Science, 604,* 57–81.

Turner, J. C. (1982). Towards a cognitive redefinition of the social group. In H. Tajfel (Ed.), *Social identity and intergroup relations* (pp. 15–40). Cambridge, UK: Cambridge University Press.

Turner, J. C., Hogg, M. A., Oakes, P. J., Reicher, S. D., & Wetherell, M. S. (1987). *Rediscovering the social group: A self-categorization theory.* Oxford, UK: Blackwell.

Wessely, S. (2004). When being upset is not a mental health problem. *Psychiatry, 67,* 153–157.

Wessely, S. (2005). Editorial: Don't panic! Short and long term psychological reactions to the new terrorism: The role of information and the authorities. *Journal of Mental Health, 14,* 1–6.

Williams, R. (2007). The psychosocial consequences for children of mass violence, terrorism and disasters. *International Review of Psychiatry, 19,* 263–277.

Williams, R., & Drury, J. (2009). Psychosocial resilience and its influence on managing mass emergencies and disasters. *Psychiatry, 8,* 293–296.

Williams, R., & Drury, J. (2010). The nature of psychosocial resilience and its significance for managing mass emergencies, disasters and terrorism. In A. Awotona (Ed.), *Rebuilding sustainable communities for children and their families after disasters: A global survey* (pp. 121–148). Newcastle-upon-Tyne, UK: Cambridge Scholars Publishing.

Williams, R., & Drury, J. (in press). Personal and collective psychosocial resilience: Implications for children, young people and their families involved in war and disasters. In D. Cook, J. Wall, & P. Cox (Eds.), *Children and armed conflict.* Basingstoke, UK: Palgrave Macmillan.

12 Social cure or social curse?

The psychological impact of extreme events during the Kosovo conflict

Blerina Kellezi
Stephen D. Reicher
University of St. Andrews

INTRODUCTION: THE PSYCHOLOGY AND POLITICS OF HUMILIATION

As this volume attests, being and feeling part of a group matters for our well-being. Even – perhaps especially – in the most extreme circumstances, the group makes a difference. Sometimes the difference between life and death. A number of authors have pointed to the fact that those who belonged to cohesive groups – political groups, religious groups, and others – were more likely to cope with the Nazi concentration camp system and even to survive it (Cohen, 1988; Langbein, 1994; Levi, 1988; Rousset, 1965). In part, this was doubtless due to the superior conditions accorded to members of some of these groups. In part it was due to the practical acts of mutual support between group members. To quote Langbein, for instance (himself quoting Wijnen, a Dutch inmate of Buchenwald): "the great strength of the Russians consisted in their doing everything in groups" (1994, p. 164). But there was more to survival than that.

Rousset, a survivor of the Buchenwald camp, explains that a sense of collective identity, of collective purpose, and collective meaning was important in itself. For those who had no such identity, who could not make sense of why they were in the camps, it was the end. They were the ones who became the so-called Muselmänner (Levi, 1996): those who no longer cared, who no longer hoped, the drowned, the walking dead, soon to be actual corpses.

Primo Levi illustrates this point in an account of his own survival during the terrible period just before liberation in January 1945 (see the chapter "The story of ten days" in Levi, 1996). In conversation with Levi, the author Philip Roth picks this up. He suggests that Levi survived precisely because he was civilised and showed concern for others rather than just himself. Levi replies:

> Exactly – you hit the bull's eye. In those memorable ten days, I truly did feel like Robinson Crusoe, but with one important difference. Crusoe set to work for his individual survival, whereas I and my two

French companions were consciously and happily willing to work at last for a just and human goal, to save the lives of our sick comrades.

(Roth, 1996, p. 180)

The Nazis were well aware of the power of the group. Their constant concern was that those concentrated in their camps would forge bonds of common identity and of solidarity. As Sofsky (1997) meticulously documents, the organisation of the camp system was specifically designed to ensure that, despite their physical density, inmates felt psychologically isolated; that "their orientation is not to each other, but past one another" (p. 154). To this end, they employed a wide variety of techniques designed to set prisoners against each other, to engender distrust, and to disrupt supportive human relations.

Humiliation was key amongst these techniques – an excess of humiliation that began on entry to the camps. Sofsky, for instance, cites the experience of being inducted into the system:

A female prisoner . . . grabbed my hand and began to tattoo the next number: 55908. It seemed she wasn't actually pricking my arm, she was jabbing me in the heart. From that moment on, I ceased to be a human being. I stopped feeling, thinking. I no longer had a name, an address. I was prisoner no. 55908. And that same moment, with every jab of the needle, a piece of my life dropped away.

(Sofsky, 1997, p. 82)

Primo Levi sums up through a seemingly trivial detail the way that humiliation was a deliberate strategy that permeated every aspect of camp existence. He describes the lack of a spoon. "Without a spoon", he relates, "the daily soup could not be consumed in any other way than by lapping it up as dogs do". And he continues:

When the camp at Auschwitz was liberated, we found in the warehouse thousands of brand-new transparent plastic spoons, besides tens of thousands of spoons made of aluminium or even silver that came from the luggage of deportees as they arrived. So it was not a matter of thrift, but a precise intent to humiliate.

(Levi, 1988, p. 91)

Levi's point here is not just about the intent to humiliate, but also about how humiliation functions. It is partly about asserting the power of the oppressor to do exactly what they want to the oppressed. It is partly about reducing the oppressed to nothing in their own eyes. But it is also about diminishing the oppressed in the eyes of their fellows. How can one trust or rely upon those who lack humanity? How could solidarity (that relies not only on supporting others but upon believing that they will support you) be possible amongst those without dignity or morality?

We can take these arguments about humiliation and the consequences of humiliation one step further. In the examples we have used so far, humiliation is about removing all signs of human being from the inmates or else getting them to act in ways that violate the standards that one would expect of any human being. Often, however, humiliation was more finely calibrated to the nature of particular social groups: it was about removing the signs that specifically made one a member of these groups or else getting people to violate specific group norms. A sense of this can be gleaned by returning to the moment of entry into the camps.

Primo Levi, like Sofsky, points to the impact of the tattooed number: it is an indelible mark, the mark with which slaves and cattle are branded. But to orthodox Jews it bears special significance: "precisely in order to distinguish Jews from the barbarians, the tattoo is forbidden by Mosaic law (Leviticus 19:280)" (Levi, 1988, p. 95). Another aspect of the initiation was what Levi (1988) calls "the coercion of nudity", something that began on arrival but continued on a daily basis. As Levi explains, nudity had some basis in necessity (for showers or medical examinations) but was offensive due to its useless redundancy. Women in particular were forced to parade past SS men and were subject to obscene mockery. Like tattooing, the performance was traumatic for everybody, but it was particularly traumatising for religious Jewish women for it violated strong norms of modesty. We shall have more to say about forms of sexual violence used precisely to offend against religious and cultural sensibilities.

In these examples, it is hard to unpick the generically dehumanising aspect of Nazi practice from the specifically "deculturing" aspect. Other examples point more clearly to practices designed to humiliate Jews *as Jews*. There are many examples of Jewish people being forced to carry anti-Jewish signs; of men having their beards shaved or being forced to shave each other's beards; of Jews being forced to ride each other to the amusement of the local population. There is, for instance, an infamous photograph of Rabbi Moshe Yitzak Hengerman on the day in July 1940 – "Bloody Wednesday" – when German policemen brutalised the Jewish population of Olkusz in Poland. Hengerman is pictured barefoot, forced to don his prayer shawl and phylacteries and to pray next to a group of prostrate Jewish men.

The impact of all this was to induce shame and guilt amongst those who survived, even though survivors had no choice. They had a sense that they survived *because* they had let down themselves, their fellows, and their group. To cite Primo Levi yet again:

> Almost everybody feels guilty of having omitted to help. The presence at your side of a companion who is weaker, or less cunning, or older, or too young, hounding you with his demands for help or with his simply

being there, which is itself an entreaty, is a constant in the life of the Lager. The demand for solidarity, for a human word, advice, even only a listening ear, was permanent and universal, but rarely satisfied.

(Levi, 1988, p. 59)

At this point, the group no longer provides support for those who suffer offence. Rather, the offence, in addition to its physical impact on the victim, serves to divide the individual from the group and the group from the individual. On the one hand, how can those who have (albeit unwillingly) violated basic group norms consider themselves to be group members and call upon the solidarity of their peers? Each time they think of the offence, they are reminded of their own shame and isolation. On the other hand, how can people embrace those who are a constant reminder of their own guilt? And, in the embarrassed silence of others, the shame of the victim is further exacerbated. To the original offence, two further layers of suffering are added.

So, instead of the group serving to support its members, the humiliation that forces people to violate their own norms turns the psychology of groups *against* the individual. Instead of the group making things better for people (the social cure) it makes things worse (the social curse). Instead of facilitating resistance and survival, it promotes acquiescence and collapse. And the Nazis, either intuitively or knowingly, took advantage of this in order to run their carceral kingdoms.

This is true not just of the Nazis, and not just of the past. We can find many examples of abuse and torture involving humiliations that are measured against the cultural norms of victims and where such humiliations are often more painful than physical torture. Much of this has to do with gendered understandings of what makes a man or what makes a woman in the relevant society. To take widely known contemporary examples, at both Abu Ghraib prison in Iraq and at the detention centre at Guantanamo Bay there have been allegations that women guards smeared what was allegedly menstrual blood on Muslim men, that they forced men to masturbate and to perform (or at least mime) homoerotic acts – and then, of course, there is the infamous picture of Guard Lyndie England holding a naked Muslim man by a dog leash. Gourevitch and Morris (2008) explain that, in these acts, the Abu Ghraib Guards were putting to use the "cultural awareness" training they had been given before they shipped to Iraq. They had been told that Arab men were "sexual prudes", that they disliked been seen naked, especially by women. "What better way to break an Arab, then, than to strip him, tie him up, and have a 'female bystander' . . . laugh at him" (p. 113).

Far more often, though, violent gendered humiliations are aimed at women, especially through the use of rape as a deliberate policy – in Liberia, in Mozambique, in Rwanda, in Sri Lanka, in Uganda (Ramanathapillai, 2006; Rehn & Sirleaf, 2002; Sinderis, 2003), and (perhaps most well known in the West) in the countries of the former Yugoslavia (Rehn & Sirleaf, 2002; UNFPA, 2005; Wareham, 2000). In each case, the policy seems to have had two elements, both of which exploit the nature of patriarchal cultures. On the one hand, women have value as mothers that perpetuate the group by bearing and raising children. To impregnate women is therefore to turn the woman against both herself and the group. It makes her an agent of "ethnic cleansing" carrying the enemy in her. In some cases women were marked with scars or tattoos (for instance, of the nationalist symbol of the Serb rapist) as an external sign of their internal betrayal (Wareham, 2000). On the other hand, men's worth is built around protecting their women's virtue and their family's honour. Rape is their failure and their humiliation as well as that of the women. As a result, even where the event is tacitly known by all, it is never spoken of. Women do not tell, men do not ask.

Janine di Giovanni's memoir of the Balkan wars illustrates this destructive dynamic. At one point she tells the story of five Kosovar women in one family who were "touched" by Serbian soldiers – the language is indicative: "No one in this family said the word 'rape'. It was too harsh, too hard, too damning" writes di Giovanni (2004, p. 44). She goes on to describe the aftermath:

> Strangely, after you were all raped, you did not help each other. You did not talk to each other. No one spoke about what happened. Some of the women who were not touched taunted and teased you. You passed days and weeks and months in a strange place, a refugee camp with ten or twelve in a tent and one bathroom set up in a field for a hundred people. There was no room for your own grief. Then you did go home, eventually, but something happened to your village during the war: the fabric and culture bound together by generation after generation have frayed bit by bit, like a sweater that begins to unravel.
>
> (di Giovanni, 2004, p. 47)

Once again, we see that, where offences involve victims breaching the norms of their own group, there is no evidence of social support. People do not even acknowledge that there is anything that requires support. What is unspoken cannot be addressed. And the silence compounds the impact, for it reminds all concerned that they have done something unspeakable. That is what we mean by "the social curse".

A MODEL OF EXTREME EVENTS AND INDIVIDUAL WELL-BEING

We can express our argument somewhat more formally by drawing on the appraisal model of Lazarus and Folkman (1984). These researchers suggest that the impact of events on well-being depends upon two stages of appraisal. The first, primary appraisal, refers to one's assessment of the seriousness of the event itself and the potential impact it could have on one's well-being. The second, secondary appraisal, refers to one's assessment of the resources at one's disposal to deal with this impact. In part this has to do with the availability of coping strategies and, in part, to do with the amount of social support that one can draw from others (see Haslam, Reicher, & Levine, this volume).

There is, by now, a wealth of evidence demonstrating the importance of primary appraisal and both aspects of secondary appraisal in a broad range of domains. Nonetheless, one significant limitation of the approach is that it tends to be couched in individualistic terms (see Sani, this volume; van Dick & Haslam, this volume). That is, primary appraisal is predominantly conceptualised in terms of the idiosyncratic beliefs of the individual rather than in terms of the impact of shared systems of belief upon the significance of events (Slavin, Rainer, McCreary, & Gowda, 1991). Equally, secondary appraisal is generally associated with the personal relations we have with others and our personal ways of coping. This focus seems particularly problematic given that many of the events that have been the subject of analysis have affected whole groups in society and that individuals have been targeted precisely because of their membership of these groups (e.g., as Jews, as Kosovars).

In recent years, social identity theorists have added a group level of analysis to the appraisal process (in addition to this volume, see, for instance, Haslam, O'Brien, Jetten, Vormedal, & Penna, 2005; Haslam & Reicher, 2006). This work has primarily concentrated on the social support dimension of secondary appraisal. It draws on evidence that, when people identify themselves as members of a social group and they see others as sharing this identification, they are both more likely to support and help their fellow group members and also expect support from them (see Reicher & Haslam, 2010, for a review). Consequently, for those facing difficult circumstances, the sense of being part of a group is likely to increase support and decrease stress (Haslam et al., 2005; Haslam & Reicher, 2006). The implication, then, is that the group is generally a positive resource in the service of well-being.

We wish to extend this approach in two ways. The first concerns the impact of social identity on primary appraisal. More specifically, we suggest that the seriousness of an event will be a function of its relationship to group norms and group identity. Thus, where an extreme event involves the victim in acts that are normative, and hence where the event affirms the social identity of the individual, it will be judged as relatively less serious and less harmful to well-being. An example might be where a soldier is shot while engaging the enemy, thus confirming his valour, his mettle as a soldier, and his standing as a patriot. Conversely, when an extreme event involves the victim in acts that are counternormative, and hence where the event negates his or her social identity, it will be judged as relatively more serious and be more harmful to well-being. The individual, after all, has not only suffered in his or her physical being but also in his or her social being. We have given many examples of this: the religious person who allows the signs of his or her faith to be desecrated, the woman who is raped, the man who fails to defend his family or who is shot while running from the enemy.

Second, we consider the interaction between the impact of social identity processes on primary appraisal and on secondary appraisal. Here we suggest that, where events affirm social identity, then social support from fellow group members will be both expected and given: the hero will be lionised by the group for the glory he or she has brought them. This in turn will allow for more constructive coping strategies – for instance, it will become easier for the individual to reframe events in positive terms. The ultimate effect will be to protect the well-being of those who have suffered.

However, where events violate norms and negate social identity, individuals will not make their burden known to others, they will find it difficult to ask for help and, even if they do, it will not be granted. The victim will be shunned by the group upon which he or she has brought shame. This is likely to lead to more negative coping strategies – such as the victim blaming himself or herself for what happened. Ultimately these processes will culminate in increased harm to the well-being of the victim. To reprise the terms we have used above, the former set of processes that flow from norm affirmation constitute "the social cure". The latter set that flow from norm violation constitute "the social curse". The full model is illustrated in Figure 12.1.

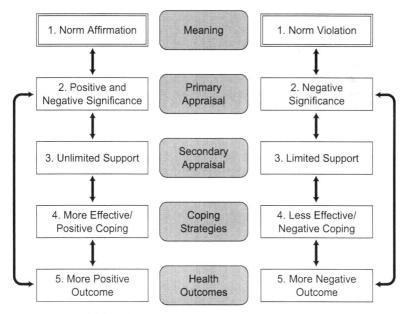

Figure 12.1 A social identity model of the impact of extreme events upon mental well-being.

EXTREME EVENTS AND MENTAL WELL-BEING IN THE KOSOVO CONFLICT

In order to interrogate this model we shall present evidence taken from a programme of research involving survivors of the 1999 war in Kosovo (Kellezi, 2006) – an event that had severe effects on almost the entire population. The war developed out of a longstanding history of conflict between Serbs and Kosovo Albanians that escalated further during the 1990s (Anzulovic, 1999; Bieber & Daskalovski, 2003; Judah, 2000; Mertus, 1999). Amongst sections of the Kosovo Albanians, there was a growing sense that peaceful movements to address their economic, social, and political grievances had proved ineffective. This led to the formation of the Kosovo Liberation Army (KLA: see Judah, 2000; O'Neill, 2002) and a split between, on the one hand, those who saw armed conflict as inevitable and necessary to preserve the Kosovar people, and on the other, those who saw war as endangering the survival of the people (Saltmarshe, 2002). In 1999, the actions of the KLA led to massive attacks on the civilian population by Serbian forces. This in turn led to the NATO bombing of Serbia. During the war more than 45 percent of the Kosovo Albanian population was forced to leave the country (often by walking to the border), an additional 22 percent were forced to live in hiding, more than 10,000 were killed, and more than 3,000 abducted. Many civilians were subjected to maltreatment and assault (both sexual and physical). Most houses in Kosovo were either partially or completely destroyed (Minervini, 2002; O'Neill, 2002; Spiegel & Salama, 2000; Suhrke, Barutciski, Garlock, & Sandison, 2000).

There is strong evidence that the aim of the war was not only to impose a military defeat on the KLA but to destroy the social and psychological integrity of the Kosovar people. In the sense of destroying Kosovars as a coherent people (rather than necessarily killing every single member of the community) the war was therefore an act of genocide. As we have already indicated, much of the violence was designed to humiliate, and there was a concerted attempt to demolish the physical infrastructure so that people could not return to their homes. Birth records and identification documents were destroyed in order to obliterate personal histories of belonging (Griffith et al., 2005; Kellezi, 2006; Meçi, 2002; Mertus, 1999). Both because of the collective nature of experiences and because of the specific form of these experiences, this conflict therefore constitutes an ideal site in which to examine our approach.

We present three studies using a range of methodologies – our strategy being (a) to determine whether there is a relationship between normativity, the appraisal process, and well-being, and then (b) to examine more directly the nature of events that become unspeakable and the experience of such unspeakability. Our first study is a survey that investigates whether the experience of war events as either identity-affirming or identity-negating impacts on levels of social support and hence on well-being. The second study then uses interviews to investigate in more detail exactly what sort of experiences are regarded as "unspeakable", whether the nature of these experiences is a function of Kosovar cultural expectations of men and women, and what the consequences of unspeakability are for survivors. The third study is based on an extended ethnography of families in three Kosovar villages. It examines how people experience different types of event – particularly those that involve norm violation – how they are treated by those around them and how this in turn impacts on their ability to bear what has happened to them.

Study 1. Identity affirmation, social support and well-being

All our studies were conducted between 2003 and 2005, 4 to 6 years after the end of the war. The survey involved a convenience sample of 127 high identifying Kosovo Albanians, primarily rural, all of whom had experienced extreme events such as loss of someone close, personal injury, or loss of their home and displacement. The sample was accessed through Kosovo Albanian health care professionals (for full details, see Kellezi, Reicher, & Cassidy, 2009).

The major issue for us was how to measure whether the experiences of our participants involved norm violation or affirmation and hence either negated or affirmed their identity as Kosovo Albanians. The difficulty lay in the fact that most people had experienced multiple events and hence it would be difficult to determine how to weight them in determining outcomes. We therefore decided to take a more global approach rooted in the two different general orientations to the war. We reasoned that for those who were in the anti-war and anti-KLA camp, all that happened in the conflict was senseless and served only to undermine group identity. Even if not actually shameful, one's ordeal could hardly be celebrated. Conversely, for those in the pro-war, pro-KLA camp, the war was an affirmation of the nation and one's sufferings could be given meaning as sacrifices for the nation. Our prediction, therefore, was that those who were pro-war (and hence for whom the events of the war as a whole were identity-affirming) would have better mental well-being than those who were anti-war (for whom these events were identity-negating) and that this would be mediated by higher levels of social support amongst the former than the latter.

Given that Kosovar villages are generally made up of people living in extended family units, comprised of people with whom one would mostly interact on a day to day basis, and from whom one would normally expect unconditional social support (Cardozo, Kaiser, Gotway, & Agani, 2003; Meçi, 2002), we measured social support in terms of levels of the ability to talk to other members of these units, to ask them for help, and to receive it. Well-being was measured using scales of self-efficacy, anxiety, and depression. Finally, we measured the use of a range of coping strategies, some positive (such as positive reframing of events) and some negative (such as self-blame).

The results concerning the relationship between appraisal of events, social support and well-being gave clear support for our model. Seeing the war as identity-affirming rather than identity-negating was positively associated with levels of support from the family unit. It was also positively associated with mental well-being on all three measures (heightened self-efficacy, lowered anxiety, and lowered depression). What is more, analysis suggested that social support mediated the link between appraisal and well-being.

The results concerning the role of coping strategies were somewhat different. For those who saw the war as identity-affirming, the use of positive coping strategies had no impact on mental well-being, while the use of negative strategies was associated with decreased well-being. Conversely, for those who saw the war as identity-negating, the use of negative coping strategies had no impact on mental well-being while the use of positive strategies was associated with improved well-being. One way of interpreting these patterns is to say that when a person saw events as positive and was supported by others, then positive coping mechanisms could not make things any better, but negative mechanisms could make things worse. Conversely, when a person saw events negatively and when he or she was isolated by others, negative coping mechanisms could not make things any worse, but positive mechanisms could make things better.

Overall, then, this first study demonstrates three things. First, it confirms the importance of group-level processes both for the appraisal process and for well-being. Second, it shows that this importance relates to both primary appraisal (the evaluation of events) and secondary appraisal (the evaluation of how events can be dealt with). Third, it suggests that the impact of the group on well-being *can* be highly positive but it can also be negative.

Nonetheless, the study is no more than a starting point. All the constructs are (necessarily) at a high level of abstraction since we are looking at overall responses to events in general, rather than examining the impact of specific events as a function of their relationship to group norms. More particularly, in our measure of appraisals of the war in general, we have used a distal proxy for the way any given event is perceived, how seriously it is seen, and how others react to what has happened. We are therefore unable to demonstrate that events that negate identities are those that are experienced as worst and where social support is least forthcoming – or even those where the group turns against the victim and adds to their burden. These are the issues we addressed in our next study.

Study 2. Gender, culture, and "unspeakability"

Between May 2003 and September 2004, we interviewed 16 women and 22 men aged between 19 and 61 who had experienced at least one extreme event during the war. We accessed the sample initially through local non-governmental organisations and then through a snowball technique. We deliberately sought a diverse sample in terms of gender, age, geographical area, and socio-economic status (for full details of the study, see Kellezi, 2006).

People were keen to talk and so our interviews, which we had intended to keep to one hour, lasted between 50 minutes and 3 hours, with a mean of approximately 90 minutes. We covered a range of topics, but for present purposes the key issues were to identify (a) the normative expectations of Kosovo Albanians (it rapidly became clear that these are highly gendered and so this developed into an analysis of the expectations of Kosovo Albanian men and women); (b) the types of experience that men and women would find most difficult to speak about and to come to terms with; (c) the types of experience that men and women would find tolerable and easy to speak of; and (d) the consequences of having undergone an "unspeakable" experience. The interviews were taped, transcribed, and analysed using thematic analysis and content analysis.

Rural Kosovo is a traditional and highly patriarchal society. This is codified in the "Kanun of Leke Dukagjini" (Dukagjini & Gjecov, 1989; Meçi, 2002), an old text that served as the foundation of Albanian traditional law and became all the more influential in Kosovo as Serbian law was rejected (Judah, 2000). Honour is a central category in the Kanun. For men, honour is defined in terms of strength and domination. The Kanun defines not only what men should do, but also what they should experience if they fail to do as they should – shame and exclusion. There are equally strong norms concerning honour and consequences of norm violation for women. But women are explicitly placed below men (a woman is "*a sack made to endure*" according to the Kanun). Their honour consists in maintaining their purity for their husbands and maintaining the family.

These ideas were equally clear in the words of our respondents. Men have to be brave and hard, to defend their honour and that of their families. A man "*should be a real man. In difficult moments he should sing*" as one interviewee put it, somewhat whimsically. Women are valued for serving their husbands and children. They are respected for the respect they show to others. They can be educated and cultured, but only so they can educate and enrich their children. As one woman put it: "*if she does not respect others she has nothing . . . always keep your head down . . . you have to be submissive, always lower and lower than the others*". Overall, content analysis showed that men, more than women, were expected to be strong, to be straight dealing, and to be protective of others. Women, more than men, were expected to be morally virtuous, well-behaved, and submissive. Both were expected to make sacrifices for the country, but men by fighting and dying in battle, women by staying at home and suffering for their children.

When it came to the speakable and the unspeakable, the tolerable and the intolerable, all could talk of events that had affirmed identity, but not of those that negated identity. Men could and would speak about appalling events as long as they had shown strength and suffered either in the cause of country or else of protecting their families. Many, like the medical doctor who told us that "*I stayed. The Kosovo Albanian army needed medical and moral support*" took pride in the fact that they had remained and suffered rather than fled the country. But men could not speak if they had suffered while fleeing, if they had failed to protect their families, or if they had shown weakness in the face of the enemy. In the words of one young woman:

> Males have to show they are strong, that is why they don't talk and they don't say what they have inside. As my grandfather used to say "Here in Kosovo, the tears of men are songs".

Women were able to speak of events where they might have died, as long as their sexual honour and their families remained intact. One woman, for instance, told us how "*I hid my son inside my breast, and I thought 'let the bullets take me, only my son should survive'*". What they were unable to speak of was the loss of honour – above all, of rape. Rape, one woman explained, is "*much worse than being beaten up and killed*".

Finally, when it came to consequences, those who were seen to have transgressed – men who had been weak, who had abandoned family or country; women who had stained family honour or been raped – were socially excluded. However, as both our qualitative and quantitative analyses showed, men were more likely to be ostracised within the community ("*he is not sent away from where he lives, but people would not speak to him*") while women were more likely to be rejected from the community ("*she is forced to leave the family and cannot help but become involved in prostitution*").

As we propose, then, suffering that affirms identity is bearable, it can be spoken of and it attracts the support of others in the group. Suffering which negates identity is unbearable and unspeakable. In the minds of Kosovo Albanians as well as in the Kanun, those who violate codes of honour are shameful both in their own eyes and in the eyes of others. And the power of this is accentuated by the fact that there is a strong consensus as to what constitutes honour. Men and women agree as to what Kosovo Albanian men and women need to do.

But there is still a gap in the analysis. We have asked a general sample what they consider to be normative, to be unspeakable and to flow from experiencing unspeakable acts. However, we have not been able to get the perspective of those who have actually had such experiences. How can you get people to speak of the unspeakable? In part the answer comes from recognising, first, that while events like rape may be unspoken they are rarely unknown in the community; second that the inability of victims to speak stems less from their own shame than from the refusal of others to hear. Hence, if there were an interlocutor they could trust and who was willing to hear, victims may tell their stories. It is part of the power of ethnography – of living amongst people for an extended period – that it is possible to build up such trust and understanding. This is the rationale for our third and final study.

Study 3. The lived experience of loss

The ethnography was conducted in three primary locations, one of which had been heavily affected by the war. On one day, 26 March 1999, Serb forces arrived and killed over 100 people, mostly men and boys. The women and children were forced to leave. For three days, without food and water, they walked to the Albanian border. Only 5 out of some 700 houses in the village escaped being burnt to the ground. In mid-2004, when the research was carried out, the village had 176 widows and 548 orphaned children. There were still 120 missing people, but most relatives had given up hope of ever finding them.

The first author (BK), herself of Albanian origin, spent a total of 70 days living with six different families in these villages, participating in their everyday lives and, through them, participating in the public life of the community. The data are based primarily on observations. On occasion, the researcher asked clarifying questions. Over time, as trust grew, she was included in conversations about events. In order to avoid disrupting social relationships, no recording devices were used. As soon as was convenient, she would write down field notes and these were written up more fully at the end of each day.

The first thing to note is that people would regularly talk about the war and they would refer to violent and harrowing events. However, there was a clear asymmetry in what was talked about and how things were talked about. As ever, the silence surrounding rape stood out given that rape had been widespread during the war. But, even if the rapes themselves were very rarely talked about, occasionally people did talk about the consequences for the victim. Sometimes they referred to the silence itself. One family, for instance, reported how they had helped a rape victim and reunited her with her family. They all joined the column of refugees walking to the border. At one point Serbian soldiers saw them all and, in front of everyone else, spoke of the rape. Since that time, neither family has ever talked of the event. The girl's family had suggested visiting the helpers to say thank you, but the visit never took place. Each time they happen to come across each other, conversations are stilted and strained.

Another woman, herself a rape survivor, explained that, at first, she had trusted a few friends and talked of her ordeal. But they had passed the information on and the experience had been almost worse than the ordeal itself. She reflected bitterly: *"It is much better for those who have not spoken. Now they have a life and they can do what they want"*. In particular, her chances of marriage were ruined because no one will accept a rape survivor:

Why don't they take me? . . . I was forced, it was against my will, and they don't have me. They leave me after they find out. It is not right! I am not jealous but I look at (other) girls and I say, why can't I be happy like them?

In referring to the unspeakable, though, there is a danger in dwelling too much on rape, lest it be thought of as an exception rather than one instance of a more general rule. So, to broaden the argument somewhat, consider the following account. On one occasion, BK met four colleagues at their work place. One was proudly introduced as a fighter in the war, another as the wife of a commander, and the third as the sister of a fighter who had died in combat. The fourth was introduced only by name. At one point, this last colleague left the room at which point the person who had done the original introductions whispered that she had lost her husband during the war as well, but as a civilian. For the rest of the visit, the conversation centred on the fighters and commanders in the war. They were praised, as were their family. Nothing was said to acknowledge the loss of the fourth woman. The silence only served to make that loss – and its difference from the other losses – all the more salient.

The contrast in treatment between those who have died in ways considered normative and those who have not was clear on a number of levels. To continue with the theme of visits, visiting the bereaved is part of the Kosovar culture of mourning. For those who lost someone in the fighting, the visits are constant. One woman, whose son died as a soldier in the war related how: "*Every day there is someone visiting. Even now after 4 years. Lots of mothers come and tell me what a wonderful boy I had and cry for him. All mothers cry for him*". Another mother of a dead soldier explained how she felt sustained by these visits: "*I just want them to come and see me and listen to me. That makes my heart better. It makes me feel better*". But for those whose close ones died as civilians there were no continuous visits and sympathy after the end of the war. At times, there was even a hint that they might have brought their fate upon themselves. To cite one participant, whose own child had died fighting: "*What were they doing at home, and not acting? Of course the Serbian army went where people did not fight so they could kill whoever they wanted. They killed them because they did not resist*".

The same asymmetry goes for public commemorations and public monuments. On the anniversaries of soldiers' deaths it is typical to set up the household as an open shrine with pictures of the dead draped in flags, with organised visits to the home or to the graveyards. A mother who had lost her daughter in the fighting reported on more than one occasion that:

All members of my town came to console me for the loss of my daughter. I have a register of memoirs from those who visited. 18,000 people came to console me. Only 6 people (and I know their names) from the whole town did not pay the traditional visit after the death of my daughter.

The graveyards for fighters are highly visible throughout the year. They are decorated with flowers, flags, some with full life engraved pictures of the fighters. Most of these graveyards are on the side of main national roads, highly visible from passing cars, soliciting a constant ritual of reverence. For instance, every time BK entered or left one town in a car or bus or even a taxi, as she passed the war graveyard, the radio would be turned off as a sign of respect. But there was no such respect for the civilian dead. No anniversary visits. In some places, there are not even separate graveyards. The victims are buried in sections of existing graveyards within villages and the only way of identifying how people died is by looking closely at the headstones.

In sum, the support of the community clearly does not extend to all those who have suffered from the war – either directly or through the deaths of others. There may be elaborate practices that embrace those whose suffering took forms that affirmed group identity. And there is evidence that such support is very important for those who receive it. It makes loss meaningful and bearable. However, the very ubiquity of these practices serves only to make the silences around identity-negating suffering all the more stark. In a context where support is expected and is highly visible, lack of support becomes highly salient. Those who have suffered are made constantly to confront the shamefulness of their predicament. And the unspeakable becomes increasingly unbearable.

CONCLUSION

Our purpose in this chapter has been to enrich the burgeoning realisation that group processes are critical to understanding our well-being, but to point out that these processes can be used to harm as well as to promote well-being. So while group psychology can be harnessed for people in order to protect them, it can also be used against people in order to break them. If people are humiliated by being forced to violate their shared standards and beliefs, then the resultant shame can come to be even more corrosive than the original act. And if others in the group either wittingly or unwittingly contribute to the sense of shame – by actively harassing the victim or by remaining silent about their plight – then they help in achieving the oppressor's original aim.

Our hunch is that oppressors are well aware of the dynamics of humiliation. That is why seemingly excessive and pointless acts of humiliation are to be found in almost every site of tyranny whether in Germany, Iraq, Guantanamo or the Balkans. Our sense is that oppressors have, at least intuitively, understood the power of humiliation in breaking groups, destroying solidarity, and undermining the likelihood of resistance from those they torment.

If this is true, it is equally important for those on the receiving end to be aware of how their culture and their groups can be used against them. It is important that they recognise how they may be induced to collude in their own downfall so that they can refuse the temptation. In a way, humiliation serves as the psychological equivalent of land-mine technology in the arsenal of war. It is not designed to kill but to maim and to leave people as burdens both to themselves, to their families and to an already weakened population. Only by identifying the sites where humiliation can be applied, by understanding the corrosive power of shame and by standing with the victims to combat shame, can the group protect its overall integrity. With insight, that is, we can ensure that the group constitute a cure and not a curse for its members.

References

Anzulovic, B. (1999). *Heavenly Serbia. From myth to genocide*. London, UK: C. Hurst & Co.

Bieber, F., & Daskalovski, Z. (2003). *Understanding the war in Kosovo*. London, UK: Frank Cass.

Cardozo, B. L., Kaiser, R., Gotway, C. A., & Agani, F. (2003). Mental health, social functioning, and feelings of hatred and revenge of Kosovar Albanians one year after the war in Kosovo. *Journal of Traumatic Stress, 16*(4), 351–360.

Cohen, E. A. (1988). *Human behaviour in the concentration camp*. London, UK: Free Association Books.

di Giovanni, J. (2004). *Madness visible: A memoir of war*. London, UK: Bloomsbury.

Dukagjini, L., & Gjecov, S. (1989). *Kanuni i Lekë Dukagjinit/The code of Lekë Dukagjini*. New York, NY: Gjonlekaj Publishing.

Gourevitch, P., & Morris, E. (2008). *Standard operating procedure*. London, UK: Picador.

Griffith, J. L., Agani, F., Weine, S., Ukshini, S., Pulleyblank-Coffey, E., Ulaj, J., et al. (2005). A family-based mental health program of recovery from state terror in Kosova. *Behavioral Science & the Law, 23*(4), 547–558.

Haslam, S. A., O'Brien, A., Jetten, J., Vormedal, K., & Penna, S. (2005). Taking the strain: social identity, social support, and the experience of stress. *British Journal of Social Psychology, 44*(Pt 3), 355–370.

Haslam, S. A., & Reicher, S. D. (2006). Stressing the group: Social identity and the unfolding dynamics of responses to stress. *Journal of Applied Psychology, 91*(5), 1037–1052.

Judah, T. (2000). *Kosovo: War and revenge*. New Haven, CT: Yale University Press.

Kellezi, B. (2006). *Social identity and trauma. The case of Kosovo Albanians*. Unpublished PhD, University of St Andrews, St Andrews, Scotland, UK.

Kellezi, B., Reicher, S., & Cassidy, C. (2009). Surviving the Kosovo conflict: A study of social identity, appraisal of extreme events, and mental well-being. *Applied Psychology: An International Review, 58*(1), 59–83.

Langbein, H. (1994). *Against all hope: Resistance in the Nazi concentration camps 1938–1945*. London, UK: Constable.

Lazarus, S. R., & Folkman, S. (1984). *Stress, appraisal and coping*. New York, NY: Springer.

Levi, P. (1988). *The drowned and the saved*. London, UK: Michael Joseph.

Levi, P. (1996). *Survival in Auschwitz*. New York, NY: Touchstone.

Meçi, X. (2002). *Kanuni i Lekë Dukagjinit. Në Variantin e Mirëditës/The code of Lekë Dukagjini. The Mirëdita version*. Tiranë/Tirana, Albania: Geer.

Mertus, J. A. (1999). *Kosovo. How myths and truths started a war*. Berkeley, CA: University of California Press.

Minervini, C. (2002). Housing reconstruction in Kosovo. *Habitat International, 26*(4), 571–590.

O'Neill, W. G. (2002). *Kosovo: An unfinished peace*. London, UK: Lynne Rienner.

Ramanathapillai, R. (2006). The politicizing of trauma: A case study of Sri Lanka. *Peace and Conflict: Journal of Peace Psychology, 12*(1), 1–18.

Rehn, E., & Sirleaf, E. J. (2002). *Women, war and peace: The independent experts' assessment on the impact of armed conflict on women and women's role in peace-building*. New York, NY: United Nations Development Fund for Women.

Reicher, S. D., & Haslam, S. A. (2010). Beyond help: A social psychology of collective solidarity and social cohesion. In S. Stürmer & M. Snyder (Eds.), *The psychology of pro-social behavior: Group processes, intergroup relations, and helping* (pp. 289–309). Oxford, UK: Blackwell.

Roth, P. (1996). A conversation with Primo Levi. Afterword to Levi, P. *Survival in Auschwitz*. New York, NY: Touchstone.

Rousset, D. (1965). *L'Univers concentrationnaire*. Paris, France: Editions de Minuit.

Saltmarshe, D. (2002). The resource profile approach: A Kosovo case study. *Public Administration and Development, 22*, 179–190.

Sinderis, T. (2003). War, gender and culture: Mozambican women refugees. *Social Science & Medicine, 56*, 713–724.

Slavin, L. A., Rainer, K. L., McCreary, M. L., & Gowda, K. K. (1991). Toward a multicultural model of the stress process. *Journal of Counselling and Development, 70*(1), 156–163.

Sofsky, W. (1997). *The order of terror: The concentration camp*. Princeton, NJ: Princeton University Press.

Spiegel, P. B., & Salama, P. (2000). War and mortality in Kosovo, 1998–99: An epidemiological testimony. *Lancet, 355*, 2204–2209.

Suhrke, A., Barutciski, M., Garlock, R., & Sandison, P. (2000). *The Kosovo refugee crisis: An independent evaluation of UNHCR's emergency preparedness and response*. Geneva, Switzerland: UNHCR.

UNFPA (2005). *Gender-based violence in Kosovo. A case study*. New York, NY: United Nations Population Fund, Women, Peace and Security Initiative Technical Support Division.

Wareham, R. (2000). *"No safe place": UNIFEM commissioned assessment of violence against women in Kosovo Albanian community*. Prishtina, Kosovo: United Nations Development Fund for Women.

Part IV

Social identity, recovery, and rehabilitation

13 Social linkage, self-concept, and well-being after severe traumatic brain injury

Jacinta M. Douglas
La Trobe University

"I don't like being alone, when I'm alone I get sad thinking about life. Better when I am around other people."

(Michael)[1]

"he (Michael) feels lost because he doesn't interact with others . . . we have to find a way he can be Michael."

(Michael's Mother, Anne)

Being a clinician and clinical researcher brings with it enormous opportunities to gain a rich understanding of the core components of meaningful living and well-being from those with whom we work. Indeed, many of the fruitful insights that I have gained into rehabilitation can be traced back to particular clinical or research encounters with people who have been grappling with the major life changes wrought by traumatic brain injury, people like Michael and his mother. Michael sustained a severe brain injury (Glasgow Coma Scale Score on admission: 3; duration of post-traumatic amnesia [PTA]: > 120 days) as a passenger in a motor vehicle crash at 20 years of age. Nearly 6 years later, Michael and his mother participated in a research project that was undertaken to gain an understanding of the personal effects of becoming engaged in group-based, community activities (Douglas, Dyson, & Foreman, 2006). Both Michael's comment above and that of his mother, Anne, capture succinctly the essence of this chapter: Social interaction and engagement facilitate well-being and the dynamic construction of self-concept after brain injury. In this chapter I focus on two related aspects of "the social cure": (1) how emotional well-being is underpinned by an individual's linkage to the social environment including community, social network, and intimate and confiding relationships; and (2) how social engagement supports identity construction. In this context, the term identity is used to encompass an individual's internal self-representation including perception of self as part of a social environment comprised of other individuals and various social groups (e.g., Brewer & Gardner, 1996; Whitbourne, Sneed, & Skultety, 2002). The overall aim of the chapter is to illustrate the potential power of social perspectives in rehabilitation through examination of selected research findings enriched by the description of personal experiences of those whose lives have been affected by severe traumatic brain injury.

WELL-BEING AND SOCIAL LINKAGE: *WHEN I'M ALONE I GET SAD THINKING ABOUT LIFE*

Severe traumatic brain injury (TBI) is an unusually prolonged and potent stressor that leads to enduring changes among those who survive the injury as well as their families. The immediate potency of the crisis stems from its sudden and unexpected onset, while long-term adjustment to challenges are associated with pervasive injury-related changes across cognitive, emotional, and social domains of functioning (Douglas & Spellacy, 1996; Karlovits & McColl, 1999; Kendall, Shum, Lack, Bull, & Fee, 2001; Kendall & Terry, 1996; Koskinen, 1998; Olver, Ponsford, & Curran, 1996; Tate, Broe, Cameron, Hodgkinson, & Soo, 2005; see also Jones, Jetten, Haslam, & Williams, this volume; Gracey & Ownsworth, this volume). Two well-established consequences of severe TBI are depression (Kreutzer, Seel, & Gourlay, 2001; Seel et al., 2003) and social isolation (Eames, Cotterill, Kneale, Storrar, & Yeomans, 1995; Hoofien, Gilboa, Vakil, & Donovick, 2001; Kozloff, 1987; Morton & Wehman, 1995; Thomsen, 1992), and ongoing or recurring periods of sadness and loneliness are described as typical experiences by those living with the everyday consequences of brain injury (Douglas & Spellacy, 2000; Lefebvre, Cloutier, & Levert, 2008; Shorland & Douglas, 2010).

Poor social engagement is a convergent finding in much of the severe TBI outcome research (Dikman, Machamer, Powell, & Temkin, 2003; Draper, Ponsford, & Schönberger, 2007; Hoofien et al., 2001; Olver et al., 1996; Schalen, Hannsson, Nordstrom, & Nordstrom, 1994; Tate, Lulham, Broe, Strettles, & Pfaff, 1989; Tate et al., 2005; Wood & Rutterford, 2006). In our own research (Douglas & Spellacy, 2000), problems with social involvement and/or lack of friendship were identified as over-riding themes in the day-to-day lives of 21 of 35 adults living in the community more than 3.5 years after sustaining a severe brain injury. These people lucidly painted a picture of reduced social linkage when they described their ongoing needs. They described the need to have friends "*to be accepted by other people, to have friends,*" and the need to be part of collective activity "*to work, to play sport*". The need to address this lack of social engagement for their loved one was expressed either directly or indirectly by almost every one of the family carers who took part in the project: "*A social activity group, somewhere for Stephen [son] to go*", "*Anything that helps, especially groups in the community . . .*". At the time of injury, all of these people were active within a social community. No-one was unemployed; 1 was retired, 7 were students, and the remaining 27 participants were employed (24 full-time and 3 part-time). However the majority, who had all survived severe to very severe injuries (mean PTA = 88.26 days, SD = 87.91) and returned home to live with their families in the community, had been unable to become involved in activities in their social contexts. Outside of watching television, they were frequently inactive, and 57 percent of them (and 60 percent of their family carers) were classified on assessment as showing significant symptoms of depression.

Friendship and involvement are clearly sources of social support, and it is generally accepted that social support plays a role in the maintenance of psychological well-being (see also van Dick & Haslam, this volume; Haslam, Reicher, & Levine, this volume). Thus, the presence of depression in the context of the social isolation frequently associated with TBI is not a surprising finding. Theoretical conceptualisations of social support traditionally have explained the positive association between social support and well-being by one of two hypotheses. The first attributes the association to an overall beneficial effect of support, irrespective of the occurrence of a stressful event. The second hypothesis is termed the buffering model and proposes that support is related to well-being only for persons under stress (Cohen & Wills, 1985). In other words, social support buffers or attenuates the effects of stress. Both of these traditional hypotheses predict that higher levels of social support will be associated with better adjustment to chronic illness or disability.

Social support can have several components serving different supportive functions (Schaefer, Coyne, & Lazarus, 1981). Social components reflect an individual's linkage to the social environment including community, social network, and intimate and confiding relationships. Networks can be described by their size, density, and the quality of relationships between members. Within theories of social process, two functions of social actions have been identified: (1) practical, tangible, or instrumental support and (2) emotional, affective, or expressive support (Caplan, 1979; Dean & Lin, 1977; Schaefer et al., 1981). The instrumental dimension involves the use of a social relationship as a means of achieving a goal. Assistance with finding a job or starting a new activity, help with caring for an injured relative, provision of transportation, and financial assistance are all examples of instrumental social support actions. In contrast to the practical functions of instrumental support, the emotional dimension emphasises the affective aspects of relationships. Sharing emotional problems, exchanging life stories, and sharing a meal or a movie with a person one likes or feels close to are examples of expressive social support actions. Problems with the instrumental or tangible functions of social support signal an individual's need for active hands-on assistance. Frequently, problems with the relational or emotional functions of social support are indicative of a lack of friendships or a lack of a relationship with a close confidant.

Applying these social support concepts in our study (Douglas & Spellacy, 2000) helped us to identify social support as an important factor that influences the distress and sadness of brain injury survivors and their family carers. As hypothesised, within the context of demographic and injury-related variables that had been associated with depression in previous research, the lack of social support was a significant and reliable indicator of depression in both adults with severe TBI and family carers. For the participants with TBI, a total of 63 percent (57 percent adjusted) of the variance in the depression measure was predicted by gender, marital status, disability level, and social support. However, social support was the only variable that made a significant unique contribution to the prediction of depression. For the family carers in this study, 50 percent (44 percent adjusted) of the variance in depression was accounted for by carer role (partner or parent), disability level of the injured family member and social support. Two of these variables, disability level and social support, both made significant unique contributions to the prediction of variance in the depression measure. When the specific functions of social support were explored further, strong-tie expressive support emerged as being crucial for maintaining the well-being of injured individuals and family carers.

These findings clearly exemplified the way social factors operate in the process of adjustment to a changed life situation. People need someone close to them with whom to share their feelings, problems, ideas and aspirations – they need a strong-tie reciprocal relationship. Unfortunately, this need was frequently not met for the participants with TBI, and this outcome was clearly illustrated by their own comments during interview: "*I want a relationship*"; "*I need to feel that I'm loved*"; and "*I feel lonely*". Further, due to their lack of involvement or social linkage in the community, those with TBI typically did not have opportunities to build new reciprocal friendships that could provide them with emotional and instrumental support. Thus, for many of these people the negative consequences of the lack of social support were unlikely to diminish over time.

In this type of scenario, there is no easy way out and emotional dysfunction is likely to remain the rule rather than the exception. If a healthy mental state requires sharing the problems one experiences with others who can empathise with them, then depression can be viewed as a problem requiring expressive action, which can be accomplished through access to, and use of, social ties that can be developed through engagement in social activity. This process is depicted schematically in Figure 13.1. Herein is the crux of the problem: the social ties are frequently absent for adults with severe TBI and also their family carers. Consequently, those with low or diminishing social resources are particularly at risk for clinical depression. Our conclusion at the time of finishing this project was simple. Efforts were needed to break the cycle of diminishing social ties feeding into poor emotional adjustment. We called for increased access to services that offer social, leisure and vocational participation programmes in the community and we proposed that helping those with severe TBI to maintain and develop reciprocal friendships could achieve two important goals. It could

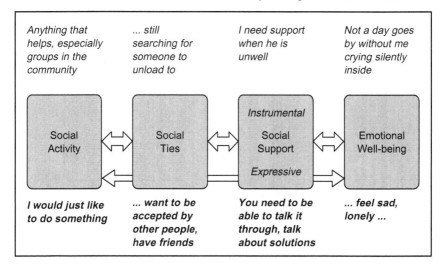

Figure 13.1 Schematic representation of the relationships between social activity, social ties, social support, and emotional well-being expressed by people with severe traumatic brain injury (TBI) and family carers.

Note: TBI participants' comments are shown in boldface italics and those from family carers are in italics. The bidirectional arrow at the bottom of the figure represents the association between social activity and emotional well-being; the smaller bidirectional arrows reflect the inter-relationships between the individual constructs and a pathway by which social activity may influence emotional well-being.

give injured individuals access to social ties and it could reduce the social support demands placed on family carers, enabling them to spend time on personal social activities and maintenance of their own social networks. But does it work?

The crucial question then is: Does becoming socially connected and involved in group community activities make a difference to the emotional well-being of people who have had a severe brain injury? We asked this very question in a subsequent research project (Douglas et al., 2006) and the results gave us some promising insights into potential answers. The project was undertaken to gain an understanding of the personal effects of becoming engaged in a community group programme. The aim of the programme was to provide adults with severe TBI opportunities to pursue leisure activities of their choice and to develop natural social networks within their own communities.

The activity programme was facilitated by regional lead agencies that provided disability services in the community and were not specific to clients with TBI. The disability service identified the interests and preferences of clients with brain injury who were living in the region and referred to their agency. Lead agencies then coordinated a calendar of activities offered within their own services or in the local community. They also coordinated shared transportation for clients to the activity venues. Given their situation within local communities, lead agencies were able to take advantage of strategies and activities that were already developed or were developing for people with disabilities in the community. Thus, they had access to a relatively large number of activities.

People with brain injury took advantage of the broad range of opportunities open to them and chose to take part in many and varied activities (e.g., sailing, indoor climbing, creative arts, lawn bowls, tennis, tenpin bowling, garden arts, health promotion, woodwork, indoor cricket, Thai cooking, creative dance, kayaking, football, music, men's activity group, indoor games, golf, computers, drama), including several activity experiences in different contexts. For example, if an individual were interested in creative arts, he or she could be supported to participate in this activity by providing education about brain injury to staff who were already running a creative arts group for people (with and without disabilities) in the local council-run activity scheme (e.g., neighbourhood house). Alternatively, if enough clients in a particular region identified an interest in an activity such as Asian cooking then an activity-specific cooking group could be provided through the lead agency. Time spent in the programme was free to vary according to client preferences from as little as 1 hour per week for one activity to as many as 6 hours per week over four activities. The programme was funded by the Transport Accident Commission, which is a compulsory, no-fault injury insurance scheme for survivors of motor vehicle-related injuries in Victoria, Australia.

We hypothesised that adults with severe TBI who commenced and maintained regular ($\geq$ weekly) participation in their chosen leisure activities over a 6-month period would show measurable positive change in community integration, social support, mental health, and quality of life (QOL). As well as using quantitative measures to evaluate change, we also conducted semi-structured interviews with the participants and their family carers, if they lived in the family home. Twenty-five participants were assessed before being involved in community activities and then re-assessed 6 months later. Participants had all sustained very severe injuries. They had a mean age of 36.95 years (SD = 10.8) and on average 10 years had elapsed since injury. None of the participants was employed at the time of assessment.

At follow-up participants had naturally divided into three groups: those who had sustained increased community activity ($\geq$ weekly activity with only short absences) over the 6-month intervening period; those who temporarily or intermittently increased activity but did not sustain it; and those who did not participate in activities. Differential outcome profiles were evident across these three groups over the 6 months. The group with sustained engagement in community activities reported significant improvement in social integration (large effect size, $d = 1.11$) and mental health (medium – large effect size, $d = 0.70$) along with significant reduction in the frequency of symptoms of depression (medium – large effect size, $d = 0.67$). They also reported fewer problems with companionship (medium effect size, $d = 0.43$) and improved quality of life (medium effect size, $d = 0.53$), but these changes were not statistically significant. Only the group of participants who sustained activity over 6 months in their chosen pursuits showed this pattern of results. Further, the group of participants who were active clearly described the social activity experience as having a positive effect on confidence and feelings of happiness (*"Activities help give me more confidence"*, *"I felt happier when doing the activities"*, *"We have a great time"*), and the experience of friendship and belonging (*"I'm in a group, us guys – all about the same level, friends"*, *"two friends – one I met at karate"*). Although the project had clear limitations and the numbers of participants per group were small, the results were supportive of the health benefits of social activity for people with severe brain injury.

As the reader will recall, it was in this project that Michael and his mother were participants, and their comments heading this chapter were taken from their first interviews. Michael maintained sustained activity in the programme and over the 6 months he sampled six activities and remained active in four of these. At the 6-month follow-up visit Anne, his mother, commented, *"Getting out has been good for Michael . . . given him more confidence, and his mood is a little better. He has off days occasionally, but he's happy when he goes out."* This sense of positive change at an individual level could also be seen quantitatively in the measures taken before involvement in the group community programme and 6 months later (see Figure 13.2). There was quite a substantial reduction in depressive symptoms [Depression Subscale of the Neurobehavioral Functioning Inventory (NFI-D); Kreutzer, Seel, & Marwitz, 1999]; a small improvement in mental health function [Medical Outcomes SF-12 v2 Survey (SFv2-MH); Ware, Kosinski, Turner-Bowker, & Gandek, 2002]; a reduction in perceived social support problems [Strong-tie Support (STS) and Lack of Involvement (LOI) subscales of the Instrumental and Expressive Social Support Scale; Ensel & Woelfel, 1986], and improvements in social integration [Community Integration Questionnaire (CIQ-SI); Willer, Rosenthal, Kreutzer, Gordon, & Rempel, 1993] and quality of life [global subjective rating (QOL); Hadorn, Sorenson, & Holte, 1995]. In addition, a comparison between Michael's first and follow-up interviews gave us a strong sense of his personal experience (see Figure 13.3).

Indeed, Michael's comments bring the assessment scores to life. Before his involvement in the group community programme Michael's limited social activity was dependent on, and only took place with, his paid carers. His social ties were his Mum and his paid carers. His family was the sole source of his social support, and he wanted to experience happiness again. After becoming a participant in the programme, Michael reported a sense of enjoyment around his now substantially increased social activity (*billiards, woodwork, social dinner, indoor cricket*). His social ties had moved

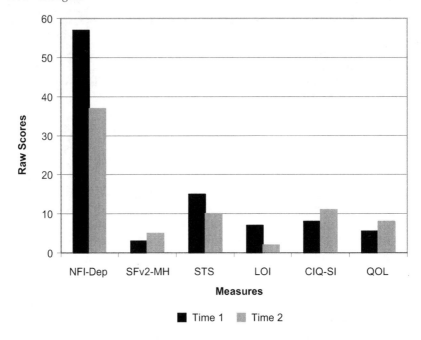

Figure 13.2 Michael's scores on measures of emotional well-being, social support, community integration, and quality of life before involvement in the community group programme and 6 months after sustained activity in the programme.

Note: NFI-Dep = Neurobehavioral Functioning Inventory – Depression Subscale. (Possible score range = 13–65. The higher the score, the more frequently the person experiences symptoms of depression.)

SFv2-MH = SF-12 v2 Mental Health. (Possible score range = 1–10. The higher the score, the better the mental health.)

STS = Strong-Tie Support from the Instrumental and Expressive Social Support Scale. (Possible score range = 3–15. The higher the score, the more frequently the person experiences problems with functions of social support.)

LOI = Lack of Involvement. (Possible score range = 2–10. The higher the score, the more frequently the person experiences problems with functions of social support.)

CIQ-SI = Community Integration Questionnaire–Social Integration subscale. (Possible score range = 0–12. The higher the score, the better the integration.)

QOL = Quality of Life, Global Subjective Rating. (Possible score range = 0–10. The higher the score, the better the person perceives his/her quality of life to be.)

beyond family and relationships bound by paid roles to include one person who Michael designated as having *similar interests* to himself and who Michael now saw as being a *friend* capable of providing expressive social support. Finally, during his second interview Michael talked about experiencing a range of feelings within his emotional adjustment, from *positive* to feeling *a bit down*. Importantly, he was also able to associate his negative feelings with a reasonable and potentially manageable cause, *tiredness*. These are not world-shattering changes, but they certainly were changes in Michael's world. Further, these changes had begun to address his mother

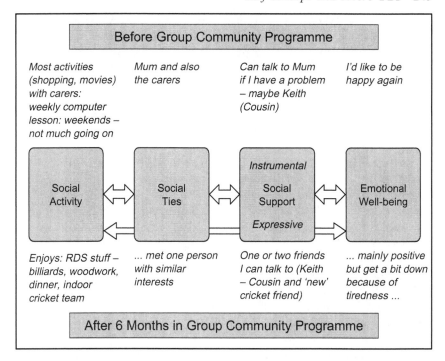

Figure 13.3 Michael's story shown through his comments applied to the schematic representation of the relationships between social activity, social ties, social support, and emotional well-being.

Note: The bidirectional arrow at the bottom of the figure represents the association between social activity and emotional well-being; the smaller bidirectional arrows reflect the inter-relationships between the individual constructs and a pathway by which social activity may influence emotional well-being.

Anne's concerns because a way for Michael *to interact with others* had been found. The possibility also existed that over time changes in Michael's social linkage could facilitate identity construction and the process of finding self after injury.

FINDING SELF: *WE HAVE TO FIND A WAY HE CAN BE MICHAEL*

We had not set out to explore connections between identity construction and social linkage through activity in the research evaluating the group community programme. However, comments describing improvements in sense of self as a consequence of social involvement signalled that direct exploration of conceptualisation of self from the perspective of adults living with the consequences of severe TBI would be a useful next step. In this study (Douglas, 2011, under review), the aim was to gain an understanding of how adults who have sustained severe brain injury view themselves several years after injury and in doing so to obtain insight into components of self-concept/identity from the insider's perspective. Sixteen men and four women living in the community with varying levels of support from family and/or paid carers volunteered to be interviewed in their own homes. Glasgow Coma Scale scores (GCS ≤ 8) or duration of PTA (PTA > 28 days) indicated they had all sustained severe to very severe TBI. None of the people involved in this study had been able to sustain paid employment since the time of injury.

Interviews and field notes were audio-recorded, transcribed verbatim, and coded using principles of grounded theory (e.g., Pigeon & Henwood, 1997) to identify emergent categories and themes. Three main themes emerged from the data, the first two themes together described a model of self-conceptualisation, while the third theme captured the insider's perspective on what had helped along the way. Table 13.1 provides a summary of the themes, the categories that emerged within each theme, and illustrative quotes from participants. The two self-concept themes were termed (a) Who I am, and (b) How I feel about myself. The first theme reflected knowledge components of self and involved two distinct domains; personal attributes and personal goals. Attributes were captured in describing statements, while goals were signalled by striving statements. The attributes category reflected straightforward descriptions of personal characteristics (e.g., *friendly*, *talkative*, *caring*, *handsome*). Notably, "brain injury" in any of its descriptive forms was absent in the personal attributes category; none of these people defined him or herself by his or her injury. Lack of reference to brain injury did not mean that the injury did not play a role in the self-narrative of these people; it simply meant that at this point in their lives it was not conceptualised as an essential attribute of the self.

The second aspect of the knowledge components of self emerged as striving statements capturing personal goals. These statements reflected four distinct categories of personal pursuits: physical, material, social-relational, and activity. These categories aligned well with domains represented in models of health and well-being [e.g., the World Health Organization's (WHO), International Classification of Functioning, Disability and Health (ICF); WHO, 2001]. It was here in these striving statements that the consequences of the brain injury became apparent in each domain. Physical disability was reflected in the majority of statements describing physical goals, and for the most part material goals were related to a desire for financial self-sufficiency. The experience of social isolation and lack of social ties clearly gave rise to the social-relational goals, while the experience of lack of involvement underpinned many of the striving statements in the activity domain.

The second major theme that emerged in the model of self-conceptualisation was the evaluative component: How I feel about myself. Again, two distinct aspects of the evaluative component emerged and these

Table 13.1 Conceptualising self: Emergent themes and categories

Theme	Category	Example Quote
Who I am: Knowledge components of self	Attributes: describing statements	. . . *sociable, friendly, honest, caring and responsible*
	Goals: striving statements	
	• Physical	. . . *increase movement in my arm*
	• Material	. . . *to have a nice car to drive to the gym*
	• Social-relational	. . . *to get a girlfriend and more friends*
	• Activity	. . . *getting back into playing sport, especially basketball*
How I feel about myself: Evaluative components of self	Attitude: describing statements	*I'm content with myself.*
	Outcomes: achieving statements	
	• Physical	*Now I'm even lifting weights.*
	• Material	. . . *have a new car*
	• Social-relational	*I have a lot of new friends – cricket . . .*
	• Activity	*I have my own page on the web.*
The things that helped: Factors that create a sense of connection between self and society	Facilitators	
	• Family	*Family, the way they are . . . they're just here.*
	• Friends	. . . *friends I had since before the accident . . . old group of guys from rehab . . . new friends from (volunteer association)*
	• Carers	. . . *ex-carers . . . carers from (group home)*
	• Pets	*I'm never lonely because I have Bess* (dog).
	• Social snacking: tangible representations	*This* (photo) *is of all of us when we finished . . .*
	• The 'self' narrative	*Telling people my story.*

described self-attitude and sense of achievement or an evaluation of "who I am" and "the outcomes I have achieved". Attitude to self spanned a full range of emotional responses from the positive, *"I'm content with myself"* to the negative, *". . . feel very sad"*. The outcome aspect of the evaluative component of self gave rise to the same four domains that were evident in the striving or goal aspect of self-conceptualisation: physical, material, social-relational, and activity. In this evaluative component of the model, these domains reflected a stocktaking list of goals achieved rather than aspirations. Thus, self-concept as it was constructed in the narratives of these people depicted a dynamic process in which evaluative components emerged as reflected outcomes of the knowledge components. The implied process whereby today's self-defined goals (represented in striving statements) become tomorrow's self-appraised outcomes (represented in achieving statements) is particularly interesting from a therapeutic perspective.

The third theme that emerged from analysis of the data encapsulated the things that helped the *finding self* process. These factors acted as facilitators whose role it was to create and maintain a sense of connection between the self and society. They included family, friends, carers, pets, social snacks or tangible representations of connection, and the biographical narrative itself. Family in all its guises (*mum, brothers, mother and father, wife, partner*) was a powerful social connector. The category of friends was exemplified by *"old"* pre-injury and *"new"* post-injury friends, and a clear link was evident between friends and activities in the community (*friends are from flyball; lots of friends at the farm, where I volunteer*). Paid carers also emerged alongside friends as facilitators of social connection. Participants acknowledged the importance of paid carers through describing them as people with whom they could share their thoughts and feelings as well as do things. These descriptions were similar to those applied to friends, but the term carer rather than friend was used distinctively when describing paid carers. The data also supported the role of companion animals in the process. For those with pets, maintaining a sense of connection was facilitated by caring for and enjoying the company of their pet (*Nugget, my cat, makes me and everyone who visits laugh*) and, additionally, having a pet opened up new avenues to social connection within the community (*A large group of friends are from dog obedience; The lady down the street has a terrier too*).

The concept of "social snacking" emerged primarily as a consequence of the interviews being run in the participants' own homes. This concept was introduced by Gardner and colleagues (Gardner, Pickett, & Knowles, 2005) in the context of their research exploring unmet belonging needs.

> When social interaction is temporarily unavailable, people appear to turn to indirect social strategies to satisfy belonging needs. We refer to these behaviors as "social snacking" because they seem to be the temporary stopgaps to be used between opportunities for true social sustenance. Some may be tangible symbols such as photos, and others

may rely on representational reminders of social connections that may even be represented as part of the self-concept. . . . Like actual snacks, we suspect none are ultimately as satisfying or as healthy as true positive and accepting interaction. However, all may be helpful in shielding one from the stings of isolation or rejection, at least temporarily.

(Gardner et al., 2005, p. 238)

The use of tangible symbols as reminders of social bonds was evident in the interview process when participants used photos, certificates and cards to trigger reminiscence of shared experiences [*I got this* (certificate) *from the communication group – we all got one*] and to affirm a sense of connection with family (*That's my son . . . he's over every 2nd weekend*) and friends (postcard from *very old friend, who has own family now, but keeps in touch*).

The final facilitator of a sense of connection that was captured in the data was the act of creating the "self" narrative. The importance of this act was evident from two perspectives. The first was linked to the activity category whereby participants chose pursuits that enabled them to tell their story (*I have my own website, so that I can tell people my story; I go to the writing group and I'm writing about it all – you know, my life*). The second perspective reflected the need to create the narrative self (*I like people to know who I am; we are all different*) as "the unique product of its own specific walk through life" (Shaddon, Hagstrom, & Koski, 2008, p. 38).

This direct exploration of conceptualisation of self from the perspective of adults living with the consequences of severe TBI sheds some light on the way in which social engagement supports identity construction. Conceptualising self can be described as a multifaceted and dynamic process culminating at any point in one's life as an organised knowledge structure, representing identity. This knowledge structure for these participants contained episodic memories of their life experiences and knowledge of personal facts. Along lines suggested by other chapters in this volume, the process of conceptualising self was influenced by a sense of social connection facilitated by social interactions and social relationships.

CONCLUSION

The work covered in this chapter is just one part of a growing body of work that is focusing on social parameters and their influence on well-being in the context of traumatic brain injury. Indeed, several other researchers have published significant findings that support the notions addressed in this chapter. Social engagement and social support have been found to be significant and reliable indicators not only of emotional adjustment, but also community integration (McColl et al., 1998), life satisfaction (Corrigan, Bogner, Mysiw, Clinchot, & Fugate, 2001; Jones, Haslam, Jetten, Williams, Morris, & Saroyan, 2011; Pierce & Hanks, 2006) and quality of life

(Steadman-Pare, Colantonio, Ratcliff, Chase, & Vernich, 2001) after severe TBI. The results recently reported by Ouellet, Morin, and Lavoie (2009) provide additional support for the psychologically protective role of social activity. These authors compared the psychological functioning of three groups of TBI survivors defined by their level of social activity and found that those who reported being active through work, study, or volunteering demonstrated significantly better psychological adjustment than those who reported no activity.

Tyerman and Humphrey (1984) were the first to report a significant negative discrepancy between post- versus pre-injury ratings of self-concept. In Nochi's (1998) qualitative work, this discrepancy experience emerged as the *loss of self by comparison* theme. Nochi (1997) also found that loss of sense of self after injury was accompanied by a reduction in the individual's field of activity in society. Other researchers have reported additional important associations between self-identity and adjustment. For example, Vickery, Gontovsky, and Caroselli (2005) found that a poorer view of self was associated with lower subjective quality of life, and Jumisko, Lexell, and Soderberg (2005) using a phenomenological approach revealed that recovering the self was a core theme in establishing the meaning of living after severe TBI. Gracey et al. (2008) have explored further the construction of self after brain injury and their findings also provide clear support for the formative role played by both social and practical activity in the personal construction of self after injury (see Gracey & Ownsworth, this volume).

In light of the strong links between social activity, self-identity, and post-injury adjustment, it seems logical to focus on these constructs in rehabilitation. Certainly work towards this end is underway. Ylvisaker and his colleagues (e.g., Ylvisaker & Feeney, 2000a, 2000b; Ylvisaker, Feeney, & Capo, 2007; Ylvisaker, McPherson, Kayes, & Pellett, 2008) have pioneered this type of approach by characterising meaningful engagement in chosen life activities and social reconstruction of identity as foundation stones of rehabilitation. It remains for us to further develop strategies and interventions that can maximise the impact of social determinants of health and ultimately to establish a reliable and valid evidence base to support the social cure.

NOTE

1 Actual names in this chapter have been replaced with pseudonyms to maintain the confidentiality of individuals.

References

Brewer, M., & Gardner, W. (1996). Who is this "we"? Levels of collective identity and self representations. *Personality and Social Psychology Bulletin, 71*, 83–93.

Caplan, T. (1979). Social support, person–environment fit, and coping. In L. A. Ferman & J. P. Gordus (Eds.), *Mental health and the economy* (pp. 89–138). Michigan: W. E. Upjohn Institute for Employment Research.

Cohen, S., & Wills, T. (1985). Stress, social support, and the buffering hypothesis. *Psychological Bulletin, 98,* 310–357.

Corrigan, J., Bogner, J., Mysiw, W., Clinchot, D., & Fugate, L. (2001). Life satisfaction after traumatic brain injury. *Journal of Head Trauma Rehabilitation, 16,* 543–555.

Dean, A., & Lin, N. (1977). The stress buffering role of social support. *Journal of Nervous and Mental Disease, 165,* 403–413.

Dikman, S., Machamer, J., Powell, J., & Temkin, N. (2003). Outcome 3 to 5 years after moderate to severe traumatic brain injury. *Archives of Physical Medicine and Rehabilitation, 10,* 1449–1457.

Douglas, J. (2008). Exploring the conceptualisation of self in people with severe traumatic brain injury. *Brain Impairment, 9,* 226–227.

Douglas, J. (2011). *Conceptualising self following severe traumatic brain injury.* Manuscript under review, La Trobe University, Melbourne, Australia.

Douglas, J., Dyson, M., & Foreman, P. (2006). Increasing leisure activity following severe traumatic brain injury: Does it make a difference? *Brain Impairment, 7,* 107–118.

Douglas, J., & Spellacy, F. (1996). Indicators of long-term family functioning following severe traumatic brain injury in adults. *Brain Injury, 10,* (11), 819–839.

Douglas, J., & Spellacy, F. (2000). Correlates of depression in adults with severe traumatic brain injury and their carers. *Brain Injury, 14,* 71–88.

Draper, K., Ponsford, J., & Schönberger, M. (2007). Psychosocial and emotional outcomes 10 years following traumatic brain injury. *Journal of Head Trauma Rehabilitation, 22,* 278–287.

Eames, P., Cotterill, G., Kneale, T., Storrar, A., & Yeomans, P. (1995). Outcome of intensive rehabilitation after severe brain injury: A long term follow up study. *Brain Injury, 10,* 631–650.

Ensel, W., & Woelfel, M. (1986). Measuring the instrumental and expressive functions of social support. In N. Lin, A. Dean, & W. Ensel (Eds.), *Social support, life events, and depression* (pp. 129–152). Orlando, FL: Academic Press.

Gardner, W., Pickett, C., & Knowles, M. (2005). "Social snacking" and "social shielding": The use of symbolic social bonds to maintain belonging needs. In K. Williams, J. Forgas, & W. von Hippel (Eds.), *The social outcast: Ostracism, social exclusion, rejection and bullying.* New York, NY: Psychology Press, pp. 227–242.

Gracey, F., Palmer, S., Rous, B., Psaila, K., Shaw, K., O'Dell, J., et al. (2008). "Feeling part of things": Personal construction of self after brain injury. *Neuropsychological Rehabilitation, 18,* 627–650.

Hadorn, D., Sorenson, J., & Holte, J. (1995). Large-scale health outcomes evaluation: How should quality of life be measured? *Journal of Clinical Epidemiology, 48,* 619–629.

Hoofien, D., Gilboa, A., Vakil, E., & Donovick, P. J. (2001). Traumatic brain injury (TBI) 10–20 years later: A comprehensive outcome study of psychiatric symptomatology, cognitive abilities and psychosocial functioning. *Brain Injury, 15,* 189–209.

Jones, J. M., Haslam, S. A., Jetten, J., Williams, W. H., Morris, R., & Saroyan, S. (2011). What doesn't kill you can make you stronger (and more satisfied with life): The impact of identity on well-being after acquired brain injury. *Psychology and Health, 26,* 353–369.

Jumisko, E., Lexell, J., & Soderberg, A. (2005). The meaning of living with traumatic brain injury in people with moderate or severe traumatic brain injury. *Journal of Neuroscience Nursing, 37,* 42–50.

Karlovits, T., & McColl, M. (1999). Coping with community integration after severe traumatic brain injury: A description of stresses and coping strategies. *Brain Injury, 13,* 845–861.

Kendall, E., Shum, D., Lack, B., Bull, S., & Fee, C. (2001). Coping following traumatic brain injury: The need for contextually sensitive assessment. *Brain Impairment, 2,* 81–96.

Kendall, E., & Terry, D. (1996). Psychosocial adjustment following closed head injury: A model for predicting outcome. *Neuropsychological Rehabilitation, 6,* 101–123.

Koskinen, S. (1998). Quality of life 10 years after a very severe traumatic brain injury: The perspective of the injured and the closest relative. *Brain Injury, 12,* 631–648.

Kozloff, R. (1987). Networks of social support and the outcome from severe head injury. *Journal of Head Trauma Rehabilitation, 2,* 14–23.

Kreutzer, J., Seel, R., & Gourlay, E. (2001). The prevalence and symptom rates of depression after traumatic brain injury: A comprehensive examination. *Brain Injury, 15,* 563–576.

Kreutzer, J., Seel, R., & Marwitz, J. (1999). *The neurobehavioral functioning inventory.* San Antonio, TX: The Psychological Corporation.

Lefebvre, H., Cloutier, G., & Levert, M. (2008). Perspectives of survivors of traumatic brain injury and their caregivers on long-term social integration. *Brain Injury, 22,* 535–543.

McColl, M., Carlson, P., Johnston, J., Minnes, P., Shue, K., & Davies, D. (1998). The definition of community integration: Perspectives of people with brain injuries. *Brain Injury, 12,* 15–30.

Morton, M., & Wehman, P. (1995). Psychosocial and emotional sequelae of individuals with traumatic brain injury: A literature review and recommendations. *Brain Injury, 9,* 81–92.

Nochi, M. (1997). Dealing with the "void": Traumatic brain injury as a story. *Disability & Society, 12,* 533–555.

Nochi, M. (1998). "Loss of self" in the narratives of people with traumatic brain injuries: A qualitative analysis. *Social Science & Medicine, 46,* 869–878.

Olver, J. H., Ponsford, J. L., & Curran, C. A. (1996). Outcome following traumatic brain injury: A comparison between two and five years after injury. *Brain Injury, 10,* 841–848.

Ouellet, M., Morin, C., & Lavoie, A. (2009). Volunteer work and psychological health following traumatic brain injury. *Journal of Head Trauma Rehabilitation, 24,* 262–271.

Pierce, C., & Hanks, R. (2006). Life satisfaction after traumatic brain injury and the World Health Organization model of diability. *American Journal of Physical Medicine & Rehabilitation, 85,* 890–898.

Pigeon, N. F., & Henwood, K. L. (1997). Using grounded theory in psychological research. In N. Hayes (Ed.), *Doing qualitative analysis in psychology* (pp. 245–273). Hove, UK: Psychology Press.

Schaefer, C., Coyne, J., & Lazarus, R. (1981). The health-related functions of social support. *Journal of Behavioral Medicine, 4,* 381–405.

Schalen, W., Hannsson, L., Nordstrom, G., & Nordstrom, C. (1994). Psychosocial outcome 5–8 years after severe traumatic brain lesions and the impact of rehabilitation services. *Brain Injury, 8,* 49–64.

Seel, R., Kreutzer, J., Rosenthal, M., Hammond, F., Corrigan, J., & Black, K. (2003). Depression after traumatic brain injury: A National Institute on Disability and Rehabilitation Research Model Systems multicentre investigation. *Archives of Physical Medicine and Rehabilitation, 84,* 177–184.

Shaddon, B., Hagstrom, F., & Koski, P. (2008). *Life stories and the narrative self.* San Diego, CA: Plural Publishing.

Shorland, J., & Douglas, J. (2010). Understanding the role of communication in maintaining and forming friendships following traumatic brain injury. *Brain Injury, 24,* 569–580.

Steadman-Pare, D., Colantonio, A., Ratcliff, G., Chase, S., & Vernich, L. (2001). Factors associated with perceived quality of life many years after traumatic brain injury. *Journal of Head Trauma Rehabilitation, 16,* 330–342.

Tate, R., Broe, G., Cameron, I., Hodgkinson, A., & Soo, C. (2005). Pre-injury, injury and early post-injury predictors of long-term functional and psychosocial recovery after severe traumatic brain injury. *Brain Impairment, 6,* 75–89.

Tate, R., Lulham, J., Broe, G., Strettles, B., & Pfaff, A. (1989). Psychosocial outcome for the survivors of severe blunt head injury: The results from a consecutive series of 100 patients. *Journal of Neurology, Neurosurgery, and Psychiatry, 52,* 1128–1134.

Thomsen, I. V. (1992). Late psychosocial outcome in severe traumatic brain injury. Preliminary results of a third follow-up study after 20 years. *Scandinavian Journal of Rehabilitation Medicine, 26,* 142–152.

Tyerman, A., & Humphrey, M. (1984). Changes in self-concept following severe head injury. *International Journal of Rehabilitation Research, 7,* 11–23.

Vickery, C., Gontovsky, S., & Caroselli, J. (2005). Self-concept and quality of life following acquired brain injury: A pilot investigation. *Brain Injury, 19,* 657–665.

Ware, J., Kosinski, M., Turner-Bowker, D., & Gandek, B. (2002). *Version 2 of the SF-12 Health Survey.* Lincoln, RI: QualityMetric, Inc.

Whitbourne, S., Sneed, J., & Skultety, K. (2002). Identity processes in adulthood: Theoretical and methodological challenges. *Identity: An International Journal of Theory and Research, 2,* 29–45.

Willer, B., Rosenthal, M., Kreutzer, J. S., Gordon, W. A., & Rempel, R. (1993). Assessment of community integration following rehabilitation for traumatic brain injury. *Journal of Head Trauma Rehabilitation. 8,* 75–87.

Wood, R., & Rutterford, N. (2006). Psychosocial adjustment 17 years after severe brain injury. *Journal of Neurology, Neurosurgery, and Psychiatry, 77,* 71–73.

World Health Organization [WHO]. (2001). *International classification of functioning disability and health.* Geneva, Switzerland: WHO.

Ylvisaker, M., & Feeney, T. (2000a). Reflections on Dobermanns, poodles and social rehabilitation for difficult-to-serve individuals with traumatic brain injury. *Aphasiology, 14,* 407–431.

Ylvisaker, M., & Feeney, T. (2000b). Reconstruction of identity after brain injury. *Brain Impairment, 1,* 12–28.

Ylvisaker, M., Feeney, T., & Capo, M. (2007). Long-term community supports for individuals with co-occuring disabilities after traumatic brain injury: Cost effectiveness and project-based intervention. *Brain Impairment, 8,* 276–292.

Ylvisaker, M., McPherson, K., Kayes, N., & Pellett, E. (2008). Metaphoric identity mapping: Facilitating goal-setting and engagement in rehabilitation after traumatic brain injury. *Neuropsychological Rehabilitation, 18,* 713–741.

14 Deciding to disclose: The importance of maintaining social relationships for well-being after acquired brain injury

Janelle M. Jones
University of Queensland

Jolanda Jetten
University of Queensland

S. Alexander Haslam
W. Huw Williams
University of Exeter

Acquired brain injury (ABI) is often seen as one of the most debilitating conditions that can affect individuals. This is largely because the neurological damage resulting from ABI can produce significant changes in individuals' physical, behavioural, cognitive, and emotional capabilities. For instance, individuals with ABI may experience symptoms such as motor impairments, attention deficits, speech difficulties, memory loss, or emotional lability (e.g., Kendall & Terry, 1996; Knox & Douglas, 2009; Kwok, Lee, Leung, & Poon, 2008; Strandberg, 2009; Willmott, Ponsford, Hocking, & Schonberger, 2009). However, while these symptoms vary as a function of their nature and severity, it is their visibility that can have more of an impact in the long term. Because functional changes resulting from ABI may not always be immediately visible to others, ABI is often referred to as the "invisible disability". Moreover, in those cases where the functional changes associated with ABI are largely invisible, individuals with ABI may have the choice of whether or not they disclose their injury to others. Some will decide to talk quite openly about their injury, whereas others may avoid the topic, or – depending on the nature of the functional change – will choose to conceal their injury. As a result, they will not routinely be identified as someone who has sustained an ABI.

All of this makes ABI a complex condition to manage not only because of the multitude of functional changes that individuals may experience, but also because the way a person communicates their injury to the world can be critical to both their adjustment and long-term well-being. In this chapter, we attempt to unpack some of the social psychological processes that determine whether ABI is associated with negative or positive well-being. We start from the assumption that ABI represents a negative life transition that affects the way that people think about themselves (i.e., their personal identity) as well as their social connections and belongingness to social groups more generally (i.e., their social identity). In this transition, concealing ABI – if this is possible – may be an important strategy for managing the consequences of the injury. When individuals choose not to disclose their injury to others, acknowledgment of the impact and consequences of the injury are likely to be minimized (publicly at least). Yet when individuals choose to disclose their injury to others, this process is likely to be associated with private and public recognition that the self has changed.

We propose that both disclosure and nondisclosure will affect well-being because they affect self-definition, the portrayal of the self to others, and the nature of relationships with others. In this chapter we draw on social psychological research on stigma and identity processes more generally to understand when disclosing one's injury to others may affect well-being negatively but also when it may be tied to recovery by paving the way for a *social cure*.

THE STIGMA SURROUNDING ABI

Once an individual has sustained an ABI a period of readjustment typically follows during which he or she attempts to come to terms with the differences, impairments, or limitations that may result from the injury. Difficulties of adjustment can be compounded by the fact that relationships with others change – sometimes for the better, but more often for the worse. There are a number of reasons for this. First, most people have little knowledge of ABI and the condition is not well understood by the general public (Simpson, Mohr, & Redman, 2000). Negative responses in this case may result from ignorance about the nature or seriousness of the neurological damage that ABI can produce. In addition, regardless of whether functional changes are minor or major, individuals with ABI are often erroneously stigmatized on the basis of the behaviours that they exhibit. For example, because neurological damage may not be visible, perceivers may fail to attribute behaviour to the injury and, as a result, those with an ABI may be considered odd and weird, or even as mentally ill or drunk (e.g., Linden, Rauch, & Crothers, 2005). As a result of this misattribution, people may negatively evaluate, hold prejudices about, and discriminate against, the individual because he or she no longer appears "normal".

Even though those who are closer to the individual with ABI know the cause of the changed behaviour, and may therefore be less likely to misattribute behaviour, ABI often changes the nature of the social interactions with those who sustained the injury. The person's personality may have changed and thus, to his or her partner, friends, or family members, he or she may no longer appear to be the same person. Others may feel awkward or uncomfortable when interacting with the person with ABI, not least because they are unsure about how they should respond to any changes they notice in the individual as a result of his or her condition. As a consequence, others may choose to distance themselves from the individual with ABI. This can strain existing social relationships, leading to breakdown and loss, but also hamper the formation of new social relationships (see also Douglas, this volume).

The prospect of negative evaluations, ignorance, uncomfortable interactions, changed or broken relationships, and prejudice more generally may be an additional barrier that stands in the way of individuals' adjustment after sustaining an ABI. Not only do they have to contend with cognitive and neurological changes, but their social world is also no longer as it used to be and this presents new challenges. Fear of being ridiculed, misunderstood, or being subjected to social, financial, and interpersonal discrimination as a result of negative stereotypes can lead individuals to be wary of social encounters and to withdraw from social contact. Again, this can put strain on existing social relationships and make it difficult for individuals with ABI to initiate new social relationships.

Yet even though one would intuitively expect that these changes would necessarily impact negatively on well-being, this is not always the case. On the contrary, a range of health outcomes have been observed among individuals with ABI. Some individuals certainly struggle with adjustment. In particular, those who have difficulty managing their condition have been found to report increased levels of depression and lower self-esteem (Draper, Ponsford, & Schönberger, 2007; Fleminger, Oliver, Williams, & Evans, 2003). Others, however, appear to be able to rebuild their lives and their well-being seems relatively unaffected despite their life-changing injury. Interestingly too, compared to pre-injury, some individuals actually fare better after their injury. These individuals report *improved* quality of life after injury and *post-traumatic growth* (McGrath & Linley, 2006; Wood, 2008). They assert that the injury has changed them in a profound way – a change that, in their eyes, is a change for the better.

It thus appears that individuals' experience of positive or negative well-being is not determined by their physical condition alone. A broader process of identity change is taking place in which well-being can be sustained (and sometimes improved) either by a sense of self-continuity despite ABI or by recognition that the self has fundamentally changed. As we will argue further below, the decision to disclose one's condition to others bears upon this process because it involves either the recognition of change (i.e., through disclosure) or the desire to present the self as relatively unchanged to others (i.e., through nondisclosure). We propose that a key to understanding this dynamic lies in the fact that disclosure decisions have a critical bearing on social relationships and identity more generally.

TO DISCLOSE OR NOT TO DISCLOSE

Disclosure decisions do not simply involve a binary decision whereby one lets everyone know about the injury or does not tell anyone about it. There are many smaller, day-to-day decisions to be made that fall in between these two extremes: who to tell, what and how much to tell them, and when to tell them. Some individuals may decide to only tell their close friends and relatives about their injury. Others may tell everyone or no one. Some may decide to tell others only after having initially kept quiet about it for some time and others may stop telling people about their ABI after a while (in particular, if the injury was sustained a long time ago and no longer impacts on their current life). As suggested already, another important factor in this decision is the degree to which individuals are able to conceal the ABI. Functional changes are more visible for some than for others and this will impact both on the extent to which they have a choice about whether to conceal their ABI from others and about what information can be concealed. For example, individuals with ABI may be reluctant to disclose how the injury was acquired or the actual severity of the injury (e.g., Linden et al., 2005; Redpath & Linden, 2004; Simpson et al., 2000), but may talk freely about their symptoms. For individuals who have some control over their disclosure of their ABI, it is likely that perceptions of the stigma surrounding their injury will influence their decision.

In this context it is important to distinguish the visibility of a stigma from what Goffman calls its "know-about-ness" (1963, p. 65). In the context of ABI, know-about-ness can take different forms. Family and friends may know about the injury, but may also not quite understand the experience of having an ABI. This may mean that once the bandages are taken off and the physical signs of the injury are healed, they also assume that the individual is cured and that life can return to normal. Particularly in the case of enduring neurological damage, however, this is unlikely to be the case and, as a result, there may be a mismatch between the individual's experience and others' expectations.

As Goffman observes, know-about-ness also takes other forms. It can include the degree to which the ABI is immediately perceivable and whether the functional changes are obvious to everyone. There may actually be less miscommunication between the person that sustained the injury and the surrounding environment when the injury is obvious and the functional changes are visible for everyone. However, in those cases, individuals with ABI may not have to contend with questions about "what is wrong with him/her?" but may face exclusion because they are perceived as severely physically or mentally disabled.

Misattributions and miscommunications are more common when others perceive that there is something different about the person and it is not obvious that this change is the result of an ABI. For instance, McClure and colleagues found that attributions were affected by whether an individual's ABI was visible or not (i.e., whether or not they were wearing head bandages). Unsurprisingly perhaps, when injury was visible, individuals' behaviour was more likely to be attributed to head injury, whereas when presented without head bandages the individual in question was more likely to be perceived as a "typical teenager". What is more, when injuries were not visible, people incorrectly associated ABI with fewer functional changes than was the case with visible injuries. In this way, the absence of outward signs of injury can engender unrealistic expectations about the amelioration of ABI (McClure, Buchanan, McDowall, & Wade, 2008; McClure, Devlin, McDowall, & Wade, 2006).

Evidence also suggests that when others know that an individual has sustained an injury, difficulties in existing social relationships often arise from a range of misapprehensions: misconceptions about ABI and its impact; misattributions for behaviours associated with ABI; and misunderstanding about the nature of recovery from these injuries. Moreover, it is not just close friends and family members who may hold erroneous expectations about recovery; health professionals have also been found to be vulnerable to unrealistic recovery expectations, particularly when ABI is invisible. It appears that, because the injury cannot be seen, they are more likely to believe that individuals with ABI are exaggerating their symptoms or complaints and more likely to expect that the victim's injuries will heal like other injuries. In this, others often fail to recognize that ABI recovery involves a continual process of renegotiating, retraining, and relearning (Glover, 2003; Guilmette & Paglia, 2004; Swift & Wilson, 2001; Willer, Johnson, Rempel, & Linn, 1993; see also Douglas, this volume; Gracey & Ownsworth, this volume).

Just as with any other invisible stigmatized identity, then, individuals with ABI may have to decide whether or not they disclose their injury to others (see Hornsey & Jetten, 2011). And here concerns about how others will react to their injury may present them with a serious dilemma post-injury. Disclosing their injury may have negative consequences insofar as it compromises existing relationships and makes them a target of discrimination. Yet while withholding this information from others may be a viable option when managing an invisible stigma, this strategy may also have negative consequences insofar as it is undermines high-quality relationships (e.g., because it implies a lack of authenticity and denotes a lack of trust) and precludes opportunities for much-needed social support.

Whether or not individuals with ABI disclose their stigmatized group membership is therefore a decision that can influence the individual and his or her well-being in different ways. Figure 14.1 presents a model outlining the different paths through which disclosure and nondisclosure can affect

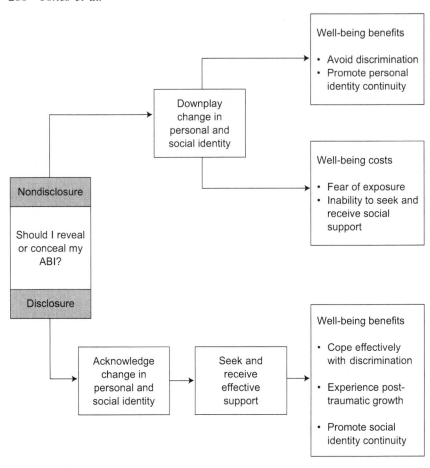

Figure 14.1 Theoretical model of the relationships between disclosure of acquired brain injury (ABI), social relationships and well-being outcomes.

well-being. The model starts from the assumption that disclosure entails a recognition that life is no longer the same as it was before the injury and that there is private and public acceptance of discontinuity between one's pre-injury and post-injury self. Nondisclosure, on the other hand, involves an attempt to present the self as rather unchanged to the outside world. In other words, people may experience functional changes, but will try to hide them from (some) others. Associated with this, they may be reluctant to discuss their symptoms with others or to seek professional help to deal with their functional changes. At the same time, when meeting new people, they may prefer not to mention their injury. In this way, nondisclosure allows the individual (and others) to maintain the perception, which may or may not be grounded in reality, of continuity between the past (before injury) and the present (after injury).

COSTS AND BENEFITS ASSOCIATED WITH NONDISCLOSURE

How then do disclosure decisions affect well-being among those who have sustained an ABI? Starting with nondisclosure, we propose that concealment may be associated with benefits to well-being because it enables individuals with ABI to minimize the impact of their stigma on their relationships with others. That is, disclosure entails the risk of exposing oneself to negative responses and telling others about a stigma can mean that one's social relationships suffer. Others may struggle to accept the individual with ABI or they may be uncomfortable in their presence. For instance, recent research suggests that HIV-positive individuals were more likely to conceal their HIV-positive status from others if they perceived members of this group to be targets of discrimination. In turn, this lack of disclosure meant that they reported lower perceived levels of personal discrimination and higher levels of physical and psychological well-being (i.e., good health, mood, and quality of life; Molero, Fuster, Jetten, & Moriano, 2011). This suggests that if individuals believe that they will face discrimination from others, then concealing their stigma enables them to avoid personal discrimination and this protects well-being.

In addition, and related to the previous point, by concealing an ABI, individuals may give the impression to the outside world that despite the injury they have sustained, their life has not changed much (indeed, concealment may involve avoiding reference to anything that might imply the possibility of change). In this, nondisclosure may be a successful coping strategy that allows those with ABI to pass as "normal" and thereby take part in activities from which they might otherwise be excluded (e.g., employment, driving; see Jetten & Pachana, this volume). That is, concealment will help individuals to maintain their existing social relationships with others. The suggestion of continuity (imagined or real) may have additional positive effects on well-being because individuals are able to sustain a coherent narrative of themselves and the social groups to which they belong (Sani, Bowe, & Herrera, 2008). In particular, continuity of social relationships before and after the ABI may be important because it helps in the management of functional changes associated with their injury. Social relationships tether individuals to the past, allowing them to function in the present, and offering them a window to the future as well as providing an opportunity to further develop existing social relationships. In this vein, recent research by Haslam and colleagues provides evidence that perceived continuity of social relationships over time is an important predictor of the extent to which individuals adjust successfully after a particular form of ABI: stroke (Haslam et al., 2008). These researchers found that those who were able to maintain previously important group memberships after their stroke (and who thus experienced high levels of continuity) reported higher life satisfaction after the stroke.

Although nondisclosure can have well-being benefits, it can also entail costs – particularly if concealment extends over a long period. Individuals who hide their injury may worry about being found out and they may become overly concerned about the impression they make on others (Pachankis, 2007). Even though successful concealment may also mean that people are not exposed to negative responses and discrimination, they may become hypersensitive to negative stereotypes and this in itself can be a source of distress (Quinn & Chaudoir, 2009). They may also feel overly unique and this has also been associated with negative well-being consequences (Frable, Platt, & Hoey, 1998). This suggestion is consistent with research which shows that nondisclosure is associated with increased stress and fear of discovery. It may also explain why nondisclosure can lead individuals to distance themselves from, and lose, social relationships (Crocker & Major, 1989; Pachankis, 2007; Quinn, 2006).

Another cost of nondisclosure is that it does not allow individuals to draw upon effective social support from others who have also suffered an ABI or from other people more generally. Indeed, the failure to receive social support that helps in the successful management of one's condition has been found to weigh heavily on well-being among those who choose not to disclose their potentially stigmatizing condition to others. For example, research with gay men that examines the long-term health effects of hiding their sexual identity has found that concealment is related to higher rates of cancer and increased incidence of infectious diseases (Cole, Kemeny, Taylor, & Visscher, 1996). Furthermore, for men who are HIV-positive, concealment was positively related to the speed of disease progression (Cole, Kemeny, Taylor, Visscher, & Fahey, 1996). It seems likely that these negative effects arise from feelings of loneliness and social isolation that are associated with keeping one's problems to oneself. Indeed, if it is the case that "a trouble shared is a trouble halved", then it follows from this proverbial wisdom that "a trouble concealed is a trouble doubled". As we will discuss more in the next section, another reason why this might be the case is that the lack of shared group membership makes those who hide a potentially stigmatizing condition more vulnerable to the negative views that mainstream society holds because it limits their ability to develop a *collective* coping response (Crabtree, Haslam, Postmes, & Haslam, 2010). Individuals suffer in silence rather than working with others to overcome their difficulties and possibly bring about social change (see Branscombe, Fernández, Gómez, & Cronin, this volume; Kellezi & Reicher, this volume).

COSTS AND BENEFITS ASSOCIATED WITH DISCLOSURE

Disclosure may be difficult for people not only because it potentially makes them vulnerable to negative responses, but also because it communicates a sense that "I'm not who you think I am" or "I am no longer the person I used to be". The act of disclosing is thus as much about telling others as it is about negotiating self-definitions and perhaps even taking a first step in coming to terms with change. As we have already intimated, what is critical in the context of ABI is that it involves the recognition, negotiation, and communication of *self-change* – relating to the fact that one's pre-injury self is not necessarily the same as one's post-injury self. Of course, there is a sense in which this is an issue that arises in relation to most significant life transitions (including any accident or illness, marriage and divorce, going to university or retiring; Jetten, Haslam, Iyer, & Haslam, 2010). Nevertheless, in the case of ABI this issue can be especially acute precisely because the change in question often has a direct impact on the experience and expression of self (e.g., as manifest in changed language ability, altered personality; see Gracey & Ownsworth, this volume).

Yet even though disclosure may expose people to negative responses, the act of disclosing also makes it possible to counteract the negative effects of discrimination on well-being. In particular, disclosure allows members of stigmatized groups to identify with these groups and this social identification may play an important role in buffering and counteracting the negative effects of perceived discrimination on well-being (e.g., Branscombe, Schmitt, & Harvey, 1999; Crabtree et al., 2010; see also Branscombe et al., this volume; van Dick & Haslam, this volume). For example, in their study of men who were HIV-positive, Molero and colleagues (2011) found that the personal costs of disclosure were to some extent offset by benefits that identification with others provided. In particular, disclosing their HIV-positive status allowed individuals to develop a sense of shared identification with others who were in the same situation. This, in turn, enhanced the likelihood of endorsing collective action to improve the fate of the group as a whole, and this sense of collective empowerment was positively associated with well-being (Drury, Cocking, Beale, Hanson, & Rapley, 2005).

It thus appears that, in addition to a path whereby nondisclosure protects individuals from exposure to discrimination, there is another more collective route through which disclosure has positive well-being effects because it provides a basis for social identification that facilitates collective coping responses. The power of this buffering role of group membership should not be underestimated. Indeed, the capacity for people to respond collectively to discrimination is almost certainly one of the main reasons why in the larger literature on coping and stigma there is little evidence that being a member of a stigmatized group is consistently associated with negative outcomes on measures of well-being (Crocker, Major, & Steele, 1998).

Yet whether disclosure leads to such beneficial well-being effects depends very much on the extent to which it is a basis either for seeking out new sources of social support or for consolidating existing social relationships. To do this, individuals need to accept that, as a result of their injury, they are no longer the same person that they were before the injury and that their relationship with others as well as their personal identity have both changed (although the extent of this change will obviously vary considerably from person to person). Disclosing the injury and publicly acknowledging this change then allows the individual to seek out the social and professional support that has the potential to help him or her deal with his or her changed life and the functional changes he or she experiences. Consistent with this assertion, there is now considerable evidence that social relationships and the social support that comes with these relationships are related to positive health and well-being outcomes when individuals are contending with a range of illnesses, injuries, impairments, or life transitions (Cohen, 2004; Haslam et al., 2008; House, Landis, & Umberson, 1988; Putnam, 2000; Stinson et al., 2008; for reviews see Sani, this volume, van Dick & Haslam, this volume).

Our own recent research provides support for the idea that the strengthening of social relationships and the social support that is derived from these relationships has a critical role to play in adjustment and life satisfaction after an ABI (Jones et al., 2011). In a sample of over 600 individuals with ABI, our initial analyses revealed – somewhat surprisingly – that as the reported severity of individual's ABIs increased, so too did their reported levels of life satisfaction. In other words, rather than compromising well-being, severity of injury was actually associated with a certain amount of post-traumatic growth (see Mailhan, Azouvi, & Dazord, 2005, for a similar finding). Although this effect was small and, at first sight, appears counterintuitive, we were able to explain it after taking account of the way in which injury severity precipitated both personal and social change.

In the first instance we found that the more severe the injury, the more individuals reported experiencing positive *personal changes*. This had two distinct aspects: first, individuals reported having acquired a stronger sense of who they were and what they stood for (something we refer to as personal identity strength; Jetten, Haslam, Pugliese, Tonks, & Haslam, 2010); second they were more likely to self-categorize as a survivor. Both these changes epitomize the process of growing stronger in the process of change. Moreover, both speak to the fact that severe injury had led individuals to reconsider and to redefine the self.

In addition to this we also found that severity of injury was associated with positive *social changes*. Again this had two aspects. First, participants indicated that as a result of their injury their relationships with significant others (e.g., family and friends) had improved; second they indicated that as a result of their injury they had been able to benefit from the help provided by relevant support agencies. In sum, as the model presented in Figure 14.2 suggests, severe brain injury fundamentally strengthened a constellation of factors that bear upon both personal and social identity and thereby promoted successful coping with injury.

It would appear, then, that the strengthening of personal identity and embeddedness in social groups can create positive spirals that help to drive

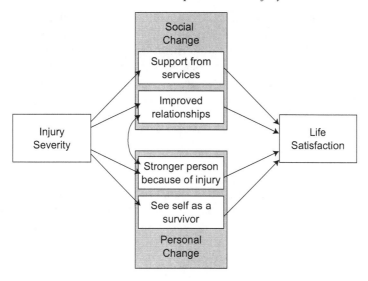

Figure 14.2 Model of the role played by personal and social changes in mediating between injury severity and life satisfaction (Jones et al., 2011).

the post-traumatic growth that some individuals report after injury. Again, it is the coming to terms with the fact that life has changed which seems to be key to such reports. Illustrative of this point, Goffman (1963) cites a mother who was permanently disabled by polio as saying:

> By now, far away from the hospital experience, I can evaluate what I have learned. For it wasn't only suffering: it was also learning through suffering. I know my awareness of people has deepened and increased, and those who are close to me can count on me to turn all my mind and heart and attention to their problems. I could not have learned *that* dashing all over the tennis court.

(p. 22)

This observation that people can construe their suffering as a blessing in disguise is consistent with other findings that examine the way that members of stigmatized groups respond to perceived group-based discrimination. Here again, individuals report experiencing growth as a result of having confronted and overcome the adversity presented by their membership of the stigmatized group (e.g., Branscombe et al., 1999; Crocker & Major, 1989; Shih, 2004).

It is not just severity of the injury that can convey to individuals that identity has changed in a fundamental way. The decision to disclose one's injury to others may also publicly signal that life has changed and this may pave the way for seeking and receiving social support to cope with a changed reality (see Figure 14.1). Again, recent research supports this prediction. For example, in a sample of gay men and lesbians, Beals and her colleagues found that voluntarily mentioning one's sexual orientation to others when the opportunity presented itself was associated with lower levels of depression and higher levels of self-esteem. Importantly too, this relationship between disclosure and well-being was mediated by perceived social support (Beals, Peplau, & Gable, 2009).

This is also an issue that we have explored in our own research by seeking to discover whether disclosure affects the well-being of individuals with visible ABI. An initial study examined individuals with mild to moderate ABI 6 months after their discharge from the emergency department in a hospital in the south west of England (Jones et al., 2010). To understand the way that visibility and stigma surrounding the injury affects well-being, individuals with ABI were compared to individuals with orthopaedic injuries. These injuries share a number of important features: both can result from similar incidents (e.g., falls), both are treated within hospital emergency departments, and both may be associated with lasting functional changes. Where they differ is in (a) their location (i.e., head versus upper limb); (b) their visibility (with orthopaedic injuries typically being visible whereas ABI tends to be invisible); and (c) the stigma surrounding ABI that is absent in the case of orthopaedic injuries (Redpath & Linden, 2004).

We found that ABI and orthopaedic injured groups did not differ in their perceptions of the severity of their injuries, personal changes, changes to social relationships, or in their well-being after injury. What we did find, however, was that these two groups differed in the extent to which individuals disclosed their injuries to others. Specifically, individuals with ABI were less willing to tell others about their injury, were more likely to report experiencing greater emotional disturbances, and that their injuries had a substantial impact on their lives. More fine-grained analysis indicated that among (and only among) individuals with ABI a lower willingness to disclose one's injury was related to a greater belief that one's injury had a negative personal impact and this in turn was related to lower levels of life satisfaction. These findings therefore provide preliminary support for our argument that there can be well-being costs associated with nondisclosure for individuals with invisible ABI.

In follow-up research, we examined more closely the relationship between disclosure, anticipated discrimination, maintenance of social relationship, and well-being (Jones et al., 2011). This involved recruiting a sample of individuals with mild to severe ABI via Headway UK (a charitable organization that provides informational, interpersonal, and practical support to individuals with ABI and their families; Glover, 2003). In our analyses, we focused on respondents who indicated that they were able to conceal their injury. We then examined respondents' experiences of stigma and discrimination as a result of injury. Specifically, we assessed the extent to which respondents (a) had disclosed their injury (e.g., by means of questionnaire items such as: "I find it hard to tell others that I have sustained a brain injury"); (b) had experienced negative changes to their social relationships (including relationship loss); and (c) had high or low levels of life satisfaction, and self-esteem.

Our results indicated that the more individuals expected to encounter discrimination as a result of having ABI, the more reluctant they were to disclose their injury to others. This finding is consistent with previous research (Molero et al., 2011) and suggests that concealment is an important strategy for protecting oneself from negative outcomes. However, we also found that respondents who were more willing to disclose their injury to others reported higher levels of self-esteem and life-satisfaction. Moreover, injury disclosure was associated with fewer relationship breakdowns, and this in turn was related to higher levels of life satisfaction and self-esteem. Caution is warranted in interpreting these relationships, since the causal sequences here are impossible to establish clearly. Nevertheless, the general patterns here are certainly consistent with claims that among individuals with ABI, nondisclosure will tend to impact negatively on well-being. In addition, it extends the findings of our earlier study by showing that the costs to well-being that arise from nondisclosure can be partly attributed to relationship breakdown. Looked at the other way round, we can also see that individuals who disclosed their injury were more likely to maintain social relationships and to experience higher levels of well-being.

CONCLUSION

In this chapter we have sought to understand the pathways through which disclosure affects the well-being of those with ABI. For individuals in this predicament, the nature of their social relationships appears to be a key factor in their recovery from injury. However, individuals with ABI are often left with substantial functional changes that are invisible to others. In weighing the decision to disclose these injuries to others, individuals may also have to evaluate the extent to which disclosure influences their ability to maintain and develop the social relationships needed to help them to manage injury. However, there are costs and benefits associated with both disclosure and nondisclosure and, at least initially, it may not be all that obvious how each of these management strategies will help one to progress along the long road to recovery. In particular, the effects of disclosure or nondisclosure on well-being depend very much on the extent to which this decision helps to maintain social relationships or to increase access to new groups. In that sense, both disclosure and nondisclosure can hold keys to successful adjustment after ABI, and both may be important in the unfolding dynamics of the recovery process.

Despite the fact that the model we have presented is not yet fully tested, preliminary evidence is quite promising. In particular, this evidence suggests that when considering adjustment to ABI, in addition to examining neurological and other physical symptoms (including injury severity and functional changes), it is also important to examine how and whether individuals communicate their injury to others. This is because disclosure appears to affect the well-being of individuals who are contending with an invisible stigmatizing health condition by virtue of the effect that the revelation or withholding of information about their condition has on social relationships.

In a number of different ways, our research thus highlights the social underpinnings of well-being among those with ABI. This is an important point because it suggests that aside from the physical and neurological changes that individuals have to contend with, their well-being is also significantly affected by the way they manage their relationships with others (see also Douglas, this volume; Gracey & Ownsworth, this volume). In this regard, our findings also underscore the importance of interventions that help rebuild social relationships among those with ABI. By helping individuals to travel down the positive pathways we have identified these interventions hold real promise not only for recovery but also for unanticipated growth.

References

Beals, K. P., Peplau, L. A., & Gable, S. L. (2009). Stigma management and well-being: The role of perceived social support, emotional processing, and suppression. *Personality and Social Psychology Bulletin, 35*, 867–879.

Branscombe, N. R., Schmitt, M. T., & Harvey, R. (1999). Perceiving pervasive discrimination among African Americans: Implications for group identification and well-being. *Journal of Personality and Social Psychology, 77*, 135–149.

Cohen, S. (2004). Social Relationships and Health. *American Psychologist, 59*, 676–684.

Cole, S. W., Kemeny, M. E., Taylor, S. E., & Visscher, B. R. (1996). Elevated physical health risk among gay men who conceal their homosexual identity. *Health Psychology, 15*, 243–251.

Cole, S. W., Kemeny, M. E., Taylor, S. E., Visscher, B. R., & Fahey, J. L. (1996). Accelerated course of human immunodeficiency virus infection in gay men who conceal their homosexual identity. *Psychosomatic Medicine, 58*, 219–231.

Crabtree, J. W., Haslam, S. A., Postmes, T., & Haslam, C. (2010). Mental health support groups, stigma and self-esteem: Positive and negative implications of group identification. *Journal of Social Issues 66*, 553–569.

Crocker, J., & Major, B. (1989). Social stigma and self-esteem: The self-protective properties of stigma. *Psychological Review, 96*, 608–630.

Crocker, J., Major, B., & Steele, C. M. (1998). Social stigma. In S. Fiske, D. Gilbert, & G. Lindzey (Eds.), *The handbook of social psychology* (pp. 504–553). Boston, MA: McGraw-Hill.

Draper, K., Ponsford, J., & Schönberger, M. (2007). Psychosocial and emotional outcomes 10 years following traumatic brain injury. *Journal of Head Trauma Rehabilitation, 22*, 278–287.

Drury, J., Cocking, C., Beale, J., Hanson, C., & Rapley, F. (2005). The phenomenology of empowerment in collective action. *British Journal of Social Psychology*, *44*, 309–328.

Fleminger, S., Oliver, D. L., Williams, W. H., & Evans, J. (2003). The neuropsychiatry of depression after brain injury. *Neuropsychological Rehabilitation, 13*, 65–87.

Frable, D. E. S., Platt, L., & Hoey, S. (1998). Concealable stigmas and positive self-perceptions: Feeling better around similar others. *Journal of Personality and Social Psychology, 74*, 909–922.

Glover, A. (2003). An exploration of the extent to which attending Headway enhances quality of life after traumatic brain injury. *Disability & Rehabilitation, 25*, 750–760.

Goffman, E. (1963). *Stigma: Notes on the management of spoiled identity*. New York, NY: Simon & Schuster.

Guilmette, T. J., & Paglia, M. F. (2004). The public's misconceptions about traumatic brain injury: A follow up survey. *Archives of Clinical Neuropsychology, 19*, 183–189.

Haslam, C., Holme, A., Haslam, S. A., Iyer, A., Jetten, J., & Williams, W. H. (2008). Maintaining group membership: Identity continuity and well-being after stroke. *Neuropsychological Rehabilitation, 18*, 671–691.

Hornsey, M. J., & Jetten, J. (2011). Impostors within groups: The psychology of claiming to be something you are not. In J. Jetten & M. J. Hornsey (Eds.), *Rebels in groups: Dissent, deviance, difference, and defiance* (pp. 158–180). London, UK: Wiley-Blackwell.

House, J. S., Landis, K. R., & Umberson, D. (1988). Social relationships and health. *Science, 241*, 540–545.

Jetten, J., Haslam, S. A., Iyer, A., & Haslam, C. (2010). Turning to others in times of change: Social identity and coping with stress. In S. Stürmer & M. Snyder (Eds.), *The psychology of pro-social behavior: Group processes, intergroup relations, and helping* (pp. 139–156). Oxford, UK: Blackwell.

Jetten, J., Haslam, C., Pugliese, C., Tonks, J., & Haslam, S. A. (2010). Declining autobiographical memory and loss of identity: Effects of well-being. *Journal of Clinical and Experimental Neuropsychology, 32*, 408–416.

Jones, J. M., Haslam, S. A., Jetten, J., Williams, W. H., Morris, R., & Saroyan, S. (2011). That which doesn't kill us can make us stronger (and more satisfied with life): The contribution of personal and social changes to well-being after acquired brain injury. *Psychology and Health, 26*, 353–369.

Jones, J. M., Jetten, J., Haslam, S. A., & Williams, W. H. (2011). *Disclosure difficulty after acquired brain injury: Identity changes influence well-being*. Manuscript submitted for publication.

Jones, J. M., Williams, W. H., Jetten, J., Haslam, S. A., Harris, A., & Gleibs, I. H. (2011). *The role of symptoms and group memberships in reducing the risk of post-traumatic stress after injury*. Manuscript submitted for publication.

Kendall, E., & Terry, D. J. (1996). Psychosocial adjustment following closed head injury: A model for understanding individual differences and predicting outcome. *Neuropsychological Rehabilitation, 6*, 101–132.

Knox, L., & Douglas, J. (2009). Long-term ability to interpret facial expression after traumatic brain injury. *Brain and Cognition, 69*, 442–449.

Kwok, F. Y., Lee, T. M. C., Leung, C. H. S., & Poon, W. S. (2008). Changes of cognitive functioning following mild traumatic brain injury over a 3-month period. *Brain Injury*, *22*, 740–751.

Linden, M. A., Rauch, R., & Crothers, I. R. (2005). Public attitudes towards survivors of brain injury. *Brain Injury*, *19*, 1011–1017.

Mailhan, L., Azouvi, P., & Dazord, A. (2005). Life satisfaction and disability after severe traumatic brain injury. *Brain Injury*, *19*, 227–238.

McClure, J., Buchanan, S., McDowall, J., & Wade, K. (2008). Attributions for behaviours of persons with brain injury: The role of perceived severity and time since injury. *Brain Injury*, *22*, 639–648.

McClure, J., Devlin, M. E., McDowall, J., & Wade, K. (2006). Visible markers of brain injury influence attributions for adolescents' behaviour. *Brain Injury*, *20*, 1029–1035.

McGrath, J. C., & Linley, P. A. (2006). Post-traumatic growth in acquired brain injury. A preliminary small scale study. *Brain Injury*, *20*, 767–773.

Molero, F., Fuster, M. J., Jetten, J., & Moriano, J. A. (2011). Living with HIV/AIDS: A psychosocial perspective on coping with prejudice and discrimination. *Journal of Applied Social Psychology*, *41*, 609–626.

Pachankis, J. E. (2007). The psychological implications of concealing a stigma: A cognitive-affective-behavioral model. *Psychological Bulletin*, *133*, 328–345.

Putnam, R. D. (2000). *Bowling alone: The collapse and revival of American community*. New York, NY: Simon & Schuster.

Redpath, S. J., & Linden, M. A. (2004). Attitudes towards behavioural versus organic acquisition of brain injury. *Brain Injury*, *18*, 861–869.

Quinn, D. M. (2006). Concealable versus conspicuous stigmatized identities. In S. Levin & C. van Laar (Eds.), *Stigma and group inequality: Social psychological perspectives* (pp. 83–103). London, UK: Lawrence Erlbaum Associates.

Quinn, D. M., & Chaudoir, S. R. (2009). Living with a concealable stigmatized identity: The impact of anticipated stigma, centrality, salience, and cultural stigma on psychological distress and health. *Journal of Personality and Social Psychology*, *97*, 634–651.

Sani, F., Bowe, M., & Herrera, M. (2008). Perceived collective continuity and social well-being: Exploring the connections. *European Journal of Social Psychology*, *38*, 365–374.

Shih, M. (2004). Positive stigma: Examining resilience and empowerment in overcoming stigma. *The ANNALS of the American Academy of Political and Social Science*, *591*, 175–185.

Simpson, G., Mohr, R., & Redman, A. (2000). Cultural variations in the understanding of traumatic brain injury and brain injury rehabilitation. *Brain Injury*, *14*, 125–140.

Stinson, D. A., Logel, C., Zanna, M. P., Holmes, J. G., Cameron, J. J., Wood, J. V., et al. (2008). The cost of lower self-esteem: Testing a self-and-social-bonds model of health. *Journal of Personality and Social Psychology*, *94*, 412–428.

Strandberg, T. (2009). Adults with acquired traumatic brain injury: Experiences of a changeover process and consequences in everyday life. *Social Work in Health Care*, *48*, 276–297.

Swift, T. L., & Wilson, S. L. (2001). Misconceptions about brain injury among the general public and non-expert health professionals: An exploratory study. *Brain Injury*, *15*, 149–165.

Willer, B., Johnson, W. E., Rempel, R. G., & Linn, R. (1993). A note concerning misconceptions of the general public about brain injury. *Archives of Clinical Neuropsychology, 8,* 461–465.

Willmott, C., Ponsford, J., Hocking, C., & Schonberger, M. (2009). Factors contributing to attentional impairments after traumatic brain injury. *Neuropsychology, 23,* 424–432.

Wood, R. Ll. (2008). Long-term outcome of serious traumatic brain injury. *European Journal of Anaesthesiology, 25,* 115–122.

15 The experience of self in the world

The personal and social contexts of identity change after brain injury

Fergus Gracey

The Oliver Zangwill Centre for Neuropsychological Rehabilitation

Tamara Ownsworth

Griffith University

The consequences of brain injury are well documented and include a range of difficulties across emotional, cognitive, physical, and social domains. In the social domain, loss of opportunity, support, or capacity to manage the demands of situations in the workplace, community, with family and friends is common. Research is beginning to focus on changes in both social and personal identity following brain injury, and theoretical frameworks are being drawn upon that allow consideration of the relationship between biological, psychological, and social factors. Social identity is defined by social roles, and group memberships and also provides an important means through which we form and maintain our sense of self (see Jetten, Haslam, & Haslam, this volume).

This chapter aims to integrate literature relevant to understanding self and identity change following brain injury, including empirical findings concerning biopsychosocial perspectives on adjustment and the role of social context and personal meaning. Discussion will focus on the processes pertinent to the brain-injured person's capacity to internalise an adaptive and coherent post-injury identity. This will be supported by a series of conceptual frameworks which aim, in progressive detail, to explain the complex interplay between biological, psychological, and social domains. Particular emphasis is placed on individual's experience of personal and social discrepancy, or the tendency to view current self in a negative light relative to both the pre-injury self and to other people. We also consider implications for rehabilitation and describe intervention approaches that aim to support both personal and social identity reformation in the context of post-injury adjustment.

THE PROBLEMS ASSOCIATED WITH ACQUIRED BRAIN INJURY

Acquired brain injury (ABI) is a major cause of disability. Every year in the UK, around 275 people per 100,000 suffer from head injuries that require hospital admission. Additionally, 20 people per 100,000 under the age of 65 experience a stroke each year (Royal College of Physicians, 2003). ABI can impair physical, cognitive, behavioural, emotional, and social functions, with moderate-severe disability reported by 50 percent of head injury patients 1 year post-injury (Thornhill et al., 2000). Emotional and behavioural problems are particularly common (with rates as high as 84 percent reported in the literature), and are of most concern in the long term for the family (Thomsen, 1974). The frontal lobes are especially vulnerable in traumatic brain injury (TBI) and are often compromised by stroke (Mattson & Levin, 1990). Damage to these brain areas can cause a general deficit in self-regulation of emotion and behaviour (the "dysexecutive syndrome"; Baddeley & Wilson, 1988). The consequence of executive and other cognitive impairments are played out in day-to-day tasks, personal relationships, and in the individual's own thoughts about him- or herself (Gracey, Brentnall, & Megoran, 2008). Strain on relationships may be exacerbated by lack of awareness, reduced motivation, emotional indifference, and disinhibition.

Individuals are typically at heightened risk of developing emotional disorders after ABI due to the changes in life circumstances and the sense of loss that they often experience (Williams & Evans, 2003). Prevalence rates of depression following TBI vary considerably, with 15–61 percent reported across studies (Fleminger, Oliver, Williams, & Evans, 2003; Kim et al., 2007). Further, there is increased incidence of suicide compared with rates in the general population (Teasdale & Engberg, 2001). Anxiety is also frequently experienced, with one meta-analysis (Epstein & Ursano, 1994) identifying a prevalence of 29 percent for anxiety disorders following TBI. Although depression and anxiety will resolve for some, others will experience long-term problems. The risk of suicide, the potential barriers to psychotherapy of concurrent cognitive and other changes, and the impact of these difficulties on return to productive activity and on family caregivers, creates a pressing need for the development of effective therapies. Such therapy approaches need to be guided by research and clinical insights concerning the adjustment process.

There is likely to be a combination of factors that interact to determine emotional and behavioural outcomes including neurologically based changes to cognitive and emotional brain systems, pre-injury factors, psychological adjustment issues, and the nature of social and family support. In our view, to inform appropriate interventions, it is necessary to understand the interplay between these various domains.

Stress and adjustment following brain injury

The event of ABI is typically stressful and traumatic for individuals and their family. Stressors in the more acute phase can include the development of odd and even life-threatening symptoms, emergency procedures to save the person's life, extensive medical investigations, diagnosis of a serious neurological condition, and invasive or prolonged treatments. Most individuals face uncertainty regarding the future in terms of their survival, level of recovery, and outcome (Godfrey, Knight, & Partridge, 1996). As individuals leave the hospital or treatment setting and attempt to return to pre-injury activities and roles they are typically confronted with the ongoing functional implications of their injury, including altered abilities, increased dependency on others, loss of productivity and vocation, relationship strain, financial difficulties, and difficulty accessing support (Karlovits & McColl, 1999; Turner, Ownsworth, Cornwell, & Fleming, 2009). Due to the long-term nature of ABI and its consequences, individuals are faced with chronic stress as well as more specific periods of adjustment relating to relevant transitions (e.g., leaving hospital, moving to a more independent living situation, trying to return to work). During this process, individuals vary considerably in their adjustment and sense of well-being, irrespective of the severity and nature of their ABI and functional limitations. In particular, some individuals may experience poor adjustment and develop a psychological disorder, whilst others report positive psychological outcomes including growth and life satisfaction (Gangstad, Norman, & Barton, 2009; Jones et al., 2011 see Jones, Jetten, Haslam, & Williams, this volume).

A biopsychosocial perspective on adjustment

Like many other chronic health conditions, individuals' adjustment to ABI has been conceptualised within a biopsychosocial framework (Engel, 1977; Ownsworth, Fleming, Desbois, Strong, & Kuipers, 2006b; Williams & Evans, 2003). As represented in Figure 15.1, this framework broadly proposes that post-injury adjustment relates to the relative contribution of, and dynamic interplay between, the neuropathology of brain injury, personal or psychological characteristics, and the social environmental context.

Whilst providing a generally useful structure for considering different factors that may contribute to varying individual adjustment outcomes, the nature of biopsychosocial interfaces and the likely reciprocal effects between factors is not well understood. In regard to this issue, there are many possible theoretical frameworks that could be applied (Wilson, 2002), although few incorporate explanations of what may be occurring across or at the interfaces between these three domains. In our view, attention to such processes is imperative in developing theory-based interventions. An initial

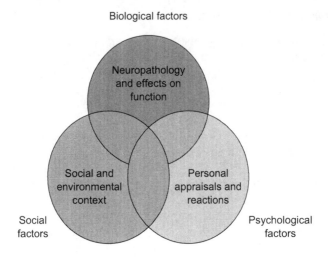

Figure 15.1 The bio-psychosocial interfaces of adjustment following brain injury.

step is to consider empirical findings concerning the link between different factors in each domain and how these covary with adjustment outcomes.

Various studies support the proposition that personal reactions and resources contribute to the post-injury adjustment process. For example, use of avoidant coping strategies and an external locus of control have been found to be related to poor psychosocial adjustment (e.g., lower productivity and greater psychological distress; Dawson, Schwartz, Winocur, & Stuss, 2007; Moore & Stambrook, 1992). In a long-term sample (> 10 years post-injury) Rutterford and Wood (2006) found that personality, appraisal and coping variables predicted various psychosocial outcomes including community integration and quality of life. Similarly, the role of social environmental factors in post-injury adjustment has been demonstrated in a small but growing body of research. For instance, pre-injury social group memberships and the capacity to maintain these after stroke were found to be associated with post-stroke life satisfaction (Haslam et al., 2008).

In contrast, other social environmental circumstances may impede adjustment; for example, in some studies involvement in litigation was a negative prognostic factor for returning to work after TBI, presumably due to reduced financial incentives (see review by Ownsworth & McKenna, 2004). Level of social support has also been positively linked to employment outcomes at 4–7 years post-injury (Vogenthaler, Smith, & Goldfader, 1989). However, the strength of individuals' social support network was related in part to whether individuals were involved with rehabilitation services, which was more likely to be the case for those assessed as having greater functional capacity for employment (Ownsworth & McKenna, 2004).

A central issue which therefore complicates understanding of how personal and social factors influence adjustment is that individuals' personal resources (such as coping, self-efficacy, and locus of control) and their social environment may alter as a function of the neuropathology of ABI, particularly the nature and severity of cognitive impairment (Curren, Ponsford, & Crowe, 2000; Krpan, Levine, Stuss, & Dawson, 2007). For instance, Krpan et al. (2007) found that negative appraisals regarding a stressful situation were associated with greater executive dysfunction and, consequently, proposed that coping and executive functions share the same neural substrate. Similarly, neuro-cognitive deficits such as impaired emotional regulation and executive function often alter communication and social skills which in turn reduce the capacity to form and maintain relationships and establish a supportive social network following ABI (McDonald & Flanagan, 2004; Yeates, Gracey, & Collicutt McGrath, 2008a).

Despite supporting the notion that the biopsychosocial domains have an interactive effect on post-injury adjustment, most studies have focused on relatively long-term samples. Such research is unable to clarify the direction of the relationship between proposed antecedents or consequences of poor adjustment. For example, depression can alternatively be viewed as a negative prognostic factor for returning to work, or an emotional consequence of difficulties in re-integrating into the workforce (Ownsworth & McKenna, 2004). Prospective longitudinal studies focusing on the early adjustment period following hospital transition provide more scope to understand the process of adjustment over time. Such research is likely to be more informative in guiding the focus of early interventions.

The influence of personal and social processes on early post-injury adjustment

Research by Ruff et al. (1993) and Felmingham, Baguley, and Crooks (2001) found that the early onset of emotional distress at either 6 months post-TBI or 6 months post-discharge was associated with poorer employment outcomes at 1–2 years follow-up. Conversely, however, Ownsworth et al. (2009) found that negative life events shortly after injury that altered the individuals' social environment (e.g., financial strain, relationship breakdown, and lack of access to therapy) after hospital discharge significantly predicted later emotional distress at 3 months post-discharge after controlling for pre-discharge emotional distress. The experience of positive life events (e.g., return to work, driving, and home and community independence) was related to better emotional adjustment at 1 month post-discharge but not at 3 months post-discharge. Interestingly, the life event that was most strongly related to depressive symptoms was lack of access to therapy. Individuals who sought therapy after discharge but were unable to access this support reported higher levels of depression at 3 months post-discharge. On this basis, Ownsworth and colleagues proposed that individuals who experienced difficulties in achieving their post-discharge goals (e.g., return to work, driving, and independence) and were unable to access a desired level of therapy or rehabilitation were particularly at risk of developing heightened emotional distress. Other literature supports the view that the early period of adjustment following discharge is a particularly uncertain time in which individuals strive for re-personalisation and personal autonomy (e.g., Conneeley, 2003). Thus, the occurrence of these accumulated stressors is likely to threaten a person's sense of self and his or her sense of belonging in society.

A further consideration regarding the occurrence of life events that alter the social environment is the individual's appraisals of his or her significance. The Transactional Model of Stress and Coping (Lazarus & Folkman, 1984; see also van Dick & Haslam, this volume) has been applied and empirically investigated in the context of ABI by many authors (e.g., Kendall & Terry, 2009; Rutterford & Wood, 2006). Longitudinal research by Kendall and Terry (2009) found that the mediating and/or moderating effects of personal appraisals and coping were most apparent at the early adjustment phase 1 month post-discharge. Specifically, individuals most at risk of early emotional distress were those who perceived greater threat and experienced lower self-efficacy regarding their post-discharge situation. Interestingly, these appraisal and coping variables influenced more long-term adjustment (9 months post-discharge) through their impact on early adjustment, whilst family support directly predicted long-term emotional adjustment.

In the longer-term, it has also been demonstrated that after ABI individuals can experience positive personal appraisals and psychological growth. This may relate to increased sense of challenge, greater personal strength, and enhanced appreciation of life or relationships with others (Gangstad, Norman, & Barton, 2009; see Jones et al., this volume). These appraisals are generally found to increase over time, well beyond the post-discharge phase, and may occur even in the context of severe injury or cognitive impairment (Powell, Ekin-Wood, & Collin, 2007). Most typically, post-traumatic growth has been found to be inversely related to emotional distress (Gangstad et al., 2009). The qualitative study by Nochi (2000) looking at the narratives of people with TBI who considered themselves well-adjusted, identified themes of being worthwhile despite the injury or because of the injury. These narratives incorporate views of the injury that provide positive meanings for the individual. Such findings underscore the view that individuals with ABI can derive benefits and experience positive psychological changes through personal adversity.

A key issue likely to impact personal and social identity change is the extent to which individuals are aware of their post-injury impairments and the implications of these for everyday living (e.g., impact on relationships and work). As with other adjustment processes, the development of self-awareness is understood to be related to neurocognitive, psychological, and social factors. Research by Ownsworth et al. (2007) identified four different awareness typologies that varied according to level of executive dysfunction (error self-regulation) and personality style (defensiveness). Amongst their ABI participants, poorer psychosocial outcomes (i.e., independent living, work and relationship difficulties) were experienced by two particular typologies, namely, those with poor awareness related to executive dysfunction and those with heightened awareness of their deficits who displayed low defensiveness. A confounding issue with these findings, however, is that individuals' post-injury circumstances (conceptualised as "psychosocial outcomes") may have actually shaped individuals' awareness of their deficits. Consistent with this view, the process of returning to work and receiving specialised vocational assistance has been found to be associated with increased awareness of post-injury deficits over time (Ownsworth, Desbois, Grant, Fleming, & Strong, 2006a). At the interpersonal level, Schönberger, Humle, and Teasdale (2006) found that awareness of deficits and engagement in rehabilitation were related to better therapeutic alliance between the person with brain injury and the "primary therapist" in rehabilitation. Thus, opportunities and experiences within the social environment, such as access to work trials and feedback, and safe and supportive relationships are likely to facilitate the development of self-awareness. Individuals with severe executive dysfunction may be viewed as less likely to benefit from these opportunities, thus limiting their engagement in activity and social contexts that support the development of self-awareness and identity change. Overall then, as Figure 15.2 suggests, the relationships between personal resources, the social environment, and adjustment after ABI appear to be complex and multi-directional.

The literature summarised above is therefore helpful in providing a broad framework for considering the interplay between social and psychological processes as the person with brain injury leaves hospital and engages in attempts to re-engage with meaningful social and activity contexts. However, as noted by Riley, Brennan, and Powell (2004), global conceptual frameworks of adjustment do not cast much light on the nature of altered subjective and personal identity. Yet experiences of changed sense of self or identity, or judgements by others of altered personality are commonly reported by those who are affected by ABI and their families (Yeates et al., 2008a). These issues may be important for understanding the link between the personal and the social self, perhaps underpinning the particular personal appraisals one might make, and the choice of coping strategies an individual may engage in.

Self-discrepancy in long-term adjustment: bridging the personal and the social

Aside from studies on coping, a common theme emerging in the literature on the process of adjustment relates to a person's sense of "self-discrepancy".

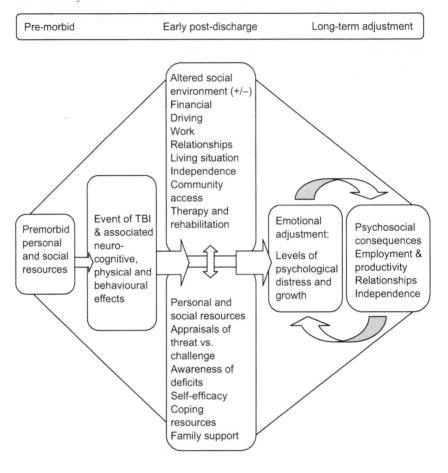

Figure 15.2 The interactive influence of personal and social environmental factors in early and more long-term post-injury adjustment.

Tyerman and Humphrey (1984) were the first to conduct research into this topic, identifying the significant ways in which people with severe TBI see current self in a more negative light compared with pre-injury self and with others. Nochi (1998) described narratives of people with TBI where the common theme was "loss of self". Participants described how gaps in autobiographical memories, perceptions of others, and pre–post injury comparisons were all associated with loss of self. Studies by Ellis-Hill and Horn (2000) and Secrest and Zeller (2007) also identified discontinuity and discrepancy of self in participants following stroke, with higher ratings of current-pre stroke discrepancy being associated with poorer emotional outcome. Along similar lines, Cantor et al.'s (2005) study of self-discrepancy and adjustment following TBI found that increased ratings of current-pre and current-ideal discrepancy were associated with increased symptoms of anxiety and depression.

Riley et al. (2004) investigated the relationship between subjective threat appraisals, task or activity avoidance, and anxiety following brain injury. The authors proposed that the experience of failure or difficulties in situations gives rise to a sense of threatened self and a related heightened level of anxiety. In order to reduce anxiety and return to a less threatened self (in the short term) the person is likely to withdraw from the situation and try to avoid it in the future. Accordingly, the researchers observed that people with brain injury often made subjective appraisals of threat relating to dealing with people (e.g., being seen as stupid, feeling embarrassed), doing things (e.g., "when things go wrong it reminds me of my injury"), awkward situations (e.g., not fitting in) as well as personal safety (e.g., fear of getting another head injury).

Also focusing on the subjective level, Gracey et al. (2008) examined the personal constructs of individuals with ABI elicited through a structured exercise of comparing pre-injury, current, and "ideal" selves. The study was based on personal construct theory (Kelly, 1955) that provides an analysis of how people make sense of the world through the active construction of meaning from their experiences. Thematic analysis revealed a key theme as "self in the world", which relates to both the subjective experience of self and a social or activity context. Bipolar constructs in this theme included "feeling part of things vs. do not fit in, (or) belong"; "doing things that reinforce who I am vs. loss of key activities, not doing personally important things"; "struggle to be part of a group, a burden vs. feel useful and able to contribute". Along the lines of Riley's study, this work emphasises the importance of subjective sense-making that involves blending together the personal and social domains. It is also consistent with social identity approaches, where it is argued that self-identity is intrinsically linked to social contexts through social group memberships that provide means through which individuals make sense of their situation and draw on social support to help them cope.

The ongoing process of experiencing poor adjustment post-injury can thus be conceptualised as a spiral of increased failures in tasks and social contexts, the perception or experience of self as different or changed, and an increased sense of pre-current or current-ideal self-discrepancy. As Figure 15.2 suggests, the presence or absence of particular life events (such as relationship breakdown, loss of independence, family or other social support) may also influence the nature and extent of such changes. In this regard, threatened personal identity appears to be closely linked to social threat, such as negative judgements by others and threat of, or actual, exclusion from groups (see Douglas, this volume). The activation of threat meanings associated with these self-discrepancies gives rise to emotions and related cognitive and behavioural coping responses. These may be based on dominant pre-injury coping styles, shaped by the presence of acquired impairments (e.g., Krpan et al., 2007), and serve to reduce distress and maintain a coherent sense of self in the short term. Over time, threat to self and actual changes to identity through loss of important social groups may serve to maintain or increase self-discrepancies. For instance, changes in cognitive, communication or other abilities due to the injury may lead to disruption to important social roles. Related emotional changes and coping involving avoidance or withdrawal is likely to result in loss of social support opportunities, which social group memberships provide. This will impact on sense of pre-current or current-ideal self-discrepancy and emotional distress, thus feeding into a cycle of maladjustment.

Neuropsychological contributions to personal and social adjustment

Consistent with a biopsychosocial perspective, the aforementioned self-discrepancies and personal and social threat reactions can be linked to various neuropsychological processes, as shown in Figure 15.3. The components represented and their interconnections are based on an integration of established biological models of self and autobiographical memory (Conway, 2005; Damasio, 1999; Teasdale & Barnard, 1993), models of social identity (Tajfel & Turner, 1979) as well as those relevant to fear (LeDoux, 1995) and executive function (Shallice & Burgess, 1996).

The top of the three bands in Figure 15.3 refers to experiences and outcomes in the social domain and is the locus of social identity processes: events, activities, opportunities, relationships, and social groups. The processes within the middle band provide a summary of what LeDoux (1995) described as the "quick and dirty" route to fear or threat reactions (e.g., to negative social judgement or pre-current self-discrepancy). Broadly speaking, these processes map onto systems involving the thalamus, amygdalae, somatosensory, and parietal cortex. The processes within the bottom band map onto frontotemporal control and autobiographical memory consolidation and access systems. These are considered to be relatively slower and deal with processing of context and higher-order control processes and are thought to support the ability to consciously monitor and reflect on one's own experiences, and therefore either communicate one's needs clearly to others, or self-regulate mood or behaviour. There are a number of more detailed processes inferred within this model that we will not describe in detail here. The key point to highlight is how acquired cognitive impairments in executive, attention, and memory processes may not only lead to the now well-known and well-described difficulties in day-to-day life. Such impairments may also present barriers to the emotional adjustment process, for example by preventing accurate self-monitoring and therefore awareness of both strengths and weaknesses, accurate recollection of positive achievements or experiences, processing of self-representations to "update" to a new, post-injury self, and behaviour that might elicit the kind of caring and

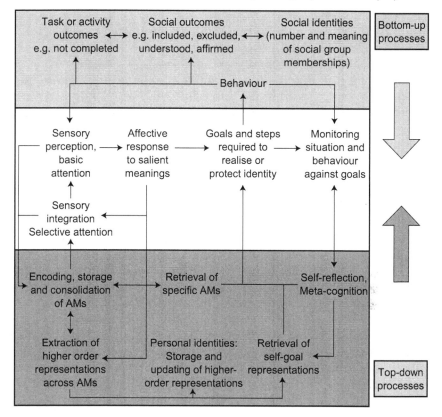

Figure 15.3 Neuropsychological processes potentially involved in social and psychological adjustment.

Note: Pale grey = social domain and locus of social identity processes; white = sensory, attention, and working memory cognitive processes; dark grey = higher order autobiographical memory domain and locus of personal identity or self-representational processes. AM = autobiographical memory.

supportive responses from others that would reduce the threat response and facilitate better self-awareness.

So, by integrating existing neuropsychological ideas about executive, memory, and identity processes, this framework provides a means of thinking about the impact of acquired impairments on the potential to experience sense of self, develop a new post-injury identity, manage the distress associated with "threats to self", inhibit emotionally driven behaviour, or reflect on oneself as a "coherent entity" over time. This model could also account for the influence of therapeutic working alliance on the development of awareness in rehabilitation (Schönberger et al., 2006). The implication is that if the person is feeling safe, understood, and that his or her failures or difficulties will not be socially judged, then he or she will have an increased capacity to draw on frontal and temporal systems that would otherwise be inhibited under activation of the threat system.

The social and interpersonal context therefore becomes a foundation and a resource for creating and supporting a process of change and post-traumatic growth. This perspective begins to shift the focus away from discrete psychological or social processes to relational processes which extend cognition outward from the individual into the social and environmental context, and reciprocally extend social structures and processes into individual psychological processes.

IMPLICATIONS FOR REHABILITATION – A SOCIAL NEUROPSYCHOLOGICAL CURE?

The term "social neuropsychology" has been used by Haslam and colleagues (Haslam et al., 2008; Jones et al., 2011) to describe a social turn in a traditionally individual and bio-cognitive field. Consistent with this approach, Figure 15.3 demonstrates how social processes form the raw material from which self-representations or personal identities may be formed. Definitions of rehabilitation emphasise increased social participation as a desired outcome. However, the social neuropsychological account we present here suggests that it should be considered an important input. In this sense, rehabilitation can be seen not as a linear process but rather as a set of interventions that support iterative cycles of social participation (and social identity development) and psychological adaptation (and personal identity development). This account also highlights how emotion, cognition, and personal identity representations may interact together and with social contexts, events, and resources (see also Douglas, this volume). Maladaptive cycles may lead to increased self-discrepancy, increased use of unhelpful coping, and increased social disruption. However, adaptive cycles may also arise in which supportive relationships and maintained social group membership, facilitate more adaptive cognitive-emotional processes, allow for updating and integration of self-representations and lead to more favourable psychosocial outcomes.

Clinically, attention to the social context, events, and resources may therefore be critical to facilitating positive outcomes. In using the social domain as a resource for new experiences and meanings to update identity in rehabilitation, consideration needs to be given to those specific impairments (especially of autobiographical memory and executive functioning) that restrict individuals' capacity to internalise their social experiences into a coherent and positive self-identity. For example, an individual experiencing difficulties on a given task may need support to self-reflect in the moment and halt automatic (including emotional threat-based) responses that may contribute to a pattern of maladaptive behaviours. Similarly, support may be needed to process and consolidate experiences in order for these to be integrated into higher-order self-representations. It is also possible that higher-order goals and values that characterised pre-injury identity (e.g., being a good friend or parent, making a valuable contribution to society) can still be drawn upon. However, in the context of disability, the means by which such goals are achieved may need to change, to include adaptations, strategies, change of context or expectations. Access to both therapy and supportive relationships in the early post-injury period may be key to guard against the overactivation of the threat system whilst also allowing the person to re-appraise his or her identity post-injury in more adaptive terms (see Douglas, this volume).

For example, the case ('VO') reported by Dewar and Gracey (2007) highlights how damage to right temporal and frontal areas, related impairments in face recognition, perception of social cues, autobiographical memory, and anxiety regulation created a cycle of heightened threat reactions and failure to process positive social and family situations effectively. Here there was a combination of real and personally threatening deficits and changes, alongside specific impairments to systems implicated in updating self-representations. VO experienced herself as "cancelled, a 'was'", and at the outset of rehabilitation many situations including most therapy appointments triggered extreme anxiety. Interdisciplinary rehabilitation with a high level of family involvement tackled the various impairments through compensatory strategies, with a brief anxiety management strategy being practised at the start of each session. VO's negative predictions about practical and family sessions were explored and recorded using forms or video, which were then used to support reflection on her predictions or beliefs and update her negative view of herself. As anxiety reduced, understanding of the nature of her strengths and weaknesses, and confidence to be open about her difficulties with others improved, so VO was able to move forward and increase her social participation and associated sense of identity, in her words to became an "am" not a "was". However, ongoing difficulties with autobiographical memory and face recognition presented continued challenges to fully feeling and believing in her adjusted identity, meaning that she continues to rely on a caring husband and family, and compensatory memory strategies, to be reminded of her achievements and what these mean to her.

Yeates et al. (2008b) described a case in which external alerts delivered via a paging service for people with memory impairment used within cognitive analytic therapy were effective in prompting clients to reflect more adaptively on their post-injury identity with associated improvements in mood. However, if becoming "conscious" of oneself as an "extended entity over time" (see Damasio, 1999) triggers thoughts about loss of self, or changes between pre and post-injury that are potentially very distressing, then avoidance of such broad reflections of one's situation may arise as a means of avoiding negative affect. In clinical practice some of our clients have resisted executive "stop think" strategies, and over time it has emerged that for them, to stop and think is to engage directly in the negative affect associated with post-injury changes.

As a further example of the interplay between organic, cognitive, psychological, and social processes, apparent changes in cognition and behaviour that could be attributed to an organic-based executive impairment could, at least in part, be accounted for in terms of chronic psychological threat activation. This possibility is suggested in the case described by McGrath (1997) in which a person who had sustained a minor head injury with no evidence of cerebral damage, exhibited impairments in cognition on testing. The post-traumatic adjustment symptoms were successfully treated with a cognitive behavioural intervention and, in addition, there was a marked improvement in behaviours previously attributed to the head injury (cognitive and "personality" changes) and seen as enduring rather than treatable.

In line with the above arguments, there is an increasing recognition of the need for rehabilitation to adopt a more complex and subtle view of the interplay between neurocognitive, emotional, and social processes of change, as represented in contemporary models, including Ylvisaker and Feeney's (2000) context sensitive approach, the 'Y'-shaped model (Gracey, Evans, & Malley, 2009; Wilson, Gracey, Malley, Bateman, & Evans, 2009), and the metacognitive contextual approach (Ownsworth, Fleming, Shum, Kuipers, & Strong, 2008a). Based on our own clinical experiences, the guiding principles and applications of the latter two approaches will now be discussed.

The Y-shaped model of rehabilitation change processes

To bridge the social and personal, the Y-shaped model describes an evolution of the holistic or comprehensive neuropsychological rehabilitation process (e.g., Ben-Yishay, 2008) that first seeks to engage with and understand social and personal discrepancies (e.g., "who I am now" vs. "who I used to be, who I want to be"), represented by the top of the Y. The model provides a framework for developing interdisciplinary interventions that attempt to link cognitive deficits, the threat to self of changed abilities and circumstances and social participation. Rehabilitation based on this model tackles issues of threat, self, and social discrepancy and coping, through "behavioural experiments" as carried out in CBT (based on learning through the "plan–do–reflect" cycle, see McGrath and King, 2004). These provide scaffolding for the client, family and team to (a) identify the subjective appraisals a person may be making, (b) formulate an understanding of how these link with underlying threats and discrepancies, and then (c) address these discrepancies through targeted activity. In this way, the "new" post-injury reality can be titrated in a supportive way so as to allow updating of pre-injury identity. Resulting reduction in social and self-discrepancies are represented by the convergence of the two prongs at the top of the Y, where the point at which they meet represents a subjective realisation of accurate and nonthreatened sense of self. In clinical practice individuals and their close friends and family describe a sense of the "old me" coming back. Specific rehabilitation interventions such as strategies for managing memory, planning, communication and emotional changes are conducted and practiced as behavioural experiments (very much in line with those described by McGrath & King, 2004). Common questions used to support self-reflection together with the client (and spouse, or other family members, team members) on the outcome of such experiments, are "what have I learned about myself?" and "what have I learned about this strategy or skill?" (Gracey, Evans, & Malley, 2009).

As with Ylvisaker and Feeney's (2000) "identity mapping" technique, the approach also highlights the need for a shared understanding across the team, client, and family, which is supported by a visual "formulation" (see Wilson et al., 2009). As the individual begins to find that pre-injury values and broad objectives may be achievable (albeit through altered means), new, adaptive or "constructive formulations" detailing the link between specific experiences post-injury, retained or re-learnt skills and strategies, subjective experience of self and desired outcomes are drawn upon to support the change process. The ongoing journey of exploring and consolidating new, adaptive self-representations in new or adapted social contexts is represented by the lower "tail" of the Y.

Gracey, Brentnall and Megoran's (2009) case of a young woman, Judith, who acquired significant attention and executive problems following a severe TBI illustrates this approach. In addition to the cognitive difficulties, Judith also presented with a range of anxiety symptoms with features of obsessive compulsive disorder, social anxiety, and panic with agoraphobia. When anxious, her attention and executive problems were doubly compromised, resulting in heightened impulsive behaviour, verbal aggression, difficulty attending to nonthreat-related stimuli (e.g., what the therapist was saying). The intervention process involved formulating the underlying threat, exploring Judith's anxious predictions associated with this threat through behavioural experiments, addressing cognitive impairments that impacted upon task performance and supporting strategy and skill development to compensate for these. Systems for collating objective information from the experiment were used – for example, video recordings or systematic written data collection by an observer using a monitoring sheet devised collaboratively with Judith. She also attended a number of group and individual sessions supporting understanding of brain injury and development of skills and strategies. Once the threat system was less activated and Judith's self-efficacy with some cognitive and mood management strategies improved, we developed a new formulation based on positive experiences that were strongly linked to a specific identity affirming experience from pre-injury.

In Judith's case we also drew upon the techniques of Mooney and Padesky (2000) and Ylvisaker and Feeney (2000) for drawing out the rich, positive, subjective components of this experience and identifying what this meant to her as an individual, using metaphors. The experience she chose to discuss involved a motorbike riding lesson, where, as a slightly built woman driving a heavy machine, her male instructor goaded her that she would not be able to complete a u-turn on a narrow stretch of road. She recounted this episode with glee, noting how she pulled the bike round smoothly, opened the throttle, and turned to make a rude gesture to her instructor. The experience brought a sense of her defiance and ability to overcome challenges, which she was then able to connect with her post-injury recovery from serious injuries, and the emotional challenges of rehabilitation. Positive experiences were then used to help up-regulate positive affect associated with previously threatening situations. Reflections on experiences arising during rehabilitation were reflected upon in therapy to enrich and consolidate this new, more adaptive and positive notion of self. Whilst changes did not generalise extensively, significant improvements in anxiety, confidence, and abilities maintained over time were noted in the specific areas targeted in behavioural experiments (e.g., cooking, and attending a very crowded bike racing event). Overall, Judith's sense of social and self-discrepancy reduced and she began to experience some specific areas of her life as less threatening, and so avoided these less. She summarised her adjustment in the shift from believing "I am no good" to feeling "I am a person, just like everyone else".

The metacognitive contextual approach

Another approach to rehabilitation that was developed to jointly target personal and social factors which may impede or facilitate adjustment to ABI is metacognitive contextual training. This person-centred and goal-directed approach combines training or retraining of skills and strategy use with systematic enhancement or modification of the social environment (Ownsworth et al., 2008a). Examples of the latter include selecting personally relevant activities and supportive environments within which to train awareness of deficits and new skills (e.g., in the home setting or group therapy), providing meaningful feedback on task performance and structured learning opportunities, educating and involving family members and other natural social supports, and specifically training for application outside the learning environment (Fleming & Ownsworth, 2006; Ownsworth et al., 2006b). The metacognitive focus refers to training self-knowledge (recognition of changes to personal abilities since the injury), self-monitoring (the capacity to identify difficulties as they occur during everyday activities), and self-regulation skills (the ability to correct or adjust performance and effectively apply strategies).

The key distinction from the Y-shaped model is that this approach highlights specific processes relating to self-monitoring, awareness, adjustment, and goal attainment in practical situations, whereas the Y-shaped model has evolved as a development of holistic neuropsychological rehabilitation, and emphasises personal and social discrepancy and sense of threat as key. However, these are differences of emphasis, and there is much conceptual and practical overlap. As with the Y-shaped model, an essential component of metacognitive contextual training is to closely monitor and support emotional reactions (e.g., shock, bewilderment, anxiety, and despair) that can occur as people begin to confront and make sense of their impairments and altered life circumstances (Ownsworth & Clare, 2006). A good rapport and strong therapeutic alliance is fundamental here, in order to buffer the potential threat that these techniques can represent to self-esteem, personal control, and independence. Ultimately, through this training, individuals typically learn that more accurate self-appraisal and increased self-regulatory skills actually enhance self-esteem, personal control and independence. A brief illustration of the key personal and social factors related to poor adjustment for two individuals with ABI and their tailored intervention approaches for restructuring of self in this context is presented in Table 15.1 (for more details see Ownsworth, 2005; Ownsworth, Turpin, Andrew, & Fleming, 2008b).

As highlighted by these case illustrations, the metacognitive contextual approach and the approach based on the Y-shaped model do not only focus on developing awareness of deficits and strategy use, but occur in the context of a broader intervention to improve other aspects of functioning such as emotional well-being, social functioning, independence, and vocational outcome. As emphasised by Ownsworth and Clare (2006), it would be futile and potentially harmful for an intervention to focus on increasing a person's capacity to recognise and monitor his or her post-injury impairments unless such metacognitive changes were directed towards achieving gains in other personally valued areas of functioning (e.g., returning to work and improving social relationships). Therefore, both of these approaches aim to support the process of restructuring personal and social identity in a synchronised manner. These rehabilitation approaches highlight the need for iterative cycles between the social and personal, with attention to addressing cognitive impairments that may hinder the return to an adaptive trajectory of personal and social identity development.

In accordance with the model presented in Figure 15.3, these approaches could also be seen as addressing top-down regulation of behaviour by identifying, developing, and activating an alternative identity. Their desired objective is to integrate new self-representations with pre-injury self-representations, and encapsulate personally compelling higher-order goals and feelings. The process of change is facilitated by providing cognitive supports to reduce working memory load, heightening integration of emotion and experience, supporting abstraction of meaning across experiences (e.g., using behavioural experiment reflection sheets, video recordings, or other memory supports) and by linking these processes with more traditional

Table 15.1 A summary of metacognitive contextual training interventions for two individuals with acquired brain injury

	CP	JK
Injury circumstances	A 28 year old male who experienced a right thalamic stroke 4 years ago. Severe deficits in visuo-spatial function and processing speed.	A 45 year old woman who sustained a severe TBI in a motor vehicle accident 5 years ago. Mild to moderate impairments in memory and processing speed.
Personal reactions impeding adjustment	Impaired self-awareness of post-stroke changes and unrealistic goals (to return to work full-time in his previous occupation). CP was clearly aware of and frustrated by his lack of success in finding work, but was unable to account for his failed pursuits or understand how he could improve his situation.	Highly defensive personality style, avoidant coping and progressive withdrawal from social and activity contexts which revealed her deficits. She instead adopted a highly simplified, unchallenging and repetitive daily routine to avoid being "thrown".
Social environmental barriers to adjustment	Lack of feedback after unsuccessful employment pursuits (job interviews and work trials). Absence of supportive opportunities to learn about post-injury changes during task performance (i.e., "in the moment" feedback and prompting) and develop corrective strategies.	Repetitive medico-legal assessments which served to highlight her deficits but also question the validity of these problems. Unexpected and unavoidable social interaction (telephone calls from lawyers and visits from family).
Pre-intervention emotional reactions and self-perceptions	Mild depression and severe hopelessness. Fluctuations in mood and perceptions of work capacity (e.g., full-time in former position vs. "I'll never be job ready"). Concerns about social identity: "I am not normal. . . . I am still a second-class citizen".	Severe social anxiety, secondary depression. Felt "stupid" and "embarrassed" around others and came to dread social situations; "I don't have any control" and "I'll never be a patch on who I was" (Ownsworth, 2005, p. 88).
Intervention summary	12 individual sessions, commenced in the therapy room and shifting to real life activities in community settings. Components included psychoeducation, roleplays, video-based self-observation during cooking, adjustment counselling, work sampling with self-predictions, self-evaluations and feedback, and post-session therapy debriefings.	13 sessions of individual therapy and 3 group therapy sessions. Nonconfrontational approaches used to initially build rapport, psychoeducation, cognitive-behavioural techniques to explore, test and challenge dysfunctional self-beliefs and social threat, and attendance in group therapy sessions.

continues

Table 15.1 (*continued*)

	CP	JK
Intervention outcomes	Achieved durable part-time work, altered and realistic goals, improved self-awareness and mood status. Perceived the programme to be "a confidence building process".	Social anxiety, stress and depression all in the normal range (anxiety in the "mild" range), reduced defensiveness in therapy, and greatly increased social and activity participation.

strategies (e.g., stop-think, arousal reduction, assertiveness, memory aids) as required.

SUMMARY

It is clear from the research and our clinical experiences that following brain injury the social and the personal are intimately connected and closely associated with emotional adjustment and quality of life. We have proposed that, for many who struggle with the adjustment process, it is the actual or feared negative experience of self in social contexts, and the resulting attempts to manage "threats to self" that result in a long-term maladjustment process. This is marked by increased self-discrepancy and failure to develop an updated and adaptive post-injury identity. Systematically and empathically exploring and developing a shared understanding of the individual's subjective threat is a necessary starting point. Exploring alternative meanings through structured and contextualised activity such as behavioural experiments, implementing cognitive strategies, and developing skills for self-awareness and self-regulation may help to re-establish the brain injured person's social participation and enhance success in valued pursuits. The re-engagement in meaningful social groups, roles and activities can then establish a developmental trajectory within which the person's personal and social identity is continually fed through his or her social experiences. It is through this "social cure" that experience of "self in the world", and realisation of a valued and worthwhile social identity, can be achieved in the face of serious neurological compromise.

References

Baddeley, A., & Wilson, B. (1988). Frontal amnesia and the dysexecutive syndrome. *Brain and Cognition*, 7, 212–230.

Ben-Yishay, Y. (2008). Foreword to Special Issue on the Self and Identity in Rehabilitation. *Neuropsychological Rehabilitation*, 18, 513–521.

Cantor, J. B., Ashman, T. A., Schwartz, M. E., Gordon, W. A., Hibbard, M. R.,

Brown, M., et al. (2005). The role of self-discrepancy theory in understanding post-traumatic brain injury affective disorders: A pilot study. *Journal of Head Trauma Rehabilitation, 20,* 527–543.

Conneeley, A. L. (2003). Quality of life and traumatic brain injury: A one-year longitudinal study. *British Journal of Occupational Therapy, 66,* 440–446.

Conway, M. A. (2005). Memory and the self. *Journal of Memory and Language, 53,* 594–628.

Curran, C. A., Ponsford, J. L., & Crowe, S. (2000). Coping strategies and emotional outcome following traumatic brain injury: A comparison with orthopaedic patients. *Journal of Head Trauma Rehabilitation, 15,* 1256–1274.

Damasio, A. (1999). *The feeling of what happens.* London, UK: Heinemann.

Dawson, D. R., Schwartz, M. L., Winocur, G., & Stuss, D. T. (2007). Return to productivity following traumatic brain injury: Cognitive, psychological, physical, spiritual and environmental correlates. *Disability & Rehabilitation, 29,* 301–313.

Dewar, B. K., & Gracey, F. (2007). "Am not was": Cognitive behavioural therapy for adjustment and identity change following herpes simplex encephalitis. *Neuropsychological Rehabilitation – Special Issue: Encephalitis, 17,* 602–620.

Ellis-Hill, C. S., & Horn, S. (2000). Change in identity and self-concept: A new theoretical approach to recovery following a stroke. *Clinical Rehabilitation, 14,* 279–287.

Engel, G. L. (1977). The need for a new medical model. *Science, 196,* 129–136.

Epstein, R. S., & Ursano, R. J. (1994). Anxiety disorders. In J. M. Silver, S. C. Yudofsky, & R. E. Hales (Eds.), *Neuropsychiatry of traumatic brain injury* (pp. 3–41). Washington, DC: American Psychiatric Press.

Felmingham, K., Baguley, I., & Crooks, J. (2001). A comparison of acute and post-discharge predictors of employment 2 years after traumatic brain injury. *Archives of Physical and Medical Rehabilitation, 82,* 435–439.

Fleming, J., & Ownsworth, T. (2006). A review of awareness interventions in brain injury rehabilitation. *Neuropsychological Rehabilitation, 16,* 474–500.

Fleminger, S., Oliver, D. L., Williams, W. H., & Evans, J. J. (2003). The neuro-psychiatry of depression after brain injury. *Neuropsychological Rehabilitation, 13,* 65–87.

Gangstad, B., Norman, P., & Barton, J. (2009). Cognitive processing and post-traumatic growth after stroke. *Rehabilitation Psychology, 54,* 69–75.

Godfrey, H. P. D., Knight, R. G., & Partridge, F. M. (1996). Emotional adjustment following traumatic brain injury: A stress-appraisal-coping formulation. *Journal of Head Trauma and Rehabilitation, 11,* 29–40.

Gracey, F., Brentnall, S., & Megoran, R. (2009). Judith: learning to do things 'at the drop of a hat': Behavioural experiments to explore and change the 'meaning' in meaningful functional activity. In B. A. Wilson, F. Gracey, J. J. Evans, & A. Bateman (Eds.), *Neuropsychological rehabilitation: Theory, models, therapy and outcome.* Cambridge, UK: Cambridge University Press.

Gracey, F., Evans, J. J., Malley, D. (2009). Capturing process and outcome in complex rehabilitation interventions: A "Y-shaped" model. *Neuropsychological Rehabilitation, 19,* 867–890.

Gracey, F., Palmer, S., Rous, B., Psaila, K., Shaw, K., O'Dell, J., et al. (2008). "Feeling part of things": Personal construction of self after brain injury. *Neuropsychological Rehabilitation, 18,* 627–650.

Haslam, C., Holme, A., Haslam, S. A., Iyer, A., Jetten, J., & Williams, W. H.

(2008). Maintaining group memberships: Social identity continuity predicts well-being after stroke. *Neuropsychological Rehabilitation, 18*, 671–691.

Jones, J. M., Haslam, S. A., Jetten, J., Williams, W. H., Morris, R., & Saroyan, S. (2011). That which doesn't kill us can make us stronger (and more satisfied with life): The contribution of personal and social changes to well-being after brain injury. *Psychology and Health, 26*, 353–369.

Karlovits, E. T., & McColl, M. A. (1999). Coping with community reintegration after severe brain injury: A description of stresses and coping strategies. *Brain Injury, 13*, 845–861.

Kelly, G. (1955). *The psychology of personal constructs.* New York, NY: W. W. Norton.

Kendall, E., & Terry, D. (2009). Understanding the adjustment following traumatic brain injury: Is the goodness of fit coping hypothesis useful? *Social Science & Medicine, 67*, 1217–1224.

Kim, E., Lauterbach, E. C., Reeve, A., Arciniegas, D. B., Coburn, K. L., Mendez, M. F., et al. (2007). Neuropsychiatric complications of traumatic brain injury: A critical review of the literature (A report by the ANPA committee on research). *Journal of Neuropsychiatry and Clinical Neuroscience, 19*, 106–127.

Krpan, K., Levine, B., Stuss, D., & Dawson, D. R. (2007). Executive function and coping at one-year post traumatic brain injury. *Journal of Clinical and Experimental Neuropsychology, 29*, 36–46.

Lazarus, R. S., & Folkman, S. (1984). *Stress, appraisal, and coping.* New York, NY: Springer.

LeDoux, J. E. (1995). Emotion: Clues from the brain. *Annual Review of Psychology, 46*, 209–235.

Mattson, A. J., & Levin, H. S. (1990). Frontal lobe dysfunction following closed head injury. A review of the literature. *Journal of Nervous and Mental Disease, 178*, 282–291.

McDonald, S., & Flanagan, S. (2004). Social perception deficits after traumatic brain injury: Interaction between emotion recognition, mentalizing ability, and social communication. *Neuropsychology, 18*, 572–579.

McGrath, J. (1997). Cognitive impairment associated with post-traumatic stress disorder and minor head injury: A case report. *Neuropsychological Rehabilitation, 7*, 231–239.

McGrath, J., & King, N. (2004). Acquired brain injury. In J. Bennet-Levy, G. Butler, M. Fennell, A. Hackman, M. Mueller, & D. Westbrook, *The Oxford Guide to Behavioural Experiments in CBT.* Oxford, UK: OUP.

Mooney, K. A., & Padesky, C. A. (2000). Applying client creativity to recurrent problems: Constructing possibilities and tolerating doubt. *The Journal of Cognitive Psychotherapy: An international quarterly, 14*, 149–161.

Moore, A. D., & Stambrook, M. (1992). Coping strategies and locus of control following traumatic brain injury: Relationship to long-term outcome, *Brain Injury, 6*, 89–94.

Nochi, M. (1998). "Loss of self" in the narratives of people with traumatic brain injuries: A qualitative analysis. *Social Science & Medicine, 7*, 869–878.

Nochi, M. (2000). Reconstructing self-narratives in coping with traumatic brain injury. *Social Science & Medicine, 51*, 1795–1804.

Ownsworth, T. (2005). The impact of defensive denial upon adjustment following traumatic brain injury. *Neuro-Psychoanalysis, 7*, 83–94.

Ownsworth, T., & Clare, L. (2006). The association between awareness deficits and rehabilitation outcome following acquired brain injury. *Clinical Psychology Review, 26*, 783–795.

Ownsworth, T., Desbois, J., Grant, E., Fleming, J., & Strong, J. (2006a). The associations among self-awareness, emotional well-being and employment outcome following acquired brain injury: A 12-month longitudinal study. *Rehabilitation Psychology, 51*, 50–59.

Ownsworth, T., Fleming, J., Desbois, J., Strong, J., & Kuipers, P. (2006b). A metacognitive contextual intervention to enhance error awareness and functional performance following traumatic brain injury: A single case experimental design. *Journal of the International Neuropsychological Society, 12*, 54–63.

Ownsworth, T. L., Fleming, J., Nalder, E., Cornwell, P., Haines, T., Kendall, M., et al. (2009). *Occurrence of sentinel events and emotional adjustment during the hospital to home transition following acquired brain injury.* Paper presented and proceedings of the International Neuropsychological Society meeting, Helsinki, Finland, August 2009.

Ownsworth, T. L., Fleming, J., Shum, D., Kuipers, P., & Strong, J. (2008a). A randomised controlled trial (RCT) for facilitating goal attainment and improving psychosocial function following acquired brain injury: Comparison of three intervention formats. *Journal of Rehabilitation Medicine, 40*, 81–88.

Ownsworth, T., Fleming, J., Strong, J., Radel, M., Chan, W., & Clare, L. (2007). Awareness typologies, long-term emotional adjustment and psychosocial outcomes following acquired brain injury. *Neuropsychological Rehabilitation, 17*, 129–150.

Ownsworth, T., & McKenna, K. (2004). Investigation of factors related to employment outcome following traumatic brain injury: A critical review and conceptual model. *Disability and Rehabilitation, 26*, 765–784.

Ownsworth, T. L., Turpin, M., Andrew, B., & Fleming, J. (2008b). Participant perspectives on an individualised self-awareness intervention following stroke: A qualitative case study. *Neuropsychological Rehabilitation, 18*, 692–712.

Powell, T., Ekin-Wood, A., & Collin, C. (2007). Post-traumatic growth after head injury: A long-term follow-up. *Brain Injury, 21*, 31–38.

Riley, G. A., Brennan, A. J., & Powell, T. (2004). Threat appraisal and avoidance after traumatic brain injury: Why and how often are activities avoided? *Brain Injury, 18*, 871–888.

Royal College of Physicians (2003). *Rehabilitation following acquired brain injury. National Clinical Guidelines.* London, UK: Royal College of Physicians & British Society of Rehabilitation Medicine.

Ruff, R., Marshall, L., Crouch, M., Klauber, M., Levin, S., Barth, J., et al. (1993). Predictors of outcome following severe head trauma: Follow up data from the Traumatic Coma Data Bank. *Brain Injury, 7*, 101–111.

Rutterford, N. A., & Wood, R. L. (2006). Evaluating a theory of stress and adjustment when predicting long-term psychosocial outcome after brain injury. *Journal of the International Neuropsychological Society, 12*, 359–367.

Schönberger, M., Humle, F., & Teasdale, T. W. (2006). The development of the therapeutic working alliance, patients' awareness and their compliance during the process of brain injury rehabilitation. *Brain Injury, 20*, 445–454.

Secrest, J. A., & Zeller, R. (2007). The relationship of continuity and discontinuity, functional ability, depression, and quality of life over time in stroke survivors. *Rehabilitation Nursing, 32*, 158–164.

Shallice, T., & Burgess, P. W. (1996). The domain of supervisory processes and the temporal organisation of behaviour. *Philosophical Transactions of the Royal Society of London* B, *351*, 1405–1412.

Tajfel, H., & Turner, J. C. (1979). An integrative theory of intergroup conflict. In W. G. Austin & S. Worchel (Eds.), *The social psychology of intergroup relations* (pp. 33–47). Monterey, CA: Brooks-Cole.

Teasdale, J. D., & Barnard, P. J. (1993). *Affect, cognition and change*. Hove, UK: Lawrence Erlbaum Associates.

Teasdale, T. W., & Engberg, A. W. (2001). Suicide after traumatic brain injury: A population study. *Journal of Neurology, Neurosurgery and Psychiatry, 71*, 436–440.

Thomsen, I. V. (1974). The patient with severe blunt head injury and his family. A follow-up of 50 patients. *Scandinavian Journal of Rehabilitation Medicine*; *6*, 180–183.

Thornhill, S., Teasdale, G. M., Murray, G. D., McEwen, J., Roy, C. W., & Penny, K. I. (2000). Disability in young people and adults one year after head injury: Prospective cohort study. *British Medical Journal, 320*, 1631–1635.

Turner, B., Ownsworth, T. L., Cornwell, P., & Fleming, J. (2009). Re-engagement in meaningful occupations during the transition from hospital to home for individuals with acquired brain injury and their family caregivers. *American Journal of Occupational Therapy, 63*, 609–620.

Tyerman, A., & Humphrey, M. (1984). Changes in self-concept following severe head injury. *International Journal of Rehabilitation Research, 7*, 11–23.

Vogenthaler, D. R., Smith, K. R., & Goldfader, P. (1989). Head injury, a multivariate study: Predicting long-term productivity and independent living outcome. *Brain Injury, 3*, 369–385.

Williams, W. H., & Evans, J. J. (2003). Brain injury and emotions: An overview to a special issue on biopsychosocial approaches in neurorehabilitation. *Neuropsychological Rehabilitation, 13*, 1–11.

Wilson, B. A. (2002). Towards a comprehensive model of cognitive rehabilitation. *Neuropsychological Rehabilitation*, 12, *97–110.*

Wilson, B. A., Gracey, F., Malley, D., Bateman, A., & Evans, J. J. (2009). The Oliver Zangwill Centre approach to neuropsychological rehabilitation. In B. A. Wilson, F. Gracey, J. J. Evans, & A. Bateman (Eds.), *Neuropsychological rehabilitation: Theory, models, therapy and outcome*. Cambridge, UK: Cambridge University Press.

Yeates, G. N., Gracey, F., & Collicutt McGrath, J. (2008a). A biopsychosocial deconstruction of 'personality change' following acquired brain injury. *Neuropsychological Rehabilitation, 18*, 566–589.

Yeates, G., Hamill, M., Sutton, L., Psaila, K., Gracey, F., Mohamed, S., et al. (2008b). Dysexecutive problems and interpersonal relating following frontal brain injury: Reformulation and compensation in Cognitive Analytic Therapy (CAT). *Neuro-Psychoanalysis, 10*, 43–58.

Ylvisaker, M., & Feeney, T. (2000). Reconstruction of identity following brain injury. *Brain Impairment, 1*, 12–28.

16 The importance of remembering and deciding together

Enhancing the health and well-being of older adults in care

Catherine Haslam
University of Exeter

Jolanda Jetten
University of Queensland

S. Alexander Haslam
Craig P. Knight
University of Exeter

> Memory performs the impossible for man by the strength of his divine arms; holds together past and present, beholding in both, existing in both, abides in the flowing, and gives continuity and dignity to human life.
>
> (Emerson, 1893, p. 64)

In the above observation, Emerson captures the pivotal role that our memories play in maintaining self-continuity throughout life. He goes further in saying that memory is "the thread on which the beads of man are strung, making the personal identity which is necessary to moral action" (Emerson, 1893, p. 63). Thus, by providing the means to connect our past and present lives, memory helps us to make sense of who we are. It is not surprising, then, that when memory fades, as it does in dementia, so too does one's understanding of self. Yet despite the claim that the memory loss associated with dementia destroys the person, there are also reports that some elements of self, particularly from the distant past, survive even in advanced stages of the disease (Cohen-Mansfield, Golander, & Arnheim, 2000; Davis, 2004; Kitwood, 1993; Klein, Cosmides, & Costabile, 2003; Sabat & Harré, 1992). Importantly, these remnants can provide a foundation from which the self can, to some extent at least, be reconstructed. However, it is not entirely clear how best to harness these remnants and how to build upon them in order to achieve this outcome.

In addition, for many people residing in care, memory loss is not the only threat to self that they confront. For, over time, they often develop an increasing sense of powerlessness, particularly as decisions about care are increasingly made on behalf of residents and hence, are no longer under their *control*. Unsurprisingly, this too has a major impact on people's sense of who they are and can in turn affect their well-being. Thus, it has been found that when residents' control over the environment (e.g., choices about care and daily activities) is limited, they tend to see their lives as more impersonal and institutionalized (Kane & Wilson, 2001). At the same time, other research suggests that empowering people to take some control over their lives can increase motivation and self-esteem (e.g., Deci & Ryan, 1987; Folkman & Lazarus, 1988) and enhance well-being (Rodin & Langer, 1976). However, in contexts where individuals become increasingly dependent on care, allowing them to remain in control of their lives may not always be possible and such initiatives may not fit well with care needs. These constraints raise the question of whether it is possible to empower those who are in care at all – especially if their situation is compounded by memory difficulties.

In this chapter we argue that group-based interventions that promote a sense of shared social identification and collective empowerment have the potential to reduce the threat to identity that results from increasing loss of memory and diminishing control. To make this case, we focus on findings from two intervention studies that we recently conducted. In the first of these we examined the impact of reminiscence therapy on cognitive performance. In the second, we looked at the impact of empowering residents to make decisions about the décor in their home on cognition and well-being as well as on their use of communal space. As we will see, the reminiscence intervention was effective in bolstering memory only when it was administered to a group. In a similar vein, we show that allowing people to choose their décor collectively had a positive impact on well-being and perceived control.

In line with the theoretical principles that informed the design of these studies, we argue that both sets of findings are best understood in terms of a social identity perspective on health and well-being (e.g., see Haslam, Jetten, Postmes, & Haslam, 2009). This points to the benefits that developing a sense of shared group membership can have for a person's quality of life, and suggests that this may be a particularly important pathway for both understanding and improving the lives of people residing in care.

IDENTITY MAINTENANCE AND RECONSTRUCTION: THE CONTRIBUTION OF SOCIAL IDENTITY APPROACHES

For the person experiencing memory loss as a result of dementia, disintegration of personality is a distinctive feature of disease progression.

While there are reports that individuals can demonstrate preserved knowledge of their personality in this condition, this appears to be the case only for the distant self. Klein et al. (2003) provide a clear example of this in their description of KR, an individual suffering from Alzheimer's disease. As the authors observe, the self that KR knew was "out-of-date" (Klein et al., 2003, p. 157).

This observation is consistent with previous research that has shown that both the quality and strength of identity is compromised as a result of autobiographical memory loss. As an illustration of this point, Addis and Tippett (2004) assessed autobiographical memory and personal identity in older adults both with and without a diagnosis of Alzheimer's disease. What they found was that the group with dementia recalled fewer auto-biographical memories and generated fewer self-statements in response to the question "Who am I?". Moreover, these statements were superficial and lacked detail. Thus, relative to those without memory impairment, people with dementia demonstrated the predicted pattern of identity loss (see also, Della Sala, Freschi, Lucchelli, Muggia, & Spinnler, 1996; Hirst, 1994).

At the same time, however, there is also evidence from other research that elements of self can remain intact well into the disease process. KR is a case in point. Here, Klein and colleagues (Klein et al., 2003) found that, despite evidence of a significant decline in many of KR's abilities, knowledge of her personality traits was largely preserved. However, along lines suggested above, this was restricted to knowledge of traits from the distant past as she was unable to update this aspect of self-knowledge. Consistent with this analysis, there is evidence that KR's knowledge about others' traits was accurate for people she had known from the past (e.g., her daughter) but not for those with whom she was recently acquainted (e.g., her primary caregiver). According to Kitwood (1993), this means that something of the past is known even in the context of declining memory in dementia. An important question then, is whether we can harness this residual knowledge to protect the self or indeed, to reconstruct and develop new dimensions of identity.

When considering ways in which to reconstruct identity by building on these remaining memories from the past, we can take several approaches. First, if we adopt the view that self or identity is derived from an individual's unique attributes (Eysenck, 1953; or what Turner, 1982, referred to as *personal identity*), then the process of identity reconstruction might proceed by focusing on personal traits and characteristics. This strategy – of *personal identity reconstruction* – might focus, say, on the fact that a given individual has become increasingly "conscientious". Attempts to increase understanding of this aspect of self might then involve helping the person to recall recent times in his or her life when this personality characteristic was particularly salient (e.g., in the garden, planning a meal). While this might appear a reasonable approach, for the person experiencing memory loss as a result of dementia, consolidation of recently acquired personality traits may prove unsuccessful given the greater vulnerability of this aspect of self-knowledge in disease progression. Moreover, in focusing on consolidation of recently acquired traits, such an approach would probably fail to establish continuity between past and present knowledge, and many have argued that this is key in maintaining a coherent sense of self (e.g., Addis & Tippett, 2004, 2008; Bluck & Alea, 2008; Locke, 1694/1970).

An alternative approach to identity reconstruction is provided by the work of social identity researchers. Working within the framework provided by social identity (Tajfel & Turner, 1979) and self-categorization (Turner, 1982; Turner, Oakes, Haslam, & McGarty, 1994) theories, this emphasizes the social dimensions of identity, and highlights the important role that group memberships play in providing structure and meaning to the self. According to this view, personal identity and self-knowledge is derived from the relationships we have with important social groups (e.g., family, work, religious, and sporting groups) and it is from these relationships that we come to know ourselves (e.g., Turner, Reynolds, Haslam, & Veenstra, 2006). This approach therefore suggests a different approach to remedial intervention in the case of identity loss – one of *social identity reconstruction*. Here, rather than focus on purely personal aspects of identity, the emphasis is on facilitating group interaction with a view to strengthening old social identities as well as developing new ones.

There is growing evidence that socially directed interventions of this form can improve cognition and general well-being in healthy older adults (e.g., Barnes, Mendes de Leon, Wilson, Bienià, & Evans, 2004; Ertel, Glymour, & Berkman, 2008; Mendes de Leon, Glass, & Berkman, 2003). Furthermore, evidence suggests that these may offer some protection against Alzheimer's disease and vascular dementia (e.g., Fratiglioni, Wang, Ericcson, Maytan, & Winblad, 2000; Wang, Karp, Winblad, & Fratiglioni, 2002). Maintaining valued social networks also allows for social identity continuity and has been shown to improve well-being during recovery from stroke (Haslam et al., 2008). It has also been found to be an important predictor of subjective well-being in a range of groups that are faced with the threat of identity loss (e.g., see Bluck & Alea, 2008; Iyer, Jetten, & Tsivrikos, 2008). In sum, and in line with the general thesis of this book, there is a growing body of evidence that points to the health benefits of an active and diverse social life (for reviews see Haslam et al., 2009; Jetten, Haslam, Haslam, & Branscombe, 2009; Jetten, Haslam, & Haslam, this volume).

WHAT REMAINS OF SELF WHEN MEMORY FADES?

Previous work thus suggests that there might be an important role for social groups and collectives in counteracting the effects of identity threat and loss – regardless of whether this arises from failing memory or from diminishing control. Some recent evidence that supports this analysis emerged from a study on which the first three authors collaborated (Jetten, Haslam, Pugliese, Tonks, & Haslam, 2010). This examined the impact of autobiographical memory and identity loss on the well-being of three groups of older adults who differed in their care needs. One group was living in the community and received no care; a second group had moderate needs and was living in residential care; a third group had high needs and was receiving specialist (i.e., dementia) care.

In the study we explored two factors that previous research suggests might be important in determining well-being in these populations. On the basis of cognitive theorizing, deficiencies in intellectual abilities – most notably, *memory impairment* – would be predicted to compromise or threaten well-being. On the other hand, social theorizing suggests that well-being will be predicted by a person's *identity integrity* (i.e., the degree to which he or she has a clear understanding of who he or she is). In other words, a memory model anticipates that well-being will be correlated with level of cognitive function, while an identity model anticipates that it will be correlated with strength of identity.

Unsurprisingly, the study found that memory loss declined progressively with increasing levels of care need. More interestingly, however, integrity of identity and well-being did not follow the same pattern. For while the groups residing in care reported lower identity strength and well-being relative to the community group, there was no difference between those receiving moderate and high levels of care. Further analyses also revealed that personal identity strength mediated the impact of care level on well-being but that this was not true for memory ability. In contrast, cognitive functioning did not mediate the relationship between memory impairment and well-being. There was also evidence that identity strength was increased as a result of belonging to multiple social groups. In short, then, a strong sense of personal identity was a much better predictor of residents' well-being than their level of cognitive impairment, and this sense of identity was itself associated with a person's sense that he or she had multiple sources of social identity.

In this study, though, it is unclear what it was that supported identity strength and well-being in those with more severe memory loss. One suggestion is that reduced awareness of memory loss among those with severe dementia may have protected their well-being (in the sense that "ignorance is bliss"). Consistent with this idea, Naylor and Clare (2008) studied people in the early stages of dementia and found that low awareness of memory difficulties was associated with weaker autobiographical recall (particularly from the mid-life period), and a stronger sense of identity. On this basis the researchers concluded that reduced awareness may "serve a protective function against threats to the self" (p. 590). Related to this, it is also possible that, because memory loss leads to a confusion of the past with the present (so that these are no longer clearly differentiated), those in the severe dementia group were released from reality constraints and therefore able to reconstruct a present identity based on accessible past memories.

Whatever its cause, the critical finding in this study was that some semblance of self either survived or was able to be reconstructed even among those suffering from severe dementia. This supports anecdotal reports of people's ability to maintain a sense of self even when faced with severe memory decline (e.g., Cohen-Mansfield et al., 2000). The overall pattern of findings also suggests four things. First, that identity strength plays a greater role in determining well-being than cognitive ability per se. Second, that personal identity has some basis in social group memberships (as suggested by Turner et al., 2006). Third, that because identity remains partially intact even among those with progressive dementia, members of this population are still able to enjoy a reasonable quality of life. Fourth, and most importantly for the purposes of the present chapter, if we put these points together it would appear that there is scope for this quality of life among this population to be enhanced by inventions that aim to maintain or enhance a sense of identity. More particularly, the study's findings suggest that even among dementia sufferers, there remains a foundation upon which identities can be built and reconstructed. Accordingly, it would appear that among vulnerable populations (e.g., those suffering from, or at risk of, dementia) there might be value in interventions that try to reconstruct identity either by working with memory or by building group ties, or both.

Improving memory and well-being through group reminiscence and group games

One intervention which appears to hold out particular promise as a means of shoring up or rebuilding identity is reminiscence. This is one of the most widely used interventions for older people (with and without dementia) and is increasingly used in residential care. In essence, the intervention involves the recollection of past memories and experiences. This is often facilitated by using tangible materials such as objects, music, and photographs from various time periods (Woods, Spector, Jones, Orrell, & Davies, 2005). It can be delivered in either a one-to-one or a group setting, but the latter is more common. The intervention is particularly relevant to the present chapter because it aims to stimulate memory and strengthen personal identity while also improving communication, mood, and well-being (see Woods et al., 2005).

Nevertheless, studies that have investigated the effects of reminiscence on memory, general cognitive performance, and well-being produce mixed results. Some reports indicate that it leads to improved performance on the Mini-Mental Status Examination (MMSE; Folstein, Folstein, & McHugh, 1975) – a measure of basic cognitive functioning often used with older adults (e.g., Lai, Chi, & Kayser-Jones, 2004; Tadaka & Kanagawa, 2007). There is also evidence that it can enhance mood (e.g., Cook, 1991), well-being (Brooker & Duce, 2000; Cook, 1998; Rattenbury & Stones, 1989), and social interaction (Head, Portnoy, & Woods, 1990). Participants also report finding reminiscence activities generally enjoyable (Baines, Saxby, & Ehlert, 1987). However, other studies have found the therapy to have few beneficial effects and report no change on key measures following its administration (e.g., Goldwasser, Auerbach, & Harkins, 1987; Ito, Meguro, Akanuma, Ishii, & Mori, 2007; Thorgrimsen, Schweitzer, & Orrell, 2002). Yet, apart from indirect evidence of enhanced social interaction, none of these studies speaks to the impact of reminiscing on identity integrity. In the context of the present discussion, this is a significant omission given that building and preserving identity is identified as one of the main goals of the therapy.

In addition, perhaps the greatest limitation of reminiscence, and hence of investigations into its effectiveness, is the failure to consider and evaluate the mechanisms that underlie any of its therapeutic benefits (Haslam et al., 2010). One of the few studies that has attempted this was undertaken by Woods and colleagues in their influential Cochrane review (Woods et al., 2005). In line with some of the above observations, in this review the authors suggest that reminiscence may capitalize on the relatively preserved memory for the past in dementia sufferers. That is, there is speculation that the greater accessibility of distant memories may facilitate the process of recollection and encourage participants to actively connect their past and present memories. This in turn may strengthen a sense of continuity between the past and the present and thereby contribute to the overall integrity of identity. Although plausible, this *memory continuity* explanation has yet to be tested as identity processes are typically neither measured nor discussed in studies that have investigated the efficacy of reminiscence.

Arguably too, it is precisely in situations when the evidence base is mixed (as it is in the case of reminiscence studies), that theorizing is needed to help identify the critical elements of an intervention. On the basis of the foregoing review it would appear that social identity theorizing has the potential to provide theory-based explanation of this form. In particular, because the majority of reminiscence work is undertaken in groups, it seems likely that the process of collective recollection of memories may increase a sense of shared identification among members of the group and this also enhances cognitive performance and general well-being.

In order to explore these possibilities, we conducted a study that was designed to examine the beneficial effects of reminiscence interventions more closely (Haslam et al., 2010). In this, 73 residents in receipt of either standard or specialized (i.e., dementia) care were randomly assigned to one of three interventions.[1] One intervention involved reminiscing in a small group context; a second involved reminiscing with another person who facilitated the activity; a third involved taking part in a group control activity that, in this case, was to play skittles.[2] The control group was included to provide a baseline against which the effects of group reminiscence and individual reminiscence could be compared.

Each intervention was facilitated by members of our research team who first received training in how to deliver reminiscence. The intervention took place weekly over a period of six weeks, with each session lasting about half an hour. Each resident was interviewed prior to and immediately after the intervention. During these interviews, residents were asked to complete a measure of general cognitive ability, which included a memory component (i.e., Addenbrooke's Cognitive Examination Revised, ACE-R; Mioshi, Dawson, Mitchell, Arnold, & Hodges, 2006), in addition to measures of identity strength (both personal and social) and general well-being. To assess the efficacy of the various treatments, post-intervention scores on each of these measures were subtracted from pre-intervention scores.

On the basis of a memory continuity account we would predict that it is the process of connecting past and present memories that is critical to the efficacy of reminiscence and hence that it would not matter whether this therapy is administered in either an individual or a group context – as both should be equally effective. In contrast, social identity theorizing would lead us to expect that group reminiscence would produce better treatment outcomes than individual delivery because only the former promotes a shared sense of social identification.

In line with the latter suggestion, the results supported the idea that group activity was the critical factor in facilitating well-being and enhancing cognitive performance. First, reminiscing led to a significant increase in general cognitive performance – due largely to enhanced memory – but *only* when this was experienced in a group setting. In fact there was a 12 percent increase in memory performance after group reminiscence and essentially no change in the remaining interventions. Second, there was also evidence that the group activity led to a significant improvement in well-being. Interestingly, though, this was observed amongst those residents who took part in the control intervention of skittles, rather than those who received the group reminiscence intervention. In this case the data showed that group skittles increased well-being by 10 percent, compared to a 2 percent reduction after group reminiscing and a 5 percent decline after one-to-one reminiscence. This suggests that the facilitation we observed in cognitive performance was not due simply to mood enhancement (a suggestion that has been made on the basis of previous studies; see Woods et al., 2005). Importantly too, the results indicated that, rather than being confined to one group of residents, the therapeutic benefits that followed group reminiscence and skittles were experienced by those receiving both standard and specialized care.

In summary, then, only group-based interventions led to improved outcomes and these were dependent on the particular intervention received. The group intervention with a cognitive focus (i.e., group reminiscence) led to enhanced memory performance, whilst the group intervention with a social focus (i.e., playing group skittles) led to enhanced well-being. Thus, while we attribute these benefits primarily to social group membership, the *form* of the intervention seemed to influence the particular *aspect* of health (i.e., cognition or well-being) that was enhanced. These findings were also mirrored in the residents' own comments on the study. For example, after taking part in a reminiscence group one resident observed that it made her "want to concentrate more on what others say" and another that it "brought your memory back to you". Following the skittles activity another resident remarked: "You're never too old to learn . . . it was a pleasure. I will miss it. It's something to look forward to. It's nice to know that people are still interested even though you are old."

Clearly, though, a key question here is whether these positive outcomes can be attributed to either personal or social identity development. Examination of data on our measure of personal identity strength showed no change following any of the interventions. This, however, could be seen to reflect a ceiling effect in light of the fact that, prior to the intervention, residents generally reported having a strong and clear understanding of who they were (with mean scores of between 4.0 and 4.2 on a 5-point scale in each of the three conditions). This finding is consistent with previous reports of personal identity preservation in this population (as noted above; see also Jetten et al., 2010) and suggests that there may have been little room for any intervention to make this any stronger.

Importantly, though, results were much clearer on our measure of social identification. Moreover, as with our focal dependent variables, scores on this measure were significantly different across conditions. First, it was apparent that the social identification of residents in the two group-based conditions (group reminiscence and skittles) did not change as a result of the intervention – their affiliation with others in their care home was as strong after the intervention as it had been before (and in fact slightly, but nonsignificantly, higher). In contrast, though, those who reminisced individually reported a significant decrease over time in their identification with other residents.

This pattern is consistent with suggestions that group-based interventions achieved their results in part because they helped maintain (or enhance) individuals' sense of shared social identity. As a corollary, individual-based interventions that actually eroded this sense of social identification had no discernable therapeutic benefits. This pattern fits with other evidence in the literature which suggests that a lack of perceived connectedness to others has negative long-term effects for well-being (Branscombe, Schmitt, & Harvey, 1999; Cohen & Syme, 1985; Jetten, O'Brien, & Trindall, 2002; Schmitt & Branscombe, 2002; Wegge, Van Dick, Fisher, Wecking, & Moltzen, 2006). As we have argued elsewhere, a key reason for this is that social identity that is developed through social interaction not only reduces a sense of social isolation (Berkman & Glass, 2000; House, Landis, &

Umberson, 1988; Putnam, 2000) but also provides a basis for receiving and benefiting from social support (Haslam, O'Brien, Jetten, Vormedal, & Penna, 2005; Haslam et al., 2009; Jetten, Haslam, Iyer, & Haslam, 2009; see also Branscombe, Fernández, Gómez, & Cronin, this volume; Matheson & Anisman, this volume; van Dick & Haslam, this volume).

It is worth emphasizing the point that the experimental design of this study meant that individual and group reminiscence were identical in all but one respect (i.e., whether they were administered in a group or one-to-one). Thus the length of the intervention, the general content from week to week, the prompts used to facilitate recollection, and the person delivering the therapy were all controlled for. Were it simply the process of strengthening connections between past and present memories during the act of reminiscing that was important (as a memory continuity account suggests), we would expect no difference between these conditions. The fact, then, that we found evidence of improved cognitive performance only among those receiving group reminiscence suggests that it is the process of *collectively sharing* past memories that is a critical factor in the intervention's effectiveness, as a social identity account would predict. Evidence from the control condition in which groups played skittles also supports this social identity account. This was the other condition in which sustained social identification was found and here group activity was observed to lead to improved well-being over time.

The moral of this story is that group-based interventions have much to offer to older adults residing in care, including those suffering from dementia. Importantly, the study represents the first theoretically driven evaluation of reminiscence, and it provides a clear rationale and evidence to support the use of group-based interventions in care settings. Moreover, by helping to maintain a sense of social identity with fellow residents, we predict that other forms of activity that involve both social engagement and social interaction have the capacity to produce similarly beneficial outcomes.

Improving cognitive and social engagement through group decision making

Memory decline and other cognitive problems are not a pre-requisite for feeling powerless. Clearly, even among those who do not experience cognitive problems, feelings of disempowerment can be common – whether in the workplace, in the family, or other social contexts (e.g., see Reicher & Haslam, 2006). However, it is also the case that cognitive problems, which are more likely to occur and increase in severity as we age, exacerbate feelings of reduced control. One might also expect these perceptions to be particularly pronounced among older people who reside in care, since they find themselves in an environment where key decisions are often made for them, and where their power and voice are routinely limited (Hauge & Heggen, 2007).

However, it follows from this that interventions which seek to empower care residents by allowing them to make decisions about aspects of their care (e.g., meal choices, leisure activities, room furnishings, and decoration) may help to reduce feelings of disempowerment. More importantly though, in thinking about ways to empower people in care, it follows from the arguments laid out in the preceding sections that there might be particular value in doing this in ways that strengthen group-based ties and social identity. Not least, this is because increasing residents' sense of connectedness to others should have benefits for both social interaction and well-being (Moos, 1981).

Recently we were offered the opportunity to test these ideas by developing and evaluating an intervention that aimed to empower residents who were in the process of moving into a new care facility. As is common in such situations, it typically falls upon care staff and managers to design and decorate communal areas. While this helps to ensure that these areas meet health and safety standards, this process can clearly undermine residents' sense of autonomy. For while before entering care they would have made such decisions as a matter of course – in the process of making their own houses into homes – now they typically have fewer opportunities to do so. One consequence of this, however, is that communal spaces can often hold little personal meaning for residents. Accordingly, it is perhaps not surprising that these spaces are often poorly used and that residents retreat into the comfort of their own rooms (Hauge & Heggen, 2007). Yet while this strategy enhances residents' comfort it also constitutes a significant problem in light of evidence that social isolation is one of the greatest threats to well-being and health (particularly for older people; e.g., Cornwell & Waite, 2009). How then should this problem be addressed?

In line with social identity theorizing, we reasoned that one way in which it might be tackled is by empowering residents to make their own decisions about the decoration of communal space in ways that also serve to build their sense of shared social identity. There is certainly evidence from previous research that when residents are given choice, they feel more in charge of their lives (for example, if they are encouraged and allowed to decorate their own rooms, see Brink, 1993; Dixon, 1991; Feingold & Werby, 1990). However, we reasoned that this sense might be augmented by allowing residents to make such choices *collectively*. Moreover, because social interaction is one of the key ways in which people develop a shared sense of identification with others (Postmes, Haslam, & Swaab, 2005) we felt that this might have additional benefits. In particular, as well as increasing social support and well-being (along lines suggested above), heightened social identification has been found to enhance trust and to encourage acts of citizenship (e.g., Ashforth & Mael, 1989; Haslam, 2004; Haslam, Eggins, & Reynolds, 2003). Theoretically then, we reasoned that a range of health-related and social benefits might result from the process of empowering residents to make collective decisions about the physical environment in the new home into which they were moving. In this context too, it is worth noting that the process of moving into a new home is one that has previously been found to be particularly confronting and stressful for people (e.g., Dickinson, Vosen, & Biedermann, 2006).

To test these ideas we conducted a study with 27 residents who were about to move from their old residential facility into a newly refurbished home (Knight, Haslam, & Haslam, 2010). These residents had not been diagnosed either with dementia or any serious physical disability and were moving onto the same floor of the new building as they had occupied in the old one (either the ground floor or the first floor). This provided us with an opportunity to conduct a natural experiment in which the residents from one floor were involved collectively in decisions about the decoration of their new communal space (the *identity empowered* condition) while those on the other floor had their communal spaces decorated for them (the unempowered, or *control condition*). Random assignment to condition was not possible, so to reduce the influence of pre-existing differences, it was decided to assign those on the first floor to the empowered intervention as, prior to the move, these residents had been the least satisfied with their living conditions. Importantly, the standard of decoration in the control condition was very high, and an equivalent amount of money was spent on the two floors.

Over several sessions, residents in the empowered condition met as a group with the researchers, care home managers and staff from an interior landscaping company. As a group, these residents were able to select from a design palette the pictures and plants that they wanted to have in their corridors, lounge and dining rooms. The residents then organized formal and informal meetings in which, independent of input from managers and designers, they made decisions as a group about how these pictures and plants should be arranged.

For the purposes of assessment, residents in both conditions were interviewed individually at three time points: 4 weeks before the move and then 4 weeks and 4 months after the move. On each occasion they were asked to rate the strength of their identification with others (residents and staff independently), their life satisfaction, and physical health. Care staff were also asked to rate the general alertness, life satisfaction, and physical health of each resident. Finally, observational data were collected to record the use of communal spaces. This involved counting the number of residents in the dining and lounge rooms at two set times (11 am and 7 pm) on seven consecutive days at each time point.

In line with predictions derived from social identity theorizing, outcomes on these various measures were consistently and significantly superior in the empowered condition (see Knight et al., 2010). Thus, over time, residents in the empowered group identified more strongly with other residents and staff, reported greater life satisfaction and better physical health than those in the unempowered condition. Carers also rated residents in the empowered condition to be healthier and to have a higher quality of life.

Furthermore, there was also a significant difference in the two groups' use of communal space. Prior to the move, residents in the control condition had used both dining and lounge rooms more than those in the empowered condition (a fact that reflected their greater satisfaction with their living conditions). After the relocation, however, this pattern was dramatically reversed. Indeed, one month after the intervention, those in the empowered group were using their new communal areas 57 percent more than they had been previously, while those in the control group were using them 60 percent less. This meant that the residents' lounge was used nearly four times as much by those in the empowered condition, and 4 months later it was still being used more than twice as much.

In summary, this study provided clear evidence that the process of increasing social identification among residents by engaging them in the process of collective decision making had a number of substantial benefits. Most importantly, it contributed to their feeling happier, healthier and more engaged with their environment and the people in it. Critically, this was not confined to residents' feelings but also had an impact on their physical activity – so that those in the empowered condition were much more likely to engage with others through their use of communal space. In a sense, then, the intervention had the effect of making residents feel "at home" rather than "in a home" and, in this, it dramatically reduced their risk of social isolation. Together these findings suggest that there are particular benefits which accrue from activities which sustain or heighten people's sense of shared social identity – and the sense of connectedness, belonging, and trust that flows from this.

SOCIAL INTERVENTIONS PAVE THE WAY

We are not alone in promoting the view that social interventions involving collective interaction, engagement and companionship can protect health and well-being. Similar views have been advanced in a range of disciplines including medicine, epidemiology, nursing, and economics. People who are socially active live longer than people who are more socially isolated (e.g., House et al., 1988; Marmot, Siegrist, & Theorell, 2005). They are less prone to physical illness (Cohen, Doyle, Turner, Alper, & Skoner, 2003), memory decline (Ertel et al., 2008), and general cognitive deterioration (Barnes et al., 2004; Mendes de Leon et al., 2003). In line with these ideas, evidence suggests, for example, that stroke sufferers who have meaningful social relationships can reduce their risk of a subsequent medical event (i.e., second stroke, myocardial infarction, or death) by half compared to those who are more socially isolated (Boden-Albala, Litvak, Elkind, Rundek, & Sacco, 2005). There is also evidence that being able to maintain important social group memberships, which provides the basis for social identity continuity, can enhance well-being and this helps people make the most of their recovery following stroke (Haslam et al., 2008). Such effects are far from trivial and as the volume of research on this topic increases, it is apparent that even those who have been firmly wedded to the medical model are starting to take the social determinants of health much more seriously (see Haslam et al., 2009; Malec, 2009).

This increased understanding is particularly important when it comes to the residential care population that has been the focus of this chapter. Concerns about the care needs of an ageing population are growing, and these are particularly high in the case of those who suffer from dementia; a condition estimated to affect 24 million people worldwide (Ferri et al., 2005). With increasing questions about the value of pharmacological interventions as a means of managing the cognitive and other problems associated with this condition, there is a clear and, some would argue, urgent need to seek alternatives.

Group-based interventions informed by a social identity approach appear to offer a timely means of tackling this problem. Moreover, this approach provides a rich base from which to develop other interventions. In this chapter we have focused primarily on the health benefits of interventions that involve group reminiscence and decision making. Yet the theory points to the potential for other group interventions to produce similar health benefits – providing that the groups are both valuable and meaningful to those who take part in them.

Throughout this chapter we have argued that declining memory and power need not erase identity. As previous research (e.g., Addis & Tippett, 2004; Naylor & Clare, 2008) and anecdotal reports from family and carers attest, it is of course the case that the richness and complexity of older adults' identity is likely to be diminished if they either suffer from dementia or feel disempowered. Nevertheless, we would suggest that it is a mistake to see this change – or that in general cognitive ability – as a reason to "write off" older people who find themselves in care. For the evidence we have presented here suggests that residual memories, and the sense of personal and social identity they support, can be a solid foundation upon which to build successful care interventions. This appears to be critical in helping to counteract the negative consequences of ageing, and feeds into issues at the heart of our common humanity. Indeed, we would suggest that by helping older people to retain and rediscover their sense of who they are, our efforts may also help to clarify and ennoble our own social identities as members of caring communities.

ACKNOWLEDGMENTS

We wish to thank the staff and residents of Somerset Care Limited and Cornwall Care Limited who took part in the studies reported in this chapter. Work on this paper was supported by a grant from the Economic and Social Research Council (RES-062-23-0135).

NOTES

1 Residents in this study were in receipt of these two levels of care. The main criteria for receipt of specialized care are that a person has a general medical diagnosis of dementia together with a greater need for both personal care and a safe stimulating environment. Those in receipt of standard care were physically frail who could possibly, though not necessarily, be in the early stages of dementia.

2 Skittles is a game commonly played in Britain, very similar to bowling, in which the aim is to knock down up to nine skittles (or pins) with a ball.

References

Addis, D. R., & Tippett, L. J. (2004). Memory of myself: Autobiographical memory and identity in Alzheimer's disease. *Memory, 12*, 56–74.

Addis, D. R., & Tippett, L. J. (2008). The contributions of autobiographical memory to the content and continuity of identity: A social-cognitive neuroscience approach. In F. Sani (Ed.), *Self continuity: Individual and collective perspectives* (pp. 71–84). New York, NY: Psychology Press.

Ashforth, B. E., & Mael, F. (1989). Social identity theory and the organization. *Academy of Management Review, 14*, 20–39.

Baines, S., Saxby, P., & Ehlert, K. (1987). Reality orientation and reminiscence therapy: A controlled cross-over study of elderly confused people. *British Journal of Psychology, 151*, 222–231.

Barnes, I., Mendes de Leon, C. F., Wilson, R., Bienià, J., & Evans, D. A. (2004). Social resources and cognitive decline in a population of older African Americans and whites. *Neurology, 63*, 2322–2326.

Berkman, L. F., & Glass, T. (2000). Social integration, social networks, social support and health. In L. F. Berkman & I. Kawachi (Eds.), *Social epidemiology* (pp. 137–174). New York, NY: Oxford.

Bluck, S., & Alea, N. (2008). Remembering being me: The self-continuity function of autobiographical memory in younger and older adults. In F. Sani (Ed.), *Individual and collective self-continuity: Psychological perspectives.* Cambridge, UK: Cambridge University Press.

Boden-Albala, B., Litvak. E., Elkind, M. S. V., Rundek, T., & Sacco, R. L. (2005). Social isolation and outcomes post-stroke. *Neurology, 64*, 1888–1892.

Branscombe, N. R., Schmitt, M. T., & Harvey, R. D. (1999). Perceiving pervasive discrimination among African-Americans: Implications for group identification and well-being. *Journal of Personality and Social Psychology, 77*, 135–149.

Brink, S. (1993). Elderly empowerment. New rights and research are enhancing nursing-home life. *US News & World Report Journal, 114*, 65–66, 69–70.

Brooker, D., & Duce, L. (2000). Wellbeing and activity in dementia: A comparison of group reminiscence therapy, structured goal-directed group activity and unstructured time. *Aging and Mental Health, 4*, 354–358.

Cohen, S., Doyle, W. J., Turner, R. B., Alper, C. M., & Skoner, D. P. (2003). Sociability and susceptibility to the common cold. *Psychological Science, 14*, 389–395.

Cohen, S., & Syme, S. L. (1985). *Social support and health.* Orlando, FL: Academic Press.

Cohen-Mansfield, J., Golander, H., & Arnheim, G. (2000). Self-identity in older persons suffering from dementia: Preliminary results. *Social Science & Medicine, 51*, 381–394.

Cook, E. A. (1991). The effects of reminiscence on psychological measures of ego integrity in elderly nursing home residents. *Archives of Psychiatric Nursing, 5*, 292–298.

Cook, E. A. (1998). Effects of reminiscence on life satisfaction of elderly female nursing home residents. *Health Care for Women, 19*, 109–118.

Cornwell, E. Y., & Waite, L. J. (2009). Social disconnectedness, perceived isolation and health among older adults. *Journal of Health and Social Behavior, 50*, 31–48.

Davis, D. (2004). Dementia: Sociological and philosophical constructions. *Social Science & Medicine, 58*, 369–378.

Deci, E. L., & Ryan, R. M. (1987). The support of autonomy and control of behaviour. *Journal of Personality and Social Psychology Bulletin, 53*, 1024–1037.

Della Sala, S., Freschi, R., Lucchelli, F., Muggia, S., & Spinnler, S. (1996). Retrograde amnesia. No past, new life. In P. W. Halligan & J. C. Marshall (Eds.), *Method in madness: Case studies in cognitive neuropsychiatry* (pp. 209–233). Hove, UK: Psychology Press.

Dickinson, L., Vosen, X., & Biedermann, S. (2006). *Living well in a nursing home: Everything you and your folks need to know.* Alameda, CA: Hunter House Publishers.

Dixon, S. (1991). *Autonomy and dependence in residential care: Evaluation of a project to enhance resident choice in an elderly people's home.* London, UK: Age Concern Institute of Gerontology.

Emerson, R. W. (1893). *Natural history of intellect and other papers.* Cambridge, MA: Riverside Press.

Ertel, K. A., Glymour, M. M., & Berkman, L. F. (2008). Effects of social integration on preserving memory function in a nationally representative US elderly population. *American Journal of Public Health, 98*, 1215–1220.

Eysenck, H. J. (1953). *The structure of human personality.* London, UK: Methuen.

Feingold, E., & Werby, E. (1990). Supporting the independence of elderly residents through control over their environment. *Journal of Housing for the Elderly, 6*, 25–32.

Ferri, C. P., Prince, M., Brayne, C., Brodaty, H., Fratiglioni, L., Ganguli, M., et al. (2005). Global prevalence of dementia: A delphi consensus study. *Lancet, 366*, 2112–2117.

Folkman, S., & Lazarus, R. S. (1988). The relationship between coping and emotion: Implications for theory and research. *Social Science & Medicine, 26*, 309–317.

Folstein, M. F., Folstein, S. E., & McHugh, P. R. (1975). 'Mini-mental state': A practical method for grading the cognitive state of patients for the clinician. *Journal of Psychiatric Research, 12*, 189–198.

Fratiglioni, L., Wang, H. X., Ericsson, K., Maytan, M., & Winblad, B. (2000). Influence of social network on occurrence of dementia: A community based longitudinal study. *The Lancet, 355*, 1315–1319.

Goldwasser, A. N., Auerbach, S. M., & Harkins, S. W. (1987). Cognitive, affective, and behavioral effects of reminiscence group therapy on demented elderly. *International Journal of Aging & Human Development, 25*, 209–222.

Haslam, C., Haslam, S. A., Jetten, J., Bevins, A., Ravenscroft, S., & Tonks, J.

(2010). The social treatment: The benefits of group interventions in residential care settings. *Psychology and Aging, 25,* 157–167.

Haslam, C., Holme, A., Haslam, S. A., Iyer, A., Jetten, J., & Williams, W. H. (2008). Maintaining group memberships: Social identity continuity predicts well-being after stroke. *Neuropsychological Rehabilitation, 18,* 671–691.

Haslam, S. A. (2004). *Psychology in organizations: The social identity approach.* London, UK: Sage.

Haslam, S. A., Eggins, R. A., & Reynolds, K. J. (2003). The ASPIRe model: Actualizing social and personal identity resources to enhance organizational outcomes. *Journal of Occupational and Organizational Psychology, 76,* 83–113.

Haslam, S. A., Jetten, J., Postmes, T., & Haslam, C. (2009). Social identity health and well-being: An emerging agenda for applied psychology. *Applied Psychology: An International Review, 58,* 1–23.

Haslam, S. A., O'Brien, A., Jetten, J., Vormedal, K., & Penna, S. (2005). Taking the strain: Social identity, social support and the experience of stress. *British Journal of Social Psychology, 44,* 355–370.

Hauge, S., & Heggen, K. (2007). The nursing home as a home: A field study of residents' daily life in the common living rooms. *Journal of Clinical Nursing, 17,* 460–467.

Head, D. M., Portnoy, S., & Woods, R. T. (1990). The impact of reminiscence groups in two different settings. *International Journal of Geriatric Psychiatry, 5,* 295–302.

Hirst, W. (1994). The remembered self in amnesics. In E. Neisser & R. Fivush (Eds.), *The remembering self: Construction and accuracy in the self narrative* (pp. 252–277). New York, NY: Cambridge University Press.

House, J. S., Landis, K. R., & Umberson, D. (1988). Social relationships and health. *Science, 241,* 540–545.

Ito, T., Meguro, K., Akanuma, K., Ishii, H., & Mori, E. (2007). A randomized controlled trial of the group reminiscence approach in patients with vascular dementia. *Dementia and Geriatric Cognitive Disorders, 24,* 48–54.

Iyer, A., Jetten, J., & Tsivrikos, D. (2008). Torn between identities: Predictors of adjustment to identity change. In F. Sani (Ed.), *Individual and collective self-continuity* (pp. 187–197). Mahwah, NJ: Lawrence Erlbaum Associates.

Jetten, J., Haslam, C., Haslam, S. A., & Branscombe, N. R. (2009). The social cure. *Scientific American Mind, 20,* 26–33.

Jetten, J., Haslam, C., Pugliese, C., Tonks, J., & Haslam, S. A. (2010). Declining autobiographical memory and the loss of identity. *Journal of Clinical and Experimental Neuropsychology, 32,* 408–416.

Jetten, J., Haslam, S. A., Iyer, A., & Haslam, C. (2009). Turning to others in times of change: Social identity and coping with stress. In S. Stürmer & M. Snyder (Eds.), *The psychology of prosocial behavior: Group processes, intergroup relations, and helping* (pp. 139–156). Oxford, UK: Blackwell.

Jetten, J., O'Brien, A., & Trindall, N. (2002). Changing identity: Predicting adjustment to organizational restructure as a function of subgroup and superordinate identification. *British Journal of Social Psychology, 41,* 281–297.

Kane, R. A., & Wilson, K. B. (2001). *Assisted living at the crossroads: Principles for its future.* Portland, OR: Jessie F. Richardson Foundation.

Kitwood, T. (1993). Towards a theory of dementia care: The interpersonal process. *Aging and Society, 13,* 51–67.

Klein, S. B., Cosmides, L., & Costabile, K. A. (2003). Preserved knowledge of self in a case of Alzheimer's dementia. *Social Cognition, 21*, 157–165.

Knight, C., Haslam, S. A., & Haslam, C. (2010). In home or at home? Evidence that collective decision making enhances older adults' social identification, well-being, and use of communal space when moving into a new care facility. *Aging and Society, 30*, 1393–1418.

Lai, C. K., Chi, I., & Kayser-Jones, J. (2004). A randomized control trial of a specific reminiscence approach to promote the well-being of nursing home residents with dementia. *International Psychogeriatrics, 16*, 33–49.

Locke, J. (1970). *An essay concerning human understanding* (2nd ed.). Yorkshire, UK: The Scholar Press. (Original work published in 1694)

Malec, J. F. (2009). Ethical and evidence-based practice in brain injury rehabilitation. *Neuropsychological Rehabilitation, 19*, 790–806.

Marmot, M., Siegrist, J., & Theorell, T. (2005). Health and the psycho-social environment at work. In M. Marmot & R. Wilkinson (Eds.), *Social determinants of health* (pp. 105–127). New York, NY: Oxford University Press.

Mendes de Leon, C. F., Glass, T. A., & Berkman, L. F. (2003). Social engagement and disability in a community population of older adults: The New Haven EPESE. *American Journal of Epidemiology, 157*, 633–642.

Mioshi, E., Dawson, K., Mitchell, J., Arnold, R., & Hodges, J. R. (2006). The Addenbrooke's Cognitive Examination Revised (ACE-R): A brief cognitive test battery for dementia screening. *International Journal of Geriatric Psychiatry, 21*, 1078–1085.

Moos, R. (1981). Environmental choice and control in community care settings for older people. *Journal of Applied Psychology, 11*, 23–43.

Naylor, E., & Clare, L. (2008). Awareness of memory functioning, autobiographical memory and identity in early-stage dementia. *Neuropsychological Rehabilitation, 18*, 590–606.

Postmes, T., Haslam, S. A., & Swaab, R. (2005). Social influence in small groups: An interactive model of identity formation. *European Review of Social Psychology, 16*, 1–42.

Putnam, R. D. (2000). *Bowling alone: The collapse and revival of American community*. New York, NY: Simon & Schuster.

Rattenbury, C., & Stones, M. J. (1989). A controlled evaluation of reminiscence and current topics discussion groups in a nursing home context. *The Gerontologist, 29*, 768–771.

Reicher, S. D., & Haslam, S. A. (2006). Tyranny revisited: Groups, psychological well-being and the health of societies. *The Psychologist, 19*, 46–50.

Rodin, J., & Langer, E. J. (1976). Long-term effects of a control relevant intervention with the institutionalized aged. *Journal of Personality and Social Psychology, 35*, 897–902.

Sabat, S. R., & Harré, R. (1992). The construction and deconstruction of self in Alzheimer's disease. *Aging and Society, 12*, 443–461.

Schmitt, M. T., & Branscombe, N. R. (2002). The meaning and consequences of perceived discrimination in disadvantaged and privileged social groups. *European Review of Social Psychology, 12*, 167–199.

Tadaka, E., & Kanagawa, K. (2007). Effects of reminiscence group in elderly people with Alzheimer's disease and vascular dementia in a community setting. *Geriatrics & Gerontology International, 7*, 167–173.

Tajfel, H., & Turner, J. C. (1979). An integrative theory of intergroup conflict. In W. G. Austin & S. Worchel (Eds.), *The social psychology of intergroup relations* (pp. 33–47). Monterey, CA: Brooks/Cole.

Thorgrimsen, L., Schweitzer, P., & Orrell, M. (2002). Evaluating reminiscence for people with dementia: A pilot study. *The Arts in Psychotherapy, 29*, 93–97.

Turner, J. C. (1982). Towards a cognitive redefinition of the social group. In H. Tajfel (Ed.), *Social identity and intergroup relations* (pp. 15–40). Cambridge, UK: Cambridge University Press.

Turner, J. C., Oakes, P. J., Haslam, S. A., & McGarty, C. A. (1994). Self and collective: Cognition and social context. *Personality and Social Psychology Bulletin, 20*, 454–463.

Turner, J. C., Reynolds, K. J., Haslam, S. A., & Veenstra, K. (2006). Reconceptualizing personality: Producing individuality through defining the personal self. In T. Postmes & J. Jetten (Eds.), *Individuality and the group: Advances in social identity* (pp. 11–36). London, UK: Sage.

Wang, H. X., Karp, A., Winblad, B., & Fratiglioni, L. (2002). Late-life engagement in social and leisure activities is associated with a decreased risk of dementia: A longitudinal study from the Kungsholmen Project. *American Journal of Epidemiology, 155*, 1081–1087.

Wegge, J., Van Dick, R., Fisher, G. K., Wecking, C., & Moltzen, K. (2006). Work motivation, organizational identification, and well-being in call centre work. *Work and Stress, 20*, 60–83.

Woods, B., Spector, A., Jones, C., Orrell, M., & Davies, S. (2005). Reminiscence therapy for dementia. *Cochrane Database of Systematic Reviews* (Issue 2. Art. No.: CD001120). doi: 10.1002/14651858.CD001120.pub2

Part V
Conclusion

17 Advancing the social cure

Implications for theory, practice, and policy

Catherine Haslam
University of Exeter

Jolanda Jetten
University of Queensland

S. Alexander Haslam
University of Exeter

The key message of this book is that social relationships – in particular, those that are framed by people's membership of social groups – influence our health and well-being in tangible ways. Regardless of whether these relationships are part of our experience in families, organizations, or communities, they have the capacity to affect mood, life quality, cognitive decline, and even life span. This basic message is conveyed through the findings reported in every one of the preceding chapters; findings that point to the important role that groups play in determining people's life satisfaction, their experience of stress, stigma and symptoms associated with illness, their adjustment to a range of life changes (e.g., ageing, neurological disease, and trauma), their decisions about health behaviour, and their responses to more extreme events (e.g., disasters and following war). Moreover, this basic message emerges from field data gathered across a broad range of populations faced with very different circumstances as well as from a large body of experimental and laboratory research. Regardless of researchers' particular foci or methods, all the work contained in this volume resonates with, or has been inspired by, the theoretical framework provided by a social identity approach to health and well-being – an approach that represents an application of social identity and self-categorization principles more generally. This, then, is where the strength of this volume lies – in its capacity to provide a social analysis based on a theoretical framework that has applicability across a range of contexts and conditions.

In this concluding chapter, our goal is to abstract some of the main lessons that emerge from the contributions that precede it. Our focus is on lessons that are relevant to three key constituencies: researchers who are concerned primarily with questions of *theory*; practitioners, clinicians, and health care professionals who are most concerned with issues of *practice*; and policy makers, advocate groups and representatives of various agencies who are concerned largely with matters of *policy*. In reality, of course, the interests of these groups (and of readers more generally) are not neatly compartmentalized in this way, and neither are the issues themselves so clearly differentiated. Nevertheless, we see some utility in structuring our discussion along these lines, as it allows us both to highlight the broad range of implications that emerge from the volume as a whole and to clarify how these can be used to advance the social cure more generally.

THEORETICAL IMPLICATIONS OF THE SOCIAL IDENTITY APPROACH

As noted above, many authors in this volume use the principles of social identity and self-categorization theories to understand the ways in which group memberships, and the sense of social identity that is derived from them, are key to health and well-being. Perhaps most pertinent to those who are interested in the theoretical framework that the social identity approach provides, is the question of whether it can be further developed and enriched by examining the role that identity plays in health and well-being. More specifically, does the work in this volume provide new insights into the operation of self and identity processes?

The traditional focus of social identity theorizing

Historically, social identity theory (Tajfel, 1972; Tajfel & Turner, 1979, 1986) was developed to explain intergroup processes, dynamics and behaviour. Two chapters in particular – those published by Tajfel and Turner in 1979 and 1986 – addressed how acting in terms of a given group membership affects people's responses to others who are perceived as belonging to other groups. These chapters played a pivotal role in formalizing the key principles of social identity theory and provided important insights into the nature of intergroup perceptions, discrimination, and prejudice. This represented a major shift in the field at the time, heralding a move away from explanations based on notions of personality and realistic conflict between groups towards one that distinguished between, on the one hand, behaviour that is shaped by interpersonal factors, and, on the other, behaviour that is informed by an internalized sense of group membership (i.e., social identity). These ideas were later refined and extended in self-categorization theory (Turner, Hogg, Oakes, Reicher, & Wetherell, 1987), to include important insights into the operation of self and *intra*group processes. After three decades of research inspired by these theories, there is now a vast evidence base that supports the claim that attitudes, beliefs, and behaviour differ fundamentally as a function of whether people act as individuals (i.e., in terms of personal identity) or as members of groups that stand in a particular relationship to other groups (e.g., see Ellemers, Spears, & Doosje, 1999; Haslam, 2004; Oakes, Haslam, & Turner, 1994; Postmes & Jetten, 2006).

Although the primary emphasis of social identity theory in particular, was to explain intergroup relations, it would be misleading to suggest that those who pioneered this work had no interest in the implications of identity for health and well-being. Indeed, in developing social identity theory, Tajfel and Turner (1979) explicitly observed that membership in social groups is "associated with positive or negative value-connotations" (p. 40) and that the value of one's groups has implications for the individual and their sense of self. As we noted in Chapter 1, the search for a positive social identity – that would furnish individuals with a positive sense of self – was assumed to be one of the driving forces behind group behaviour. Indeed, as we and other contributors to the current volume have argued, this quest for positive self-definition implicates social identity processes in health and well-being in quite fundamental ways. Consistent with this analysis, in the 1980s and 1990s there was an upsurge in research which investigated the ways in which group members strive to achieve a positive identity (in particular, see Hogg & Abrams, 1990). Unfortunately, however, this research tended to have a relatively narrow focus in being concerned more or less exclusively with questions of self-esteem. What is more, empirical findings tended to be mixed (e.g., see Rubin & Hewstone, 1998) and this led most social identity researchers to lose interest in this aspect of the theory (Turner, 1999).

Yet the move away from a narrow focus on self-esteem also had some fortunate consequences, particularly in encouraging researchers to stand back and consider questions of a broader nature. As a result, in the intervening years there has been exponential growth in research which explores the relationship between identity and health (for a discussion, see Haslam, Jetten, Postmes, & Haslam, 2009). Indeed, this volume is testament to this burgeoning of interest, as well as to the diversity of topics in the field – such that it deals, amongst other things, with issues of physical and mental health, symptom perception and treatment, stress, coping, rehabilitation, life satisfaction, cognitive function, and recovery.

This polymorphism is exciting for a number of reasons. Most obviously, it has served to bring together a broad-based network of researchers who are able to draw on multiple bodies of knowledge and different disciplinary skills in the process of seeking to develop a more comprehensive appreciation of the relationship between social identity and health. Not only has this stimulated research in many fields (e.g., audiology, epidemiology, neuropsychology, health economics) but, as we will outline below, it can also be used to develop concrete recommendations about ways in which social identity theorizing can ultimately be translated into beneficial health outcomes.

In this process, it is reassuring to discover that many core social identity principles prove to be both applicable and useful. Returning to the principles that we discussed in Chapter 1, on the basis of social identity theory we can predict that as an individual's sense of shared identification with others in his or her social groups increases, so too does the likelihood that he or she will use those groups to maintain a positive self-image (e.g., see Branscombe, Férnandez, Gómez & Cronin, Chapter 7; Douglas, Chapter 13; van Dick & Haslam, Chapter 10), and this is fundamental in deriving positive health outcomes from social groups. Moreover, we can go further if we invoke the principles of self-categorization theory to predict that, under these conditions, people gain the power to influence, and be influenced by, social groups in ways that affect health at individual and societal levels (e.g., see Haslam, Reicher, & Levine, Chapter 9; Tarrant, Hagger, & Farrow, Chapter 3). As the evidence in several of the foregoing chapters attests, together these principles explain not only how belongingness to social groups affects health under conditions of stress (see van Dick & Haslam, Chapter 10), illness (St. Claire & Clucas; Chapter 5), disability (see Branscombe et al., Chapter 7), and trauma (Douglas, Chapter 13; Gracey & Ownsworth, Chapter 15; Jones, Jetten, Haslam, & Williams, Chapter 14), but also how groups can be critical vehicles for responding to, and effecting, change (see Drury, Chapter 11; Haslam, Jetten, Haslam, & Knight, Chapter 16; Tarrant et al., Chapter 3). Importantly too, using these same principles we can also predict when and why social groups sometimes fail to encourage or achieve positive health outcomes (see Haslam et al., Chapter 9; Kellezi & Reicher, Chapter 12; Sani, Chapter 2).

New theoretical insights

While it is encouraging to see that social identity principles retain currency once researchers apply them to the task of understanding health outcomes, it is also clear that by focusing on a relatively new set of empirical questions – those pertaining to health and well-being – social identity theorizing has also been advanced. For example, St. Claire and Clucas (Chapter 5) examine the way in which self-categorization (e.g., as a cold sufferer) informs the perception of symptoms and shapes subsequent health behaviour. Van Dick and Haslam (Chapter 10) demonstrate how group identification structures an individual's appraisal of, and response to, stressors in organizational contexts. Kellezi and Reicher (Chapter 12) show how living up to internalized group norms can bolster health and well-being, just as being unable to do so is corrosive. In these various contributions we see that the traditional focus of social identity theory on the intergroup context – typically where there is an "us" versus "them" distinction (see Turner et al., 1987; Turner, Oakes, Haslam, & McGarty, 1994) – is not necessarily of paramount importance when it comes to the relationship between identity and health. Instead, it is often more important to focus on those features of health-relevant contexts that inform a particular self-definition as "I"/"me" versus "we"/"us".

What then are the new theoretical insights that have been developed as a result of these shifts in focus? From the many that are discussed in the various chapters, there are three that we wish to draw particular attention to. The first is that social identities should be seen as valuable *resources* that people can draw upon in responding to diverse life stressors. The second is that the availability of social identity *networks* proves critical when responding to those same stressors. The third is that the *trajectories* of social identities – spanning past, present, and future – are also of vital importance for health and well-being. To clarify the significance of these ideas, we consider each in turn.

1. The importance of social identities as resources

Previous research has emphasized the way in which the behaviour of group members is shaped by the specific context and content of group-based identities, as well as by their sense of commitment to their group (e.g., see Ellemers et al., 1999). In this, social identities provide individuals with a framework for self-definition, which in turn is the basis for orienting the self to the social and physical world. When individuals are committed to their social groups, the specific values and norms of that group become a guide to individual thought and behaviour. All these aspects of group member-ship remain central to analysis of the impact of social factors on health. However, closer examination of this topic draws our attention to other aspects of identity that have yet to be fully explored in social identity research and theorizing (see Ashforth, Harrison, & Corley, 2008, for similar observations in the organizational domain). Perhaps most important in this regard is the realization that social identities are not simply aspects of the self-concept that researchers need to understand, but that they are tangible *resources* from which people can draw strength when undergoing poten-tially stressful life changes. As resources they offer a buffer against the negative consequences of change, illness, and stress. Important too is the prediction that as the size of a person's social identity resource increases, so too does their likelihood of deriving beneficial health outcomes.

The *buffering* property of social identity resources is theorized in many of the foregoing chapters. For example, Helliwell and Barrington-Leigh (Chapter 4) argue that social identities are a form of capital. Moreover, they show compellingly that people can benefit from this resource as much as – if not more than – they do from economic capital (e.g., household income). Branscombe and colleagues (Chapter 7) demonstrate how group identification serves as a buffer that counteracts the negative effects of exposure to group-based discrimination. Haslam and colleagues (Chapter 9) show how group identification also determines the extent to which people are able to benefit from social support. Jones and colleagues (Chapter 14) offer a model to explain how those who have sustained brain injury can buffer against adverse well-being effects by disclosing their injury to others and self-identifying as a survivor. And finally, Drury (Chapter 11) reveals how even groups comprised of perfect strangers – groups without a past or future – can furnish people with an emergent sense of social identity that allows them to deal effectively with the dangers posed by a mass emergency.

The realization that group membership can be a social and psychological resource opens up new terrain for both theorists and practitioners (a point we develop further below). First, it allows us to think of ways in which groups can be developed to maximize their resource potential (see Branscombe et al., Chapter 7, for an analysis of the conditions that allow groups to provide an effective coping resource). Second, it can help us to target interventions more effectively, to ensure that we create and maintain groups capable of providing such a resource for individuals who are confronted with specific stressors. Along these lines, chapters by Douglas (Chapter 13), Gracey and Ownsworth (Chapter 15), and Haslam and colleagues (Chapter 16) all provide excellent examples of the way in which thinking about social identity as a resource proves useful in conceptualizing and managing processes of rehabilitation and recovery.

2. The importance of social identity networks

A second new insight arises from focusing on entire social networks rather than just single identities, with a view to capitalizing on the many social identities that people can use as a basis for self-definition. Even though it is clear that at any moment in time identities differ in the extent to which they are salient (as suggested by self-categorization theory), it is also clear that those other identities that exist in the background do not necessarily become irrelevant. Instead non-salient but potentially accessible identities remain influential and are highly relevant in determining people's response to stressors (Jetten & Pachana, Chapter 6). To understand how people respond to challenges such as life transitions, identity loss, trauma, and work demands, it is therefore clear that in addition to mapping out the way in which a salient identity is affected, one also needs to take a range of other factors into account. These include how rich an individual's identity network is, whether he or she can fall back on other identities, how central the immediately affected identity is relative to other identities, and how different identities stand in relation to each other (e.g., whether their values and norms are compatible or incompatible).

Of course, assessing the impact that a whole spectrum of group identities has on a person is a complex undertaking. Certainly, examining the effect of a given event on just one identity (e.g., how Alice feels as a result of being a member of a stigmatized group) is likely to be easier than doing this for all the identities that may be indirectly implicated in the experience (i.e., her feelings as a parent, a woman, a member of a particular profession). On the positive side, though, research shows that these other identities can be a source of important benefits. For example, people generally appear to be much better equipped to cope effectively with various challenges if they have more than one social identity to fall back on (Haslam et al., Chapter 16). The social support drawn from these additional identities may have the potential to further enhance health effects in the context of counteracting negative effects of identity change. People also appear to be quite flexible and adaptive when managing their identity networks and can choose to re-evaluate or strategically emphasize the importance of the various identities within their networks.

In this way, *identity choice* is an important component of well-being (e.g., "now that I am retired, I can develop my volunteer identity"). Indeed, the effects of this can be seen to constitute a form of social creativity akin to that envisaged within original statements of social identity theory (Tajfel & Turner, 1979). Such flexibility is clearly important for understanding successful coping pathways and also forms an important starting point for interventions aimed at building new or existing identities (e.g., see Douglas, Chapter 13).

Another positive consequence of broadening social identity theorizing to consider the larger network of a person's identities is that the insights gained can be enriched by, and used to inform, theorizing in other disciplines. In particular, these considerations draw attention to important parallels between social identity research and work in the social capital tradition (Putnam, 2000; see Helliwell & Barrington-Leigh, Chapter 4). Within this tradition there is a long-standing interest in the impact of group life on such things as happiness, life satisfaction, life span, and mortality, and it would appear that all parties stand to gain from the cross-fertilization of ideas across traditional disciplinary boundaries (e.g., Lim & Putnam, 2010).

3. The importance of social identity trajectories

Although social identity theorists have long recognized the importance of taking the trajectory of social identities into account (e.g., Doosje, Spears, & Ellemers, 2002), the ways in which identities develop and the impact of this on individual self-construal and behaviour, has largely been over-looked. The temporal aspects of identities become particularly important when one wants to understand the relevance of identity networks for well-being. For identities do not operate in a temporal vacuum (Levine, 2003); people have a clear sense of whether they have lost group memberships that were important in the past (e.g., as a driver; Jetten & Pachana, Chapter 6), whether they have acquired new identities (e.g., as someone with a brain injury, Jones et al., Chapter 14), and may also have an awareness of the future viability of those identities (e.g., whether they are likely to be main-tained or are threatened as a result of discrimination; Matheson &

Anisman, Chapter 8). Indeed, in many situations perceptions of identity loss (both prospective and retrospective) may be at least as important as the accessibility of alternative or multiple social identities in the present.

Such observations highlight the importance of understanding how different social identities relate to each other over time. This also means that to understand the way that people utilize social identity resources, we need to understand the individual trajectories of identity and how these link to past, current, and potential future group memberships. However, just as the move to study multiple identities adds complexity to the research process, so too would any move to account for trajectories of group membership. Here again, though, we would argue that such an approach is likely to yield considerable dividends when it comes to understanding health and well-being. Indeed, evidence that this is the case emerges from work by Sani (Chapter 2; see also Sani, 2008) and Jetten and Pachana (Chapter 6) that, in the case of valued groups, shows people's perceptions of social identity continuity to be a unique and powerful predictor of well-being.

PRACTICAL IMPLICATIONS OF THE SOCIAL IDENTITY APPROACH

Having clarified the implications of a social identity approach to health for theorizing, the next obvious task is to identify the practical implications of this approach for the promotion of health and well-being. In this section we focus on two important realms of practice within which social identity principles can be brought to bear – those of *risk assessment* and *intervention* – and use these to support a decision-making model that can assist in the design of interventions. However, before going into details of these, we need first to discuss two caveats that must inform such practices more generally.

Practical caveats

1. Social identities cannot be taken for granted

One of the most dangerous assumptions we can make about social relations and social identities is that they are easy to develop and sustain. Because it is not particularly difficult to induce a sense of social identification with others in the laboratory (e.g., in the minimal group paradigm; Tajfel, Flament, Billig, & Bundy, 1971) and also because there are a range of situations in which social identity is an emergent product of social relations and social context (e.g., see Drury, Chapter 11), it is sometimes assumed that people only need minimal encouragement in order to engage in social interaction with others and to benefit from the experience. As many practitioners can attest, this is not the case. Social relationships are often challenging and fraught (e.g., see Haslam et al., Chapter 9; Kellezi & Reicher, Chapter 12) and may also be hard to come by. Accordingly, meaningful social identities and enduring social capital can be difficult to build and to maintain and they are not something that can simply be taken for granted.

This is likely to be especially true during those periods when people experience social identity change (e.g., when leaving home, starting a new job, having a baby, moving house, retiring, having a serious accident, becoming ill). It is during these periods that we are most vulnerable – emotionally, physically, and psychologically – due largely to the uncertainty that each transition brings. Some people manage these transitions well. In line with observations in the previous section, there is evidence that prior experience with social groups, and particularly multiple social groups, is a critical factor in building new relationships in times of change (e.g., Iyer, Jetten, Tsivrikos, Postmes, & Haslam, 2009). However, some people require help in managing transitions. When this is the case, care should be taken to ensure that interventions are appropriately targeted.

In this regard, simply telling people that they should seek social contact, perhaps by joining an existing group in the community, is unlikely to succeed because this ignores the *source* from which socially driven cures emerge – in much the same way as edicts from white middle-class professionals tend to have suboptimal impact on the health behaviours of members of disadvantaged minority groups (Oyserman, Fryberg, & Yoder, 2007; see Tarrant et al., Chapter 3). In part, this is because when there is no meaningful basis for mutual identification between curative agents (e.g., health professionals) and their targets, potentially curative support is neither given nor received (see Kellezi & Reicher, Chapter 12; Haslam et al., Chapter 9).

As several authors in this volume stress, it is therefore not social contact in and of itself, but *social identification* with others that is the basis for cure (e.g., Sani, Chapter 2). To develop such identification there must be a meaningful basis for aligning oneself with a particular group (e.g., perhaps because this is based on perceived common interest, fate, motivations and aspirations, beliefs, or values; see Drury, Chapter 11). Moreover, a failure to take such dynamics into account helps explain why simple encouragement and random attempts to slot people into groups often fail.

2. Social groups are not always a source of support

A different, but equally damaging assumption, is that *all* social groups are good for us. The rationale for such a belief is that because social groups have the capacity to benefit health and well-being, it should not matter what form these groups take. But social groups can both heal and harm, and we need to be aware of the core features of groups that produce these different outcomes. Sani captures this point succinctly, arguing that curative relationships are "based on cooperation, trust, and mutual support" (p. 21, Chapter 2), but as Kellezi and Reicher (Chapter 12) demonstrate, the opposite experience – one that involves exploitation, mistrust, and humiliation – characterizes harmful relationships.

Within the clinical literature, opposing outcomes tend to be seen as a product of people's contact with different *types* of groups, but this is often not the critical consideration. A group (e.g., a work department) can enhance health and well-being when its members share identification as group members (e.g., so that they are both aligned with their employers' mission), but it can also be detrimental to health if that commonality is lost or violated for some reason (e.g., if the group leader does not consult members about relevant organizational changes, or if some group members bully others; see van Dick & Haslam, Chapter 10). More important than the type of group, then, is its psychological status as ingroup or outgroup, and the individual's standing within the group (e.g., as a central or peripheral member). In this way, our experience of the group, and our relationship to other group members, plays a central role in determining its curative potential. Failure to appreciate this point is another common reason why social interventions fail.

The assessment of social identity risk

With these caveats in mind, we can start to reflect on ways in which practitioners can build or develop health-promoting identity networks. An important first step is to use risk assessment to determine whether social intervention is required at all, and, if it is, how much is needed. Following on from points made previously, here it is important to assess three distinct features of people's *social identity landscape*: their existing social groups and networks (from which they derive current social identities), their prospects for maintaining existing social groups and networks (from which they derive social identity continuity), and their opportunities to develop new social groups (from which they can create new social identities). We consider these in turn and link each to particular scales described in the Appendix that can be used for assessment purposes.

1. Assessing existing social identity resources

Examination of *existing* social groups involves consideration of the number, type, importance, and quality of a person's current relationships. This could be determined simply by asking people to describe their social relationships and networks, both in the present and in the past (see the *multiple identities* measures presented in the Appendix). From this information details about the number of valued social relationships will emerge that provides an index of the social identity resources, or *social identity capital*, potentially available to a person.

Evidence suggests that the more sources of social support we have the better the effect on our health (Iyer et al., 2009; Jetten & Pachana, Chapter 6; Putnam, 2000). However, it is also important to stress that there is no optimal number here. Accordingly, when focusing on the number of groups that people belong to, it is just as important to determine whether these resources are *sufficient* to support their needs. One way of establishing this is by assessing the perceived importance of a person's various social group memberships together with his or her ability to enact membership of those groups that are perceived to be important. These things can be indexed by measures of *social provisions, social isolation, generation and consumption of social support,* and *unsupportive interactions* (as detailed in the Appendix).

Assessment of a person's existing social identity resources is the first step in establishing whether he or she is likely to benefit from a social identity intervention. If it emerges that the individual in question has multiple well-established and well-maintained connections with social groups that are both important and supportive, then there will often be little reason to intervene (at least on social grounds). However, in the absence of such support, assessment of two particular risks should be prioritized. The first involves examining potential threats to the maintenance of valued social identities; the second involves appraising an individual's potential to benefit from the development of new social identities.

2. Assessing opportunities to maintain existing social identities

As we have noted already, our ability to maintain valued social group memberships tends to be under greatest threat during periods of life transition (e.g., when moving house, divorcing, retiring). Here loss of relationships will contribute to *social identity discontinuity* and this has the proven potential to compromise both mental health and well-being (e.g., Haslam et al., Chapter 16; Jetten & Pachana, Chapter 6; Gracey & Ownsworth, Chapter 15). The disruption to such continuity can be assessed informally, by simply asking people about the social relationships they have and have not been able to maintain, or more formally through measures of *social identity continuity* provided in the Appendix.

When attempting to examine the potential threat to health that results from social identity discontinuity, it is important to bear in mind our second caveat: that not all social relationships are curative. Accordingly, it is not the case that all forms of social identity maintenance are good for a person's health and well-being. Some social groups are unhelpful (e.g., when disclosing an injury, Jones and colleagues, Chapter 14; when adjusting to disability, Branscombe and colleagues, Chapter 7) and others can be distinctly harmful (e.g., when they promote conflict, exploitation, or destructive health behaviours, Sani, Chapter 2; Tarrant et al., Chapter 3). These possibilities can be captured by measures of *unsupportive interactions* (see Appendix).

Where the assessment of opportunities for social identity maintenance exposes some risk, there is a need to intervene. Yet it is only when we consider the impact of both helpful and harmful relationships that we can target interventions more effectively to overcome potential barriers in retaining those groups that offer the greatest benefit to health.

3. Assessing opportunities to create new social identities

Having raised the importance of social identity continuity, we must also acknowledge that people are not always in a position to maintain those groups they value. This will be less of a problem if the person has a broad network of social identity resources, so that the threat caused by loss of one identity can be compensated for by the maintenance or strengthening of another. However, where a person has a limited number of existing identity resources (so that they have all their social identities "in one basket"), and these can no longer be maintained, this can prove to be a particular risk. In this context, there is considerable value in exploring opportunities for the development of new social identities.

Consistent with this point, the work of Douglas (Chapter 13), Gracey and Ownsworth (Chapter 15), and Haslam and colleagues (Chapter 16), shows that building new social identities can play an instrumental role in helping people adjust to the identity loss associated with many different life events (e.g., neurological disease, trauma, moving into care). For these populations, social identity reconstruction was achieved either by encouraging individuals to join new groups (e.g., a cookery class; Douglas, Chapter 13), or by creating new groups for them to join (e.g., a reminiscence group; Haslam and colleagues, Chapter 16). In either case, practitioners need to be sensitive both (a) to the opportunities for new group memberships that are both available and viable, and (b) to the social identity resources that would have greatest value, meaning, and purpose for the individual in question. In this context, it is also important to recognize the potential benefits that can be gained from joining groups that may be devalued or stigmatized in society at large (e.g., support groups associated with a disabling condition). Indeed, these groups can be especially useful in helping individuals both (a) to come to terms with the specific challenges they confront and (b) to devise and engage in collective strategies for successfully overcoming them (e.g., see Branscombe et al., Chapter 7).

It is obviously the case that assessment of the form that we have outlined in this section is already a component of good practice in many clinical domains (e.g., on the part of psychologists, occupational therapists, or social workers). Nevertheless, it is equally true that a great deal of clinical practice either ignores these factors or deals with them rather unsystematically. In part, this reflects the fact that health professionals tend to be given only broad recommendations to encourage and promote social relationships while lacking either a theoretical framework for doing so or a set of explicit procedures (and tools) to guide them. The theoretically and empirically grounded approach to assessment that we have presented here constitutes an initial attempt to address these twin lacunae.

The treatment of social identity risk

If risk assessment points to the value of intervention as a means of ameliorating threats to social identities, then this raises the question of what form intervention should take. One clear message from the social identity approach is that practitioners should move beyond individual-centred strategies and instead develop interventions that are *group-based* (or at least *group-focused*), in order to capitalize upon the potential for a social cure. More specifically, intervention should involve the maintenance or creation of one or more social groups that (a) offer meaning and purpose for the person at risk, and which, in turn, can (b) provide the basis for shared identification with other group members.

In striving for these goals, it is important that interventions are flexible and tailored to the social needs of the individuals and groups concerned, rather than being prescriptive "off the peg" solutions. The importance of this is illustrated in the strategies reported in several of the chapters in this volume where groups are used to achieve positive health outcomes. Thus the intervention reported by Douglas (Chapter 13) focused on patient interests and preferences that led to them to join either existing groups (e.g., sporting, dance, computing, drama) or new groups (e.g., a Thai cookery class). Gracey and Ownsworth (Chapter 15) show how the process of reconnecting with a past social identity (as a motorbike rider) helped Judith develop a positive self-image (as someone able to overcome challenges) after her brain injury (see also Jones et al., Chapter 14). Two rather different interventions with groups of care home residents were developed and tested by Haslam and her colleagues (Chapter 16); one involved the residents reminiscing about their past and the other involved them making decisions about the décor in their care home. Despite the differences in approach, the authors of these chapters arrive at similar conclusions about the basis for enhanced health outcomes – attributing them to the positive sense of collective self that is achieved by maintaining or gaining a sense of connection and identification with others through shared social group membership. Equally dramatic effects have been reported more recently as a result of other forms of social intervention (establishing 'water clubs' to counteract dehydration among care home residents; Gleibs, Haslam, Haslam, & Jones, in press; facilitating "gentlemen's groups" to counteract social isolation among men in care, Gleibs et al., 2011).

Together, these studies show that very different social interventions are all capable of achieving similar, and equally positive, health outcomes. Theoretically and practically, what is common to these various interventions is the fact that the social identities with which they engage prove to be *meaningful* to those who take part in them. As group members, participants come to see the group as "us" not "them" and this emergent sense of "us-ness" lies at the heart of their curative experience.

Model for designing social group interventions

Figure 17.1 summarizes some of the key points that emerge from the foregoing discussion and presents a model to assist practitioners in the strategic design of social group interventions. In line with our earlier arguments, we suggest three discrete foci that need to be considered when planning intervention. The first of these involves determining whether there are barriers to the maintenance of existing social identities that can be overcome. Some of these barriers may be material (e.g., lack of access to transport, lack of funds to participate in a given activity). Others may be psychological – either cognitive (e.g., being unable to concentrate) or emotional (e.g., being anxious about one's status within the group). Either type of barrier may make it difficult or unwise for the individual in question to try to retain membership of particular groups, but if these barriers can be removed, there may well be no need for further intervention.

Sometimes it may not be possible to maintain existing group memberships, and under these circumstances it may be helpful to pursue a second focus by establishing whether the individual needs and wishes to develop new group memberships. If this is the case, it is important to ascertain both (a) the identity-related aspirations and interests upon which these might be built and (b) the availability of relevant existing groups in the community which might cater for these identity-related needs. If no existing groups can fulfil these needs, then a third focus of decision making can involve exploring opportunities to create new groups, centred on the *social identity potentialities* of the individual – that is, those aspects of the self that might form the basis for a shared identity with others.

The exploration of existing group memberships and opportunities to build new groups can certainly occur simultaneously. Indeed, being a member of multiple groups has been shown to be better for health, so where possible it would be important to reinforce existing group memberships whilst exploring opportunities for new memberships. Overall though, if we are serious about harnessing the potential for a social cure, then we need models of this form to provide a strategic approach to assessment of social risk and its intervention. Of course, this model is based on the existing research to date, and hence over time, other factors may be identified as key to this process. Importantly, though, it offers a practical template for putting the social identity approach to health into practice.

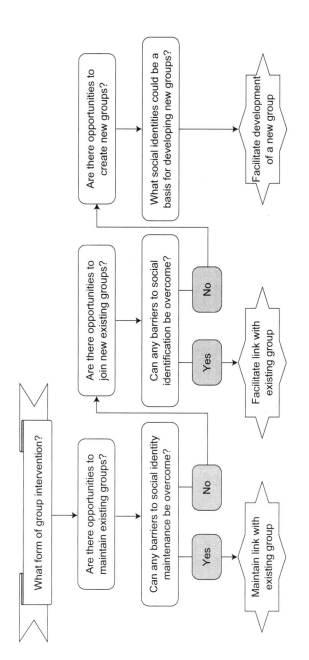

Figure 17.1 Model for designing interventions to address social identity risk.

POLICY IMPLICATIONS OF THE SOCIAL IDENTITY APPROACH

It is unfortunate that, despite considerable progress in specifying the relationship between social identity and health, very few policy initiatives have sought explicitly to capitalize upon the potential to use social groups as a means of improving health and well-being. One of the main stumbling blocks in policy development has been the failure to fully conceptualize key concepts (e.g., see Hawe & Shiell, 2000). In this volume, many contributors have tried to address this criticism directly by identifying and developing the core principles of theory that need to be promoted and implemented in practice. On this basis we would assert that the critical question is no longer one of conceptualization, but rather one of determining how social identity resources can be developed and mobilized with a view to promoting health and well-being both within specific populations and in societies at large.

In this section we tackle the issue of how policy makers can help to develop and sustain the socially engaging communities required to benefit from "social cures". To meet this agenda, we suggest two strategic initiatives. The first follows from our assertion that groups – and the sense of social identity that underpins them – represent substantial, tangible assets rather than mere ephemera. Thinking about social identities in this way means that their value needs to be incorporated into cost–benefit analyses that are used to make decisions about resource allocation. The second initiative relates the development of specific strategies targeted at health promotion. Here we suggest that there is considerable value in moving beyond traditional approaches to health and well-being that are grounded in individualized treatment and the imposition of solutions by "external" agencies. This is because the evidence presented in this volume suggests that the social cure works best when it is both (a) focused at a collective level, but also (b) delivered in partnership with those to whom it is administered.

Social identity as an economic resource

There is growing emphasis on quantifying both the cost of impoverished social relations and the benefits of social capital for society. This is particularly apparent in fields of economics, political science, organizational psychology, and epidemiology. As a consequence, we are steadily gaining a far better appreciation of the size of the problems societies face if they ignore the social dimensions of health, as well as the benefits of taking these dimensions seriously. Organizations, for example, are now acutely aware of the damage that workplace stress can do to their financial bottom line (see van Dick & Haslam, Chapter 10) and, at a national level, governments are increasingly sensitive to the economic advantages of having a cohesive society in which individuals are trusting of their neighbours, have friends and colleagues they can count on, and are engaged with their communities (see Helliwell & Barrington-Leigh, Chapter 4). Moreover, it would appear that an emergent sense of shared social identity is a vital source of social capital that proves critical when tackling the exigencies of natural disaster or public emergency (e.g., earthquakes, bombings; see Drury, Chapter 11).

In all these circumstances the evidence that has been surveyed in this book suggests that social identity – and the things which flow from it (e.g., support, trust, solidarity) – is a far more valuable economic commodity than financial wealth and material resources (see also Akerlof & Kranton, 2010; Van Boven & Gilovich, 2003). Furthermore, in line with the observations of Turner (2005), this evidence suggests that when they do prove important, material resources tend to *flow from* social identity rather than having any utility in their own right. We can use care home research to illustrate this point (see Haslam et al., Chapter 16). In economic terms, the cost of decorating a care home with or without input from groups of residents is identical. However, it is only where groups of residents are involved in this process – where policy engages with, and mobilizes, social identities – that this investment proves to be worthwhile in terms of the residents' health and well-being.

In this regard, it is apparent that a prevailing problem with conventional public health policy is that, although it is largely well-intentioned, its approach is often paternalistic. This is a problem, because by *imposing* solutions on potential beneficiaries, this tends to undermine the sense of shared identity (and the associated sense of *agency*; Reicher & Haslam, 2006) that is necessary for practical support to have its desired impact (see Drury, Chapter 11; Haslam et al., Chapter 9; Tarrant et al., Chapter 3). A key point here, then, is that in order to prove successful, policy needs to work with the grain of citizens' social identities rather than to go against it.

In tackling these issues, it is again helpful to see social identities not as abstract entities but as concrete resources that can either be diminished, maintained, or grown. By doing this we may also arrive at new answers to questions about how best to effect social change. For example, if we are interested in enhancing population health, does it make sense to prioritize the delivery of tax breaks (thereby increasing household income) or to build and support sustainable communities (see Helliwell & Barrington-Leigh, Chapter 4)? We suggest that it will be easier both to pose and to correctly answer questions of this form when the outcomes of social identity-based interventions have a clear price tag, as this allows policy makers to make less constrained economic choices. Indeed Putnam adopts this approach in his evaluation of the effect of social capital on smoking: "If you smoke and belong to no groups it is a toss up statistically whether you should stop smoking or start joining" (Putnam, 2000, p. 331). In the process of weighing the benefits and costs, Putnam concludes that: "These findings are in some ways heartening: it's easier to join a group than to lose weight, exercise regularly, or quit smoking" (p. 331).

It is also the case that in many instances it is no more expensive to deliver a health programme that caters to people's social identity needs than it is to deliver one that ignores them. Indeed, a common reason for using groups as the basis for intervention is that they are often considerably cheaper (representing a more effective use of both time and money) than therapy which is delivered one-on-one. Assuming that such group-based interventions are tailored to specific identity needs (see Figure 17.1), this makes not only good economic sense but can deliver many additional benefits. Moreover, it is worth noting that this is a policy implication which makes social cures as attractive to those on the right of the political spectrum as they are to those on the left.

Social identities as forethought rather than afterthought

There are various arguments about whether "an ounce of prevention is worth a pound of cure", but this aphorism has particular resonance in the context of social identity resources. The destruction of communities, the decline of social capital, and the lack of effective social support all have health costs, which are often most visible when the social identity resource has vanished and it is too late to intervene. In the British context, there is, for example, a certain irony to the fact that the Conservative government has recently heralded the value of "The Big Society" (Cameron, 2009; see Evans, 2010) when, in its previous term in office, the Conservative leader Mrs Thatcher had proudly pronounced that "there is no such thing as society". In this regard, we are reminded of a public address by Anthony Clare, formerly Professor of Psychiatry at the Maudsley Institute, in which he wistfully lamented the fact that politicians seem only ever to appreciate the value of community once they have destroyed it (Clare, 2002).

Some corporeal sense of this point is provided in the last panel of the triptych by the artist Stephen Willats "Living without the certainty that I will see someone tomorrow" (see Figure 17.2, last panel). This vividly depicts in three panels the life of an elderly woman living in a West London tower block. In the picture we see that the quality of the woman's life flows straightforwardly from her state of physical isolation. Moreover, the picture centres on her plaintive question "What do you propose is the way for me to form new relationships within this isolated tower?"

This situation is grim for a number of reasons. First, and perhaps most importantly, the social context no longer lends itself to fulfilling social identities. The modern housing arrangements depicted here make it difficult to meet others and to build social relationships. There is no space for people to get together and develop a sense of community. The result is loneliness, depression, lack of trust, and alienation. Moreover, it seems hard to imagine how these effects can be treated successfully through manualized, one-on-one psychological intervention (e.g., in the form of cognitive behaviour therapy). Helpful as they may be in the short term, they

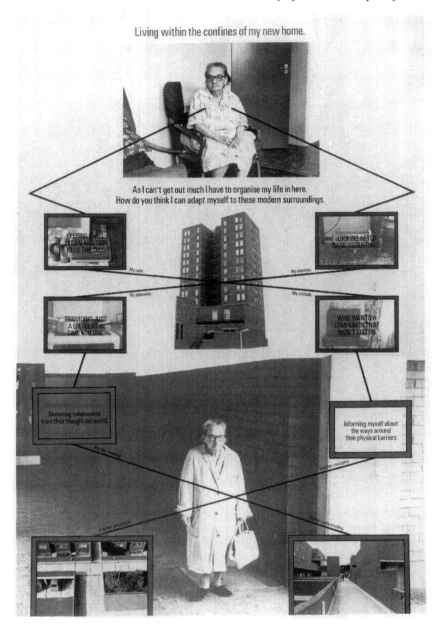

Panel 1

Figure 17.2 Stephen Willats "Living with practical realities" (reproduced with permission).

Living with the present day limitations of a small income.

When deciding what I need it's not much use looking at other people.
Can you find a solution that will help me change the economic realities I now face.

Panel 2

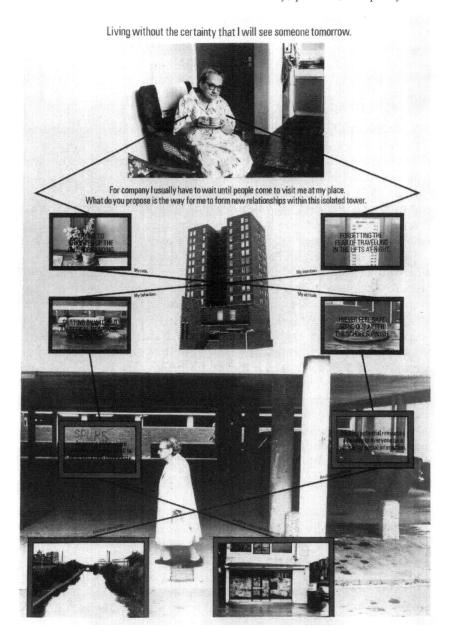

Panel 3

fail to target the underlying problem caused by the physical environment of the tower block.

The point we are seeking to emphasize here is that although in this book we have focused largely on the process whereby the health and well-being of vulnerable populations can be improved by developing and maintaining social identity, it is equally important for policy makers to be aware of the fact that failing to maintain social identities (or acting in ways that undermines them), can serve to transform healthy and happy communities into vulnerable ones. As Cohen and Janicki-Deverts (2009, p. 376) observe, "social environments play an essential role in the health and well-being of people who are neither challenged by major life stressors nor by serious disease".

Again, one of the key problems here is that policy makers tend to be more attuned to the value of social identity when it is lacking (e.g., as a result of critical life events), than when it is working – albeit invisibly – to support community health and well-being. From a policy perspective, it therefore behoves policy makers to take stock of the social identity resources that people have at their disposal (whether through work, family, friendship, or local community ties) and to think about ways in which these may be affected by any policy initiative that they are planning (e.g., in seeking to restructure an organization, to make new legislation, to set new targets). Indeed, just as developers are required by law to conduct an Environmental Impact Assessment (EIA) before they commence a new building project, so we would urge policy makers to conduct a "Social Identity Impact Assessment" before they implement any new social policy. Indeed, there is economic logic in this, as it is a lot cheaper to maintain or build upon existing social identity resources than it is to build them from scratch once they have been depleted. This is a realm in which it is often the case that "you don't know what you've got till it's gone", and this is all the more reason to handle social identities with care.

At a practical level then, we suggest that, as with any form of effective *leadership* (see Haslam, Reicher, & Platow, 2011), policy implementation in particular communities needs to be informed by knowledge of existing social identity resources gained through localized engagement with them. Importantly, these resources need to be appraised in terms of the social identities and group memberships that are meaningful to people, rather than in terms of the demographics (or other population characteristics) of a particular community (e.g., as in the strategy of Ascertaining Identity Resources, or AIRing; Eggins, O'Brien, Reynolds, Haslam, & Crocker, 2008).

It could, of course, be argued that the policy initiatives suggested by the social identity approach are too hard, too time-consuming, and too expensive – especially in a time of fiscal austerity. Yet we would argue that it is precisely during periods of austerity and challenge that we stand to gain the most from mobilizing social identity resources. For it is when people confront collective challenge that societal health and well-being are most under threat and where the remedial benefits of social identification are most needed and most likely to be felt (e.g., see Branscombe et al., Chapter 7; Matheson & Anisman, Chapter 8). In this context, the costs associated with developing and sustaining social identity resources will surely be far outweighed by gains in societal health and well-being. This assertion is not only supported by the work presented in this volume, but also by a growing international and cross-disciplinary evidence base. Indeed, given the abundant evidence, the pertinent question for policy makers is not whether society can afford the social cure that the social identity approach promises, but whether it can afford not to have it.

CONCLUSION

If there is one basic message to take from this book, it is that social factors are every bit as important to our health as other factors that have traditionally been emphasized in health and social policy. The epidemiological, social, and economic evidence clearly supports this conclusion. Nevertheless, our tendency to take social factors for granted and to prioritize medical, pharmacological, and technological initiatives has the unfortunate consequence of creating an ongoing imbalance in theory, practice, and policy. In this regard, the full potential of the social identity approach will only be realized if it secures a higher place on the intellectual and policy agenda, and if its claims are recognized as legitimate, practicable, and fundable. A key purpose of this book has been to make the case for recognition of precisely this form.

Applying social identity principles to the study of health and well-being has consolidated existing theorizing, but it has also led to a number of important refinements that can inform both practice and policy. The evidence base that supports the application of social identity principles to these latter activities is in its infancy, but in the growing number of studies that have been conducted there is compelling evidence that points to the immense benefits for health and well-being that flow from enabling people to maintain and develop social identities that are capable of supporting fulfilling group lives. This volume bears testimony to the enormous strides that have been made in taking this agenda forward. Our sense, however, is that we have only just scratched the surface when it comes to appreciating and harnessing the benefits that such an approach can bring.

References

Akerlof, G., & Kranton, R. (2010). *Identity economics: How identities shape our work, wages and well-being.* Princeton, NJ: University of Princeton Press.

Ashforth, B. E., Harrison, S. H., & Corley, K. G. (2008). Identification in organizations: An examination of four fundamental questions. *Journal of Management, 34*, 325–374.

Cameron, D. (2009, November, 11). *The big society*. Hugo Young Lecture, London. Available online at http://www.conservatives.com/News/Speeches/2009/11/David_Cameron_The_Big_Society.aspx

Clare, A. W. (2002). *Clinical psychology and the community*. Paper presented at the Group of Trainers in Clinical Psychology Annual Conference, 31 October–2 November.

Cohen, S., & Janicki-Deverts, D. (2009). Can we improve our physical health by altering our social networks? *Perspectives on Psychological Science, 4*, 375–378.

Doosje, B., Spears, R., & Ellemers, N. (2002). Social identity as both cause and effect: The development of group identification in response to anticipated and actual changes in the intergroup status hierarchy. *British Journal of Social Psychology, 41*, 57–76.

Eggins, R. A., O'Brien, A. T., Reynolds, K. J., Haslam, S. A., & Crocker, A. S. (2008). Refocusing the focus group: AIRing as a basis for effective workplace planning. *British Journal of Management, 19*, 277–293.

Ellemers, N., Spears, R., & Doosje, B. (Eds.) (1999). *Social identity: Context, commitment, content*. Oxford, UK: Blackwell.

Evans, S. (2010). 'Mother's boy': David Cameron and Margaret Thatcher. *British Journal of Politics and International Relations, 12*, 325–343.

Gleibs, I., Haslam, C., Haslam, S. A., & Jones, J. (in press). Water clubs in residential care: Is it the water or the club that enhances health and well-being? *Psychology and Health*.

Gleibs, I., Haslam, C., Jones, J., Haslam, S. A., McNeil, J., & Connolly, H. (2011). No country for old men? The role of a Gentlemen's Club in promoting social engagement and psychological well-being in residential care. *Aging and Mental Health. 15*, 456–466.

Haslam, S. A. (2004). *Psychology in organizations: The social identity approach* (2nd ed.). London, UK: Sage.

Haslam, S. A., Jetten, J., Postmes, T., & Haslam, C. (2009). Social identity, health and well-being: An emerging agenda for applied psychology. *Applied Psychology: An International Review, 58*, 1–23.

Haslam, S. A., Reicher, S. D., & Platow, M. J. (2011). *The new psychology of leadership: Identity, influence and power*. London, UK: Psychology Press.

Hawe, P., & Shiell, A. (2000). Social capital and health promotion: A review. *Social Science & Medicine, 51*, 871–885.

Hogg, M. A., & Abrams, D. (1990). Social motivation, self-esteem and social identity. In D. Abrams & M. A. Hogg (Eds.), *Social identity theory: Constructive and critical advances* (pp. 28–47). London, UK: Harvester Wheatsheaf.

Iyer, A., Jetten, J., Tsivrikos, D., Postmes, T., & Haslam, S. A. (2009). The more (and the more compatible) the merrier: Multiple group memberships and identity compatibility as predictors of adjustment after life transitions. *British Journal of Social Psychology, 48*, 707–733.

Levine, R. M. (2003). Times, theories and practices in social psychology. *Theory and Psychology, 13*, 53–72.

Lim, C., & Putnam, R. D. (2010). Religion, social networks, and life satisfaction. *American Sociological Review, 75*, 914–933.

Oakes, P. J., Haslam, S. A., & Turner, J. C. (1994). *Stereotyping and social reality*. Oxford, UK: Blackwell.

Oyserman, D., Fryberg, S. A., & Yoder, N. (2007). Identity-based motivation and health. *Journal of Personality and Social Psychology, 93,* 1011–1027.

Postmes, T., & Jetten, J. (2006). *Individuality and the group: Advances in social identity.* London, UK: Sage.

Putnam, R. D. (2000). *Bowling alone: The collapse and revival of American community.* New York, NY: Simon & Schuster.

Reicher, S. D., & Haslam, S. A. (2006). On the agency of individuals and groups: Lessons from the BBC Prison Experiment. In T. Postmes & J. Jetten (Eds.), *Individuality and the group: Advances in social identity* (pp. 237–257). London, UK: Sage.

Rubin, M., & Hewstone, M. (1998). Social identity's self-esteem hypothesis: A review and some suggestions for clarification. *Personality and Social Psychology Review, 2,* 40–62.

Sani, F. (Ed.) (2008). *Self-continuity: Individual and collective perspectives.* New York, NY: Psychology Press.

Tajfel, H. (1972). La catégorisation sociale. In S. Moscovici (Ed.), *Introduction à la psychologie sociale* (Vol. 1, pp. 272–302). Paris, France: Larousse.

Tajfel, H., Flament, C., Billig, M. G., & Bundy, R. F. (1971). Social categorization and intergroup behaviour. *European Journal of Social Psychology, 1,* 149–177.

Tajfel, H., & Turner, J. C. (1979). An integrative theory of intergroup conflict. In W. G. Austin & S. Worchel (Eds.), *The social psychology of intergroup relations* (pp. 33–47). Monterey, CA: Brooks-Cole.

Tajfel, H., & Turner, J. C. (1986). The social identity theory of intergroup behavior. In S. Worchel & L. W. Austin (Eds.), *Psychology of intergroup relations* (2nd ed., pp. 7–24). Chicago, IL: Nelson-Hall.

Turner, J. C. (1999). Some current issues in research on social identity and self-categorization theories. In N. Ellemers, R. Spears, & B. Doosje (Eds.), *Social identity: Context, commitment, content* (pp. 6–34). Oxford, UK: Blackwell.

Turner, J. C. (2005). Explaining the nature of power. A three-process theory. *European Journal of Social Psychology, 35,* 1–22.

Turner, J. C., Hogg, M. A., Oakes, P. J., Reicher, S. D., & Wetherell, M. S. (1987). *Rediscovering the social group: A self-categorization theory.* Oxford, UK: Blackwell.

Turner, J. C., Oakes, P. J., Haslam, S. A., & McGarty, C. A. (1994). Self and collective: Cognition and social context. *Personality and Social Psychology Bulletin, 20,* 454–463.

Van Boven, L., & Gilovich, T. (2003). To do or to have? That is the question. *Journal of Personality and Social Psychology, 85,* 1193–1202.

Appendix
Measures of identity, health, and well-being

As most of the chapters in this volume attest, researchers who are interested in exploring issues of identity, health, and well-being have generally found it necessary to measure these constructs in ways that are both valid and reliable. This appendix presents details of a sample of different measures that have been developed for this purpose and includes most of the measures that are referred to in the chapters above. The reason for collating these measures is two-fold: first, to give readers a sense of exactly how key constructs are typically assessed and, second, to provide researchers with a resource that brings together the range of assessment options that are available for use in their own research.

The measures are organized into three sections. The first includes measures of identity and identification, the second presents a range of relevant psychological measures (e.g., those assessing social isolation and social support), and the third includes instruments designed to assess health and well-being. In most cases we include all the items in a given scale, but in the case of longer scales (i.e., those with more than 10 items) we include only a representative subset of items and refer the reader to the article or source where they can find all items.

As in other domains, no single measure is appropriate for all settings and it may be necessary to adapt a given measure to suit the particular circumstances of the assessment context and the particular questions that the research is addressing. Exactly which measure a researcher chooses to use will thus depend on factors such as the research setting (e.g., laboratory or field), the time available for assessment, the research budget, the response format (e.g., multiphase or one-shot), and the number and capacity of respondents.

IDENTITY MEASURES

Personal identity strength

This 5-item scale was developed primarily for use with older adults to assess the extent to which people have a clear understanding of who they are (see

Haslam, Jetten, Haslam, & Knight, this volume). The items were adapted from a self-clarity scale developed by Campbell et al., (1996) and a personal identity strength scale devised by Baray, Postmes, and Jetten (2009). First used by Jetten, Haslam, Pugliese, Tonks, and Haslam (2010) and Haslam et al., (2010), the scale has reported internal reliabilities that range between .65 and .81. Participants are asked to respond on a 5-point scale, although in Haslam et al.'s (2010) study, symbols were used instead of numbers on all identity measures to make the scale easier to use (i.e., 1 = – – to 5 = ++). Higher ratings indicate a stronger understanding of self.

---

1. I know what I like and what I don't like

    do not agree at all   – –   –   o   +   ++   agree completely

2. I know what my morals are

    do not agree at all   – –   –   o   +   ++   agree completely

3. I have strong beliefs

    do not agree at all   – –   –   o   +   ++   agree completely

4. I know what I want from life

    do not agree at all   – –   –   o   +   ++   agree completely

5. I am aware of the roles and responsibilities I have in my life

    do not agree at all   – –   –   o   +   ++   agree completely

---

Social identification

This scale was developed by Doosje, Ellemers, and Spears (1995) and first used to measure Dutch students' identification with the category "psychology student". The items are widely used by social and organizational psychologists (e.g., see Haslam, 2001), and the scales global nature makes it suitable as a measure of social identification that can be used with a wide range of groups. The items can easily be adapted for use in health-related settings by substituting the name of a relevant group or an organization (e.g., as discussed by van Dick & Haslam, this volume). Different dimensions of identification can be assessed using other more elaborate measures (e.g., Leach, van Zomeren, Zebel, Vliek, & Spears, 2008).

1. I see myself as a member of [relevant group]

   do not agree at all   1 2 3 4 5 6 7   agree completely

2. I am pleased to be a member of [relevant group]

   do not agree at all   1 2 3 4 5 6 7   agree completely

3. I feel strong ties with members of [relevant group]

   do not agree at all   1 2 3 4 5 6 7   agree completely

4. I identify with other members of [relevant group]

   do not agree at all   1 2 3 4 5 6 7   agree completely

Crowd identification

Crowds are not usually perceived as a typical social group, but seminal studies by Reicher (1987) demonstrated that the same social identity/self-categorization principles that shape group behaviour also operate in large and novel crowd events. Drury (this volume) indexes crowd identification retrospectively with a 2-item scale, $r = .81$, which was originally developed by Drury et al. (2009, study 2). These items emphasized the particular crowd context that the authors investigated (i.e., evacuating a rail station) and hence, to make them more amenable to any context, we have included reference to a generic crowd.

1. I felt a sense of unity with others [in the crowd]

   disagree strongly   1 2 3 4 5 6 7 8 9 10 11   agree strongly

2. I felt a sense of togetherness with others [in the crowd]

   disagree strongly   1 2 3 4 5 6 7 8 9 10 11   agree strongly

Social identity continuity

This measure is referred to in several chapters of this volume (e.g., Haslam, Jetten, Haslam & Knight; Gracey & Ownsworth) and was first reported in research by Haslam et al. (2008) to assess the degree to which stroke survivors were able to maintain their pre-stroke social group memberships. The scale typically has good internal reliability ($\alpha > .90$).

1. After [life transition] I still belong to the same groups I was a member of before [life transition]

    do not agree at all   1 2 3 4 5 6 7   agree completely

2. After [life transition] I still join in the same group activities as before [life transition]

    do not agree at all   1 2 3 4 5 6 7   agree completely

3. After [life transition] I am friends with people in the same groups as I was before [life transition]

    do not agree at all   1 2 3 4 5 6 7   agree completely

4. After [life transition] I continue to have strong ties with the same groups as before [life transition]

    do not agree at all   1 2 3 4 5 6 7   agree completely

Multiple identities

This measure is used to assess the extent to which people belong to multiple social groups and is cited in several chapters in this volume (Haslam, Jetten, Haslam, & Knight; Jetten & Pachana). It has been used with a range of groups including stroke survivors (Haslam et al., 2008), students entering university (Iyer, Jetten, Tsivrikos, Postmes, & Haslam, 2009), and older adults residing in care (Jetten et al., 2010). It can be used to index multiple forms of group activity at the point where people are anticipating some life change (i.e., as a Time 1 measure; Iyer et al., 2009) or retrospectively after life change (e.g., Haslam et al., 2008). The measure has been adapted and used as a 2-item (Jetten et al., 2010) and 4-item scale (Haslam et al., 2008) with good internal reliability (2-item scale, $r = .44$; 4-item scale: $\alpha = .93$).

Haslam et al. (2008), 4-item scale

---

1. Before [life transition] I belonged to lots of different groups

    do not agree at all 1 2 3 4 5 6 7 agree completely

2. Before [life transition] I joined in the activities of lots of different groups

    do not agree at all 1 2 3 4 5 6 7 agree completely

3. Before [life transition] I had friends who were members of lots of different groups

    do not agree at all 1 2 3 4 5 6 7 agree completely

4. Before [life transition] I had strong ties with lots of different groups

    do not agree at all 1 2 3 4 5 6 7 agree completely

Jetten et al. (2010), 2-item scale

---

1. I am a member of lots of different social groups

    do not agree at all 1 2 3 4 5 6 7 agree completely

2. I have friends who are in lots of different social groups

    do not agree at all 1 2 3 4 5 6 7 agree completely

Haslam et al. (2008) also developed a multiple-identity scale that requires participants to write down up to six groups that are (or were) important to them. They are then are asked to reflect on these groups and to indicate (a) how important this group is (or was) to them, and (b) the compatibility of this group to the other groups to which they belong. This measure provides a rich source of data that can be used to examine the influence of the (a) number of group memberships, (b) type of group memberships that respondents list, and (c) types of group memberships that are compatible with other identities. Note too that the measure can be used to assess the groups that respondents belonged to *before* their life-changing event (see example below) and then again to assess the groups that respondents belong to *after* the life-changing event.

The instructions and response sheet are as follows:

This questionnaire refers to the types of groups that you [used to belong to] [and] [now belong to]. These groups could take **any** form – for example, they could be leisure or social groups (e.g., book group or gardening club); community groups (e.g., church group); sporting groups (e.g., rugby club); work groups (e.g., sales team); professional groups (e.g., trade union); or any others you can think of.

In the first column, list up to 6 groups that you belong[ed] to [**before/ after**] [the life-changing event]. Then indicate how much you agree with the items in the next two columns.

1. Group memberships before [life-changing event]	2. How important was this group to you **before** [life-changing event]. → Circle one number for each group	3. How well did this group fit with your other groups **before** [life-changing event]? → Circle one number for each group
1.	not important 1 2 3 4 5 6 7 very important	not well 1 2 3 4 5 6 7 very well
2.	not important 1 2 3 4 5 6 7 very important	not well 1 2 3 4 5 6 7 very well
3.	not important 1 2 3 4 5 6 7 very important	not well 1 2 3 4 5 6 7 very well
4.	not important 1 2 3 4 5 6 7 very important	not well 1 2 3 4 5 6 7 very well
5.	not important 1 2 3 4 5 6 7 very important	not well 1 2 3 4 5 6 7 very well
6.	not important 1 2 3 4 5 6 7 very important	not well 1 2 3 4 5 6 7 very well

PSYCHOLOGICAL MEASURES

Social isolation

This measure was developed for screening purposes in collaboration with Huw Williams (see Reicher & Haslam, 2006). With a sample of over 300 members of the general public it proved to have good reliability ($\alpha = .83$). Items 3 and 4 are reverse-scored.

1. Do you have someone close in whom you can confide?

   not at all   1 2 3 4 5 6 7   definitely

2. Do you see yourself as a loner?

   not at all   1 2 3 4 5 6 7   definitely

3. Do you see yourself as a sociable person? (R)

   not at all   1 2 3 4 5 6 7   definitely

4. Are your relationships important to you? (R)

   not at all   1 2 3 4 5 6 7   definitely

Social support

Several measures of social support have been referenced in this volume. One measure, referred to in the chapters by van Dick and Haslam and Haslam, Reicher, and Levine is a shortened version of a 10-item measure originally developed by Haslam, O'Brien, Jetten, Vormedal, and Penna (2005) to assess stress in patients recovering from heart surgery. The long version has high reliability ($\alpha = .81$), and this is not compromised by shortening (in various shorter versions, comprising between 4 to 7 items, αs range between .79 and .86). The measure incorporates items designed to assess the four distinct aspects of social support identified by House (1981): (a) emotional support (relating to an individual's sense of acceptance and self-worth); (b) companionship (affiliation and help from others); (c) instrumental support (concrete aid, material resources, financial assistance); and informational support (advice to help understand and cope with one's circumstances).

1. Do you get the emotional support you need from other people?

   not at all   1 2 3 4 5 6 7   completely

2. Do you get the help you need from other people?

   not at all   1 2 3 4 5 6 7   completely

3. Do you get the resources you need from other people?

   not at all   1 2 3 4 5 6 7   completely

4. Do you get the advice you need from other people?

   not at all   1 2 3 4 5 6 7   completely

Matheson and Anisman (this volume) also use three further measures of perceived social support: social provisions, generation and consumption of social support, and unsupportive interactions.

Social provisions

This scale was developed by Cutrona and Russell (1987) to assess perceptions of the social support provided by parents, friends, and their intimate partners. The scale comprises 12 items on which respondents indicate whether support was provided by each of these sources on a 3-point rating scale (no = 1, not sure = 2, yes = 3). Mean scores are then calculated with higher scores reflecting greater perceived social support from each source. Indicative items are as follows:

---

1. Are there friends you can depend on to help you, if you really need it?

	1	2	3
	no	not sure	yes

2. Are there friends who enjoy the same social activities that you do?

	1	2	3
	no	not sure	yes

3. Do your relationships with friends provide you with a sense of emotional security and well-being?

	1	2	3
	no	not sure	yes

4. Do you feel your competence and skill are recognized by your friends?

	1	2	3
	no	not sure	yes

Generation and consumption of social support

This measure was developed by Bertera (1997) and can be modified to make reference to support from various sources (e.g., ingroup or outgroup members; see Matheson & Anisman, this volume). This scale was originally validated within a geriatric and a low socioeconomic status population comprising people from a range of ethnic backgrounds (Bertera, 1997). Responses are made to 12 behavioural items reflecting receipt of social support, as well as support given, along a 5-point scale ranging from 0 (not at all) to 4 (about every day). Indicative items are as follows:

Provision of support

---

1. You gave information to others on how to do something

    not at all   0 1 2 3 4   about every day

2. You have pitched in to help others do something that needed to be done

    not at all   0 1 2 3 4   about every day

3. You have expressed interest and concern in the well-being of others

    not at all   0 1 2 3 4   about every day

Receipt of support

---

1. You received some information from others which helped you to understand a situation

    not at all   0 1 2 3 4   about every day

2. You were helped by others to do something that needed to be done

    not at all   0 1 2 3 4   about every day

3. You received interest and concern from others in your well-being

    not at all   0 1 2 3 4   about every day

Unsupportive interactions

Unsupportive interactions have been linked to reduced psychological well-being, over and above the perceived unavailability of social support or the effects of stressor experiences (Ingram, Betz, Mindes, Schmitt, & Smith, 2001; Ingram, Jones, Fass, Neidig, & Song, 1999). The Unsupportive Social Interactions Inventory (Ingram et al., 1999, 2001) can be used to index this construct and comprises 24 items tapping into four types of unsupportive responses – namely, distancing, minimizing, bumbling, and blaming. The scale can be modified to refer to the extent to which people experience unsupportive interactions with others in general, with specific sources, or as applied by Matheson and Anisman (this volume), with members of relevant ingroups and outgroups. Participants respond to each item on a 5-point scale, ranging from 0 (not at all) to 4 (a lot). This measure has been successfully used across diverse social and ethnic populations in North America (Cole, Matheson, & Anisman, 2007; Ingram et al., 1999; Jorden, Matheson, & Anisman, 2009). Indicative items are as follows:

1. When I was talking with someone about the issue/situation, s/he did not give me enough of his/her time or made me feel like I should hurry.

   not at all   0 1 2 3 4   a lot

2. The person didn't seem to know what to say, or seemed afraid of saying/doing the "wrong" thing.

   not at all   0 1 2 3 4   a lot

3. The person said "I told you so", or made some similar comment to me about my situation.

   not at all   0 1 2 3 4   a lot

4. The person felt that I should stop worrying about the situation and just forget about it.

   not at all   0 1 2 3 4   a lot

Disclosure/concealment

Two single-item measures were used by Jones and colleagues (this volume) to assess whether individuals were willing to disclose information about their clinical condition (in their research, acquired brain injury), as well as whether they perceived the condition to be concealable.

Disclosure

I find it hard to tell people about my [condition]

strongly disagree   1 2 3 4 5 6 7   strongly agree

Concealment

I can conceal my [condition] from other people

strongly disagree   1 2 3 4 5 6 7   strongly agree

HEALTH AND WELL-BEING MEASURES

Burnout (chronic stress)

This measure is an extension of the 7-item measure developed by Haslam and Reicher to measure stress in the BBC Prison Experiment (see Haslam & Reicher, 2006; Reicher & Haslam, 2006). It has three subscales that correspond to the three core components of burnout identified by Jackson, Schwab, and Schuler (1986) and Maslach, Jackson, and Leiter (1996): (a) exhaustion, (b) lack of accomplishment, and (c) callousness (lack of concern for others). Studies in which various versions of this scale have been used indicate that the scale as a whole forms a reliable single measure (e.g., in a study of care workers, Gaffney & Haslam, 2002, report $\alpha = .67$ for a 6-item version; see also van Dick & Haslam, this volume). Likewise, the three subscales also generally have good reliability (Haslam & Reicher obtained αs between .59 and .82 across two phases of their study). One item in each subscale is reverse-scored.

Exhaustion

1. I feel I am working too hard
do not agree at all   1 2 3 4 5 6 7   definitely
2. I feel exhausted
do not agree at all   1 2 3 4 5 6 7   definitely
3. I feel energetic (R)
do not agree at all   1 2 3 4 5 6 7   definitely

Lack of accomplishment

4. I feel I am failing to achieve my goals
do not agree at all   1 2 3 4 5 6 7   definitely
5. I feel frustrated
do not agree at all   1 2 3 4 5 6 7   definitely
6. I feel I am accomplishing many worthwhile things (R)
do not agree at all   1 2 3 4 5 6 7   definitely

Callousness

---

7. I am concerned about the welfare of others (R)

   do not agree at all   1 2 3 4 5 6 7   definitely

8. I don't really care what happens to people any more

   do not agree at all   1 2 3 4 5 6 7   definitely

9. I feel I am becoming callous towards other people

   do not agree at all   1 2 3 4 5 6 7   definitely

Traumatic experiences

The Traumatic Life Events Questionnaire (TLEQ; Kubany et al., 2000) assesses exposure to a range of potentially traumatic events. Matheson and Anisman (this volume) have added "an experience of discrimination due to race, gender or religion" to the list of possible experiences. The TLEQ has been validated with wide range of samples, including substance abusers, Vietnam war veterans, and battered women (Kubany et al., 2000). Events are presented in behaviourally descriptive terms (consistent with the DSM-IV Axis I stressor criterion) and the frequency of occurrence of each event is indicated using a 7-point scale, ranging from 0 (never) to 6 (more than five times). When events are endorsed, respondents indicate whether they had experienced intense fear, helplessness, or horror (the PTSD Axis II criterion in the DSM-IV), along with when the event occurred. If the event had occurred more than once, respondents are asked to report the timing of the first and most recent occurrences. The frequencies of each event that are reported to cause fear, helplessness, and/or horror are summed to create five trauma types based on a combination of conceptual and empirical considerations (Breslau, Chilcoat, Kessler, & Davis, 1999). These include (1) discrimination; (2) shocking events involving an accident in which someone was seriously injured or killed, a natural disaster, or a life-threatening illness; (3) traumas from events occurring to others, including life-threatening events; (4) death of a loved one; and (5) assault from a stranger or a familiar other, including childhood physical or sexual abuse, and spousal violence. Indicative items are as follows:

For each of the following events, please indicate whether you personally have had any of the described experiences ...

a personal experience of discrimination
(e.g., based on your sex, ethnic group
membership, religion etc).   yes ☐ no ☐

a) How many times did this happen, or how many
such events do you remember experiencing? ....

b) If this happened, in the most serious
instance, did you experience fear, helplessness,
or horror when it happened?   yes ☐ no ☐

c) When did it happen?
    Most recent incident:
        In the past year .... ☐
        2–5 yrs ago .... ☐
        6–10 yrs ago .... ☐
        10–15 yrs ago .... ☐
        When you were less than 5 years old   ☐

    First incident (if different from above):
        In the past year .... ☐
        2–5 yrs ago .... ☐
        6–10 yrs ago .... ☐
        10–15 yrs ago .... ☐
        When you were less than 5 years old   ☐

    For what period of time were you discriminated against,
    in the longest instance?
        It only happened once .... ☐
        It took place a number of times over
        the course of several days .... ☐
        A month .... ☐
        Several months .... ☐
        A year .... ☐
        Several years .... ☐

Post-traumatic stress

The Impact of Events Scale (IES-R; Weiss & Marmar, 1997) is among the measures used by Matheson and Anisman (this volume) to index post-traumatic stress. It is a 22-item measure that assesses three dimensions of trauma symptoms, including intrusiveness, avoidance, and hyperarousal. These dimensions can be analysed separately, but the correlations among them are often relatively high, thereby justifying examination of a single summated index. This measure is frequently regarded as an index of post-traumatic stress disorder symptoms, demonstrating excellent specificity and sensitivity (Brewin, 2005). Participants use a 5-point scale, ranging from 0 (not at all) to 4 (extremely), to indicate how distressing each symptom has been during the past seven days as a result of their most severe prior trauma (or if they did not indicate any trauma, to consider the "stressful event that has most troubled you during the past few years"). The following are indicative items:

Reflecting on your trauma, during the past seven days:

1. Has any reminder brought back feelings about it?

        not at all   0 1 2 3 4   extremely

2. I had trouble staying asleep

        not at all   0 1 2 3 4   extremely

3. Other things kept making me think about it

        not at all   0 1 2 3 4   extremely

4. I felt irritable and angry

        not at all   0 1 2 3 4   extremely

5. I avoided letting myself get upset when I thought about it or was reminded of it

        not at all   0 1 2 3 4   extremely

6. I thought about it when I didn't mean to

        not at all   0 1 2 3 4   extremely

7. I felt as if it hadn't happened or wasn't real

        not at all   0 1 2 3 4   extremely

8. I stayed away from reminders about it

        not at all   0 1 2 3 4   extremely

Affect

Positive and negative affect

Several standard measures of affect have been used as measures of subjective well-being (e.g., Helliwell & Barrington-Leigh, this volume). The *Positive and Negative Affect Scale* (*PANAS*; Watson, Clark, & Tellegen, 1988) is used to gauge the incidence or preponderance of exhibited feelings and behaviours associated with positive affect and, as an independent construct, negative affect. The scale consists of 10 descriptors for positive affect – attentive, interested, alert, excited, enthusiastic, inspired, proud, determined, strong, and active – and 10 descriptors for negative affect – distressed, upset-distressed, hostile, irritable-angry, scared, afraid-fearful, ashamed, guilty, nervous, and jittery. For these 20 items respondents are asked to indicate how they feel on a 5-point scale (1 = very slightly, 5 = extremely).

Happiness

Several scales are used to index happiness (see Helliwell & Barrington-Leigh, this volume). Single-item measures can be used to access more transient affective states, rather than global, longer term, or general cognitive evaluations of life quality. An example is as follows:

Presently would you describe yourself as:				
1	2	3	4	5
very happy	somewhat happy	somewhat unhappy	very unhappy	no opinion

Helliwell and Putnam (2004) compare happiness and life satisfaction equations for world values survey data, and find them to have very similar structures, with slight differences consistent with the less evaluative nature of the happiness responses.

Depression

The 21-item *Beck Depression Inventory* (Beck, Ward, Mendelson, Mock, & Erbaugh, 1961) is the most commonly used instrument to index depression and comprises items that tap into symptoms of depression, feelings of guilt and punishment, and physical changes. Respondents are asked to indicate how they have been feeling in the past week and a value of 0 to 3 is assigned to each item. Scores for all individual items are then summed to provide a total score, where higher scores are indicative of higher levels of depression. A sample item is as follows:

---

(0) I do not feel sad
(1) I feel sad
(2) I am so sad all the time and I can't snap out of it
(3) I am so sad or unhappy that I can't stand it

A scale assessing the frequency of depressive thoughts and feelings has been used among undergraduate students thinking about entering university (e.g., Iyer et al., 2009; see Jetten & Pachana, this volume) and African-Americans reflecting on group-based discrimination (Branscombe, Schmitt, & Harvey, 1999). The scale is adapted from Diener, Larsen, Levine, and Emmons (1985) who showed that respondents can accurately report the frequency of these negative emotions. Coefficient alphas are generally quite high (e.g., .86, Iyer et al., 2009; .89, Branscombe et al., 1999).

How often do you feel or experience the following emotions?

depression

    very infrequently   1 2 3 4 5 6 7 8 9   very frequently

weariness

    very infrequently   1 2 3 4 5 6 7 8 9   very frequently

helplessness

    very infrequently   1 2 3 4 5 6 7 8 9   very frequently

lifelessness

    very infrequently   1 2 3 4 5 6 7 8 9   very frequently

sadness

    very infrequently   1 2 3 4 5 6 7 8 9   very frequently

unhappiness

    very infrequently   1 2 3 4 5 6 7 8 9   very frequently

anxiety

    very infrequently   1 2 3 4 5 6 7 8 9   very frequently

Life satisfaction

Helliwell and Barrington-Leigh (this volume) have used several measures to index life satisfaction. Satisfaction with Life (*SWL*) is typically indexed with the following single item:

> All things considered, how satisfied are you with life as a whole these days?

This is answered on a 1 to 10 or 0 to 10 numerical scale with verbal anchoring points at the extremes (0/1 = completely dissatisfied, 10 = completely satisfied). Coarser scales can have the advantage of allowing verbal descriptions to be provided for each possible response, but this seems to be outweighed by the benefit of having more resolution in an 11-point scale with anchoring descriptions at the top and bottom.

Satisfaction with Life Scale (SWLS)

This popular 5-item scale was developed by Diener et al. (1985) who argued that multiple items were required to index life satisfaction as a cognitive-judgemental process. That said, only one of the questions includes the word "satisfied". The index may have greater statistical integrity than single-items, but is costlier to include in large-scale surveys.

> 1. In most ways my life is close to ideal
>   strongly disagree   1 2 3 4 5 6 7   strongly agree
> 2. The conditions of my life are excellent
>   strongly disagree   1 2 3 4 5 6 7   strongly agree
> 3. I am satisfied with life
>   strongly disagree   1 2 3 4 5 6 7   strongly agree
> 4. So far I have gotten the important things I want in life
>   strongly disagree   1 2 3 4 5 6 7   strongly agree
> 5. If I could live my life over, I would change almost nothing
>   strongly disagree   1 2 3 4 5 6 7   strongly agree

Cantril Self-Anchoring Striving Scale

This scale, sometimes called the "Cantril Ladder", is similar in response format to the single-item SWL measure. However, this poses the following question:

> Please imagine a ladder with steps numbered zero at the bottom to ten at the top. Suppose we say that the top of the ladder represents the best possible life for you and the bottom of the ladder represents the worst possible. If the top step is 10 and the bottom step is 0, on which step of the ladder do you feel you personally stand at the present time?

For some waves, the Gallup World Poll contained both the Cantril ladder and an SWL question, on the same 0 to 10 scale. Helliwell and colleagues (Helliwell, Barrington-Leigh, Harris, & Huang, 2010) fitted the same model to both sets of data and found essentially identical coefficients, and closer fitting equations if the two measures were averaged. The reliability and validity of several measures of subjective well-being are reviewed by Diener, Lucas, Schimmack, and Helliwell (2009, pp. 67–84).

Job satisfaction

A range of short scales exist to measure job or work satisfaction. One of the most commonly used is the 3-item satisfaction scale from the Michigan Organizational Assessment Questionnaire. This was developed by Cammann, Fichmann, Jenkins, and Klesh (1979) and generally has high reliability (typical $\alpha = .80$; see also Spector, 1997). Measures of this form were used in research discussed by van Dick and Haslam (this volume). The second of the three items is reverse-scored.

> 1. All in all I am satisfied with my job
>   do not agree at all   1 2 3 4 5 6 7   agree completely
> 2. In general I don't like my job (R)
>   do not agree at all   1 2 3 4 5 6 7   agree completely
> 3. In general I like working here
>   do not agree at all   1 2 3 4 5 6 7   agree completely

Personal self-esteem

Self-esteem is commonly measured using Rosenberg's (1965) 10-item self-esteem measure. This was originally developed on the basis of responses from over 5,000 adolescent high-school students in New York. Respondents use a 5-point scale to indicate the extent to which they agree with each item. Half the items (2, 5, 6, 8, 9) are reverse-scored. Previous studies have indicated that the scale has high reliability (αs in the range .72 to .88; Gray-Little, Williams, & Hancock, 1997).

Rosenberg self-esteem measure

---

1. On the whole, I am satisfied with myself

    strongly disagree 0 1 2 3 4   strongly agree

2. At times, I think I am no good at all (R)

    strongly disagree 0 1 2 3 4   strongly agree

3. I feel that I have a number of good qualities

    strongly disagree 0 1 2 3 4   strongly agree

4. I am able to do things as well as most other people

    strongly disagree 0 1 2 3 4   strongly agree

5. I feel I do not have much to be proud of (R)

    strongly disagree 0 1 2 3 4   strongly agree

6. I certainly feel useless at times (R)

    strongly disagree 0 1 2 3 4   strongly agree

7. I feel that I'm a person of worth, at least on an equal plane with others

    strongly disagree 0 1 2 3 4   strongly agree

8. I wish I could have more respect for myself (R)

    strongly disagree 0 1 2 3 4   strongly agree

9. All in all, I am inclined to feel that I am a failure (R)

    strongly disagree 0 1 2 3 4   strongly agree

10. I take a positive attitude toward myself

    strongly disagree 0 1 2 3 4   strongly agree

Although Rosenberg's scale is very popular, it is worth noting that self-esteem can also be measured using the following single item:

> I have high self-esteem
>
> strongly disagree 0 1 2 3 4   strongly agree

Robins, Hendin, and Trzesniewski (2001) report that this single-item measure – whose use they pioneered and argue strongly for – has high convergent validity with the Rosenberg 10-item measure and nearly identical correlations with a range of criterion measures (e.g., social desirability, psychological and physical health, academic outcomes, and demographic variables). It has the obvious advantage of being far easier to administer.

U-index

This measure was developed by Kahneman and Krueger (2006) to quantify societal well-being. The "U" in the index refers to "unpleasant" or "undesirable". The index is calculated by aggregating over respondents the proportion of time in which the highest rated recalled feeling was negative. This provides a way to compare and aggregate over individuals where there are idiosyncratic differences in the scales they use to describe their own affect. For instance, Kahneman and Krueger suggest asking respondents to rate each episode in a day according to the strength of positive feelings ("Happy", "Enjoying myself", "Friendly") and negative ones ("Depressed", "Angry", "Frustrated"), and to classify each episode simply according to whether the single strongest-rated feeling was positive or negative. The U-index is then calculated as the proportion of those episodes in which the predominant rating is negative.

References

Baray, G., Postmes, T., & Jetten, J. (2009). When "I" equals "We": Exploring the relation between social and personal identity of extreme right-wing political party members. *British Journal of Social Psychology*, *48*, 625–648.

Beck, A. T., Ward, C. H., Mendelson, M., Mock, J., & Erbaugh, J. (1961). An inventory for measuring depression. *Archives of General Psychiatry*, *4*, 561–571.

Bertera, E. (1997). Consumption and generation of social support scale: Psychometric properties in low socioeconomic status elderly. *Journal of Clinical Geropsychology*, *3*, 139–147.

Branscombe, N. R., Schmitt, M. T., & Harvey, R. D. (1999). Perceiving pervasive discrimination among African Americans: Implications for group identification and well-being. *Journal of Personality and Social Psychology*, *77*, 135–149.

Breslau, N., Chilcoat, H. D., Kessler, R. C., & Davis, G. C. (1999). Previous exposure to trauma and PTSD effects of subsequent trauma: Results from the Detroit area survey of trauma. *American Journal of Psychiatry*, *156*, 902–907.

Brewin, C. (2005). Systematic review of screening instruments of adults at risk of PTSD. *Journal of Trauma Stress, 18*, 53–62.

Cammann, C., Fichmann, M., Jenkins, D., & Klesh, J. (1979). *The Michigan Organizational Assessment Questionnaire.* Ann Arbor, MI: University of Michigan.

Campbell, J. D., Trapnell, P. D., Heine, S. J., Katz, I. M., Lavallee, L. F., & Lehman, D. R. (1996). Self-concept clarity: Measurement, personality correlates, and cultural boundaries. *Journal of Personality and Social Psychology, 70*, 141–156.

Cole, B., Matheson, K., & Anisman, H. (2007). Academic performance and well-being: The moderating role of ethnic identity and social support. *Journal of Applied Social Psychology, 37*, 592–615.

Cutrona, C., & Russell, D. (1987). The provisions of social relationships and adaptation to stress. *Advances in Personal Relationships, 1*, 37–67.

Diener, E., Larsen, R. J., Levine, S., & Emmons, R. A. (1985). Intensity and frequency: Dimensions underlying positive and negative affect. *Journal of Personality and Social Psychology, 68*, 653–663.

Diener, E., Lucas, R., Schimmack, U., & Helliwell, J. F. (2009). *Well-being for public policy.* New York, NY and Oxford, UK: Oxford University Press.

Doosje, B., Ellemers, N., & Spears, R. (1995). Perceived intragroup variability as a function of group status and identification. *Journal of Experimental Social Psychology, 31*, 410–436.

Drury, J., Cocking, C., Reicher, S., Burton, A., Schofield, D., Hardwick, A., et al. (2009). Cooperation versus competition in a mass emergency evacuation: A new laboratory simulation and a new theoretical model. *Behavior Research Methods, 41*, 957–970.

Gaffney, C., & Haslam, S. A. (2002). *Burnout in care workers: The role of social identification.* Unpublished manuscript, University of Exeter, UK.

Gray-Little, B., Williams, V. S. L., & Hancock, T. D. (1997). An item response theory analysis of the Rosenberg Self-Esteem Scale. *Personality and Social Psychology Bulletin, 23*, 443–451.

Haslam, C., Haslam, S. A., Jetten, J., Bevins, A., Ravenscroft, S., & Tonks, J. (2010). The social treatment: Benefits of group reminiscence and group activity for the cognitive performance and well-being of older adults in residential care. *Psychology and Aging, 25*, 157–167.

Haslam, C., Holme, A., Haslam, S. A., Iyer, A., Jetten, J., & Williams, W. H. (2008). Maintaining group memberships: Social identity continuity predicts well-being after stroke. *Neuropsychological Rehabilitation, 18*, 671–691.

Haslam, S. A. (2001). *Psychology in organizations: The social identity approach.* London, UK: Sage.

Haslam, S. A., O'Brien, A., Jetten, J., Vormedal, K., & Penna, S. (2005). Taking the strain: Social identity, social support and the experience of stress. *British Journal of Social Psychology, 44*, 355–370.

Haslam, S. A., & Reicher, S. D. (2006). Stressing the group: Social identity and the unfolding dynamics of responses to stress. *Journal of Applied Psychology, 91*, 1037–1052.

Helliwell, J. F., Barrington-Leigh, C. P., Harris, A., Huang, H. (2010). International evidence on the social context of well-being. In D. Kahneman, E. Diener, & J. F.

Helliwell (Eds.), *International differences in well-being*. Oxford, UK: Oxford University Press.

Helliwell, J. F., & Putnam, R. D. (2004). The social context of well-being. *Philosophical Transactions of the Royal Society B: Biological Sciences, 359,* 1435–1446.

House, J. S. (1981). *Work stress and social support*. Reading, MA: Addison-Wesley.

Ingram, K. M., Betz, N. E., Mindes, E. J., Schmitt, M. M., & Smith, N. G. (2001). Unsupportive responses from others concerning a stressful life event: Development of the Unsupportive Social Interactions Inventory. *Journal of Social and Clinical Psychology, 20,* 174–208.

Ingram, K. M., Jones, D. A., Fass, R. J., Neidig, J. L., & Song, Y. S. (1999). Social support and unsupportive social interactions: Their association with depression among people living with HIV. *AIDS Care, 11,* 313–329.

Iyer, A., Jetten, J., Tsivrikos, D., Postmes, T., & Haslam, S. A. (2009). The more (and the more compatible) the merrier: Multiple group memberships and identity compatibility as predictors of adjustment after life transitions. *British Journal of Social Psychology, 48,* 707–733.

Jackson, S. E., Schwab, R. L., & Schuler, R. S. (1986). Toward an understanding of the burnout phenomenon. *Journal of Applied Psychology, 71,* 630–640.

Jetten, J., Haslam, C., Pugliese, C., Tonks, J., & Haslam, S. A. (2010). Declining autobiographical memory and the loss of identity: Effects on well-being. *Journal of Clinical and Experimental Neuropsychology, 32,* 408–416.

Jorden, S., Matheson, K., & Anisman, H. (2009). Supportive and unsupportive social interactions in relation to cultural adaptation and psychological symptoms among Somali refugees. *Journal of Cross-Cultural Psychology, 40,* 853–874.

Kahneman, D., & Krueger, A. B. (2006). Developments in the measurement of subjective well-being. *Journal of Economic Perspectives, 20,* 3–24.

Kubany, E. S., Hanes, S., Leisen, M., Owens, J., Kaplan, A., Watson, S., et al. (2000). Development and preliminary validation of a brief broad-spectrum measure of trauma exposure: The traumatic life events questionnaire. *Psychological Assessment, 12,* 210–224.

Leach, C. W., van Zomeren, M., Zebel, S., Vliek, M. L. W., & Spears, R. (2008). Group-level self-definition and self-investment: A hierarchical (multicomponent) model of ingroup identification. *Journal of Personality and Social Psychology, 95,* 144–165.

Maslach, C., Jackson, S. E., & Leiter, M. P. (1996). *Maslach Burnout Inventory manual* (3rd ed.). Palo Alto, CA: Consulting Psychologists Press.

Reicher, S. D. (1987). Crowd behaviour as social action. In J. C. Turner, M. A. Hogg, P. J. Oakes, S. D. Reicher, & M. S. Wetherell (Eds.), *Rediscovering the social group: A self-categorization theory* (pp. 171–202). Oxford, UK: Blackwell.

Reicher, S. D., & Haslam, S. A. (2006). Rethinking the psychology of tyranny: The BBC Prison Experiment. *British Journal of Social Psychology, 45,* 1–40.

Robins, R. W., Hendin, H. M., & Trzesniewski, K. H. (2001). Measuring global self-esteem: Construct validation of a single-item measure and the Rosenberg Self-Esteem scale. *Personality and Social Psychology Bulletin, 27,* 151–161.

Rosenberg, M. (1965). *Society and the adolescent self-image*. Princeton, NJ: Princeton University Press.

Spector, P. E. (1997). *Job satisfaction: application, assessment, cause, and consequences*. Thousand Oaks, CA and London, UK: Sage.

Watson, D., Clark, L. A., & Tellegen, A. (1988). Development and validation of brief measures of positive and negative affect: The PANAS scales. *Journal of Personality and Social Psychology, 54,* 1063–1070.

Weiss, D. S., & Marmar, C. R. (1997). The impact of events scale – revised. In J. Wilson & T. Keane (Eds.), *Assessing psychological trauma and PTSD: A practitioner's handbook* (pp. 399–411). New York, NY: Guilford Press.

Author index

Subject index

Note: References in **bold** indicate figures and tables.